PERSONAL INJURY AND WRONGFUL DEATH DAMAGES CALCULATIONS: TRANSATLANTIC DIALOGUE

CONTEMPORARY STUDIES IN ECONOMIC AND FINANCIAL ANALYSIS

Series Editors: Robert J. Thornton and
J. Richard Aronson

Recent Volumes:

Volume 83: Foreign Direct Investment in the United States
Edited by W. L. Casey

Volume 84: Colombia: An Opening Economy?
Edited by C. M. Callahan and F. R. Gunter

Volume 85: The Irish Economy in Transition: Success, Problems and Prospects, Edited by J. R. Aronson, V. Munley and R. J. Thornton

Volume 86: Asia Pacific Financial Markets in Comparative Perspective: Issues and Implications for the 21st Century, Edited by J. A. Batten and T. A. Fetherston

Volume 87: Developments in Litigation Economics
Edited by P. A. Gaughan and R. J. Thornton

Volume 88: European Responses To Globalization: Resistance, Adaptation And Alternatives
Edited by Janet Laible and Henri J. Barkey

Volume 89: Globalization: Perspectives from Central and Eastern Europe, Edited by Katalin E. Fabian

Volume 90: Privatization in Transition Economies: The Ongoing Story, Edited by Ira W. Lieberman and Daniel J. Kopf

CONTEMPORARY STUDIES IN ECONOMIC AND FINANCIAL ANALYSIS VOLUME 91

PERSONAL INJURY AND WRONGFUL DEATH DAMAGES CALCULATIONS: TRANSATLANTIC DIALOGUE

EDITED BY

JOHN O. WARD
University of Missouri-Kansas City, MO, USA

ROBERT J. THORNTON
Lehigh University, Bethlehem, PA, USA

Emerald

United Kingdom – North America – Japan
India – Malaysia – China

JAI Press is an imprint of Emerald Group Publishing Limited
Howard House, Wagon Lane, Bingley BD16 1WA, UK

First edition 2009

British Library Cataloguing in Publication Data
A catalogue record for this book is available from the British Library

ISBN: 978-1-84855-302-6
ISSN: 1569-3759 (Series)

CONTENTS

THE TRANSATLANTIC DIALOGUE: AN INTRODUCTION

John O. Ward and Robert J. Thornton

1. BACKGROUND TO THE DIALOGUE

This collection of original papers had its origin in a series of annual meetings of the National Association of Forensic Economics (NAFE) held in Great Britain, Ireland, Italy, and the United States from 2004 to 2008.[1] NAFE sponsored these meetings to explore common research areas in the calculation of damages in personal injury and death litigation in Western Europe and the United States. NAFE was founded in 1986 and is the largest association of economists and other damages experts specializing in the calculation of economic damages in litigation in the United States and Canada. The *Journal of Forensic Economics* (JFE) is the journal of NAFE and has been the primary outlet of peer-reviewed research in forensic economics over the past 22 years. The field of forensic economics has generated a substantial literature on methodologies and empirical research in the calculation of damages in personal injury, death, employment, and commercial litigation; and the use of that literature in the United States and Canadian courts by economists, Certified Public Accounts (CPAs), and actuaries has become commonplace in the past two decades (Thornton & Ward, 1999).[2]

The intent of the first international meeting of NAFE in Edinburgh in 2004 was to compare U.S. methodologies for calculating economic damages in personal injury and death litigation with those procedures used in the

Personal Injury and Wrongful Death Damages Calculations: Transatlantic Dialogue
Contemporary Studies in Economic and Financial Analysis, Volume 91, 1–10

ISSN: 1569-3759/doi:10.1108/S1569-3759(2009)0000091003

United Kingdom and other European Union (EU) members. In the United Kingdom prior to 1999, economic damages in such litigation were typically assessed by individual judges using "rule of thumb" multipliers with little actuarial or economic input or content. In 1999 in a case titled *Wells v. Wells*[3] before the House of Lords, the courts took judicial notice of actuarially derived multipliers used in the calculation of lost wages in personal injury and death litigation. These actuarially derived multipliers were the "Ogden" tables, named after Sir Michael Ogden. Ogden was the force behind the development of the tables in the 1980s through the work of the Law Commission and the Ogden Working Group, as described by Matthias Kelly, QC, in the following chapter of this volume. After the *Wells v. Wells* decision in 1999 by the House of Lords, there began a process of examination of methodologies appropriate to the calculation of economic damages in personal injury and death litigation in the United Kingdom involving lawyers, actuaries, and economists. The Ogden Working Groups that followed that decision have included the participation of several authors of chapters in this volume and have utilized the best available statistical, actuarial, and economic methodologies in creating future Ogden tables. These have included the examination of forensic economic methodologies used in the United States.

Two of the contributors to this volume, Robert McNabb and Victoria Wass, coauthored a paper in 2003 with Lewis and Robinson titled "Loss of Earnings Following Personal Injury: Do the Courts Adequately Compensate Injured Parties?" (Lewis, McNabb, Robinson, & Wass, 2002[4]). The paper reviewed the development of forensic economic methodologies and concepts in the United States and concluded that, while the current Ogden tables were a substantial improvement over "rule of thumb" verdicts by judges prior to the *Wells v. Wells* decision, the "U.S. model" offered even greater accuracy in the forecasting of lost earnings. The authors also outlined an agenda for future research in the United Kingdom to incorporate improvements into future Ogden tables. It was this agenda that was the focus of the 2004 NAFE meetings in Edinburgh with both Robert McNabb and Matthias Kelly participating.

At the NAFE 2005 meetings in Dublin, Steve Haberman, Richard Verrall, and Zoltan Butt presented their research on enhanced Markov work life tables for the United Kingdom as an addition to the 2006 Ogden tables. Their research parallels that done in the United States by Gary Skoog, James Ciecka, and Kurt Krueger. Haberman, Verrall, and Butts also prepared a paper on their Markov work life calculations for the NAFE meetings in Boston in 2006 (Verrall, Haberman, & Butt, 2006).

In 2007, the NAFE meetings in Florence, Italy, explored the topic of awards for noneconomic damages, focusing on research by Giovanni Comandé on a European model for non-pecuniary damages awards. Comandé later proposed a similar non-pecuniary damages model for the United States in a paper that he presented at the NAFE meetings in Chicago in 2007. Papers were also presented in Florence and Chicago by John Ward and Robert Minnehan on the development of Ogden-type multipliers for the United States, particularly in class-action cases.

The exchange of ideas on forensic economic methodologies between economists and actuaries who attended the NAFE meetings described above has been most fruitful. It has opened new paths for cooperative research and stimulated new ways of thinking about both economic and noneconomic damages in personal injury and death torts in the United States and Europe. And the original papers in this volume serve to capture the essence of the dialogue described above.

2. OVERVIEW OF CHAPTERS

In this section, we provide summary overviews of each of the chapters (largely in the words of the authors themselves). The volume begins with Matthias Kelly's contribution, "The Development of an Actuarial Approach to the Calculation of Future Loss in the UK." The chapter is a history of the adoption of actuarial methods for calculating and awarding pecuniary damages by the courts of the United Kingdom during the past two decades. The author examines the case law leading to the *Wells v. Wells* decision that officially recognized the Ogden tables as the mechanism for determining compensation in personal injury litigation, and also the work of the Law Commission in recognizing the need for actuarial precision in making such awards. The chapter discusses the evolution of the Ogden tables and the role of Sir Michael Ogden, QC, in gaining acceptance for the tables. The work of the Ogden Working Party in addressing issues of discounting, adjusting losses for inflation, and addressing rising health care costs through periodic payments is also reviewed. Finally, the author outlines the areas of damages calculation that remain to be addressed as well as the need for continued input by the Ogden Working Party and the Law Commission to address those issues.

The next chapter is by John Ward and is entitled "Economic Damages and Tort Reform: A Comparative Analysis of the Calculation of Economic Damages in Personal Injury and Death Litigation in the United States and the United Kingdom." The chapter compares the traditional actuarial method of calculating pecuniary damages for personal injury litigation in the United States with the system of scheduled pecuniary damages (the Ogden tables) in the United Kingdom in the contexts of both exactness of measurement and the goals of tort reform. In the United States, the presentation of a pecuniary-damages claim is commonly made by an economic expert to a jury, while in the United Kingdom the judge directly decides upon damages and may rely upon published actuarial multipliers in arriving at the level of pecuniary damages to award. The chapter lays out the design of the actuarial model used by experts in the United States and how that design has been incorporated into the Ogden tables in the United Kingdom. It also discusses the possibility of developing a system of scheduled damage multipliers for pecuniary-damages awards in the United States and offers a model for the design of such multipliers. Finally, the Ogden tables, the multipliers derived from the damages model of the September 10, 2001, Victim's Compensation Fund, and U.S. scheduled damages model multipliers are each applied to hypothetical personal injury cases. The results are then compared, along with their implications for the accuracy of damages calculations and for tort reform.

In "Accounting for the Effects of Disablement on Future Employment in Britain," Victoria Wass and Robert McNabb first note that UK law generally provides that any person injured through the fault of another may claim monetary compensation in the form of damages. The quantum of damages is determined by means of a formula, the multiplier–multiplicand formula, in which an annual sum for posttax earnings (the multiplicand) is multiplied by the number of years to retirement (the multiplier), with the latter discounted by a real rate of return and the risks of both mortality and nonemployment prior to retirement age. In contrast to U.S. courts, courts in the United Kingdom have been reluctant to engage labor market data or economic expertise in the determination of employment risks. Instead, normal practice has been the arbitrary adjustment of multipliers in the form of judicial discretion. Such adjustments set precedents and become established. One such precedent is the *Smith v. Manchester* award of between 6 and 24 months post-injury earnings in response to the increased risk of nonemployment over a lifetime for a claimant who is disabled but who retains the capacity to work.

There is surprisingly little UK research on the labor market effects of disability, and none that looks at the effects of disability over a working lifetime. However, the research that does exist indicates a much greater employment disadvantage than that assumed by the courts. Nonparticipation rates for the disabled are generally about twice that of the nondisabled, and the trend is upwards. While acknowledging the difficulties in measuring disability-induced employment effects, the authors proceed to develop a simple two-state increment–decrement model to estimate worklife expectancies (WLE) by age, sex, and employment and disability status. The authors use this model to estimate individual WLEs before and after injury. The use of empirically based disability-adjusted multipliers in the calculation of post-injury earnings precludes the need to make arbitrary adjustments to the lump sum for the purpose of accounting for the employment effects of disability. A comparison of WLE by disability status indicates that the impact of disablement on employment exceeds 24 months by a substantial margin. Finally, using a sample of 100 awards adjudicated in the UK courts during the 1990s, the authors use their model to recalculate the award for future loss of earnings in each case and compare this hypothetical figure with that actually awarded by the court to reveal a situation of substantial under-compensation.

The next chapter, "Estimating and Using Work Life Expectancy in the UK," is by Zoltan Butt, Steve Haberman, Richard Verrall, and Victoria Wass. The starting point for this chapter is the deficiencies in the estimated employment risks contained in the Ogden tables for use in the traditional multiplier–multiplicand calculation, namely the use of average (unconditional) employment rates and the absence of account of the impact of disability. (These points were also raised in the previous chapter.) The focus of this chapter is to provide a suitable modification to the multiplier–multiplicand calculation, since this is the approach that lawyers are committed to using, and to reestimate the parameters of the formula to more accurately account for employment risks.

The parameters of the multiplier–multiplicand formula are contained within the Ogden tables. The baseline multiplier is the discounted life expectancy, and the reduction for employment risks is a discounted WLE expressed as a proportion of the discounted number of years alive to retirement. The authors provide improved estimates of the reduction factors (RFs) for employment risks. WLE and RFs are modeled within the framework of a multiple-state Markov process and, as in the previous chapter, are conditioned upon age, sex, starting employment status, and disability. In this chapter, the authors make use of the longitudinal element of the labor force survey (LFS) and a more sophisticated from of modeling. One of the benefits of this approach is the addition of a further covariate – educational achievement. The combination of disability and skill level proved to be powerful in the determination of employment.

The new RFs estimated in this study, and the adaptation to the calculation to formally incorporate the effects of disability on the multiplier, were adopted in the latest version of the Ogden tables (Sixth Edition, May 2006). However, the law is slow to change. Incorporation of the disability-induced employment disadvantage into the quantum of damages has proved to be controversial with both insurance companies and with the judiciary. The focus of their concern is the magnitude of the impact (compared to the *Smith v. Manchester* award) and the consequent implication for the level of damages. A case example (*Conner v. Bradman*) shows how the courts, while adopting the new approach, use judicial discretion to reduce its effect on the award of damages.

Judicial discretion is the perfectly reasonable response to imprecision in the RFs, which are estimated for broad categories of the working population and not for individual claimants. However, the decision in *Conner v. Bradman* suggests a need for further guidance on the magnitude of discretionary adjustments away from the average RF. In this regard, the authors look to important developments in the U.S. forensic economics literature in which the average RF is treated as a random variable whose distribution can be estimated through simulation techniques.

In the next chapter, "Markov Work Life Table Research in the United States," Gary Skoog and James Ciecka summarize worklife-related research in the United States over the last 25 years. They point out that striking theoretical and empirical developments have occurred over this period. The switch, first of all, from life-table-based constructs to Markov process models was seminal. The probabilistic implications of Markov models have been captured theoretically and estimated with large, current, and nationally representative data sets. Parametric and nonparametric worklife models have been estimated, along with models of full-time and part-time worklife as well as occupation-specific worklife models. Skoog and Ciecka also note that worklife research has progressed along quite different paths in the United States and the United Kingdom over the last 25 years. The chapter concludes with a glimpse at the likely direction of future worklife-related research.

The focus switches again to the United Kingdom in the next chapter, "Periodical Payments Awards and the Transfer of Risk." Richard Cropper and Victoria Wass point out that personal injury claims for future loss in the United Kingdom have been settled traditionally by lump sum payments. Although structured settlements have long been available as a remedy, they have rarely been used. But as of April 2005, an amendment to the Damages Act of 1996 introduced a new approach to claims in the United Kingdom in which the court is required to consider (and potentially impose) an award of damages in the form of a structured settlement. In contrast to the existing structured settlement, the new form of award is to be called a "periodical payment" and is to be determined on a "bottom up" basis where the claimant's needs are paramount. This approach has been described as "the most fundamental change in 150 years in the quantification of bodily injury claims" (London International Insurance and Reinsurance Market Association, 2003).

As the authors explain, under a lump sum award it is the *claimant* who bears the risk of uncertain mortality and investment returns. However, periodical payments were designed to transfer these risks to the *tortfeasor* where, for reasons of justice, equity, and efficiency, they ought properly to lie. Yet the statutory provision for periodical payments left the issue of indexation unresolved. The UK retail price index (RPI) was the default measure, and the first order for a periodical payment was linked to this index. However, historically earnings have risen faster than have prices in the United Kingdom; and, since the largest component of any care plan is the wages of the "carers" (caregivers), uprating the annual cost of care by the RPI would very likely leave the claimant unable to afford the cost of future care from his/her damages. The risk of a shortfall was high – in fact, it was almost a certainty – and with annual sums often in the region of £250 thousand, the magnitude of the shortfall was also high. The indexation issue was to prove critical to the success of periodical payments. The benefits to the claimant of the transfer of risk were acknowledged by both the parties and the courts. However, indexation to an inappropriate measure, in which the failure of the annual sum to meet the rising cost of the expenditure is all but guaranteed, threatened to jeopardize the reform in its entirety. In this chapter, the authors outline the arguments in favor of replacing the RPI with an earning-based measure for the indexation of annual care costs. As things turned out, these arguments were to prevail in both the High Court and the Court of Appeal so that the very considerable potential benefits to the claimant of the transfer of mortality and investment risks to the defendant were able to be realized. The authors were the lead expert witnesses in a series of test cases centered on the issue of indexation of periodical payments during 2006–2007.

The next chapter, "The United States Approach to Computing Economic Damages due to Personal Injury and Wrongful Death," was written by Kurt Krueger and Gary Albrecht. As the authors point out, tort damage law in the United States allows the claimant to recover economic damages incurred because of injury when the injury causes reduced individual productivity. The level of economic damages recoverable is a function of the difference between the pre-injury and the post-injury values of the claimant's economic output. Although state jurisdictions in the United States show marked variations in their compensable economic damages, there are nonetheless certain "core" economic methods that are used in all jurisdictions to determine economic damages in tort cases. This chapter presents the generally accepted economic theories and methodologies which comprise what has been called the "U.S. approach" to computing economic damages.

The following chapter crosses the Atlantic once more, this time directing attention to the Republic of Ireland. In "Principles of Compensation for Injury and Wrongful Death in Ireland," Shane Whelan lays out the fundamental processes underlying the assessment of damages in Ireland by reference to landmark statutes and precedents. The principal focus of the chapter, however, is on how damages in Ireland are computed in practice. The discussion highlights those assumptions to which the quantum of damages is most sensitive while also noting the more debatable ones. In particular, Whelan discusses and analyzes the sensitivity of the lump sum to the discount rate(s), to future mortality improvements, and to future taxation. The expert witnesses relied on by the Irish courts to capitalize future pecuniary losses have for many decades been actuaries, and their original market-consistent approach influenced practice in the United Kingdom following the adoption of the Ogden tables. In more recent years, Irish actuaries and Irish courts have had to adopt a less theoretically sound approach to setting the discount rate, consequent on the failure of an index-linked bond market to develop in Ireland from the mid-1980s.

The focus next turns to Italy, with Giovanni Comandé's "Doing Away with Inequality in Loss of Enjoyment of Life." The aim of this chapter is to show the viability and the benefits for the United States of experimenting with awarding methods for non-pecuniary losses in light of European experiences. A comparison of innovative methods shows that the use of "European style" guidelines would help the review process while safeguarding the jury's independence and enabling courts to consider the legitimate evidential factors that evoked the specific jury verdict. A better understanding of non-U.S. solutions would at least bring about more consistency in striving for individual justice while retaining judicial "discretion."

In their chapter, "Scheduled Damages and the American Tort Environment," Steven Shapiro and A.E. Rodriguez return to the United States to compare caps on noneconomic damages with proposals to adopt "scheduling" of such damages. In comparing scheduling with caps on noneconomic damages, the authors conclude that caps do not eliminate horizontal and vertical inequities. In addition, caps can create greater incentives for victims to underinsure, they can lessen incentives to avoid injury, and they may lead to larger awards for economic damages. By contrast, scheduling is a second-best solution to a status quo of unconstrained awards for noneconomic damages by jurors. Scheduling does provide greater horizontal and vertical equity for litigants. However, scheduling requires using information based on past awards or on subjective judgments by legislators in order to construct schedules. Hence, problems of suboptimal deterrence and insurance are not necessarily reduced.

In "Examples of Scheduled Damages Used in Europe and the United States," Robert Minnehan describes nine selected examples of "Schedules of Damages" from Europe and the United States that illustrate the range of complexity found in such schedules. The author distinguishes between "general" and "special" damages, which are specific concepts in American and British laws, and provides examples of how both types of concepts are formulated and specified. The general damages compensation schemes vary from relatively simple – with only a few levels of awards – to much more complex schemes – with as many as 29 levels of awards in one example or with awards based on the percent of disability in another. The special damages compensation schemes, which focus on quantifiable economic or pecuniary losses, are formula-based calculations with either a few factors or with many factors considered in the calculations. These examples also vary from simple to relatively complex. Although not a specific focus of this chapter, differences in potential award levels across countries can be observed in these descriptions.

The concluding chapter in the volume is entitled "International Data and the Forensic Economist: A Guide to Sources and Uses." As the authors, Michael Piette and David Williams, note, forensic economists are often asked to calculate economic damages in cases that are tried in the United States but involve the death or injury of a citizen or resident of a foreign country. Commonly called "international cases," they can range from a single tourist who is killed or injured when visiting the United States to mass torts such as plane crashes or product liability claims. In international cases, macroeconomic data compiled by various governmental or private sources within the United States are of very limited use in preparing economic loss estimates. Rather, the decedent or injured party's economic, demographic, and social environment may differ significantly from that of an individual living in the United States. In this regard, plaintiffs are impacted by the macroeconomic conditions of their country of domicile. The purpose of this chapter is to provide an overview of the data sources that are available as well as the limitations of these sources in preparing economic loss estimates in international cases.

We hope that the exchange of ideas on forensic economic methodologies contained herein will be both useful and enlightening for practitioners. We also hope that the exchange will continue to create opportunities for cooperative research on both sides of the Atlantic as well as stimulate new ways of thinking about damages estimation in torts involving personal injury and death.

NOTES

1. The European meetings were held in Scotland, Dublin, and Florence; and the U.S. meetings were held in Boston and Chicago in conjunction with the meetings of the Allied Social Sciences Association.
2. See Thornton & Ward (1999) for a history of the development of the field of forensic economics in the United States.
3. *Wells v. Wells* (1999) 1 AC 345.
4. The paper was based on an earlier one, "Methods of Calculating Damages for Loss of Future Earnings," in the *Journal of Personal Injury Law*, 2002, No. 2.

REFERENCES

Thornton, R. J., & Ward, J. O. (1999). The economist in tort litigation. *Journal of Economic Perspectives*, *13*(2), 101–112.

Lewis, R., McNabb, R., Robinson, H., & Wass, V. (2003). Loss of earnings following personal injury: Do the courts adequately compensate injured parties? *The Economic Journal* (November), 568–584.

Verrall, R., Haberman, S., & Butt, Z. (2006). The impact of dynamic measurement of worklife expectancy on the loss of earnings multipliers in England and Wales. Presented at the meetings of the National Association of Forensic Economics meetings in Boston, January 6, 2006.

THE DEVELOPMENT OF AN ACTUARIAL APPROACH TO THE CALCULATION OF FUTURE LOSS IN THE UK

Matthias Kelly[1]

1. THE HISTORICAL BACKGROUND

In the common law of the United Kingdom the objective of any award of damages in personal injuries litigation is to achieve as nearly as possible full compensation for the claimant in respect of the injury sustained.[2] To achieve that objective the court seeks to award such sum as is notionally required to be laid out in the purchase of an annuity which will provide an annual amount equivalent to the loss for the whole period of the loss.[3] The basis of the calculation is an assumed annuity. The court makes an assumption about how the award will be invested.[4] Lord Fraser of Tullybelton in *Cookson v. Knowles*[5] put it thus:

> The assumed annuity will be made up partly of income on the principal sum awarded, and partly of capital obtained by gradual encroachment of the principal. The income element will be at its largest at the beginning of the period and will tend to decline, while the capital element will tend to increase until the principal is exhausted.

Personal Injury and Wrongful Death Damages Calculations: Transatlantic Dialogue
Contemporary Studies in Economic and Financial Analysis, Volume 91, 11–34

ISSN: 1569-3759/doi:10.1108/S1569-3759(2009)0000091004

The court is not, in fact, concerned with how the award will be spent:

> How the Plaintiffs will in fact invest their damages is, of course, irrelevant. That is a question for them. It cannot affect the calculation.[6]

In *Tameside & Glossop Acute Services NHS Trust* (2008) EWCA Civ 5 [17/1/08] the Court of Appeal re-affirmed this principle saying that a claimant of full age and capacity 'had the right to receive his damages as a lump sum and to spend (or squander) them entirely as he wished'.[7]

2. THE ABOLITION OF TRIAL BY JURY IN PERSONAL INJURY ACTIONS

Originally in England and Wales,[8] juries assessed damages. They merely awarded a lump sum that 'seemed' right. There was criticism that jury assessment of damages created inconsistent awards.[9] The law was reformed in 1933 but it was not until 1966 that jury trial ceased to be the norm in personal injury trials. Such trials continued in Northern Ireland until 1987.

Section 6 of the Administration of Justice (Miscellaneous Provisions) Act, 1933 gave a right to trial by jury to a party in the Queen's Bench Division where fraud was alleged against that party, or a claim was made for libel, slander, malicious prosecution, false imprisonment, seduction, or breach of promise of marriage. Then for all the remaining cases (which include personal injury cases) it provided: 'but, save as aforesaid, any action to be tried in that Division may, in the discretion of the court or a judge, be ordered to be tried either with or without a jury'. There was, thus, a residual power to order trial by jury. That continued until the 1960s.

In *Ward v. James* (1966) 1 QB 273 the Court of Appeal restricted trial by jury to cases involving 'exceptional circumstances'. Lord Denning put it thus:

> The judge ought not, in a personal injury case, to order trial by jury save in exceptional circumstances.

Trial by jury was, subsequently ordered in *Hodges v. Harland & Wolff* (1965) 1 WLR 523. There was a further attempt to obtain trial by jury in *H v. Ministry of Defence* (1991) 2 QB 103. At first instance jury trial was ordered but on appeal the Court of Appeal re-asserted that there was, in the United Kingdom 'a bias against jury trials in civil cases'.

It re-affirmed its approach that

> save in exceptional circumstances, trial by jury was inappropriate in personal injury actions where compensatory damages were to be assessed, since such assessment was made by

reference to conventional scales known to a judge but not to a jury and justice required consistency of approach; that although the plaintiff's injuries were unusual and traumatic, such consistency demanded that the assessment of the damages should be in conformity with the conventional scales; that, further, in retaining a judicial discretion for exceptional cases, Parliament was not to be taken as necessarily having contemplated that such cases would arise in the context of personal injury actions; and that, accordingly, the plaintiff's claim was not exceptional so as to justify an order for trial by judge and jury; that the judge had exercised his discretion on a wrong principle and his order would be set aside.

When juries were effectively abolished in claims for personal injuries and death, the award was capable of being precisely calculated to meet the objective of full compensation. That objective was called into question with the rapid inflation of the late 1960s and early 1970s.

3. THE EFFECT OF INFLATION UPON THE AWARD OF DAMAGES

The English courts set their face against overt changes to the multiplier or multiplicand to allow for inflation. The claimant is compensated at present day values. Whilst it is accepted that money loses its value through inflation, the judicial approach has been to leave inflation to be dealt with by investment decisions, the assumption being that properly invested funds will keep place with inflation. Quite how the average recipient of a medium-sized award was supposed to negotiate the financial markets was not made clear by the courts. In the United Kingdom the relevant sum is fixed at the time of trial.

In my view, the only practicable course for courts to adopt in assessing damages awarded under the Fatal Accidents Acts is to leave out of account the risk of further inflation, on the one hand, and the high interest rates which reflect the fear of it and capital appreciation of property and equities which are the consequence of it, on the other hand. In estimating the amount of the annual dependency in the future, had the deceased not been killed, money should be treated as retaining its value at the date of the judgment, and in calculating the present value of annual payments which would have been received in future years, interest rates appropriate to times of stable currency such as 4 per cent to 5 per cent should be adopted. (Per Lord Diplock in *Mallett v. McMonagle* (1970) 1 AC 166 at p. 176.)

As for the suggestion that either the multiplier or the multiplicand should be adjusted to take account of inflation in *Cookson v. Knowles* (1979) AC 556, Lord Diplock was clear:

Quite apart from the prospects of future inflation, the assessment of damages in fatal accidents can at best be only rough and ready because of the conjectural nature of so many of the other assumptions upon which it has to be based. The conventional method

> of calculating it has been to apply to what is found upon the evidence to be a sum representing 'the dependency', a multiplier representing what the judge considers in the circumstances particular to the deceased to be the appropriate number of years' purchase. In times of stable currency the multipliers that were used by judges were appropriate to interest rates of 4 percent to 5 percent whether the judges using them were conscious of this or not. For the reasons I have given I adhere to the opinion Lord Pearson and I had previously expressed which was applied by the Court of Appeal in *Young v. Percival* [1975] 1 W.L.R. 17, 27-29, that the likelihood of continuing inflation after the date of trial should not affect either the figure for the dependency or the multiplier used. Inflation is taken care of in a rough and ready way by the higher rates of interest obtainable as one of the consequences of it and no other practical basis of calculation has been suggested that is capable of dealing with so conjectural a factor with greater precision.[10]

Thus the principle that inflation ought not to affect either the multiplier or multiplicand was established. In the assessment of future loss, save in exceptional circumstances, inflation was to be disregarded and was left to look after itself, the fall in the value of money being balanced by increased interest rates and capital appreciation.[11]

However, in 1981 the UK Government made available to investors index-linked government stocks (ILGS). This stock transformed the outlook for the risk adverse investor, the investor in a similar position to a claimant seeking security, minimum risk and protection from inflation. From that point onwards many thought that ILGS were the perfect vehicle for the assumed annuity referred to by Lord Fraser of Tullybelton in *Cookson v. Knowles*.[12] However, it was not until *Wells v. Wells*, some 19 years later that such an approach received the approval of the courts. To achieve this transformation the attitude of the courts towards expert evidence, from, for example, actuaries, economists and accountants, had to undergo significant change.

4. THE SELECTION OF THE MULTIPLIER

In *Mallett*,[13] Lord Diplock described the process of selection of the multiplier:

> The starting point in any estimate of the number of years that a dependency would have endured is the number of years between the date of the deceased's death and that at which he would have reached normal retiring age. That falls to be reduced to take account of the chance, not only that he might not have lived until retiring age, but also the chance that by illness or injury he might have been disabled from gainful occupation. The former risk can be calculated from available actuarial tables. The latter cannot. There is also a chance that the widow may die before the deceased would have reached normal retiring age (which can be calculated from actuarial tables) or that she may

> remarry and thus replace her dependency from some other source which would not have been available to her had her husband lived.[14]

Up to that stage it was somewhat unclear why one figure rather than another was chosen as the multiplier. In *Mallett* Lord Diplock explained:

> In cases such as the present where the deceased was aged 25 and his widow about the same age, Courts have not infrequently awarded 16 years' purchase of the dependency. It is seldom that this number of years' purchase is exceeded. It represents the capital value of an annuity certain for a period of 26 years at interest rates of 4 percent, 29 years at interest rates of 4½ percent or 33 years at interest rates of 5 percent. Having regard to the uncertainties to be taken into account, 16 years would appear to represent a reasonable maximum number of years' purchase where the deceased died in his 20's. Even if the period were extended to 40 years, when the deceased would have attained the age of 65, the additional number of years' purchase at interest rates of 4 percent would be less than 4 years, at 4½ percent will be less than 2½ years, and at 5 percent would be little more than 1 year.[15]

In an article in 1995 the late Sir Michael Ogden QC records that during his years at the Bar 16 became established as the conventional maximum multiplier.[16] The following can be deduced as representing the law pre *Wells v. Wells*:

i. 'In times of stable currency the multipliers that were used by judges were appropriate to interest rates of 4 to 5 per cent whether the judges using them were conscious of this or not.'[17]
ii. A stable currency was presumed.
iii. The appropriate multiplier was selected by deciding upon what capital sum would have to be invested at a real rate of return of 4–5 per cent to produce the multiplicand.
iv. There was a ceiling of 16–17[18] upon the multiplier.

This approach was unsatisfactory. Since the object of the law was to achieve full compensation, a cap of 16, 17 or even 18 was inconsistent, particularly in the case of a younger claimant. The case of *Corbett v. Barking and Havering Health Authority* (1990) 1 WLR provides a good illustration. In a fatal accident claim the multiplier is determined as at the time of the accrual of the cause of action. In *Corbett* the cause of action of the claimant arose upon his mother's death at his birth. The overall multiplier, selected at her death, for the claimant, was 12. By the time the case came to trial he was 11 years and 6 months old. His loss of dependency (to age 18) was set at 6 months (12 years less 11 years 6 months). That had the result that the court awarded him 6 months to cover 6 and a half years loss. In the case of a 21 year old with a lifetime loss the maximum multiplier was 20[19] even if he had a life expectancy of 55 years. In short the approach resulted in under-compensation through assuming unrealistic investment strategies, capped multipliers and effectively excluding actuarial evidence.

5. THE GENERAL PRINCIPLES

(1) All damages, whether general or special, are to be assessed on the basis that 'the fundamental purpose of an award of damages is to achieve, as nearly as possible, full compensation for the injury sustained'.[20]
(2) The award should be equitable to both sides. The claimant should recover no more and no less than he/she lost.[21]
(3) At common law, damages are assessed at the time of trial with future losses assessed as a lump sum. Provisional damages, periodical payments and structured settlements are exceptions.
(4) It was, formerly, a fundamental assumption underlying the award of a lump sum that it will be invested in a normal spread of investments.[22]
(5) In the assessment of future loss, save in exceptional circumstances, inflation is to be disregarded and is left to look after itself, the fall in the value of money being balanced by increased interest rates and capital appreciation.[23]

6. ACTUARIAL EVIDENCE

Actuarial evidence had, in the past, been regarded with scepticism by, at least, some of the judges. That scepticism was reflected in judicial views. Lord Pearson felt actuarial calculations gave a 'false appearance of accuracy and precision'.[24] Sir Gordon Wilmer felt that actuarial calculations were 'concerned with averages only'.[25] Lord Denning, the then master of the Rolls, felt that the use of actuarial evidence would lead to 'colossal' awards.[26] Webster J in *Robertson v. Lestrange* (1985) 1 All ER 950 expressed some bewilderment as to how a multiplier was to be decided upon. He described the exercise as 'artificial', quoting Lord Diplock in *Cookson v. Knowles* (1979) AC 556 at p. 568, 'artificial and conjectural'. He was unsure whether the exercise was a fact finding one or 'at least where multipliers are concerned, as one of impression, common sense, estimation, selection, choice, convention, discretion or practice, since each one of those words have been used, most of them, I think, in the House of Lords in the last few years'. He concluded that 'the selection of the appropriate multiplier has become, to a considerable extent, a matter of impression and discretion, taking into account all the circumstances, but circumscribed by the range of multipliers adopted in practice by the courts'.

Perhaps the most colourful contribution came from Oliver LJ, later Lord Oliver, in *Auty v. National Coal Board* (1985) 1 WLR 784:

> Actuarial evidence is no doubt of the greatest assistance where one is seeking to value interests in a fund of ascertained amount for the purposes of purchase, sale or exchange. Indeed, such valuations are the foundation of virtually all schemes propounded under the Variation of Trusts Act 1958. But as a method of providing a reliable guide to individual behaviour patterns, or to future economic and political events, the predictions of an actuary can be only a little more likely to be accurate (and will almost certainly be less entertaining) than those of an astrologer. The judge was, in my judgment, right to reject evidence of this type as admissible for the purposes or which it was sought to adduce it in the case before him.[27]

In a paper[28] in 1985 the actuarial profession hit back. Its authors expressed their understated view that 'there is clearly a problem of communication between the actuarial profession and the judiciary'. Of that there was little doubt at the time.

The climate, however, had begun to 'thaw' by the time of the decision in *Hunt v. Severs* (1994) AC 350. By then the courts were prepared to treat the Ogden tables as 'a check' on the 'conventional' model. Today the tables are the starting point and determine the multiplier unless there is compelling evidence pointing to another different figure.[29] Today no one doubts the admissibility, relevance and accuracy of such evidence.

7. THE ROLE OF THE LAW COMMISSION

The Law Commission has played a pivotal role in the reform of the law in the United Kingdom, nowhere more marked than in its contribution to the reform of the law of damages in personal injury and fatal accident claims. It has provided clear intellectual analysis, conducted research and made clear logical proposals for reform. Its work encouraged the lawyers involved in this area of law to take a group of cases that transformed the calculation of future loss: *Wells v. Wells*, *Thomas v. Brighton Health Authority* and *Page v. Sheerness Steel PLC*,[30] commonly referred to as '*Wells v. Wells*' which resulted in the House of Lords delivering its momentous reforming judgement.

That process began when the Law Commission published a report in 1973 on Personal injury litigation. It summarised the then existing common law in this way:

> (a) the use of the multiplier has been, remains and should continue to remain, the ordinary, the best and the most satisfactory method of assessing the value of a number of future annual sums both in regard to claims for lost dependency under the Fatal Accidents Acts and claims for future loss of earnings or future expenses;
>
> (b) the actuarial method of calculation, whether from expert evidence or from tables, continues to be technically admissible and technically relevant but its usefulness is confined, except perhaps in very unusual cases, to an ancillary means of checking a computation already made by the multiplier method.[31]

The Law Commission recommended that the use of actuarial evidence should be promoted by legislation. That led to exchanges in Parliament during the passage of the Administration of Justice Bill 1982. The then Lord Chancellor invited the relevant professions (lawyers and actuaries) to form a working party to consider the issue of actuarial tables. The Bar of England and Wales took the lead and established 'The inter-professional working party on the actuarial assessment of damages in personal injury and fatal accident litigation.' That group, with its unwieldy title, became known as 'The Ogden Working Party' and ultimately produced what are universally known as 'The Ogden tables'. The tables are actually produced by the Government Actuary and the process is overseen by the working party who provide the written guidance as to their application and use. The working party consists of actuaries and lawyers from all parts of the United Kingdom appointed by their respective professional bodies.

The first set of tables was produced in 1984. However, the arrival of the tables did not produce a change in the approach of the courts, the predominant approach then being one of 'feel', 'instinct' or 'impression'.

The Law Commission returned to the topic, as part of a planned review[32] in 1992 and issued a consultation paper.[33] In that consultation paper they expressed their provisional view:

> We believe, as we did in 1973,[34] in the value of actuarial methods of assessing future loss. Our provisional conclusion is that actuarial methods should be given greater prominence in the awarding of lump sums. However, it is important to bear in mind that despite elaborate calculations concerning mortality, the assessment of loss could be falsified by application of an inappropriate discount rate. The present interest rate and projections of its future movement are both subject to continuous adjustment. But the presumption is that the Court will always abide by its figure of 4.5 percent as appropriate in determining the discount. Insurance companies do not take decisions based on such simplistic assumptions. Annuities involve such companies in making a promise to make

payments over a long period of time on the basis of more sophisticated methods of predicting future interest rates and hedging the risk of interest rate movement. We therefore believe that the need for actuarial methods to be given greater prominence goes hand in hand with the need for more thought to be given to the choice of the appropriate discount rate when selecting multipliers in individual cases.[35]

Two-thirds of those who responded to the Law Commission's consultation paper supported the use of index-linked government securities rates as a method of determining fair compensation. There was broad agreement that the assumption of a 4–5 per cent rate of return over time was 'crude and inflexible'[36] and could lead to over- or under-compensation and hence to injustice.

8. THE LAW COMMISSION REPORT OF 1994 (NO. 224, CM. 2646)

The commission, having completed its public consultation and consideration of the existing law concluded:

We share the views of the majority of those who responded to us, that a practice of discounting by reference to returns in ILGS would be preferable to the present arbitrary assumptions. The 4 percent to 5 percent discount, which emerged from the case law, was established at a time when ILGS did not exist. ILGS now constitute the best evidence of the real return on any investment where the risk element is minimal, because they take account of inflation, rather than attempt to predict it as conventional investments do. Capital is redeemed under ILGS at par and index-linked to the change in the Retail Price Index since issue. Income remains constant in real terms, rising with increases in the RPI. There is no premium available for risk because there is no risk.[37]

Thereafter some momentum developed in the debate. The Government responded to the commission's report by saying on 23 March 1995[38] in the House of Commons: 'The Government welcome the report and will introduce legislation implementing all the recommendations made in it, both on the rationalisation of the structured settlements system and on other aspects of the law of damages, when a suitable opportunity arises.'

There then followed The Civil Evidence Act 1995 in which by section 10 the actuarial tables prepared by the Ogden Working Party were rendered admissible in evidence, without the need to formally prove them. In addition Parliament passed The Damages Act 1996 which enabled the Lord Chancellor to prescribe a rate of return. It provided in section 1:

(1) In determining the return to be expected from the investment of a sum awarded as damages for future pecuniary loss in an action for personal

injury the court shall, subject to and in accordance with rules of court made for the purposes of this section, take into account such rate of return (if any) as may from time to time be prescribed by an order made by the Lord Chancellor.

(2) Subsection (1) above shall not however prevent the court taking a different rate of return into account if any party to the proceedings shows that it is more appropriate in the case in question.

(3) An order under subsection (1) above may prescribe different rates of return for different classes of case.

(4) Before making an order under subsection (1) above the Lord Chancellor shall consult the Government Actuary and the Treasury; and any order under that subsection shall be made by statutory instrument subject to annulment in pursuance of a resolution of either House of Parliament.

Unfortunately the Lord Chancellor did not exercise his power until 2001 when he made the Damages (Personal Injury) Order 2001.[39] That was after *Wells v. Wells* had been decided and the rate of return on investments, including ILGS, had fallen further than the 3 per cent rate prevailing when *Wells* was decided. He set the rate at 2.5 per cent, which was higher than the then current ILGS rate, thus provoking a furious debate. He explained his reasons in a paper as being based on the fact that the Court of Protection invested damages it controlled in 'multi-asset portfolios, including an equity element', which he concluded would produce returns in excess of 2.5 per cent. This was despite the House of Lords having decided in *Wells* that it was irrelevant as to how the award was invested as 'it cannot affect the calculation'.[40]

In prescribing that rate the Lord Chancellor was in a difficult position. As a minister in the government, as well as head of the judiciary he wore two hats. In addition, as a minister he was part of a government likely to be directly affected by the choice of rate. Many government departments were, and are, litigants before the courts in personal injury and fatal accident claims (e.g. the Ministry of Defence, the NHS). Nevertheless the rate stood and still stands. Attempts have been made to persuade the courts to apply a different rate. All have been rebuffed. In *Warriner v. Warriner* [2002] EWCA Civ 81 Dyson LJ said at paragraph 33:

> We are told that this is the first time that this court has had to consider the Act, and that guidance is needed as to the meaning of 'more appropriate in the case in question' in section 1(2). The phrase 'more appropriate', if considered in isolation, is open-textured. It prompts the question: by what criteria is the court to judge whether a different rate of return is more appropriate in the case in question? But the phrase must be interpreted in

> its proper context, which is that the Lord Chancellor has prescribed a rate pursuant to section 1(1) and has given very detailed reasons explaining what factors he took into account in arriving at the rate that he has prescribed. I would hold that in deciding whether a different rate is more appropriate in the case in question, the court must have regard to those reasons. If the case in question falls into a category that the Lord Chancellor did not take into account and/or there are special features of the case which (a) are material to the choice of rate of return and (b) are shown from an examination of the Lord Chancellor's reasons not to have been taken into account, then a different rate of return may be 'more appropriate'.

The Court of Appeal in *Cooke v. United Bristol Health Care* (2003) EWCA Civ. 1370 was faced with an attempt to use revised multiplicands with stepped increases over time to reflect the faster rise in care costs in comparison with retail price index (RPI). The court rejected the approach. Laws LJ at paragraph 30 said:

> Once it is accepted that the discount rate is intended in any given personal injury case to be the *only* factor (in the equation ultimately yielding the claimant's lump sum payment) to allow for any future inflation relevant to the case, then the multiplicand cannot be taken as allowing for the same thing, or any part of it, without usurping the basis on which the multiplier has been fixed. And it must be accepted that the discount rate was so intended: by the House in *Wells*, by Parliament in the Act of 1996, and by the Lord Chancellor in making his order under the Act. Mr Hogg's attempt to treat his calculation of the multiplicand as a 'separate issue' from the discount rate, and counsel's submissions supporting that position, are in the end nothing but smoke and mirrors. It follows that the substance of these appeals constitutes an illegitimate assault on the Lord Chancellor's discount rate, and on the efficacy of the 1996 Act itself. [41]

9. THE ROLE OF THE OGDEN WORKING PARTY

The work of the Law Commission was augmented by the work of the Ogden group. Its tables and guidance are now in a sixth edition.

The first pioneering edition was published in May 1984. It took no account of risks other than mortality, such as the risk of loss of employment, regional variations. As a result judges stuck with 'conventional' multipliers. The second edition was published in 1994 and took account of contingencies other than mortality, such as the risk of unemployment, regional variations in economic activity, age and illness. The discounting factors for such risks were based on work carried out by Professor S. Haberman and Mrs D.S.F. Bloomfield (Haberman and Bloomfield, 1990). Their work relied on labour force studies for 1973, 1977, 1981 and 1985. Still the courts continued to be sceptical, applying discounts of as much as 20 per cent. The working party slogged on. The third edition was published in 1998. This was prompted by the publication of English Life Table number 15 showing increased life spans. The third edition also provided projections of improved mortality in future. By this time many had become convinced that the time had come for an assault upon the assumptions that underlay the adherence to a discount rate of 4–5 per cent as the rate to be applied to the notional rate of return upon the lump sum award. By the time the fourth edition was published in 2000 *Wells v. Wells* had been decided. This edition was prompted by the Law Commission's recommendation that the working party should consider how the tables should be used to produce accurate assessments of damages in Fatal Accident Act cases.[42] It was followed by the fifth edition, which was published in 2004. This edition was prompted by the need to revise the life tables[43] and reflect improved life expectancy.[44] We are, at the time of writing, now on the sixth edition, which was published in 2007, using new data to calculate contingencies other than mortality, such as education, likelihood of unemployment, disability and economic activity. This revised methodology is based on work carried out by Lewis, McNabb, and Wass (2002); by Verrall, Haberman, and Butt; as well as a separate work by Wass. The discounting tables in the sixth edition are an amalgam of these works.

The role of the Ogden group has been widely praised. In *Wells v. Wells* Lord Lloyd of Berwick paid tribute to the group:

> I turn next to the commentators and textbook writers. It was the Working Party under the chairmanship of Sir Michael Ogden Q.C. which blazed the trail.[45]

He went on to provide a good resume of the history of the issue:[46]

> In the introduction to the first edition of the Actuarial Tables published in 1984, Sir Michael Ogden refers to the then recent introduction of index-linked government stocks in 1981. They had already become an established part of the investment market. Sir Michael describes the advantages of I.L.G.S. in the following paragraph, at p. 8:
>
> Investment policy, however prudent, involves risks and it is not difficult to draw up a list of blue chip equities or reliable unit trusts which have performed poorly and, in some cases, disastrously. Index-linked government stocks eliminate the risks. Whereas, in the past, a plaintiff has had to speculate in the form of prudent investment by buying equities, or a 'basket' of equities and gilts or a selection of unit trusts, he need speculate no longer if he buys index-linked government stock. If the loss is, say, £5,000 per annum, he can be awarded damages which, if invested in such stocks, will provide him with almost exactly that sum in real terms.

In the second edition published in 1994 Sir Michael Ogden repeats the views expressed in the introduction to the first edition:

> However, there are now available index-linked government stocks and it is accordingly no longer necessary to speculate about either the future rates of inflation or the real rate of return obtainable on an investment. The redemption value and dividends of these stocks are adjusted from time to time so as to maintain the real value of the stock in the face of inflation. The current rates of interest on such stocks are published daily in the Financial Times and hitherto have fallen into the range of about 2.5 percent to 4.5 percent gross.

A little later he says:

> … the return on such index-linked government stocks is the most accurate reflection of the real rate of interest available to plaintiffs seeking the prudent investment of awards … .

The third edition of the Ogden Tables was published in April 1998, after the decision of the Court of Appeal in the present case, but before the hearing in the House. Sir Michael anticipates a fourth edition when the decision of the House is made known, and when the Lord Chancellor has had an opportunity to fix the rate of return under section 1 of the Damages Act 1996. Sir Michael will then be able, as he says, to retire from the task which he was first asked to undertake 15 years ago, and which he has performed with such conspicuous success.

The Court of Appeal expressed their concern at departing from the recommendation of the Ogden Working Party but added that the Working Party suffered from the disadvantage that the membership did not include any accountants or investment advisers. The plaintiffs challenged the truth of that observation; but in any event I would not regard it as weakening the force of the Working Party's recommendation.

In between the first and second editions of the Ogden Tables, the Law Commission published Consultation Paper No. 125 on Structured Settlements and Interim and Provisional Damages, to which there was a large response from a variety of sources, including investment advisers. The consultation paper led to Law Commission Report No. 224 (1994) (Cm. 2646). The following passages are relevant:

> 2.25 Our provisional view was that courts should make more use of information from the financial markets in discounting lump sums to take account of the fact that they are paid today. One way of doing this would be to enable courts to refer to the rate of return on ILGS as a means of establishing an appropriate rate of discount. The purpose of this would be to obtain the best reflection of market opinion as to what real interest rates will be in future. The question upon which we sought the views of consultees was whether it would be reasonable to use the return on ILGS as a guide to the appropriate discount.
>
> 2.26 Almost two-thirds of those who responded to this question supported the use of the ILGS rates to determine more accurate discounts. These consultees agreed that the

> assumption of a 4 to 5 percent rate of return over time is crude and inflexible and can lead to over- or under-compensation and hence to injustice... .
>
> 2.28 Wc sharc thc views of the majority of those who responded to us, that a practice of discounting by reference to returns on ILGS would be preferable to the present arbitrary presumption. The 4 to 5 percent discount which emerged from the case law was established at a time when ILGS did not exist. ILGS now constitute the best evidence of the real return on any investment where the risk element is minimal, because they take account of inflation, rather than attempt to predict it as conventional investments do.

This is a very strong recommendation indeed. Once again the Court of Appeal expressed concern at departing from such a recommendation, but commented that the recommendation was based on implicit assumptions as to the objective to be achieved, which they did not accept.

There is a sustained criticism of the Court of Appeal's decision in Kemp and Kemp: The Quantum of Damages vol. 1, para. 6-003/9-6-003/13, and in David Kemp Q.C.'s article in 1997 L.Q.R. vol. 113 at p. 195. I have derived much assistance from Mr. Kemp's commentary, for which I am grateful.

In the current edition of McGregor on Damages, 16th ed. (1997), Mr. Harvey McGregor Q.C. hazarded a guess that the House would endorse a rate somewhat less than the Court of Appeal's 4.5 percent but would not adopt the I.L.G.S. rate. In Mr. McGregor's view that would have been the right solution, because he regarded it as highly unlikely that a plaintiff with substantial damages would invest it all in I.L.G.S. He would be more likely to accept investment advice, and end up with a portfolio largely of equities. This would lead to over-compensation, if equities continue their upward progression.

For reasons which I have already given I would not agree with this approach. The suggestion that plaintiffs with a substantial award of damages are likely to invest in a portfolio consisting largely of equities is not supported by the research carried out for the Law Commission: see their Report No. 225 para. 10.2. In any event what an individual does with his damages is a matter for him. If he invests in equities, he may be lucky and end up by being over-compensated. But the question is whether his damages should be calculated on the basis that he is obliged to invest in equities.

Apart from McGregor on Damages, we were not referred to any other commentary or textbook which disagrees with the recommendations of the Ogden Working Party and the Law Commission.

10. RISING CARE COSTS

When providing for future care costs, there is always uncertainty. The injured claimant may live longer than anyone expected. He or she may live for a shorter period than expected. In the former case he or she will have been under-compensated by the lump sum approach. In the latter case he or she will have been over-compensated. Care cost will rise more rapidly than conventional RPI. To meet that eventuality he will have to invest more aggressively than ILGS, contrary to the approach of low-risk investment assumed in case law. To address this problem the United Kingdom has looked to periodical payments. Initially this was by way of structured settlements. The first steps were taken in the tax treatment of periodical payments in 1988 when the purchase of an annuity by a defendant or its insurer out of, and at the same time, as an award of compensation resulted in the annual payments from the annuity being tax-free in a claimant's hands. The first structured settlement was the following year. It provided for the payment to the claimant of a combination of lump sum and a stream of tax-free payments payable for his/her lifetime. Various factors limited the number of claims resolved by way of structured settlements. One major problem was that structured settlements could be implemented only with the agreement of both parties. Another was escalating care costs and the absence, in the market, of an annuity which was linked to a suitable index to meet escalating care costs.

The Damages Act 1996 [Section 2(1)] attempted to meet the problem by allowing the court to make an order that damages were wholly or partly to take the form of periodical payments. However, such an order could only be made if both parties agreed. In 2002, a working party established by the Master of the Rolls' provided a report which led to amendments[47] to the 1996 Act. As a result of these amendments, since 1 April 2005 it has been open to the court to make an order for periodical payments whether or not the parties agree. It is now mandatory, when the court is making an award of damages for future pecuniary loss in respect of personal injury, for it to consider whether the damages – or part of them – should be paid by way of periodical payments.

Periodical payments provide a guarantee for the claimant that he will continue to receive regular annual payments for the duration of his life. That has the benefit that the damages will never be exhausted. The annual payments will be free of tax, thereby removing uncertainties associated with possible future changes to the taxation of investment income. The fact that the annual payments cease on death has the result that there is less risk of large sums paid by defendants going to persons other than the injured person for whose benefit they were intended.

When a lump sum award is made, the responsibility for deciding how to invest the lump sum lies with the claimant. It is for him to manage his resources carefully, with a view to ensuring that he has the best possible chance of meeting his lifelong needs. Where the claimant has a large sum of damages and a long life expectancy, his damages will, usually, require expert financial management not only to guard against the risk that he might survive longer than the estimate of life expectancy on which the multiplier was calculated, but also to meet the cost of his annual needs, which will increase year by year from the date when the award is made.

The management of any fund involves taking decisions about risk. All investments, of course, carry with them some element of risk. The more risk an investor is prepared to take, the greater the likely returns. An investment that offers the prospect of high returns in terms of capital growth also carries with it the risk that the capital value might decrease. An investment carrying a lower rate of risk is likely to produce lower returns allied to greater security of the capital. Ideally, a claimant who is entirely reliant on his damages for his future quality of life should not be compelled to expose himself to a significant degree of investment risk. That was the rationale of *Wells v. Wells*. However, for many claimants receiving a 'once and for all' damages award, this was often unavoidable. Such claimants usually were advised to invest in a combination of low-risk and higher-risk investments, this being the only way in which it was believed that there could be any chance of meeting increasing annual care costs and the additional expense associated with a longer life expectancy.

One important effect of a periodical payments order is to transfer the risk associated with the investment of damages away from the claimant. The award will guarantee the claimant annual payments for his lifetime. Furthermore, the amendments to the 1996 Act provide for uplifts to the annual payments in accordance with RPI or another more suitable index. Provided that indexation accurately reflects actual increases in the relevant annual costs, the claimant will be protected against the effects of future increases in those costs.

If, however, the annual uplifts do not accurately reflect the actual increase in relevant care costs, most claimants will have no means of protecting themselves against the shortfall. That is a major difficulty with RPI. It is not linked to care costs, yet it is the index referred to by section 2(1) of the Damages Act 1996 as amended.[48] The transfer of risk away from the claimant results, however, in a loss of the opportunity for gain. However the reality for most claimants, if RPI is used, is that they may be caught in a situation in which the annual income falls further and further below the level which, at the time the periodical payments order was made, it was agreed or assessed as being necessary to meet his needs.

The effect of any shortfall in the damages available for future care is that the claimant could become dependent on the State to make up the balance needed to meet his care needs. Such assistance is not, in a changing economic and political climate, guaranteed. It, therefore, became necessary to address the indexation provisions. This was done in *Thompstone v. Tameside & Glossop Acute Services NHS Trust* [2006] EWHC 2904 QB. The solution arrived at was to fix the index by reference to the 75th percentile of ASHE occupational group 6115.[49] That was a course adopted by three other judges in separate cases. All came before the Court of Appeal in *Tameside & Glossop Acute Services NHS Trust v. Thompstone* (2008) EWCA Civ 5 [17/1/08). The court upheld the decision of all four judges to depart from RPI as the appropriate index and approved ASHE 6115 as a more appropriate index when making an order for periodical payments in respect of care.

11. THE 'LOST YEARS'

This is a claim brought by a living clamant for lost income in the period by which his life expectancy has been reduced due to the injury (e.g. mesothelioma). The argument is that

> The plaintiff has lost the earnings and the opportunity, which, while he was living, he valued, of employing them as he would have thought best. Whether a man's ambition is to build up a fortune, to provide for his family, or to spend his money upon good causes or merely a pleasurable existence, loss of the means to do so is a genuine financial loss. The logical and philosophical difficulties of compensating a man for a loss arising after his death emerge only if one treats the loss as a non-pecuniary loss – which to some extent it is. But it is also a pecuniary loss – the money would have been his to deal with as he chose, had he lived. (Per Lord Scarman in *Pickett v. British Rail Engineering Ltd* (1980) 1 AC 136 at p. 170.)

Up to that point English law did not permit recovery in respect of what was lost during the 'lost years'. A claimant could recover damages in respect of his future loss of earnings, provided he was likely to be alive in that period. The Law Commission[50] had criticised the position:

> There seems to be no justification in principle for discrimination between deprivation of earning capacity and deprivation of the capacity otherwise to receive economic benefits. The loss must be regarded as a loss of the plaintiff; and it is a loss caused by the tort even though it relates to moneys which the injured person will not receive because of his premature death. No question of the remoteness of damage arises other than the application of the ordinary foreseeability test.

The idea was to bring the claim into line with what could be recovered in a fatal accidents claim. In such claims the award is in respect of the loss of dependency. The convention has grown over the years that there is a conventional deduction in respect of what would have been spent on the deceased's own expenses: 33 per cent in the case of a married person without children, 25 per cent in respect of a married person with dependent children. That rule of practice was articulated in *Harris v. Empress Motors Limited* (1984) 1 WLR 212.

However, the same case suggests that in the case of a claim in respect of the lost years the deduction should be 50 per cent in the case of a married person with no children and 33 per cent in the case of a married person with a surviving spouse and children. This is difficult to justify in logic and fairness. It has attracted criticism: McGregor on Damages, 17th edition (2003), Paragraph 35-084. In the case of *Shanks v. Swan Hunter Group* [2007] EWHC B4 QB (24 May 2007), I argued the point. The judge concluded: 'Why should a married man without children recover only 50 per cent of his earnings if he sues for lost years himself, when his estate would recover 66 per cent if he dies and his estate sues in respect of the same loss?' In that case the court awarded 60 per cent.

In all fatal accident claims the loss is assessed as at the date of death. It is from then that the multiplier is calculated, unlike a claim by a living claimant where the multiplier is set at the date of trial. This is of practical significance as it may take several years for the case to come to court. The time between death and assessment under the current practice is deducted from the multiplier. This has been of concern to the Ogden group. In the fourth edition we tackled the issue. The Law Commission in its report 'Claims for Wrongful Death' (No. 263) addressed the issue. The Court of Appeal wrestled with the problem in *Corbett v. Barking and Havering Health Authority* (1991) 2 QB 408 but felt compelled to follow higher authority (*Cookson v. Knowles* [1979] AC 556). Purchas LJ[51] substituted $3^1/_2$ years for 6 months:

> The correct approach must be to calculate the multiplier from the date of death but in so doing account must be taken of the removal of many of the 'uncertainties' surrounding the provision and receipt of the dependency during the period involved. Accordingly, the discount from the 18-year period to take into account those uncertainties will itself be reduced. Other uncertainties, themselves independent of the continued existence of the beneficiary, e.g. the continued existence of the provider, will remain factors upon which the multiplier will depend and in respect of which the figure for the multiplier must be discounted.

This led the Law Commission to conclude:

> In cases such as *Corbett,* it is the duration of the claimant's need which controls the multiplier. In this type of case, the selection of the multiplier as at the date of death has no logic whatsoever: it is the claimant's circumstances, not the deceased's, which are relevant to the selection of the multiplier, and the claimant's circumstances are best viewed in the light of all the facts known at trial.[52]
>
> Although explicitly intended for use in personal injury *and fatal accident* cases, it is of crucial importance that the present date of death calculation does not enable lawyers and courts to make proper use of the Ogden tables. As laid down by the House of Lords in *Wells v. Wells* these are now to be the starting point when calculating multipliers. Multipliers under the Ogden tables are adjusted so as to reflect a discount for early receipt. This discount is calculated to take effect from the date of trial, when the claimant is assumed to receive any award due to him. It follows that multipliers derived from the present Ogden tables should only take effect from trial. If pre-trial losses are calculated as they are at present, by simply subtracting the duration of the period between death and trial from the multiplier derived from the Ogden tables, the deduction for early receipt incorrectly takes effect on pre-trial losses. For example, say the deceased was a female aged 45 at the time of death. The dependent's claim comes to trial five years later. The present approach is to take the multiplier at the date of death (which, using a three per cent discount in table 14 of the Ogden tables, would be 14.70) and for future loss to apply that multiplier minus 5 (i.e. 9.70). Yet the multiplier for a 50 year-old woman, using the same table, would be 11.78 to which there would need to be a small discount for the risk (which the present Ogden tables, geared primarily for personal injury, do not take account of) that the deceased might have died, or given up work, in any event pre-trial. We have been advised that in the above example an actuarially accurate multiplier for future loss is 11.66. On the other hand, the present approach of the courts does not factor into the calculation of pre-trial losses the possibility that the deceased would have died before trial. That is, for pre-trial loss the courts simply apply to the multiplicand the number of years before death and trial. The award for pre-trial losses therefore overcompensates the claimant. However, because the possibility that the deceased would in any event have died between death and trial is small, it is unlikely to cancel out the substantial loss resulting from the inaccuracy in relation to future loss (in the above example, the inaccuracy being the application of a multiplier of 9.70 instead of 11.66). We conclude that the present approach of the courts will result in the adoption of too low a multiplier in at least the vast majority of cases.[53]
>
> Under our preferred approach, as in personal injury cases, actuarially calculated multipliers would be used in Fatal Accidents Act cases for the purposes of calculating future losses, and thus should be applied from the date of trial. If the multiplier is controlled by the life expectancy of the deceased, it should reflect his or her life expectancy at the time of trial had he or she lived. If the multiplier is controlled by the claimant's need, the selection of the multiplier at trial should ensure greater accuracy in the compensation of the claimant's losses. In both types of case, pre-trial losses can be assessed straightforwardly as in personal injury cases, without the need to calculate a multiplier: the estimated annual loss can simply be multiplied by the number of years between death and trial. Under this approach, the only significant difference from the approach to pre-trial losses in personal injury cases is that one will then need to make a

> small deduction to take account of the possibility that the deceased might in any event have died or given up work before trial.[54]
>
> We should clarify, however, that the simple proposition – 'the multiplier should be calculated from trial, not death' – is ambiguous. This is because a straightforward application of pre-trial loss involves a multiplier, albeit a multiplier which is not actuarially calculated and which simply comprises the number of years between death and trial. We therefore think that, instead of saying that multipliers should be calculated from trial not death, our policy is more clearly expressed by saying that a multiplier which has been discounted for the early receipt of the damages shall only be used in the calculation of post-trial losses.[55]

That led them to recommend (7.14):

> In the first instance, the Ogden Working Party (which includes the Government Actuary) should consider, and explain more fully, how the existing actuarial Ogden tables should be used, or amended, to produce accurate assessments of damages in Fatal Accident Act cases (as opposed to personal injury cases). We would point out to that working party our preferred approach as set out in paragraphs 4.17 and 4.18 and, in particular, our view that a multiplier which has been discounted for the early receipt of the damages should only be used in the calculation of post-trial losses. (Paragraph 4.23).

We did consider the issue and the result was the fourth edition in 2000. The courts[56] have hitherto rejected our recommendations on the basis that they were bound by the speech of Lord Fraser in *Cookson*. In *White v. ESAB Group (UK) Ltd* [2001] EWHC QB 453, Nelson J said:

> I conclude that the Law Commission recommendations are correct and that the multiplier in respect of post trial losses in a fatal claim should be calculated as at the date of trial rather than as at the date of death. The procedure recommended in the Ogden tables 4th edition section D should be followed.
>
> Whilst these are my views as to the merits however I am bound by authority to follow the date of death calculation rule set out in *Cookson v. Knowles* and *Graham v. Dodds*. Neither of these authorities in my judgment is expressly or impliedly overruled by the decision of the House of Lords in *Wells v. Wells*. Nor does that decision provide a means of distinguishing them.

Recently the issue has again been before the Court of Appeal. In *A Train & Sons Ltd v. Fletcher* (2008) EWCA Civ. 413 the issue was whether the trial judge should have awarded full interest on all damages for dependency[57] from the date of death to the date of trial. To do so, it was argued, consistent with the approach set out in *Cookson v. Knowles* (1979) AC 556, that damages are to be assessed as at the date of death and interest to be awarded at half the ordinary rate for losses between death and trial. In that case 2 years 6 months had passed between death and trial. The claimant argued that she had been kept out of an ascertainable sum (the entire award) for that period and should receive full interest. The trial judge agreed. The

Court of Appeal agreed with Nelson J in *White v. ESAB Group (UK) Ltd* [2001] EWHC QB 453 (above) and gave leave to appeal to the House of Lords so that court might reconsider the entire matter. Hooper LJ added that the practice as adopted by the courts resulted in chronological years being deducted from the multiplier. He said 'I do not understand why chronological years are deducted from the multiplier.' The House of Lords will thus be given an opportunity to reconsider the issue.

There is judicial support, albeit not majority House of Lords support, for the approach pointed to by Lord Wilberforce in *Pickett v. British Rail* (1980) 1 AC 136 at p. 151A.

> … the amount to be recovered in respect of earnings in the 'lost' years should be after deduction of an estimated sum to represent the victim's probable living expenses during those years. I think that this is right because the basis, in principle, for recovery lies in the interest which he has in making provision for dependants and others, and this he would do out of his surplus. There is the additional merit of bringing awards under this head into line with what could be recovered under the Fatal Accidents Acts.

This was echoed by the trial judge in *Shanks v. Swan Hunter*:

> First, the difference between the conventions as to deductions for living expenses in a claim under the Fatal Accidents Acts on the one hand and a claim by a living claimant on the other has no obvious rational basis, given the principle behind allowing lost years claims by a living claimant expressed by Lord Wilberforce and the merit (as he saw it) of bringing lost years claims into line with amounts recoverable under the Fatal Accidents Act (see *Pickett*, at page 151A). Why should a married man without children recover only 50 percent of his earnings if he sues for lost years himself, when his estate would recover 66 percent if he dies and his estate sues in respect of the same loss? Of course, the former is not a dependency claim in form or substance – the jurisprudential basis of such claims being relatively uncertain, and the subject of criticism (see, e.g., McGregor on Damages, 17th edition (2003), Paragraphs 35-084 and following) – but the disparity in these potential results is curious and difficult to justify rationally.

The fact that a later claim by the dependants is generally thought to be barred where the deceased, in his lifetime recovered damages for his injury, is open to challenge. In *Pickett v British Rail* (1978) 3 WLR 955, p. 964, Lord Salmon was not prepared to express a concluded view as to whether that assumption was correct:

> Although the point has never been considered by your Lordships' House, it is generally assumed that should the plaintiff accept a sum in settlement of his claim or obtain judgment for damages in respect of the defendent's negligence, his dependents will have no cause of action under the Fatal Accidents Acts after his death. This assumption is supported by strong authority: see *Read v Great Eastern Railway Co.* (1868) L.R. 3 QB 555; *Williams v. Mersey Docks & Harbour Board* [1905] 1K.B. 804 and *Murray v Shuter* [1972] 1 Lloyd's Rep. 6, 7. No point about the correctness of this assumption arises for decision in this appeal and therefore I express no concluded opinion about it. I think,

> however, that the assumption which has held the field for upwards of 100 years is probably correct and that, for present purposes, it must be accepted. In the overwhelming majority of cases a man works not only for his personal enjoyment but also to provide for the present and future needs of his dependents. It follows that it would be grossly unjust to the plaintiff and his dependents were the law to deprive him from recovering any damages for the loss of remuneration which the defendent's negligence has prevented him from earning during the 'lost years'. There is, in my view, no principle of the common law that requires such an injustice to be perpetrated.

The unsatisfactory nature of the award in a lost years claim as seen from the dependant's perspective has recently been recognised in the House of Lords. In *Gregg v Scott* [2005] UKHL 2 Lord Phillips of Worth Matravers reflected on the position where a successful action has been brought by a living claimant in respect of his lost years, recovering less than the likely dependency figure in a fatal accidents claim for dependency. He described it as 'a poor substitute for the right of the claimant's dependants to make full recovery for loss of dependency if and when the claimant dies prematurely'.[58]

This is an area of the law of damages that is still developing. Many claimants with terminal diseases wish to have their financial position sorted out before they die and thus bring actions in their lifetime, even though they are aware of the lower percentage recovery. It will, in my view, be addressed in time.

Recent years have seen many changes in the way damages are calculated in the United Kingdom. The progress has been steady and informed by reasoned debate. The Law Commission and the Ogden Working Party have played a significant and, I venture to suggest, a positive role.

NOTES

1. The author is a practising barrister, former Chairman of the Bar of England and Wales and former Chairman of the Personal Injuries Bar Association of England and Wales. He is a former member of the Ogden Tables Working Party.

2. Livingstone v Rawyards Coal Company (1880) 5 AC 25 at p. 39 per Blackburne J, quoted with approval by Lord Scarman in Lin Poh Choo v Camden Health Authority (1980) AC 174 at p. 187, and also in Pickett v British Rail Engineering (1978) 3 WLR 955 at p. 979. Dicta approved in Wells v Wells (1999) 1 AC 345 at p. 383F, 'the 100 percent principle'.

3. Per Lord Oliver in *Hodgson v Trapp* (1989) AC 804: 'Essentially what the Court has to do is to calculate as best it can the sum of money which will on the one hand be adequate, by its capital and income, to provide annually for the injured person a sum equivalent to his estimated annual loss over the whole of the period during which that loss is likely to continue, but which, on the other hand, will not, at the end of that period, leave him in a better financial position than he would have been apart

from the accident. Hence the conventional approach is to assess the amount notionally required to be laid out in the purchase of an annuity which will provide the annual amount needed for the whole period of loss' per Lord Oliver at 826E–F.

4. Lord Lloyd of Berwick in *Wells* (1999) 1 AC 345 at p. 373.

5. (1979) AC 556 at p. 576G.

6. Lord Lloyd of Berwick, *Wells v Wells* (1999) 1 AC 345 at p. 365.

7. Paragraph 103.

8. Jury trial for personal injury claims was abolished in Northern Ireland in 1987: The Jury Trial (Amendment) (Northern Ireland) Order 1987.

9. See *H v MOD* (1991) 2 QB 103.

10. *Cookson v Knowles* (1979) AC 556 at p. 571.

11. Lord Diplock's 'rough and ready' approach in *Cookson v Knowles* at p. 571F.

12. (1979) AC 556 at p. 576G.

13. *Mallett v McMonagle* (1970) AC 166.

14. Mallett (1970) AC 166 at p. 176.

15. *Cookson v Knowles* (1979) AC 556 at p. 571G.

16. Law Society 'Gazette' of 22 March 1995.

17. Page 571G.

18. By the late 1970s and early 1980s that maximum had risen to 18, reflecting broadly a 4.5 percent rate of return.

19. See Ogden table 1, 3rd ed., 1998.

20. Per Lord Blackburn in *Livingstone v Rawyards Coal Co.* 1880 5 AC 25 at p. 39 and Lord Scarman in *Lim Poh Choo v Camden Health Authority* (1979) 3 WLR 44 and Lord Scarman in *Pickett v British Rail Engineering Ltd.* (1978) 3 WLR 955.

21. Lord Bridge in *Hodgson v Trapp* (1988) 3 WLR 1281 at p. 1285H '... it cannot be emphasised too often when considering the assessment of damages for negligence that they are intended to be purely compensatory. Where damages claimed are essentially financial in character, being the measure on the one hand of the injured plaintiff's consequential loss of earnings, profits or other gains which he would have made if not injured or on the other hand, consequential expenses to which he has been and will be put which, if not injured, he would not have needed to incur, the basic rule is that it is the net consequential loss of expense which the Court must measure. If, in consequence of the injury sustained, the plaintiff has enjoyed receipts to which he would not otherwise have been entitled, prima facie, those receipts are to be set against the aggregate of the plaintiff's losses and expenses in arriving at the measure of his damages. All this is elementary and has been said over and over again.' Also Lord Bridge in *Hussain v New Taplow Board Mills* (1988) 1 AC 514.

22. *Mallett v McMonagle* and *Cookson v Knowles*.

23. Lord Diplock's 'rough and ready' approach in *Cookson v Knowles* at p. 571F.

24. *Taylor v O'Connor* (1971) AC 115.

25. *Mitchell v Mulholland* (1972) 1 QB 65.

26. Lord Denning in *What Next in the Law*, 1982, subsequently withdrawn from sale because of other remarks made in the book.

27. Page 800H.

28. By R. Owen and P. S. Shier, JSS 29 (1986) 53–59.

29. 'The tables should now be regarded as the starting point rather than a check.' Per Lord Lloyd of Berwick, *Wells v Wells* (1999) 1 AC 354 at p. 379F.

30. Reported in (1999) 1 AC 345.
31. Law Commission paper number 56 (1973), paragraph 222.
32. The 5th programme of Law Reform, 1991, Law Commission Report No. 200, item 11.
33. Consultation Paper No. 125, 'Structured Settlements and Interim and Provisional Damages (1992)'.
34. 1973, Law Com. No. 56.
35. Consultation Paper 125, paragraph 2.21.
36. Paragraph 2.26, Law Commission Report No. 224, September 1994.
37. Paragraph 2.28, Structured Settlements and Interim and Provisional Damages, Law Commission Report No. 224, Fifth programme of law reform, September 1994.
38. Mr John M. Taylor MP, a Minister in the Lord Chancellor's Department.
39. SI 2001/2301.
40. *Wells v Wells* (1999) 1 AC 345 at p. 365C.
41. However, differential rates for future care are now used, particularly where the claimant has a substantial life expectancy and the likelihood of escalating care costs. An index different to RPI may be used: see: *Thompstone v Thameside & Glossop Acute services NHS Trust* [2006] EWHC 2904 (QB), albeit in the context of periodical payments, as opposed to a lump sum award.
42. Recommendation 7.14, Law Commission Report No. 263.
43. By removal of those tables dealing with historic mortality rates.
44. See 'Quantum' (Sweet & Maxwell), 24 January 2005.
45. *Wells v Wells* 1 AC 345 at p. 369.
46. (1999) 1 AC 345 at p. 369.
47. Contained in the Courts Act 2003.
48. Amended by the Courts Act 2003.
49. Annual Survey of Hours and Earnings (ASHE) for the occupational group of care assistants and home carers, produced by the Office of National Statistics (ONS).
50. Paragraph 90, Law Commission Report No. 56, Personal Injury Litigation – Assessment of Damages 1973.
51. With whom Farquharson LJ agreed in a court split 2–1.
52. Paragraph 4.10.
53. Paragraph 4.15.
54. Paragraph 4.17.
55. Paragraph 4.18.
56. See, for example, *White v ESAB Group* (UK) (2002) PIQR Q6.
57. Including future losses.
58. *Gregg v Scott* [2005] UKHL 2 at paragraph 182.

REFERENCES

Haberman, S., & Bloomfield, D. S. F. (1990). Work time lost to sickness, unemployment and stoppages: Measurement and application. *Journal of the Institute of Actuaries*, *117*, 533–595.

Lewis, R., McNabb, R., & Wass, V. (2002). Methods of calculating damages for loss of future earnings. *Journal of Personal Injury Law*, *2*, 151–165.

ECONOMIC DAMAGES AND TORT REFORM: A COMPARATIVE ANALYSIS OF THE CALCULATION OF ECONOMIC DAMAGES IN PERSONAL INJURY AND DEATH LITIGATION IN THE UNITED STATES AND THE UNITED KINGDOM

John O. Ward

1. INTRODUCTION

Proponents of tort reform in the United States frequently point to specific features of tort systems of Western European Countries to support their positions on such proposals as:

- the elimination of the jury system;
- the enforcement of a loser-pays-all legal fees system;
- the curtailment or elimination of contingency fee arrangements with plaintiff's attorneys;

Personal Injury and Wrongful Death Damages Calculations: Transatlantic Dialogue
Contemporary Studies in Economic and Financial Analysis, Volume 91, 35–71

ISSN: 1569-3759/doi:10.1108/S1569-3759(2009)0000091006

- the imposing of caps on nonpecuniary damages;
- the curtailing of "expert" testimony through judicial screening and scheduled damages;
- the admission of collateral income/payment sources for plaintiffs.

All of the above proposals are realities in Western Europe, and it is suggested that the adoption of such "reforms" would substantially reduce the transaction costs of providing compensation to deserving plaintiffs, improve the efficiency of the tort system, and provide manufacturers and service providers with greater predictability and "fairness" in potential tort damages in the United States.

One example of such a comparison of the United States with other Western tort systems is provided in a paper by David Bernstein entitled "Procedural Tort Reform: Lessons from Other Nations," published in 1996 in the Cato Institute publication, *Regulation* (Bernstein, 1996). Bernstein began his paper with the statement:

> By all reasonable measures, the American tort system is a disaster. It resembles a wealth-redistribution lottery more than an efficient system designed to compensate those injured by the wrongful actions of others. Modern product liability litigation is particularly problematic. As has been well documented elsewhere, product liability lawsuits have made a few plaintiffs' attorneys and their clients rich (p. 1).

Bernstein's distrust of the jury system and expert testimony in general is best summarized by his statement that:

> Perhaps the most radical and important measure that legislatures can take to eliminate the pernicious effects of civil juries is to remove the issue of damages from the jury and put it in the hands of judges. Judges are repeat players with a stake in the coherence of the system, and have some idea of what the going rate for certain injuries is (p. 3).

In a Manhattan Institute study in 2002, Stephen Presser argued that the U.S. system relies too heavily on litigation to compensate injured parties. In the European Union (EU), compensation for injured parties incorporates both social welfare programs and awards from the litigation process, and greater concern is given to a consistent regulation of the safety of products and services. Presser states that:

> Even though the European Community recently altered its tort doctrines from a pure fault-based system to strict products liability, there are features of the European legal system that lessen the effects of even strict liability. Consequently, European courts are much less likely to hand out unpredictable and disproportionate damage judgments – unlike American courts, where ruinous verdicts are a potential in too many lawsuits.

> Europe has escaped an American style litigation explosion by erecting barriers to excessive litigation. Such barriers include:
>
> - Absence of contingent fees
> - Loser pays winner's attorney fees
> - Discouragement of massive discovery filings
> - Lower damage judgments
> - Absence of punitive damages
> - Nonuse of juries in civil cases
> - Lower expectations of damages
>
> Unless similar barriers to excessive litigation are created in the U.S., American companies face an ongoing competitive disadvantage relative to European manufacturers who operate in a more predictable, less costly, and less litigious legal environment (Presser, 2002).

The opinions of Stephen Presser and David Bernstein are shared by a substantial number of policymakers in the United States. The accuracy of their opinions is greatly contested, but the process of tort reform in the United States will likely continue, with or without evidence of need. While the elimination of the jury system in civil cases is unlikely in the near future, alternative dispute resolution methods are effectively replacing jury trial in a growing number of personal injury and death cases. Other adoptions of Western European civil tort procedures and rules will likely occur. Punitive damages caps, the admissibility of collateral source payments to plaintiffs as offsets against economic damages, limits on class action suits, and/or lowered expectations of damages through caps on noneconomic damages, such as pain and suffering, have been adopted in a growing number of states.

In the United States and the EU the objective of damages awards in personal injury and death litigation is to make a plaintiff "whole," to restore the plaintiff to the position they would have enjoyed but for the tort. However, in the United States additional objectives of damage awards may be deterrence and the assignment of all damages to the defendant. An award of economic and noneconomic damages to a plaintiff by a judge or a jury should be based on the "wholeness" objective. Ideally, the methods of calculating economic damages and noneconomic damages should be predictable and consistent given the specific facts of a case. In the determination of economic damages, such as (a) a person's loss of earnings capacity, (b) the ability to perform services, or (c) needed medical care as the result of an injury, there exists a considerable literature on appropriate methodologies for making such calculations of losses in the EU and the United States.

Bernstein's suggestion that judges have some idea of the "going rate" for certain injuries and are in a better position to bring coherence to the system contains several assumptions. The idea of a "going rate" for an injury implies that judges possess knowledge of the methodologies used by economic and actuarial experts in calculating economic losses and that they are consistent in their use of such methodologies in awarding damages. There is no logical basis for such a suggestion, however. Rather, judges in the EU until recent years have relied on rule-of-thumb multipliers in calculating economic damages and that process has provided neither consistency nor predictability. In the past decade considerable effort has been expended to replace that system of rule-of-thumb damages with a system of actuarially derived multipliers, particularly in the United Kingdom.

In the United Kingdom, actuaries, economists, barristers, and legislatures have successfully adopted the use of actuarially based damages multipliers in the courts through legislation and *Wells v. Wells* in 1999. The methodologies underlying those multipliers are similar to the methodologies used by damages experts in the 50 state jurisdictions in the United States, but the process of applying the methodologies in the courts is much different. In the United Kingdom there is effectively one court system rather than the federal and 50 state tort systems of the United States. In the United Kingdom one set of multipliers (and qualifiers) is directly available to judges as a starting point for calculating damages while in the United States a presentation of economic damages by a forensic economist is unique to each personal injury or death case, and is also unique to each jurisdiction.

One aspect of damages determination in European torts that has been the focus of attention in tort reform debates in the United States has been the replacement of expert-driven damages calculations with a system of scheduled damages using multipliers. Rather than having a jury consider evidence of pecuniary losses of earnings, benefits, and services from testimony by economic, financial, and actuarial experts (loosely designated as "forensic economists") on issues of forecasting loss, the judge would direct a loss award on the basis of statutory damages schedules and multipliers that would be consistent for similar cases. Among the suggested benefits of such a system would be simplicity and uniformity of awards, predictability of awards, the diminished potential for unreasonable jury awards, and lower litigation costs by reducing or eliminating the uses of expert witnesses in the damages calculation. The Ogden tables used in the United Kingdom are one example of such a system.[1]

This chapter reviews the experience of the United Kingdom with the Ogden tables in terms of their promotion of consistency, predictability, and "wholeness" of calculated economic damages. One recent U.S. experiment with a uniform damages methodology is the Victim's Compensation Fund (VCF) to compensate victims and survivors of the September 11, 2001, World Trade Center and Pentagon attacks. The chapter also compares the results of using Ogden multipliers to those of using the VCF methodology as well as a generalized U.S. methodology in calculating economic damages in a hypothetical case. Finally, the chapter explores a system of scheduled compensation in the United States using the methodologies used by damages experts in the United States. The results of all three models, applied to the same hypothetical example, are compared and conclusions offered.

2. THE ROLES OF DAMAGES IN THE UNITED STATES TORTS

When someone is injured or dies, the person injured or survivors usually will suffer economic and noneconomic losses. Economic losses consist of losses of earnings and support, employer-paid fringe benefits, the ability to perform household services, and other family services such as advice counsel and care and medical costs. Noneconomic losses might include loss of companionship, consortium, or pain and suffering. As in loss of enjoyment of life, loss might be either economic or noneconomic depending on the law of a particular jurisdiction. Loss may extend beyond self, family, and survivors to a business or society. If the incident that generated the injury or death was not attributable to the negligence of another, the individual or society will bear the economic and noneconomic costs of injury or death. However, if the injury or death occurs in the workplace or is due to the fault or liability of someone else, then economic and noneconomic costs might be recovered as damages from the individual or institution liable for the harm.

Injuries or death in the workplace in most western industrialized nations are usually covered by workers' compensation, and no fault insurance on the part of the employer is necessary to recover losses.[2] In the United States, there is no national system of workers' compensation; rather each State administers its own system, and those systems vary widely. Moreover, railroad, seamen, and harbor workers are not covered by workers' compensation and must recover damages for injury or death through civil suits, requiring proof of negligence. In nonjob-related actions, liability usually requires some proof of negligence. Because recovery for loss in workers' compensation does not imply negligence and focuses on providing financial assistance to the injured or their survivors, the intent of the recovery is not to make the injured person or survivors whole or to punish those liable for the harm.

Where loss comes from a wrongful action or defective product (a tort), the intent of recovery in the United States is usually to make the injured person or survivors (plaintiff(s)) whole: to restore to them their full measure of economic losses and some measure of their noneconomic losses (such losses are frequently limited or capped). Moreover, tort law usually seeks to recover all economic and noneconomic losses of the plaintiff(s) from liable defendant(s). This full-recovery from the defendant is both a legal and an economic foundation of the US tort law system. Usually, evidence of collateral sources of financial and support assistance to the plaintiff(s) by third parties is not admissible in court. This exclusion also furthers the economic goal of internalizing the externalities of harm to those creating the harm and providing efficient deterrence for those who harm.

The concepts of efficient deterrence expands the concept of internalizing the externality to an appropriate, efficient standard of liability represented by Justice Hand's Rule where "B" (the expenditure on precaution against harm by the defendant) equals "p" (the probability of an accident occurring) times "L" (the cost of the harm to the plaintiff(s) resulting from the accident at an equilibrium level of precaution). As originally used by Hand as a measure for deciding the threshold of negligence for liability, if $B>pL$ the firm would not be liable for accidental harm. While the Hand rule focuses on liability, harm is also an important variable. If L is overestimated, society will exercise an inefficient level of precaution, and awards for plaintiffs will be excessive. If L is underestimated there will be too little precaution, too little compensation for plaintiffs, and too little deterrence for defendants.

L can be overestimated or underestimated on the basis of

- incorrect information about the earnings or services of the person injured or killed and their ability to mitigate any losses of such in injury cases;
- incorrect methodology used by a damages expert in forming an opinion on mitigation, future medical needs, or the present value of actuarial calculations of damages by an economist; and
- inappropriate laws that restrict information on taxes or collateral income that the damages expert cannot consider in calculating L.

Systems of scheduled damages, such as the Ogden tables, should be ultimately evaluated as to whether they would serve to improve the quality and predictability of L measurements as compared to the U.S. model and still be compatible with the make-whole principle.

In the United States, when settlement efforts fail, the recovery of losses in tort laws is in two steps: the proof of liability and the offer of proof of the economic and noneconomic losses suffered by the plaintiff(s). The plaintiff can seek a jury trial, and the evidence of losses often consists of testimony of expert damages witnesses, such as vocational/rehabilitation experts, life-care planners, and/or economists. The laws that define the recovery of losses in the various states and in federal cases are a combination of both case law and statute – but the damage award itself rests with the jury (subject to caps and the ability of judges to reduce or increase losses with or without the approval of the parties). That is not the case in most other western democracies where jury decisions have been replaced by judges' decisions based on systems of scheduled damages. Moreover, the legal and economic intents of making the plaintiff(s) whole and fully internalizing the harm created by the defendant to the defendant are not fully shared by other western democracies. In Western Europe, tort laws typically allow evidence of some collateral payments to plaintiffs and even require reductions in awards for such payments. Such payments usually include national health care payments and services. In the case of the Ogden tables, specific provision is made for incorporating such collateral payments into the damages award of the judge.

There are obvious advantages to the use of Ogden tables and similar legislated damages formulas for calculating and awarding damages in torts. Such multipliers are simple to apply, avoid expert testimony costs and conflicts, are transparent and subject to change by legislation, and offer the promise of predictability and uniformity to all parties. But are they reasonable, accurate, and economically good and sound estimators of pecuniary loss? Moreover, are they consistent with the intent of U.S. tort law?

3. THE ORIGIN OF THE OGDEN TABLES

Prior to 1999, the system by which judges in the United Kingdom calculated damages has been described as arbitrary and capricious (Lewis, McNabb, Robinson, & Wass, 2003). Rules of thumb for estimating damages evolved, which were not based on either case law or economic logic. Various multipliers were selected by judges based on their "common sense" value rather than their actuarial foundation.

In an attempt to bring some sound actuarial principles to the use of multipliers, the British Actuary's Department first prepared a set of multipliers in 1984 named "Actuarial Tables with Explanatory Notes for Use in Personal Injury and Fatal Accident Cases." Sir Michael Ogden was the chairperson of the joint committee of actuaries and lawyers who were responsible for the publication of the tables of multipliers, and the tables became known as the Ogden tables. Now in their sixth edition, the Ogden tables assist in the calculation of lost earnings or cost of care by providing a factor to multiply a person's base earnings or annual cost of care to derive a present value of economic loss in that category. These multipliers, then, incorporate actuarial data such as annual probabilities of death by age, disability status, education, and gender in combination with an assumed retirement age and a real discount rate. The sixth edition of the tables added disability status and educational levels in the multipliers. These variables are used to prepare unique multipliers for disabled individuals and individuals by level of education rather than adjusting all tables by transitional probabilities of disability or age-earnings transitions by educational level. A judge could then use these multipliers to arrive at a lump-sum award for economic damages. In their base form, the Ogden tables have the characteristics of work life tables with adjustments for growth and discounting rolled into one number. However, there have been no formal work life tables available for the United Kingdom until very recent years.[3] The tables provide multiple discount rates despite the mandated 2.5% rate and there are no bright lines for the judge in selecting a discount rate other than the legislated rate.

Judges were not required to use the Ogden tables in calculating damages until 1999. In a landmark case, *Wells v. Wells*, the House of Lords approved actuarial evidence as the primary method of calculating future pecuniary loss[4] and required the judges use the tables in forming their opinions. This decision applied to England and Wales. Scotland has its own legal system that closely parallels that of England and Wales. Matthias Kelly was a barrister in the *Wells* case and had a key role in advancing the mandatory use of the Ogden tables by the courts. He considers the mandatory use of Ogden multipliers as a substantial improvement over the prior practices of judges in arriving at pecuniary damages, although he admits that numerous deficiencies still exist in the use of Ogden tables.[5] These deficiencies include the omission of provisions for real growth in earnings and age-earnings cycle adjustments for younger workers, as well as after-the-fact postinjury risk adjustment made by judges without any particular basis in fact. Also, the treatment of unemployment probabilities amounts to adjusting multipliers up or down, and can be rather arbitrary.

4. DAMAGES IN THE UNITED KINGDOM AND DEFICIENCIES IN THE OGDEN TABLES

In their two recent papers (2002 and 2003) comparing pecuniary damages calculations in the United States and the United Kingdom, Lewis, McNabb, Robinson, and Wass have concluded that "the (United Kingdom) tort system fails to satisfy one of its main objectives in that it does not provide recipients of damages with 'full' compensation. Instead claimants are often under-compensated by the present methods used to assess loss of future earnings" (Lewis, McNabb, Robinson, & Wass, 2002). They arrive at their conclusions by first constructing a generalized U.S. model of damages largely from the literature of the *Journal of Forensic Economics* and the *Journal of Legal Economics*. This U.S. model incorporates labor force participation data, annual probabilities of death and unemployment probability adjustments, and age-earnings cycle adjustments by educational level and future productivity growth (no future real growth or age-earnings corrections are incorporated into the Ogden tables). The UK data on age-earnings trends include categories for disabled workers, which were used by the authors in calculating postinjury earnings capacity. Future losses are discounted to present value at real rates varying from 3% to 4.5%, using those rates used by UK courts for the periods where those rates applied. The hypothesis tested by Lewis et al. was whether the reluctance of courts in Britain to make use of economists in assign damages actually would make a difference to those claiming compensation.

Next, the authors examined (Lewis et al., 2002) a sample of 108 personal injury cases tried between 1990 and 1998 where economic damages were awarded. Given the facts of each case, the present values of lost earnings awarded by the courts were compared to damages calculated using the fourth edition of the Ogden tables and a generalized U.S. model. They found that

> by comparison with our alternative (US) method, the courts under-compensated future earnings loss by 88%. Of the cases in our survey, over half of the claimants adversely affected would have received at least 50 per cent more if our alternative calculation had been used, and a third of them would have more than doubled their court award (p. 164).

Some of these court awards may have been made on the basis of Ogden tables prior to 1999, but many were probably based on "rule-of-thumb" multipliers. Using Ogden tables increased average awards in most categories, but not to the levels reached with the U.S. model.

The major reasons for the differences between awards using Ogden tables and U.S. methodologies, according to Lewis et al., lie in the Ogden tables' failure to directly consider age-earnings and productivity growth of wages over a worker's life, impacts of disability on earnings of workers, and excessive reductions by UK judges for postinjury employment risks. Actual awards by UK courts in the above cases may have relied on Ogden tables, in part, prior to 1999, but judges were not required to use such tables and when they did use multipliers (either "rule-of-thumb" or Ogden variants) they frequently made rather arbitrary, significant reductions in calculations for the risks of unemployment.

In their 2003 paper in *The Economic Journal*, Lewis et al. applied four alternative models to the calculation of damages for their sample, based on varying economic assumptions, but their essential findings were that "rules of thumb" yielded very unequal damage awards under similar circumstances, and that a more scientific approach to calculating damages should be a first goal for the judicial system of the United Kingdom. The mandatory use of Ogden tables, according to them, is a first necessary step in that process, but the adoption of methodologies used in the United States would add even greater exactness to the process of determining damages. The use of forensic economic testimony would further enhance that exactness.

While Lewis et al. viewed the use of Ogden tables as a more "scientific" approach to the assessment of damages, they also believe that the tables "merely support the existing multiplier and multiplicand method and thus do not address the absence of compensation for earnings growth" (p. 165). Also, the tables in the fourth edition did not address issues of reduced capacity to work because of possible future disability for the currently able bodied.

Much of the current criticism of the use of Ogden tables in England and Wales also centers on the mandated stable net discount rate. Although reduced from 3% to 2.5% in 2001, many argue that it should be reduced much farther and that judges should have the freedom to use alternative rates when justified. Given that all earnings losses are net of taxes and that medical costs are being projected, it can be argued that a tax-free bond yield should be used in discounting. Stephen Grime, QC, writing for the Deans Court Chambers in 2003 observed that (Grime, 2003)

> The courts and the Lord Chancellor have stressed the advantage for the administration of justice in having a single relatively stable rate as it facilitates settlements and the disposal of disputed cases – see e.g. Lord Steyn in *Wells v. Wells* [1999] AC 345 at 388d and the Lord Chancellor in the reasons published on 27th July 2001 for the setting of the 2.5% rate. Allowance of greater flexibility by, for example, permitting differing rates for different heads of loss or varying the discount rate to take account of changes in investment conditions is likely to be financially favourable to claimants and detrimental to insurers and the N.H.S. – at least in the present economic climate. Therefore any attack on the single, stable rate will probably be fiercely resisted and, if the relevant criteria can be demonstrated, insurers and/or the N.H.S. would try to appeal any unfavourable decisions of the Court of Appeal to the House of Lords.

Nevertheless, Grime calls for at least a reduction of that net discount rate, if not a freeing of the rate on the basis that

> It is possible to be more sophisticated, because data is available covering both pay in the Health Service and pay received by Personal Social Service workers. The table below covers the period from 1994 to 2002 from which it can be seen that Average Earnings and Health Service pay have risen on average by 4.1% per annum against a rise of 2.5% per annum in R.P.I. – a differential of 1.6%. In the case of Personal Social Service pay (derived from date in the New Earnings Survey) the differential is 1.4%. The effect of adoption of a differential discount rate would be significant. At present the argument is being advanced on two fronts. It is said that a lower discount rate could be taken in setting a multiplier. The alternative is to make an adjustment of the multiplicand. Either of these approaches is easy to adopt given access to the Ogden Tables. The first would assume that the reduction of the discount rate should be equivalent to the excess rate of inflation in care costs. If the data from 1994 to 2002 were to be adopted, the result would probably be to reduce a discount rate of 2.5% to 1.0%. Taking the example of a 25 year old male with unimpaired life expectancy and care costs of £50,000, the effect would be to give a multiplier of 42.1 against 29.56 increasing the size of the award by £627,000 or 58%. The alternative (US and Canadian) method involves forecasting future costs for each year, discounting for accelerated payment and awarding a lump sum on the basis of the total of the discounted future costs. This is likely to give a very similar result to a simpler multiplier/multiplicand approach.

While the use of Ogden tables is mandated in England and Wales only, the tables, or a variant of them, are also commonly used in Scotland and the Republic of Ireland. However, like England and Wales, multipliers used by judges are often "rule-of-thumb" standards derived from prior cases. In 2003, Ireland established a Personal Injuries Assessment Board (PAIB) to independently assess personal injury claims. The PAIB was "inspired" by the perceived high and inconsistent levels of compensation for personal injury claims in Ireland. One of the objectives of the PAIB was to substitute a more consistent and scientific basis for making such awards than the multipliers used by judges. Presumably the PAIB will incorporate some of the Ogden methodology reforms in their analysis.

Following the two papers by Lewis et al. (2002, 2003) on the inadequacies of the Ogden tables (based on the fourth edition), significant changes were made in the fifth edition, published late in 2004, and in the sixth edition in 2006. A number of these changes resulted from the Lewis et al. criticisms and from the research of Steven Haberman, a participant in the 2005 meeting of the National Association of Forensic Economics in Dublin and the 2006 meetings in Boston (Verrall, Haberman, & Butt, 2006). The most recent Ogden tables do recognize the deficiencies of not incorporating age-earnings trends in the multipliers. However, the tables have been enhanced by allowing for extended life expectancies due to improved health, by the inclusion of disability transitions and unemployment probabilities, and by allowing ranges of assumed growth of earnings by multiple net discount rates. The tables also are categorized by levels of educational attainment. A copy of the current Ogden table multipliers for a male retiring at age 65 is contained in Appendix A (Table A1).

Previous editions of the Ogden tables gave minimal direction to the use of the tables in calculating losses to survivors in death actions. The new tables provide clearer direction for use in such cases, however. Basically the multiplicand in the calculation of loss is the loss to survivors at the time of death of the individual times the loss multiplier appropriate to the persons age, gender, and education. Traditionally the personal consumption reduction has been 25% for a husband or wife with children and 33% for a husband–wife household. These rates are comparable to those used in the United States. The calculation of loss of services in both death and injury cases is based on replacement costs, using the multipliers over a lifetime or to a specific age. The Ogden tables require calculation of loss from the date of injury or death rather than the date of trial. It has been proposed that past losses be separately calculated and that future loss begins with the date of trial, but the tables do not allow such a calculation.

One of the strengths of the U.S. methodology for calculating damages in personal injury and death litigation is that it has been the product of a competition of ideas and research by forensic economists in the crucible of the courtroom. Virtually every element of that methodology has been subject to intense debate, publication, and criticism by other forensic economists and the courts. Virtually all U.S. forensic economists would agree that projections of economic damages in personal injury and death litigation today are, on average, far superior to those of twenty, ten, or five years ago. Even so, much room for improvement remains. But the system of courts, trial by jury, and acceptance of economic expertise by the courts concerning damages provide the dynamics for such improvements.

In the United Kingdom and Ireland, with centralized systems of tort law, trial by judge or panel, and with an absence of economic expertise in the courtroom, there is no internal impetus for improvements in damages methodologies. Those reforms that have occurred, such as the Ogden tables, have been the product of external commissions and while the Ogden actuarial multipliers are a considerable improvement over prior "rule-of-thumb" multipliers, they still require rather arbitrary adjustments in practice. Moreover, with a mandated net discount rate above the market rate, they tend to undercompensate plaintiffs. In this respect the United Kingdom and Ireland could benefit from the positive features of the U.S. damages methodology and structure, and the research of Lewis et al. (2002, 2003) and Verrall et al. (2006) has been directed to this end.

5. WHAT IS BEING MEASURED? LEGAL PARAMETERS IN THE UNITED KINGDOM AND THE UNITED STATES

Although the general methodological frameworks for calculating lost-earnings capacity or value of services is fairly consistent in the variety of jurisdictions in the United States, the constraining assumptions for using that framework are not uniformly consistent. Each state in the United States has its own common law, legislative constraints, and directives for the use of the model. Federal cases usually follow the law of that state where the case is tried, but not in all cases (such as FELA cases). In general, damages are calculated on the basis of gross earnings with no reduction for taxes except for FELA and Jones Act cases. All states require a discounting of lost earnings, services, and future medical costs, but in some states, that discounting can be offset by presumed future increases in wages or costs. Only a few states legislate a discount rate. Collateral income sources are not generally allowed as deductions from earnings loss, although in some states such deductions have been permitted. Such rules do not restrict collateral payment providers (such as State Workers Compensation Insurance) from seeking recovery from a plaintiff's award. Household services lost to plaintiffs as a result of injury or death is recoverable in all state and federal courts, but common law precedents for measuring such losses can vary considerably by state. Such differences in assumptions and inputs into the damages model required by state law produce often uneven results in projecting damages throughout the United States.

In England, Wales, and Northern Ireland, where the Ogden tables are used, all earnings losses are net of taxes in personal injury and death actions.[6] Since the legal system is centralized, the framework for calculating damages is uniform in all courts. Prejudgment interest is allowed for past damages in personal injury or death cases, unlike most past damages calculations in the United States. Gratuitous collateral payments are not deducted from loss, and private insurance, pension, and disability pension payments are not subtracted from loss. But social benefit payments in the first five years from the initial cause (if greater than £2,500) are deducted from loss and repaid to providers. Sick pay or salary continuation funds, if not paid by the employer, are subtracted from loss. For other Western European countries, reductions for collateral social welfare payments are more prevalent. In death actions in the United Kingdom, losses to survivors are specified under the Fatal Accidents Act of 1976. The loss period is calculated from time of death, as is the multiplier. The multiplier is adjusted for life expectancy and the risks of death and unemployment probabilities. An assessment of loss must consider the uncertainty of whether the decedent would have provided the claimant with support. In valuing services where the decedent primarily provided services, replacement costs will be used. For the care of a child, the cost of a nanny is appropriate.

In the Republic of Ireland (where multipliers may be considered), social security injury or disability benefits received by an injured person are to be deducted from an award, and no further right of subrogation exists for the provider. No other collateral payments are deducted, and earnings losses are based on after-tax earnings. Recovery in death actions can occur under a wrongful death action or a survival action. There is no mandated net discount rate, and judges are to consider the after-tax nature of the award in selecting a net discount rate. Structured settlements are an option for a judge with the consent of parties. The creation of the Person Injuries Assessment Board (PIAB) in 2004 offers the most radical departure from traditional systems of tort recovery. The methods for calculating damages under the PIAB are still unknown in that awards have yet to be announced. A parallel to the PIAB might be the VCF special master system in the United States.

The above-mentioned, limited comparison of rules of recovery of damages in personal injury or death actions in the United States, the United Kingdom, and Ireland show a number of similarities and contrasts. The use of mandated real discount rates in the United Kingdom is in contrast to a trier-of-fact determination in the United States and Ireland, but the intent of recovery is basically the same. Reductions for taxes from lost-earnings awards exist in Ireland and the United Kingdom, but only are made in death actions in FELA and Jones Act cases in the United States. Reductions for collateral payments from social security agencies are made in the United Kingdom and Ireland, but not in the United States. Despite these differences, similarities in rules of recovery share a common law origin and are greater than differences.

6. THE RELEVANCE OF THE OGDEN TABLES TO THE UNITED STATES

In the United Kingdom and increasingly in Ireland, tort recovery is moving to a system of scheduled payments, determined by multipliers, with no juries, loser pays, substantial limits on punitive damages, substantial caps on noneconomic damages, mandatory structures in some situations, scheduled damages, and no class actions for products such as asbestos. It should also be pointed out that these tort limitations in the United Kingdom and Ireland are accompanied with substantial regulation of industries and services for the public welfare. Such regulation includes stricter oversight on product safety, quality of services offered, product marketing, and environmental impacts of manufacturers.

In the United States we have a greater "free market" mentality with respect to products and services in the marketplace as well as in the system of torts. It is argued that manufacturers are given greater leeway to produce dangerous products or externalities with the understanding that those harmed are allowed to recover damages for the harm through the tort system. A consumer harmed by an unsafe product can also recover damages that would not only compensate for harm, but also send a market signal to stop such production. That does not mean that a system of scheduled payments using multipliers such as the Ogden tables could not be useful in the United States, especially in class action cases such as asbestosis or black lung cases.

In the United Kingdom, Ireland, and Western Europe as a whole, there is a greater willingness for society to absorb the costs of torts through national health and other social programs than there is in the United States, just as there is a greater willingness to substitute public for market solutions in resource allocation. But that may be changing. The creation of the VCF following the September 11, 2001 attack is one example of a public solution to a potentially massive tort action in the United States. Over 5,000 individual claims were resolved without the assignment of liability to the airlines or to the owner's and architects of the World Trade Center through the use of a Special Master, a specified system of formulas for the calculation of damages, and through the use of public funds. Moreover, a number of collateral payments including workers compensation, disability, and social security payments were allowed as offsets against damages awarded.

7. THE SEPTEMBER 11 VICTIM COMPENSATION FUND (VCF)

The VCF was established by the U.S. Congress as a device to compensate the 2,680 persons injured and the survivors of the 2,973 persons killed in the terrorist attacks on September 11, 2001. A Special Master, Mr. Kenneth Feinberg, was appointed by the U.S. Justice Department to devise a plan to compensate these individuals on a no-fault basis, avoiding litigation and quickly. Over a period of 33 months a plan was established, and more than 97% of those injured or the survivors of those killed received compensation of over $7 billion for economic and noneconomic damages suffered. A total of 5,560 claims were paid with total fund expenses of $86.9 million, of which $76.5 million was paid to PricewaterhouseCoopers LLP for developing the loss model, calculating economic losses under the model, and processing other claims (averaging $13,760 per claim paid). This was done with minimal participation of attorneys using scheduled damages, with implicit multipliers, and with the flexibility to consider special circumstances. Although there were claimed shortcomings in the process, it was successful in most respects (Feinberg, 2004).

In a paper published in 2006 entitled "Did the 9/11 Victim Compensation Fund Accurately Assess Economic Losses," Frank Tinari, Kevin Cahill and Elias Grivoyannis, have offered a critical appraisal of the economic compensation provided to victims by the fund in a number of categories (Tinari, Cahill, & Grivoyannis, 2006). The paper outlines the development of the VCF guidelines and methodologies used to award compensation. Many individuals contributed to those guidelines and methodology over the several months of its development. As a no-fault program of compensation, there were no issues of liability, general rules of make-whole, or deterrence to consider, although by accepting VCF compensation, claimants did forego the right to sue the airlines involved in civil torts.

Collateral offsets, such as life insurance and disability payments, were subtracted from the final determination of loss; and noneconomic losses were capped at $250,000 per family, with an additional $100,000 for the spouse and each dependent of a deceased victim (although these sums could be increased on appeal). A set of tables, based on age, income, and household size, was prepared, which were in effect multipliers for the determination of wage loss compensation. The tables were capped at an income of $250,000 per year, which was much criticized by highly compensated individuals. The Special Master responded by pointing out that this was a system of financial assistance to victims rather than compensation for total loss, but claimants could seek a hearing with the Special Master or his representative to make a special claim. Since household service loss was excluded in the initial tables, these hearings became important.

We show an example of the initial VCF Damages Tables with projected awards in Appendix B. It is simple to develop the multipliers used to calculate projected economic loss (excluding services) from the tables by subtracting noneconomic damages of $250,000 and $100,000 per dependent where appropriate and then by dividing the result by the base gross income shown. In Appendix B, the multipliers for a 25-year-old single individual would be 49.4 for a single person earning $10,000 per year, 37.5 for such a person earning $30,000 per year, 36.2 for such a person earning $60,000 per year, and 35.4 for such a person earning $125,000 per year. The tables were constructed by incorporating (1) a three-year average of earnings and (2) appropriate fringe benefits, tax reductions, a work life expectancy, earnings growth, adjustments for an age-earnings cycle, unemployment probabilities, and a reduction to present value. Except for the after-tax calculation and ultimate reductions for collateral income, the methodology used was basically consistent with the methodologies used by economists in damages torts.

The Tinari's analysis of the VCF process centered on a comparison of awards where individuals used an economist in presenting damages in a hearing with the Special Master or his representative, with awards outlined in the initial multiplier tables, and with awards damages calculated by economists in those cases. Tinari concluded that final awards were larger than the multiplier damages when an economist was used. The economist's calculations of damages were, on average, larger than the multiplier damages but smaller than the final awards. He concluded that the tables were a conditional success but that special circumstances did reduce the usefulness of the tables in calculating accurate damages. Given the fact that such circumstances could be considered in special hearings did reduce that bias.

Any attempt to use the VCF approach to award compensation in civil torts would have to address the VCF's caps on noneconomic damages, after-tax calculations, reductions for collateral payments, and failure to directly address losses of services. However, such considerations can be addressed. Moreover, more exact multipliers can be developed using the state-of-the-art methodologies available to economists in the United States.

8. DAMAGES MULTIPLIER TABLES FOR THE UNITED STATES

In this section we offer a basic set of multipliers (Economic Loss Tables) for damages using the basic techniques used by forensic economists in the United States to forecast economic damages in personal injury and death torts. A first construction of Economic Loss Tables (EL Tables) for the United States should provide at least

- earnings multipliers based on age, gender, race, and level of education (EL-E);
- service multipliers based on age, gender, race, and family demographic (EL-S); and
- medical-loss multipliers based on age, gender, and race (EL-M).

This preliminary design of EL-E tables enables the calculation of a methodologically sound estimate of the present value of the average expected future earning capacity or earnings based on inputted parameters specific to a person. Although the methodologies employed in the EL tables have been accepted in the literature and are widely used by economists in the United States, no single person will be (or would have been) "absolutely" typical when compared to statistics that describe the average person. In many, if not most situations, an individual has special circumstances that can be quantified to allow an economist to improve upon the EL table presumed economic loss calculation. With that said, the EL tables are limited to providing an estimate of the presumed loss for a typical individual based on the known characteristics of a specific person.

8.1. EL-E Input Parameters

The EL tables consist of multipliers. To obtain the EL-E multiplier, it is necessary to know the age, gender, race, and level of education of the person being evaluated. With this input, multipliers are provided for combinations of discount rates and retirement ages. The chosen multiplier is applied to the individual's preevent earning capacity or earnings to arrive at the present value of his or her future earning capacity or earnings.[7]

To use the EL-E tables, it is necessary to choose a discount rate. The discount rates provided in the tables are real rates of net discount – the use of real rates obviates the need to forecast inflation as recognized by the U.S. Supreme Court in *Jones & Laughlin Steel Corporation v. Howard E. Pfeifer* case where the court suggested using a real net discount rate of between 1% and 3%. The real net discount rate considers future anticipated wage and compensation increases and future anticipated interest rates under the following standard formula:

$$r_{\text{net}} = \frac{(1+w)}{(1+R)} - 1 = \frac{(1+((1+g)(1+i)-1)}{(1+((1+r)(1+i)-1)} - 1 = \frac{(1+g)}{(1+r)} - 1$$

where w is the expected nominal future wage growth, R is the expected nominal future interest rate, g is expected real future wage growth, i is the expected nominal future inflation rate, and r is the expected real future interest rate.

Using the EL tables also requires the choice of a retirement age. This is the age at which an individual would have voluntarily and permanently exited the labor force. In some cases information regarding the age that a particular individual planned to retire is available. In other cases, the age at which the individual would have been eligible to retire with full social security retirement benefits may be a reasonable choice. If the choice of one particular age is not practical, a range of ages can be used in order to obtain a range for the loss.

8.2. Factors Imbedded in EL-E Multipliers

The EL-E tables constructed here consist of two basic tables of multipliers by gender and race combination for each age. The first table adds a life cycle earnings pattern adjustment and the second table assumes that earnings growth is limited to the constant real wage rate growth embedded in the net discount rate. Multipliers can be provided for a range of education levels, the choice of net discount rate, and the age of retirement. In the example derived here, a high school level of education is assumed. The hazards of death, disability preventing work, and other involuntary reasons for not being employed (unemployment and discouragement) reduce the expected number of full-earnings years from the beginning age through the age of retirement.

8.3. The Concept of Life Cycle Earnings Patterns

When studying the changes in earning capacity over time, economists frame their methodology within their understanding of an individual's marginal product of labor (MPL). The changes in an individual's MP_L over time are a function of changes in innate abilities, human capital, and technological conditions. In the EL-E tables, we assume that changes in technological conditions are captured by the real net discount rate. Innate abilities refer to the individual's natural mental and physical capacities that are subject to changes with age. Loss of innate ability creates negative marginal productivity growth causing earning capacity to decline (the decline can be gradual with advancing age or immediate with the onset of disability). Human capital, in contrast to innate abilities, refers to skills and positions acquired by an individual throughout life. In general, human capital is acquired early in life leading to a concave path of wages over the life cycle, ceteris paribus. The generally accepted Ben-Porath human capital model contains the derivation of the generally accepted concave life cycle earnings pattern. We summarize the Ben-Porath model as follows (Ben-Porath, 1967):

$$E_t = wC_t$$

where E_t is earning capacity, w is the wage rate per unit of human capital stock, and C_t is the number of units of human capital processed in time t.

The behavior of E_t over time will depend on the behavior of C_t over time. Increasing C_t involves an investment cost that requires the use of some portion of the existing human capital stock (i.e., the human capital stock used for investment could otherwise be used for current earnings). The individual benefit to increasing C_t is an increase in remaining lifetime earning capacity. By equating the marginal cost and marginal benefit of increasing the human capital stock, the human capital model shows that the investments will be greater at younger ages and then diminish with time, resulting in the concavity of wage rates (or earning capacity) over a worker's lifetime. To address human capital's impact on earning capacity, economists on a case-by-case basis empirically construct data for life cycle earnings patterns that coincide with the theoretical models of human capital.

8.4. The Concept of the Hazards of Death, Disability, and Nonaccess to a Job

Generally accepted theoretical models of labor supply are based on consumer demand for consumption. Income from market work depends on hours of work h and, in the simplest case, the fixed wage rate w (or earning capacity) per unit of work. Under the assumption of utility maximization, the real wage is the consumer's implicit value of his or her time at the margin between participating and not participating in the labor market. If at the margin the market's valuation of the consumer's time (w) exceeds the consumer's implicit value of his or her time when $h = 0$ (w^* or the reservation wage), then the consumer will participate in the labor market and supply a positive number of hours h of market work. A constraint to the model of labor supply for an individual includes the involuntary factors that would prevent his or her participation in the labor force. Those involuntary factors include death, disability that prevents work, and lack of access to a job due to unemployment, or discouragement from employment.

During the course of a lifetime, we expect an individual to continually face at least two different living states (able to work and not able to work) from which there is no exit. In the EL-E tables, we model such lifetime hazards using an increment–decrement Markov life table model that allows movement from one living state to the other before death. The movements between states and time are presented as transition probabilities that give the probability of being in state i at time t and in state j at time $t+n$ where n is some interval of time following time t.

We specify two fluid living states with regard to ability to be employed, active and inactive, using the annotations a and i, respectively, and we denote the absorbing state death with the letter d. The active state is ability to be employed and the inactive state is the inability to be employed. We let ${}^{m}p_x^{n}$ denote the transition probability that a person in state m at age x will be in state n at age $x+1$ where $m \in \{a, i\}$ and $n \in \{a, i, d\}$. The sums of the Markov transitions probabilities equal 1:

$$ {}^{a}p_x^{a} + {}^{a}p_x^{i} + {}^{a}p_x^{d} = 1 \tag{1} $$

$$ {}^{i}p_x^{i} + {}^{i}p_x^{a} + {}^{i}p_x^{d} = 1 \tag{2} $$

Unfortunately, mortality data by activity state are not available, so we assume that

$$^{a}p_x^d = {}^{i}p_x^d = {}^{\bullet}p_x^d \tag{3}$$

which states that the transition probabilities from active to death and inactive to death are identical and marked with a • to represent either active or inactive.

The number of active and inactive survivors at each age x is calculated recursively from

$$^{\bullet}l_x = {}^{\bullet}l_{x-1}(1 - {}^{\bullet}p_{x-1}^d) \tag{4}$$

where the beginning life table radix value of l_x is set to a positive number (usually 100,000). The number of survivors at any age is obtained from

$$^{\bullet}l_x = {}^{a}l_x + {}^{i}l_x \tag{5}$$

Following the standard life table equation, the active and inactive survivors at age x are determined recursively on the transition probabilities and survivors at age x–1 are determined from

$$^{a}l_x = {}^{a}l_{x-1} + {}^{i}p_{x-1}^a\,{}^{i}l_{x-1} - {}^{a}p_{x-1}^i\,{}^{a}l_{x-1} - {}^{\bullet}p_{x-1}^d\,{}^{a}l_{x-1} \tag{6}$$

$$^{i}l_x = {}^{i}l_{x-1} + {}^{a}p_{x-1}^i\,{}^{a}l_{x-1} - {}^{i}p_{x-1}^a\,{}^{i}l_{x-1} - {}^{\bullet}p_{x-1}^d\,{}^{i}l_{x-1} \tag{7}$$

We assume that all transitions occur evenly through the year, so that the number of person years of life, activity, and inactivity at age x are given by

$$^{\bullet}L_x^d = \frac{^{\bullet}l_x + {}^{\bullet}l_{x+1}}{2} \tag{8}$$

$$^{\bullet}L_x^a = \frac{^{a}l_x + {}^{a}l_{x+1}}{2} \tag{9}$$

$$^{\bullet}L_x^i = \frac{^{i}l_x + {}^{i}l_{x+1}}{2} \tag{10}$$

Survival and ability-to-work probabilities to any mid-year-age after age $\bar{x}$ are computed from $^{\bullet}\ell_x^{\bullet} = {}^{\bullet}L_x^{\bullet}/{}^{\bullet}l_{\bar{x}}$ where ℓ is a probability and $\bar{x}$ is the age beginning the relevant synthetic lifetime of a subcohort in the life table (e.g., if we want probabilities of state participation beyond the exact age of 35, then $\bar{x}$ equals exact age 35). From Eqs. (8) to (10), we calculate living, active, and inactive participation probabilities for each mid-year-age after age x as follows:

$$^{\bullet}\ell_x^d = \frac{^{\bullet}L_x^{\bullet}}{^{\bullet}l_{\bar{x}}} \tag{11}$$

$$^{\bullet}\ell_x^a = \frac{^{\bullet}L_x^a}{^{\bullet}l_{\bar{x}}} \tag{12}$$

$$^{\bullet}\ell_x^i = \frac{^{\bullet}L_x^i}{^{\bullet}l_{\bar{x}}} \tag{13}$$

A feature of the Markov model in computing ability-to-work attachment probabilities is that we can change the radix or beginning value of state participation at each age x to be comprised entirely of actives or inactives to reestimate the synthetic lifetime ability to work attachment probabilities for actives and inactives after that one age x. For example, suppose the life table for the entire population begins at age x. For conformity with the life table model, the radix value of $^{\bullet}l_x$ is equal to the number of survivors at age x from the mortality table. The radix values of the active able-to-work population is $^{a}l_x$, which is computed as $^{\bullet}l_x$ times the percentage of the population that is able to work at age x and the radix value of $^{i}l_x$ is $^{\bullet}l_x$ minus $^{a}l_x$. All of the remaining values of the life table are dependent on these radix values to compute the expected probabilities of active and inactive ability to work. However, if we change the radix values to $^{a}l_x = {}^{\bullet}l_x$ and $^{i}l_x = 0$, we could compute the active and inactive able-to-work probabilities by age for only those who were active at age x. Likewise, if we change the radix values to $^{i}l_x = {}^{\bullet}l_x$ and $^{a}l_x = 0$, we could compute the active and inactive able-to-work probabilities for only those who were inactive at age x. Using Eqs. (12) and (13), which do not depend on beginning ability to work state participation, and changing radix values at the beginning exact age x, we calculate active and inactive ability to work probabilities for each mid-year-age after age x as follows:

$$^{a}\ell_x^a = \frac{^{a}L_x^a}{^{\bullet}l_{\bar{x}}}, \text{ where at } \bar{x},\ {}^{a}l_x = {}^{\bullet}l_x \tag{14}$$

$$^{a}\ell_x^i = \frac{^{a}L_x^i}{^{\bullet}l_{\bar{x}}}, \text{ where at } \bar{x},\ {}^{a}l_x = {}^{\bullet}l_x \tag{15}$$

$$ {}^{i}\ell_{x}^{i} = \frac{{}^{i}L_{x}^{i}}{{}^{\bullet}l_{\bar{x}}}, \text{ where at } \bar{x},\ {}^{i}l_{x} = {}^{\bullet}l_{x} \tag{16} $$

$$ {}^{i}\ell_{x}^{a} = \frac{{}^{i}L_{x}^{a}}{{}^{\bullet}l_{\bar{x}}}, \text{ where at } \bar{x},\ {}^{i}l_{x} = {}^{\bullet}l_{x} \tag{17} $$

For all of our calculations of the hazard of death or inability to work, the EL-E multiplier begins in the active state of alive and able to work. Therefore, the Markov hazard in the EL-E tables only considers those persons dying or becoming unable to work after a specific age.

8.5. Data Source for Life Cycle Earnings and Hazards Preventing Employment

Using the monthly outgoing rotations of the Current Population Survey (CPS) from January 1998 through December 2005, from 781,056 one-year-apart matching records on individuals in the CPS, we found the average size of the U.S. noninstitutional population by age, gender, and six educational levels by the statuses of "able to work" and "not able to work." The data set used appears in Krueger's analysis with the addition of dividing the population into persons that are able to work (or are employed for age-earnings calculations) and those that are unable to work (Krueger, 2005). The *U.S. Life Tables, 2003* from the U.S. Centers for Disease Control provide data regarding the hazard of death.

Persons in the CPS that are unable to work include disabled persons, unemployed persons, and discouraged persons. Persons that are able to work include employed persons, students and homemakers who are at those activities not because of an inability to work due to disability, retired persons who did not retire due to disability nor want a job but cannot work due to disability, and other nondisabled persons. Persons are categorized in the CPS as disabled and unable to work when all of the following conditions are met:

- a person has a specific physical or mental condition that prevents the individual from working;
- the disability is not a combination of minor disabilities that normally come with advanced age; and

- the disability incapacitates a person and prevents him or her from doing any kind of work, not just the type of work at his or her last job, for at least the next six months.

Students or homemakers who want a job but cannot work due to disability are categorized as disabled and unable to work. Retired persons who retired due to disability or are retired and want a job but cannot work due to disability are categorized as disabled and unable to work. Unemployed persons are categorized in the CPS as persons able to work and who have been looking for work over the last four weeks. Discouraged persons are persons able to work but were not currently looking for work specifically because they believed no jobs were available for them. Under the above definitions, for persons aged 18–75, 10.3% of males are unable to work and 9.8% of females are unable to work.

For the EL-E tables, we have used the life cycle earnings patterns distinguished by gender and level of education. We have used 10 levels of education: less than 9th grade, 9th to 12th grade but no diploma or GED, GED, high school diploma, vocational AA degree, academic AA degree, bachelor's degree, master's degree, professional school, and doctorate degree. The earnings data are recorded from the same matched sample of persons used to compute the hazard of inability to work based on the usual weekly earnings of employed persons. Included in the calculation of earnings by age are all persons employed full-time and persons with a disability that are employed part-time.

8.6. Sample EL-E Tables

In Appendix C, we show two example EL-E tables. Both tables are for all males in the United States with a high school education with retirement at age 65. The first table in Appendix C, Table C1, includes the life cycle age-earnings adjustment and the second table, Table C2, does not. Conforming to the Ogden tables, real discount rates from 0% to 5% are shown. From Table C2, the work life period is easily gleaned from the 0% net discount rate column. For example, at age 18 there are 38.96 remaining full-years of earnings in the EL-E table without considering life cycle earnings adjustments. From Table C1, we see that when adding the life cycle earnings adjustment, the loss multiplier at age 18 increases from 38.96 to 78.17 showing that the incorporation of life cycle earnings doubles the total economic loss-of-earnings estimate. After age 46, the multipliers in Table C2 exceed those in Table C1 because of the concavity of the age-earnings equation.

9. COMPARING OGDEN, VCF, AND EL-E MULTIPLIERS

In Table 1 we provide comparisons of projections of loss of earnings in personal injury cases using the male Ogden, VCF, and EL-E tables at a net discount rate of 0%, omitting the consideration of income taxes. For the Ogden and EL-E tables, retirement is set at age 65. Since the VCF tables rely on work life statistics that include voluntary retirement, the age of retirement is not entirely compatible with those of the Ogden and EL-E tables. To minimize the discrepancy between retirement ages, we only show VCF data for persons aged 45 and under. The top part of Table 1 shows VCF and EL-E data without incorporating life cycle earnings adjustments, and the bottom part of Table 1 includes the VCF and EL-E life cycle earnings adjustment. The Ogden and VCF tables are not delineated by education, so the EL-E data we choose are for high-school-educated persons who fairly represent "average" work life for all males as used in the VCF.

As can be seen from Table 1, the VCF and EL-E tables produce similar multipliers when not considering life cycle earnings adjustments. Since the Ogden tables for able-bodied workers do not include probabilities of

Table 1. Comparing Ogden, VCF, and EL-E Multipliers at 0% Net Discount.

Age	Ogden	VCF	EL-E
Without life cycle earnings			
25	38.71	32.62	33.01
30	33.78	28.48	28.61
35	38.88	24.29	24.40
40	24.00	20.16	19.95
45	19.16	16.15	15.74
With life cycle earnings			
25		56.77	46.99
30		41.46	35.39
35		30.63	27.26
40		22.79	21.02
45		16.93	15.88

disability or unemployment that would reduce earnings, the Ogden multipliers are significantly higher than those of the VCF and EL-E tables when neither include life cycle earnings adjustments. The deficiency of the Ogden tables not including the life cycle earnings adjustment is most noticeable at early ages in the tables. The life cycle earnings adjustment in the VCF reaches a maximum at age 52 without any decline thereafter, while the life cycle earnings adjustment in the EL-E tables results in declining earnings after age 52. Therefore, even though the basic worklives contained within the VCF and EL-E tables with retirement at age 65 are comparable, the VCF table multipliers with life cycle earnings are higher because of the VCF's truncated life cycle earnings pattern. The Ogden tables, compared to the EL-L and VCF multipliers, thus appear to undercompensate young individuals and overcompensate older workers. These conclusions are consistent with those of Lewis et al. in 2002.

10. CONCLUSIONS

David Bernstein, in his 1997 paper "Procedural Tort Reform: Lessons from Other Nations," urged the adoption in the United States of a variety of features of tort law in the United Kingdom and other Commonwealth countries. In this paper we have provided a basic outline of the differences between the methodologies for calculating damages in personal injury and death litigation, rules for calculating damages, and the court structures of the United Kingdom as compared to those of the United States. Several conclusions can be drawn from these comparisons. First, the U.S. model of damages calculations, which uses an actuarial, economic methodology, testimony by economic experts, and a jury system, has produced a fairly dynamic process of continuing improvement in damages methodologies and exactness in estimates of loss. In the United Kingdom a centralized system of law, with trial by judge without the use of economic experts in the litigation process, according to Lewis et al. has led to a systematic undercompensation of plaintiffs, a situation that has improved with the adoption of the Ogden tables in 1999. With the use of actuarial Ogden tables by judges in determining damages, the compensation to plaintiffs is expected to rise, and come closer to levels found in the United States. That, in itself, will likely produce a "Tort Reform" crisis in the United Kingdom. As a recent (2004) electronic paper, "Potential Effects of Ogden Table Review on Insurance Claims and Premiums," states:

> The Tables and discount rates applied to them are consistently cited as one of the reasons for increasing liability insurance costs and therefore premiums. In addition, there has been a notable increase in the number of high-value claims, on which the Ogden Tables have the highest impact. Claims expenses have risen dramatically, with the average cost of a motor claim increasing by 23% between 1997 and 2002, and the contributing factors include the use of Ogden Tables and the discount rates applied to them. Some insurance industry experts consider that the revised Ogden Tables could lead to as much as a 9% increase in the cost of claims.[8]

In many respects, the lessons from the United Kingdom with respect to the calculation and award of damages in personal injury and death litigation are that past systems of damages calculations, on average, appear to have undercompensated plaintiffs. The Ogden commission members have incorporated sound actuarial methodologies into the multipliers used by the courts, and the database used in constructing the tables has improved over time. The sixth edition tables have incorporated disability and employment status and educational levels into the multipliers Thus the use of actuarially derived Ogden tables have improved the "wholeness" objective of damages as have promoted consistency and predictability of awards, and the use of damages methodologies used in North America would further increase awards in all probability. No doubt, a comparison of Ogden multipliers to U.S. damages projections, as done by Lewis et al. in 2003, would yield more equal results today.

However the accuracy of a damages projection rests on variables that are still not considered at all in the Ogden table multipliers. These variables include the future growth rate of earnings and the discount rate. In the above comparison of damages using Ogden, VCF, and EL multipliers, no future earnings growth and no discounting were assumed. In reality, in the U.S. methodology the forensic economist would project future earnings with some growth rate and then discount those future earnings to present value. But the Ogden multipliers leave the choice of growth rates and discounting to the judge. The discount rate is mandated by the House of Lords (Section 1 of the Damages Act of 1996) and that rate is now 2.5%, but the tables are arranged by discount rates ranging from 0% to 5%. Therefore, the judge might use a 1% rate to implicitly account for future earnings growth rather than the 2.5% rate. The judge might also incorporate age-earnings adjustments in the calculations by adjusting base earnings (the multiplicand) at specific ages (from $25,000 per year for ages 20–29 to $35,000 per year for ages 30–39). Although such devices for correcting projections for growth and discounting rates exist, their use is at the discretion of the judge, and there is no economic logic underlying their selections. In other words, legislated discount rates are not good substitutes for rates supported by economic reasoning.

As to the application of Ogden tables to litigation in the United States, several observations are in order. First, in situations like the September 11, 2001, terrorist attacks on the World Trade Center and the Pentagon, and in cases involving very large groups of plaintiffs with the same causes of action (tobacco, asbestosis, or radon litigation), multipliers offer the advantages of consistency and predictability in awards with minimal transaction costs. Moreover, multipliers can be constructed that incorporate many of the features of "expert-driven" damages methodologies used in the United States. The EL multipliers developed in this paper represent an example of such multipliers. However, the "expert-driven" system has been the source of enhancements to the projections of economic damages, including the Ogden tables, and it should remain the method by which economic damages are determined in the majority of personal injury or death cases in the United States.

NOTES

1. See Ager (2000) for a discussion of scheduled damages in other western European countries, such as Spain. He points out that schedules may create predictability in pecuniary damages, but cannot address the variability in noneconomic damages where multipliers do not exist. Also, see Bona (2003) for a discussion of the process of harmonizing compensation rules in Europe.
2. Ireland is an exception and such claims are considered torts, which has placed pressure on the court system of Ireland and has promoted movement away from trials in recent years.
3. The most recent Ogden tables, along with the methodology used to creating the tables, can be found in *Actuarial Table, with Explanatory Notes for Use in Personal Injury and Fatal Accident Cases* (6th ed.). Actuary's Department http://www.gad.gov.uk/Other_Services/Compensation_for_injury_and_death.htmGovernment
4. [1999] AC 345.
5. Based on Matthias Kelly's presentation to the First Trans-Atlantic Conference of the National Association of Forensic Economics in Edinburgh in 2004.
6. Scotland has a separate legal system within the United Kingdom, but rules for calculating damages are much the same as those in England, Wales, and Northern Ireland. Although the Ogden tables are not mandated for use in calculating damages, they are commonly used and strongly encouraged.
7. In most situations, the difference between the present value of earning capacity and earnings centers on the choice of final exit from the labor force.
8. www.icclaw.com/devs/uk/frame/isframe.htm, July 2004.

ACKNOWLEDGMENT

The author thanks Kurt V. Krueger and Gary R. Albrecht for their work on an earlier draft of this paper.

REFERENCES

Ager, J. (2000). Scheduling damage awards. *INDRET, 1*, 1–16.

Ben-Porath, Y. (1967). The production of human capital and the life cycle of earnings. *Journal of Political Economy, 75*(1), 352–365.

Bernstein, D. (1996). Procedural tort reform: Lessons from other nations. *Regulation, 19*(1). Available at www.cato.org/pubs/regulation/reg 19nle.html

Bona, M. (2003). Towards the 'Europeanization' of personal injury compensation? In: M. Bona & P. Mead (Eds), *Personal injury compensation in Europe*. Deventer: Kluwer.

Feinberg, K. (2004). *Final report of the special master of the September 11th victim compensation fund of 2001, Vol. 1*. The report and details of the fund can also be seen at http://usdoj.gov/archive/victimcompensation/

Grime, S. (2003). *Multiplier issues*. Deans court chambers. Available at www.deanscourt.co.uk/legal/multipliers.html

Krueger, K. (2005). Tables of inter-year labor force status of the U.S. population (1998–2004) to operate the Markov model of worklife expectancy. *Journal of Forensic Economics, 17*(3), 313–381.

Lewis, R., McNabb, L., Robinson, H., & Wass, V. (2003). Loss of earnings following personal injury: Do the courts adequately compensate injured parties. *The Economic Journal, 113*(491), 568–584.

Lewis, R., McNabb, R., Robinson, H., & Wass, V. (2002). Methods of calculating damages for loss of future earnings. *Journal of Personal Injury Law, 2*, 151–165.

Presser, S. (2002). How should the law of products liability be harmonized? what Americans can learn from Europeans. *Global liability issues*. Manhattan Institute, April.

Tinari, F., Cahill, K., & Grivoyannis, E. (2006). Did the 9/11 victim compensation fund accurately assess economic losses? *Topics in Economic Analysis and Policy, 6*(1), 1–42.

Verrall, R., Haberman, S., & Butt, Z. (2006). The impact of dynamic measurement of worklife expectancy on the loss of earnings multipliers in England and Wales. Paper presented at the meeting of the National Association of Forensic Economics, Boston, January 6.

APPENDIX A. THE SIXTH EDITION OF THE OGDEN TABLES: SELECTED PAGE

Table A1. Multipliers for Loss of Earnings to Pension Age 60 (Females).

Age at Date of Trial	Multipliers Calculated with Allowance for Projected Mortality from the 2004-Based Population Projections and Rate of Return of											Age at Date of Trial
	0.0%	0.5%	1.0%	1.5%	2.0%	2.5%	3.0%	3.5%	4.0%	4.5%	5.0%	
16	43.49	39.07	35.26	31.97	29.10	26.60	24.42	22.50	20.81	19.32	17.99	16
17	42.49	38.27	34.62	31.44	25.68	26.26	24.14	22.27	20.63	19.16	17.87	17
18	41.50	37.46	33.96	30.91	28.24	25.91	23.85	22.04	20.43	19.01	17.74	18
19	40.50	36.65	33.30	30.37	27.80	25.55	23.56	21.80	20.23	18.84	17.60	19
20	39.51	35.84	32.63	29.82	27.35	25.18	23.25	21.55	20.03	18.67	17.46	20
21	38.51	35.02	31.96	29.27	26.89	24.80	22.94	21.29	19.81	18.49	17.31	21
22	37.51	34.20	31.28	28.70	26.43	24.41	22.62	21.02	19.59	18.31	17.16	22
23	36.52	33.37	30.59	28.13	25.95	24.01	22.28	20.74	19.35	18.11	16.99	23
24	35.52	32.54	29.89	27.55	25.46	23.60	21.94	20.45	19.11	17.91	16.82	24
25	34.53	31.70	29.19	26.96	24.96	23.18	21.59	20.15	18.86	17.69	16.64	25
26	33.53	30.86	28.48	26.36	24.46	22.75	21.22	19.84	18.60	17.47	16.45	26
27	32.54	30.02	27.77	25.75	23.94	22.31	20.85	19.52	18.33	17.24	16.25	27
28	31.54	29.17	27.04	25.13	23.42	21.86	20.46	19.19	18.04	17.00	16.04	28
29	30.55	28.32	26.32	24.51	22.88	21.40	20.07	18.85	17.75	16.74	15.83	29
30	29.56	27.47	25.58	23.87	22.33	20.93	19.66	18.50	17.44	16.48	15.60	30
31	28.56	26.61	24.84	23.23	21.77	20.45	19.24	18.14	17.13	16.20	15.36	31
32	27.57	25.74	24.09	22.58	21.21	19.95	18.81	17.76	16.80	15.92	15.10	32
33	26.58	24.88	23.33	21.92	20.63	19.45	18.36	17.37	16.46	15.61	14.54	33
34	25.59	24.01	22.57	21.25	20.04	18.93	17.91	16.97	16.10	15.30	14.56	34

Table A1. *(Continued).*

Age at Date of Trial	Multipliers Calculated with Allowance for Projected Mortality from the 2004-Based Population Projections and Rate of Return of											Age at Date of Trial
	0.0%	0.5%	1.0%	1.5%	2.0%	2.5%	3.0%	3.5%	4.0%	4.5%	5.0%	
35	24.60	23.14	21.80	20.57	19.44	18.39	17.44	16.55	15.73	14.97	14.27	35
36	23.61	22.26	21.02	19.88	18.82	17.85	16.95	16.12	15.35	14.63	13.97	36
37	22.62	21.38	20.23	19.18	18.20	17.29	16.45	15.67	14.95	14.28	13.65	37
38	21.63	20.49	19.44	18.47	17.56	16.72	15.94	15.21	14.53	13.90	13.31	38
39	20.64	19.60	18.64	17.75	16.91	16.14	15.41	14.74	14.11	13.51	12.96	39
40	19.65	18.71	17.83	17.02	16.25	15.54	14.87	14.24	13.66	13.11	12.59	40
41	18.67	17.81	17.02	16.27	15.58	14.92	14.31	13.74	13.20	12.69	12.21	41
42	17.68	16.92	16.20	15.52	14.89	14.30	13.74	13.21	12.71	12.25	11.80	42
43	16.70	16.01	15.37	14.77	14.19	13.66	13.15	12.67	12.22	11.79	11.38	43
44	15.71	15.11	14.54	14.00	13.48	13.00	12.54	12.11	11.70	11.31	10.94	44
45	14.73	14.20	13.69	13.22	12.76	12.33	11.92	11.53	11.16	10.81	10.48	45
46	13.76	13.29	12.85	12.43	12.02	11.64	11.28	10.93	10.60	10.29	9.99	46
47	12.18	12.37	11.99	11.62	11.27	10.94	10.62	10.32	10.03	9.75	9.48	47
48	11.80	11.46	11.13	10.81	10.51	10.22	9.94	9.68	9.43	9.18	8.95	48
49	10.82	10.53	10.25	9.99	9.73	9.48	9.25	9.02	8.80	8.59	8.39	49
50	9.85	9.61	9.37	9.15	8.94	8.73	8.53	8.34	8.15	7.97	7.80	50
51	8.87	8.67	8.49	8.30	8.13	7.96	7.79	7.63	7.48	7.33	7.19	51
52	7.89	7.74	7.59	7.44	7.30	7.16	7.03	6.90	6.78	6.66	6.54	52
53	6.91	6.79	6.68	6.56	6.46	6.35	6.25	6.15	6.05	5.95	5.86	53
54	5.93	5.84	5.76	5.67	5.59	5.51	5.44	5.36	5.29	5.22	5.14	54
55	4.95	4.89	4.83	4.77	4.71	4.66	4.60	4.55	4.50	4.44	4.39	55
56	3.96	3.93	3.89	3.85	3.S1	3.78	3.74	3.70	3.67	3.64	3.60	56
57	2.98	2.96	2.93	2.91	2.89	2.87	2.85	2.83	2.81	2.79	2.77	57
58	1.99	1.98	1.97	1.96	1.95	1.94	1.93	1.92	1.91	1.90	1.90	58
59	1.00	0.99	0.99	0.99	0.99	0.99	0.98	0.98	0.98	0.98	0.97	59

APPENDIX B. SELECTED VCF SCHEDULE

Table B1. Presumed Economic and Noneconomic Loss for a Single Decedent Before Any Collateral Offset.

Age	Income								
	$10,000	$20,000	$25,000	$30,000	$35,000	$40,000	$45,000	$50,000	$60,000
25	$383,953	$502,525	$565,791	$643,072	$751,528	$877,423	$963,377	$1,051,593	$1,214,526
30	$348,755	$436,170	$482,811	$539,785	$619,743	$712,557	$775,925	$840,961	$961,080
35	$325,946	$393,171	$429,040	$472,854	$534,344	$605,721	$654,453	$704,468	$796,844
40	$310,562	$364,169	$392,772	$427,712	$476,746	$533,664	$572,525	$612,408	$686,071
45	$300,000	$337,221	$359,073	$385,766	$423,226	$466,709	$496,398	$526,867	$583,144
50	$300,000	$315,111	$331,423	$351,349	$379,313	$411,774	$433,936	$456,681	$498,692
55	$300,000	$300,000	$308,408	$322,702	$342,761	$366,047	$381,945	$398,261	$428,396
60	$300,000	$300,000	$300,000	$300,000	$312,200	$327,813	$338,473	$349,414	$369,621
65	$300,000	$300,000	$300,000	$300,000	$300,000	$302,076	$309,211	$316,533	$330,056
	$70,000	$80,000	$90,000	$100,000	$125,000	$150,000	$1750,000	$200,000	$225,000
25	$1,376,302	$1,751,060	$2,107,059	$2,281,192	$2,669,889	X,XXX,XXX	X,XXX,XXX	X,XXX,XXX	X,XXX,XXX
30	$1,080,347	$1,356,630	$1,619,085	$1,747,461	$2,034,021	$2,344,344	$2,643,787	X,XXX,XXX	X,XXX,XXX
35	$888,564	$1,101,035	$1,302,871	$1,401,596	$1,621,971	$1,860,619	$2,090,900	$2,311,844	$2,523,762
40	$759,212	$928,644	$1,089,594	$1,168,322	$1,344,055	$1,534,361	$1,717,995	$1,894,184	$2,063,174
45	$639,020	$768,460	$891,421	$951,566	$1,085,821	$1,231,208	$1,371,498	$1,506,100	$1,635,203
50	$540,404	$637,031	$728,821	$773,719	$873,940	$982,472	$1,087,198	$1,187,679	$1,284,054
55	$458,318	$527,632	$593,477	$625,684	$697,577	$775,431	$850,555	$922,634	$991,768
60	$389,685	$436,162	$480,314	$501,910	$550,116	$602,320	$652,693	$701,025	$747,381
65	$343,484	$374,589	$404,137	$418,590	$450,852	$485,789	$519,501	$551,847	$582,871

APPENDIX C. SAMPLE EL-E TABLES

Table C1. Lifetime Age-Earnings Multipliers for All Males with a High School Education with Retirement at Age 65.

Age at Loss	Selected Net Discount Rate										
	0.0%	0.5%	1.0%	1.5%	2.0%	2.5%	3.0%	3.5%	4.0%	4.5%	5.0%
18	78.17	69.09	61.34	54.71	49.02	44.11	39.86	36.17	32.95	30.14	27.67
19	71.60	63.50	56.57	50.62	45.49	41.06	37.20	33.85	30.92	28.34	26.08
20	66.01	58.75	52.51	47.14	42.49	38.46	34.94	31.88	29.18	26.82	24.73
21	61.20	54.66	49.02	44.14	39.91	36.22	33.00	30.18	27.70	25.52	23.58
22	57.03	51.10	45.98	41.53	37.66	34.28	31.32	28.71	26.42	24.39	22.59
23	53.33	47.95	43.28	39.21	35.66	32.55	29.81	27.40	25.27	23.38	21.70
24	49.99	45.09	40.82	37.09	33.82	30.95	28.42	26.18	24.19	22.43	20.86
25	46.99	42.52	38.61	35.18	32.16	29.51	27.16	25.07	23.22	21.57	20.09
26	44.28	40.19	36.60	33.44	30.66	28.20	26.01	24.07	22.34	20.79	19.41
27	41.79	38.04	34.74	31.82	29.25	26.96	24.93	23.12	21.50	20.05	18.74
28	39.49	36.05	33.01	30.32	27.94	25.81	23.92	22.23	20.71	19.35	18.12
29	37.36	34.20	31.40	28.92	26.71	24.74	22.97	21.39	19.97	18.68	17.53
30	35.39	32.49	29.91	27.61	25.56	23.73	22.08	20.60	19.27	18.06	16.97
31	33.55	30.88	28.51	26.39	24.48	22.78	21.24	19.85	18.60	17.47	16.44
32	31.83	29.39	27.20	25.23	23.47	21.88	20.45	19.15	17.98	16.91	15.94
33	30.23	27.98	25.96	24.14	22.51	21.03	19.69	18.48	17.38	16.38	15.46
34	28.71	26.64	24.78	23.10	21.59	20.21	18.97	17.83	16.80	15.86	15.00
35	27.26	25.37	23.65	22.11	20.70	19.42	18.26	17.20	16.24	15.35	14.54
36	25.88	24.15	22.57	21.14	19.84	18.66	17.58	16.59	15.69	14.86	14.09
37	24.58	22.99	21.54	20.22	19.02	17.92	16.92	16.00	15.15	14.37	13.66
38	23.33	21.88	20.55	19.34	18.23	17.21	16.28	15.42	14.63	13.90	13.23

39	22.15	20.82	19.61	18.49	17.47	16.53	15.67	14.87	14.13	13.45	12.82
40	21.02	19.80	18.69	17.67	16.73	15.86	15.06	14.32	13.64	13.00	12.41
41	19.91	18.81	17.80	16.86	16.00	15.20	14.46	13.78	13.14	12.55	12.00
42	18.86	17.86	16.94	16.08	15.29	14.56	13.88	13.25	12.66	12.11	11.60
43	17.84	16.94	16.10	15.32	14.60	13.93	13.30	12.72	12.17	11.67	11.19
44	16.85	16.03	15.27	14.57	13.91	13.30	12.72	12.19	11.69	11.22	10.78
45	15.88	15.15	14.46	13.83	13.23	12.67	12.15	11.66	11.20	10.77	10.36
46	14.95	14.29	13.68	13.10	12.56	12.06	11.58	11.13	10.72	10.32	9.95
47	14.04	13.46	12.91	12.39	11.91	11.45	11.02	10.62	10.23	9.87	9.53
48	13.16	12.64	12.16	11.70	11.26	10.85	10.47	10.10	9.75	9.43	9.12
49	12.31	11.85	11.42	11.01	10.62	10.26	9.91	9.58	9.27	8.97	8.69
50	11.46	11.06	10.68	10.32	9.98	9.66	9.35	9.06	8.78	8.51	8.26
51	10.65	10.30	9.97	9.66	9.36	9.07	8.80	8.54	8.29	8.06	7.83
52	9.85	9.55	9.27	9.00	8.74	8.49	8.25	8.02	7.80	7.59	7.40
53	9.08	8.82	8.58	8.34	8.12	7.90	7.70	7.50	7.31	7.13	6.95
54	8.34	8.12	7.92	7.72	7.53	7.34	7.17	7.00	6.83	6.68	6.53
55	7.60	7.42	7.25	7.09	6.93	6.77	6.62	6.48	6.34	6.21	6.08
56	6.85	6.71	6.57	6.43	6.30	6.17	6.05	5.93	5.82	5.71	5.60
57	6.10	5.98	5.87	5.76	5.66	5.56	5.46	5.36	5.27	5.18	5.09
58	5.34	5.26	5.17	5.09	5.00	4.93	4.85	4.77	4.70	4.63	4.56
59	4.59	4.53	4.46	4.40	4.34	4.28	4.22	4.17	4.11	4.06	4.00
60	3.84	3.80	3.75	3.71	3.66	3.62	3.58	3.54	3.50	3.46	3.42
61	3.09	3.06	3.03	3.00	2.97	2.95	2.92	2.89	2.87	2.84	2.81
62	2.35	2.33	2.31	2.30	2.28	2.26	2.25	2.23	2.22	2.20	2.19
63	1.59	1.59	1.58	1.57	1.56	1.56	1.55	1.54	1.53	1.53	1.52
64	0.81	0.81	0.81	0.81	0.80	0.80	0.80	0.80	0.80	0.79	0.79
65	0.00	0.00	0.00	0.00	0.00	0.00	0.00	0.00	0.00	0.00	0.00

Table C2. Lifetime Simple Earnings Multipliers for All Males with a High School Education with Retirement at Age 65.

Age at Loss	Selected Net Discount Rate										
	0.0%	0.5%	1.0%	1.5%	2.0%	2.5%	3.0%	3.5%	4.0%	4.5%	5.0%
18	38.96	34.87	31.36	28.34	25.74	23.48	21.51	19.79	18.28	16.95	15.77
19	38.09	34.17	30.80	27.89	25.37	23.18	21.27	19.59	18.12	16.82	15.67
20	37.23	33.48	30.24	27.44	25.01	22.89	21.03	19.40	17.96	16.69	15.56
21	36.39	32.81	29.70	27.01	24.66	22.61	20.81	19.22	17.82	16.58	15.48
22	35.57	32.15	29.17	26.59	24.32	22.34	20.60	19.06	17.69	16.48	15.40
23	34.74	31.48	28.63	26.15	23.97	22.06	20.37	18.87	17.55	16.37	15.31
24	33.87	30.76	28.04	25.66	23.57	21.72	20.09	18.64	17.36	16.21	15.18
25	33.01	30.04	27.45	25.17	23.16	21.38	19.81	18.41	17.16	16.04	15.04
26	32.15	29.34	26.86	24.68	22.76	21.05	19.53	18.18	16.97	15.88	14.91
27	31.27	28.60	26.24	24.16	22.32	20.68	19.22	17.91	16.74	15.69	14.74
28	30.38	27.85	25.61	23.63	21.86	20.29	18.89	17.63	16.50	15.48	14.57
29	29.49	27.10	24.97	23.09	21.40	19.90	18.55	17.34	16.25	15.27	14.38
30	28.61	26.35	24.33	22.54	20.93	19.50	18.20	17.04	15.99	15.04	14.18
31	27.73	25.59	23.69	21.99	20.46	19.09	17.85	16.74	15.73	14.81	13.98
32	26.85	24.84	23.05	21.43	19.98	18.68	17.50	16.43	15.46	14.58	13.78
33	25.99	24.10	22.40	20.88	19.50	18.26	17.14	16.11	15.19	14.34	13.57
34	25.12	23.35	21.75	20.31	19.01	17.83	16.76	15.79	14.90	14.09	13.35
35	24.24	22.59	21.09	19.74	18.51	17.39	16.37	15.45	14.60	13.83	13.11
36	23.37	21.82	20.42	19.15	17.99	16.94	15.97	15.09	14.29	13.55	12.87
37	22.50	21.06	19.75	18.56	17.47	16.48	15.57	14.73	13.97	13.26	12.61
38	21.64	20.31	19.08	17.97	16.95	16.01	15.15	14.37	13.64	12.97	12.35
39	20.80	19.56	18.42	17.38	16.43	15.55	14.74	14.00	13.31	12.68	12.09
40	19.95	18.81	17.75	16.79	15.90	15.08	14.32	13.62	12.97	12.37	11.82

41	19.10	18.04	17.07	16.18	15.35	14.58	13.88	13.22	12.61	12.05	11.52
42	18.26	17.29	16.40	15.57	14.80	14.09	13.43	12.82	12.25	11.72	11.23
43	17.42	16.54	15.72	14.95	14.25	13.59	12.98	12.41	11.88	11.38	10.92
44	16.58	15.77	15.02	14.32	13.67	13.07	12.50	11.98	11.48	11.02	10.59
45	15.74	15.01	14.33	13.69	13.10	12.54	12.02	11.53	11.07	10.65	10.24
46	14.91	14.25	13.63	13.05	12.51	12.00	11.53	11.08	10.66	10.26	9.89
47	14.08	13.49	12.94	12.42	11.92	11.46	11.03	10.62	10.23	9.87	9.53
48	13.27	12.74	12.24	11.78	11.33	10.92	10.53	10.15	9.80	9.47	9.15
49	12.46	11.99	11.55	11.13	10.74	10.36	10.01	9.67	9.36	9.05	8.77
50	11.65	11.24	10.85	10.48	10.13	9.79	9.48	9.18	8.89	8.62	8.36
51	10.86	10.50	10.16	9.83	9.52	9.23	8.95	8.68	8.43	8.19	7.95
52	10.07	9.76	9.46	9.18	8.91	8.66	8.41	8.17	7.95	7.73	7.53
53	9.29	9.03	8.77	8.53	8.30	8.07	7.86	7.66	7.46	7.27	7.09
54	8.55	8.32	8.11	7.90	7.70	7.51	7.33	7.16	6.99	6.82	6.67
55	7.80	7.61	7.43	7.26	7.09	6.93	6.78	6.63	6.49	6.35	6.21
56	7.03	6.88	6.73	6.59	6.45	6.32	6.19	6.07	5.95	5.84	5.73
57	6.25	6.13	6.01	5.90	5.79	5.68	5.58	5.48	5.39	5.29	5.20
58	5.47	5.38	5.29	5.20	5.12	5.03	4.95	4.88	4.80	4.73	4.66
59	4.69	4.62	4.56	4.49	4.43	4.37	4.31	4.25	4.19	4.14	4.08
60	3.91	3.86	3.82	3.77	3.73	3.69	3.64	3.60	3.56	3.52	3.48
61	3.13	3.10	3.07	3.05	3.02	2.99	2.96	2.93	2.91	2.88	2.85
62	2.37	2.35	2.34	2.32	2.30	2.29	2.27	2.25	2.24	2.22	2.21
63	1.60	1.60	1.59	1.58	1.57	1.56	1.56	1.55	1.54	1.54	1.53
64	0.81	0.81	0.81	0.81	0.80	0.80	0.80	0.80	0.80	0.79	0.79
65	0.00	0.00	0.00	0.00	0.00	0.00	0.00	0.00	0.00	0.00	0.00

ACCOUNTING FOR THE EFFECTS OF DISABLEMENT ON FUTURE EMPLOYMENT IN BRITAIN

Victoria Wass and Robert McNabb

1. INTRODUCTION AND BACKGROUND

It is a common feature of both the English and the US legal systems that any person injured through the fault of another can claim monetary compensation, in the form of damages, for the injuries sustained.[1] The objective and measure of such damages is also the same across the jurisdictions, namely to restore the individual, in financial terms and in as far as it is possible to do so, to their pre-injury position. However, the approaches adopted in the two countries towards determining the level of damages are very different. In the United States, courts make extensive use of economists (called forensic economists), economic data and econometric methods to quantify damages, particularly in the calculation of those which relate to future losses. The courts in Britain do not, favouring instead the routine application of a simplified formula which is populated by figures chosen by judges, albeit with increasing reference to published actuarial averages. There has been a long-standing antipathy on the part of the judiciary towards evidence from financial experts. This has been justified on the grounds that predicting the future is nothing more than crystal ball gazing for which a judge is as well suited as any other profession.[2]

Personal Injury and Wrongful Death Damages Calculations: Transatlantic Dialogue
Contemporary Studies in Economic and Financial Analysis, Volume 91, 73–101

ISSN: 1569-3759/doi:10.1108/S1569-3759(2009)0000091007

The formula for calculating loss of future earnings involves the product of the multiplicand, an estimated annual loss, and the multiplier, an estimated number of years over which the annual loss is to be paid (discounted for early receipt). This is the notional lump sum which, when used to purchase an 'assumed annuity', provides the annual sum (the multiplicand) in each year of loss. Traditionally, the number of future years was determined on the basis of judicial conjecture and was generally within the confines of a 4.5 percent real discount rate and a 16-year upper limit on the discounted worklife expectancy (WLE). Over the course of the 1990s, there was increasing reference to the broad actuarial averages which had been published in the Ogden Tables since 1984, at least as a 'check' on judicial impression (*Hunt v. Severs* [1991]).[3] The Ogden Tables are a set of tables of discounted life expectancies and explanatory notes which are compiled by the Ogden Working Party and published by the Government Actuary's Department. They are named after Sir Michael Ogden QC who first chaired the Working Party. Their purpose is to provide lawyers with guidance in the calculation of future pecuniary loss in claims for personal injury, clinical negligence and fatal accidents. Although available from 1984, it was 1999 that their use was formally endorsed by the House of Lords which determined that the actuarial multipliers published in the Ogden Tables should form the 'starting point' of any settlement and that any departure would require 'compelling evidence pointing to another figure' (*Wells v. Wells* [1999]).[4] The discount rate to be used in subsequent calculations was also reduced to 3 percent in this case. It was later reduced to 2.5 percent in June 2001 by the Lord Chancellor using the powers conferred on him by the Damages Act 1996.[5]

The use of the Ogden Tables has undoubtedly improved the transparency and consistency of the calculation of awards. Together with the reduction in the discount rate, it has also increased the level of awards. Nevertheless, it is the case that a number of deficiencies remain. The focus of this chapter is on those that pertain to the employment risks incorporated within the WLE. The Ogden Tables have as their subject the WLE of individuals whose working lives have been disrupted by the disabling effects of injury, yet no guidance is offered in how such effects might be measured and compensated.

In this chapter, we consider the extent to which the simple formulaic approach, which ignores both the dynamic nature of an individual's engagement with the labour market, and the impact of disability on employment risks, makes a difference to the level of damages awarded for loss of future earnings when compared with the more individual and informed approaches used in the United States. To do this, we compare the level of damages awarded by the courts in 100 cases in Britain with the level of damages calculated using an econometric analysis based upon the individual facts of each case.[6] This econometric analysis is informed by some of the more widely used practices employed in US courts. Although there is considerable variety in the methodologies and data sources used in the United States, and in the complexity of the analysis that is permissible by different states, there is a general consensus regarding appropriate methods. Brookshire and Slesnick (1997), Thornton and Ward (1999) and Martin (1999) provide details of the different approaches adopted.

The structure of the chapter is as follows. In the next section, we explain how damages for loss of future earnings are determined under the English tort system using the multiplier–multiplicand formula. In the context of loss of future earnings, the multiplier is equivalent to the WLE and is central to the estimation of loss of future earnings. We then outline the statistical concept of the WLE and review some of the US approaches to its estimation. This is followed by a description of our own approach which is based upon data on annual employment transitions collected in the UK Labour Force Survey (LFS) 2002–2004. The LFS also collects information on health and disability status, and we review research which seeks to measure the impact of disability on employment outcomes before using these methods to integrate the impact of disability into the estimation of claimants' employment prospects. In the following section, we present our findings in relation to the impact of measuring employment as the outcome of a lifetime of labour market transitions and including in the calculation the effects of disability. We later explore the implications of our results for 100 awards adjudicated in the British courts based upon the simple multiplier–multiplicand calculation and discretionary awards for labour market disadvantage. We conclude this chapter with a review of the advantages of our approach and a discussion of some of the potential sources of bias in our approach.

2. HOW THE COURTS IN BRITAIN MEASURE LOSS OF FUTURE EARNINGS

Damages for loss of future earnings are measured at the time of trial as the capital sum that will, via the purchase of an annuity, fully compensate the injured claimant for the future stream of earnings that would have been available to her/him in the absence of the injury. The calculation, which is undertaken by the court, is based on the multiplier–multiplicand method. The multiplicand is the annual loss of earnings and is the difference between the claimant's earnings before and after injury. In most cases, future pre-injury earnings are the claimant's earnings at the time of injury plus any earnings growth to the date of trial. In general, and in contrast to many US approaches, no account is taken of any potential growth in real earnings after the date of trial. Where the claimant is not working at the time of injury, due to non-participation, unemployment or, in the case of injured children, having not yet entered the labour market, the court imputes a figure for future pre-injury earnings with reference to published average earnings data such as is available in the UK Government's *Annual Survey of Hours and Earnings*.

Estimating future post-injury earnings is more speculative. Where the claimant is judged to be medically incapable of future employment, no calculation is required, and the full loss of pre-injury earnings is awarded. However, where medical evidence indicates that the claimant is capable of employment in the future, a partial loss is awarded in which the court assesses the value of future post-injury earnings, normally using average earnings for an occupational group for which the claimant is considered intellectually and physically capable. If the claimant is working at the time of trial, future post-injury earnings will be based upon the claimant's current earnings.

The Ogden Tables (Fifth Edition, 2004) contain 26 tables of discounted life expectancies to retirement age. These are the baseline multipliers. The application of a reduction factor for discounted labour market risks converts the baseline multiplier into a discounted WLE. It is the discounted WLE which converts the multiplicand into a working lifetime capital sum, the purpose of which is to provide an annual amount equivalent to the loss of earnings in each year to retirement age.

Actuarially determined baseline multipliers have been published by age, sex and discount rate in each edition of the Ogden Tables. The baseline multiplier requires downward adjustment to account for employment risks (often referred to as non-mortality risks) that would have precluded the claimant from continuous employment even in the absence of injury. Historically, the magnitude of this downward adjustment to the multiplier has been fairly arbitrary, taking the form of a percentage deduction determined by the judge and averaging around 17 percent (Luckett & Craner, 1994). From 1994, actuarially calculated percentage deductions for labour market risks by age for very broadly defined industrial/occupational and regional categories of workers have been available in the Ogden Tables

(Second Edition, 1994). These deductions are represented as reduction factors which are calculated as the proportion of the potential remaining lifetime to retirement that is likely to be spent in employment. They are based upon average employment rates and are those estimated by Haberman and Bloomfield (1990) from early years of the LFS.[7] From 1999, the courts have been required to use the 'Ogden' baseline multipliers and the associated reduction factors for labour market risks as a 'starting point' in the calculation of loss of future earnings (*Wells v. Wells* [1999]).

Although both the multiplier–multiplicand formula and the figures intended to populate the formula provided in the Ogden Tables have as their subject the potentially adverse effect of disability on the future employment of the injured claimant, no guidance is offered in this matter. In those cases where medical evidence indicates that the claimant is capable of employment in the future, but where the impact of displacement and/or residual disablement is to significantly weaken the claimant's competitive position in the labour market, the courts seek to compensate for the resulting loss of employment opportunities through an additional lump-sum payment. This award is assessed separately from the multiplier–multiplicand calculation and has come to be called a '*Smith v. Manchester*' lump sum, after the case in which the principles for such an award were established.

2.1. The Smith v. Manchester Lump Sum

The purpose of this award is to provide compensation for the 'weakening of the plaintiff's competitive position in the open labour market'.[8] The courts have experienced difficulty in formulating clear guidelines as to when such an award should apply and, where it does, how it should be evaluated. Although originally intended to cover the situation where the claimant was employed at the time of trial, it has subsequently been applied more broadly to cover those who might have been expected to gain employment or who might be expected to gain employment shortly (see Randolf, 2005). In terms of the determination of quantum, the *Smith v. Manchester* decision seemingly provides authority for judges to 'pluck from the air a suitable number of pounds sterling',[9] all the time maintaining that this is 'the best that can be done'.[10] The particular difficulty which precludes an arithmetic approach appears to arise from the 'double speculation'[11] involved in combining the risk of losing the current job and the uncertainty of when alternative employment might be secured. Despite the absence of guidelines for such an award, a *Smith v. Manchester* lump sum, according to Ritchie

(1994), would normally be in the region of 6–24 months of post-injury net earnings.[12] There is a considerable body of social science research, at least in the United Kingdom, which indicates that the average impact of disability on a future lifetime of employment (even when discounted into the future) is vastly understated by this norm.

2.2. Worked Example

We use a worked example as a means of illustrating the approach. The example is reworked later using the alternative economic analysis developed in the chapter. In this worked example, compensation for loss of future earnings is calculated using the multiplier–multiplicand formula and a conventional *Smith v. Manchester* lump-sum award for disability-induced employment disadvantage. The discounted life expectancies and the discounted non-mortality risks are those from the Fifth Edition of the Ogden Tables (2004).

The claimant is male and 30 years of age at the time of injury in 1999. He was employed as a motor mechanic at the date of injury on an annual salary of £25,000 after tax. He had no pre-injury disability. As a result of his injuries, he has continuing disability and is unable to perform his pre-injury job. At the time of trial, he is employed on a three-quarter contract as a sales assistant in a car hire firm on an annual salary of £15,000 after tax. His continued ability to perform this post-injury employment is supported by medical opinion.

The discounted life expectancy to retirement age of 65 years is 22.81 (Ogden Tables, Fifth Edition, Table 8). The reduction factor for employment risks is 0.97 (Ogden Tables, Fifth Edition, Table A). The calculation proceeds as follows:

Pre-injury expected future earnings	£25,000 × 22.81 × 0.97	+£553,143
Post-injury expected future earnings	£15,000 × 22.81 × 0.97	−£331,886
Smith v. Manchester lump sum for disability-induced labour market disadvantage		+£30,000
Total award		= £251,257

The point of note is that the WLE (23 years) and the reduction factor (0.97) are the same in the pre- and post-injury calculation. The award of compensation for loss of future earnings comprises largely the difference in annual salary due to occupational downgrading and the reduction in hours. Any additional employment risks due to the continuing disabling effects of injury are intended to be compensated in the *Smith v. Manchester* lump sum, in this case equivalent to two years' post-injury earnings.

3. MODELLING A LIFETIME OF EMPLOYMENT

The statistical concept of the WLE is central to the calculation of future loss of earnings. It is the statistical estimate of the future number of years over which the annual loss occurs, and in tort law in Britain it is known as the multiplier. For the purposes of loss of earnings' compensation in the United States, working life is defined as the time spent active in the workforce until final separation (through either death or retirement). In Britain, working life is defined as the time spent in employment. The difference is that the US definition of WLE includes time spent actively seeking employment from a state of non-employment, that is time spent in unemployment (as defined by the International Labour Office [ILO]), whereas in Britain unemployment falls outside the WLE. In the United Kingdom, the award is for loss of actual earnings and, since unemployment does not attract earnings, the UK definition is preferred. In the United States, where it is necessary to account for the impact of potential unemployment, the multiplicand is reduced accordingly. Unemployment accounts for less than 4 percent of the British working population so the distinction is likely to be of relatively modest practical significance. A further complicating difference is that in certain jurisdictions in the United States, a claimant is compensated for loss of earning capacity (as opposed to actual earnings) in which case the WLE is simply the number of years to expected retirement.

There are many different approaches to the measurement of the duration of loss of earnings in the United States (see Ciecka, 1994; Martin, 1999; Skoog & Ciecka, 2004). We provide a simple two-way taxonomy in Fig. 1, which distinguishes (i) whether or not a single 'lifetime' figure is used as opposed to a lifetime of annual figures and (ii) whether a dynamic Markov framework where the WLE is conditioned on a series of transitions from a particular starting status is used in preference to a simple demographic average. Superimposed on this classification is the distinction between whether or not the period of loss refers to potential or actual loss of earnings.

So, for example the US Bureau of Labor Statistics (BLS) tables are single-figure age-specific work life tables of the US population which are estimated from labour force transitions conditioned on an active starting status

	A single lifetime figure	Annually over a lifetime
Average based on transitions from a specified starting state	(i)	(iii)
Simple demographic average	(ii)	(iv)

(i) Nelson, 1983; Frasca and Winger, 1989; Smith, 1982, 1983,1985; BLS WLE Tables,1982.
(ii) Simple model of years to retirement
(iii) Alter and Becker, 1985; Becker and Alter, 1987; Romans and Floss, 1993.
(iv) Brookshire and Cobb, 1983; Baker and Seck, 1987.

Fig. 1. Different Approaches to Measuring Duration of Loss.

(see Smith, 1982, 1983, 1985). Other single-figure approaches, also based upon transitions, estimate the median years to retirement rather than a WLE (see, e.g. Nelson, 1983). This represents the period of potential loss of earnings. Conditional estimates of WLEs are preferred to those based upon on a static distribution of the labour force across different employment states as they more closely follow the conditional and chequered nature of individual work histories. (However, see Richards, 2000, for a contrary view.) They are estimated using dynamic models which explicitly include multiple entries into, and exits from, employment. Observations on the timing and the number of the transitions from one state to another make it possible to estimate the likelihood of the time that is spent in a particular state conditional upon age and upon the starting employment status. The theoretical and technical aspects of the application of multiple-state Markov chain models to econometric problems are now well developed in the literature, and the general consensus is that they provide a superior framework for the analysis of labour market behaviour (Butt, Haberman, Verrall, & Wass, 2008). Advances in this field in the United Kingdom have been facilitated by the availability of panel data from the early 1990s.

Conditioning future employment patterns on current employment is particularly relevant in the present context – most claimants are in employment at the time of injury and suffer displacement as a result of injury. This is illustrated by statistics taken from the claimants in the sample of 100 cases collected by the authors in the late 1990s. Of the 63 who were judged to have post-injury employment capacity, 59 were employed at the time of injury (an employment rate of 93 percent compared to a population average of 74 percent). Once disabled by injury, only 27 claimants (43 percent) had secured employment at some time between the time of injury and the time of trial. This provides a first indication that the adverse affects of injury on employment are greater than assumed in a conventional *Smith v. Manchester* award.

The alternative to the single-figure approaches is to use the year-by-year representations of labour force activity that feed into the single-figure WLEs. There are examples of this explicit life cycle approach in the US literature using both conditional probabilities based upon transition rates into and out of activity (Alter & Becker, 1985; Becker & Alter, 1987) and unconditional average life-participation-employment (LPE) rates (e.g. see Brookshire & Cobb, 1983; Romans & Floss, 1993). The Alter and Becker (1985) approach estimates transition probabilities in each remaining year of working life conditional upon starting employment status. Expected earnings at each future age are the wage rate weighted by the probability of being alive and in employment where the employment weights are conditioned on past labour market outcomes and are calculated from age-specific transition probabilities. According to this approach, the expected earnings at each age j are measured as

$$E(W_j) = \left[(W_j P_{\mathrm{aa}j} P_{\mathrm{sw}j} P_{\mathrm{s}j}) + \left(\frac{1}{2} W_j P_{\mathrm{aa}j} P_{\mathrm{lw}j} P_{\mathrm{s}j} \right) + \left(\frac{1}{2} W_j P_{\mathrm{aa}j} P_{\mathrm{sw}j} P_{\mathrm{d}j} \right) + \left(\frac{1}{2} W_j P_{\mathrm{an}j} P_{\mathrm{ew}j} P_{\mathrm{s}j} \right) \right] \quad (1)$$

where $E(W_j)$ is expected earnings at age j, $P_{\mathrm{aa}j}$ the probability of being alive and in the workforce, $P_{\mathrm{an}j}$ the probability of being alive and not in the workforce, $P_{\mathrm{sw}j}$ the probability of staying in the workforce, $P_{\mathrm{lw}j}$ the probability of leaving the workforce, $P_{\mathrm{ew}j}$ the probability of entering the workforce, $P_{\mathrm{s}j}$ the probability of surviving the year and $P_{\mathrm{d}j}$ the probability of dying during the year. The formula assumes that W_j is made in two equal biannual payments during the year and that someone who changes labour market status or dies does so halfway through the year; hence, in the last three components, each expected earnings figure is multiplied by one-half.

Loss of future earnings is simply the sum (integral) of expected earnings over the individual's working lifetime. Schieren (1993) suggests that the Alter and Becker use of year-by-year transition probabilities to estimate expected annual earnings is 'a more accurate depiction of what a person actually earns over the course of a lifetime'. It is preferred for this reason. It also offers the flexibility to vary earnings over the life cycle (to include, e.g. an age-earnings profile, anticipated promotions and predicted periods of inactivity) and to avoid the use of a fixed retirement age. In a comparison of awards calculated under different assumptions, Schieren (1993) and Ciecka (1994) note that the differences between single-figure and year-by-year approaches are relatively modest, particularly for men at younger ages.

It is common practice in the United States to use the single-figure BLS WLE estimates in the calculation of future loss of earnings (see Brookshire & Slesnick, 1997). For Britain there is no 'official' equivalent of the WLE, and any single-figure approach is predicated upon first estimating annual employment probabilities over each age-specific working lifetime. In this chapter, we estimate age-specific, year-by-year, conditional employment probabilities. In another chapter in this volume (91), we have developed the model and methodology to estimate age-specific single-figure WLEs.

The model is a simple increment–decrement Markov chain as depicted in Fig. 2 with transitions between two states of economic activity, employed and non-employed.

The age-specific transition probability p_x^{ij} is defined in terms of the retrospective (one year earlier) labour market status as follows:

$$p_{x-1}^{ij}(t=1) = \frac{n_{x-1}^{ij}}{n_{x-1}^{i}} \quad \text{for } i = 1 \text{ or } 2 \quad \text{and } j = 1 \text{ or } 2 \tag{2}$$

The term n_{x-1}^{i} is the total number of participants of age x who one year earlier were in employment state i and n_{x-1}^{ij} the number of participants who move from i to j over the age year $x-1$ to x. Transition probabilities are based upon observations of current employment status at age x and previous employment status 12 months previously at age $x-1$. The age-specific employment probabilities over any number of years t are estimated as a function of the yearly transition probabilities from Eq. (2) above, the starting employment status and age-specific survival rate making use of a recursive formula. Survival rates are the same for both economic states and are those reported in the UK Interim Life tables for 1999–2001.[13] The WLE is calculated as the integral of the expected proportion of people who

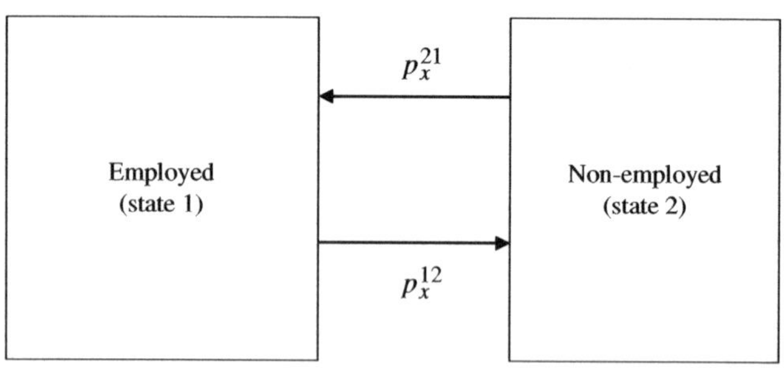

Fig. 2. Two-State Markov Model of Labour Force Transitions.

after t years will be alive and employed, conditional on their employment status at age x and being alive at age x.[14]

Current employment status is measured in each quarter of the LFS using ILO-defined categories. In the spring quarter of each year, respondents recall their employment status one year ago. It is this measure which forms the starting state from which transitions are measured. Both employment status variables include multiple (and different) categories of employment and non-employment. Owing to small sample sizes, when disaggregated by age, sex and starting employment status (and disability), and the absence of a unique map between current and past employment measures, these multiple-category variables are aggregated into two main transient states: 'employed' and 'non-employed'. At this level of aggregation the two variables share a common classification. This classification differs from the one adopted in the US WLE tables in which the dichotomy is 'active' and 'inactive' where the employed and unemployed together form the category of the 'active' workforce to be contrasted with those who are neither working nor looking for work, the 'inactive'.

Within the UK dichotomy, the unemployed form a distinctive group within the non-employed group, not least because of their greater attachment to the labour market (see Jones & Riddell, 1999). Our preference would have been to model unemployment as a separate economic state in a three-state model. However, since the unemployed account for less than 4 percent of the working population, the size of the sub-sample is insufficient to generate stable estimates when disaggregated by sex, age and disability status. The potential for bias which results from our classification is considered likely to be small and is discussed later in this chapter. We note that, in line with the United States focus on activity rather than employment, Kreider (1999) groups the unemployed with the employed, but he finds that this has 'virtually no effect on the results of the analysis' (see Kreider, 1999, footnote 16).

Two estimates of employment probabilities have been considered. The first is based on the life-employment-participation approach developed by Brookshire and Cobb (1983) and uses unconditional employment probabilities comprising the number of people of a stated age in employment divided by the total number of people of that age. In the second approach, we estimate conditional employment rates based upon transition probabilities between different employment states, and these are used to follow a type of Alter and Becker (1985) approach. For each age, we calculate the likelihood that someone who was employed 12 months ago will remain employed or become non-employed. Similar calculations are made for people who were non-employed 12 months previously. In this way, we calculate age-specific employment probabilities for males and females by each employment status at the age of injury and at the age at trial over their remaining lifetime until statutory retirement age.

4. MODELLING THE IMPACT OF DISABILITY

An analysis of the variation in employment probabilities which includes disability as a regressor invariably produces results which indicate that the presence of disability not only has a negative effect on individual employment outcomes but also that it is amongst the most important factors determining employment outcomes. Disability is a difficult concept to define and to measure. There is a distinction between condition, impairment and disability and no unique relationship between the three. Impairment refers to reduced functional ability. Disability concerns a mismatch between an individual's reduced abilities, which arise from impairment, when compared to the level of ability that is required/expected for an individual to function independently at home or at work. Disability is the more complex characteristic, which includes reference to skills and barriers, and is therefore potentially the better predictor of employment outcomes (see Ettner, 2000). However, disability is inherently subjective, and this subjectivity gives rise to the potential for exaggeration in both the prevalence rate of disability and the impact of disability on employment. These difficulties are addressed below. Nevertheless, with the average UK employment rate among those who report a disability consistently estimated to be between 30 and 40 percent (depending upon sampling and definitions; see Office of Population Censuses and Surveys (OPCS), 1985; Berthoud, 2006; Burchardt, 2000; Haardt, 2006) compared to around 80 percent for those who report the absence of a disability, the impact of disability on employment is clearly important.

Although the Ogden Tables have as their subject the WLE of individuals whose work lives have been affected by the disabling effects of injury, there are no recommendations as to how these effects ought to be quantified in damages. We saw in the case example that the WLE was identical in the pre- and post-injury earnings calculations and that compensation for the employment effects of disability was awarded in an arbitrarily determined lump sum. Our purpose here is to disaggregate the model developed in the previous section to accommodate the presence and absence of the LFS measure of disability and thereby estimate disability-adjusted employment trajectories.

There are two distinct theoretical perspectives from which to understand the labour market disadvantage associated with impairment – the economic and the social approaches. An economic model of disability views impairment as a 'form of negative human capital' (Berthoud, 2006) in which reduced skills, reduced productivity, employment displacement and high replacement ratios all limit the employment opportunities available to the disabled and contribute to their high rates of non-employment. In this model, the problem of disablement is experienced at the personal level, and policy is directed towards assisting the individual in acquiring positive human capital attributes as a counter-balance. The social model views disability as an economic identity and has as its focus the refusal of employers to recognise the productive capacity of the impaired (generally and specifically) or to adapt their premises and practices to enable them to take a job (Oliver, 1990). In this way, the functionally impaired are capable of productive work but are 'disabled' in their ability to participate by social and physical barriers (see Barnes, 1991; Oliver, 1996; Disability Rights Commission, 2005). Since the purpose here is to measure the impact of disability on employment, we are not required to choose between these alternative models. Both offer useful insights into why the observed effect of disability on employment is large and negative.

There are three surveys in the United Kingdom which include information on health and disability as well as labour market outcomes. These include two continuous surveys, the British Household Panel Survey (BHPS) and the LFS. The former is a panel survey of around 5,000 households going back to 1991. The latter is a quasi-panel based on 60,000 households interviewed over five waves over the course of a year.[15] In both surveys disability is self-reported by the respondent.[16] The Health and Disability Survey (HDS) provides a more objective measure of disability which is based upon functional impairment. This is a one-time sample survey undertaken alongside the Family Resources Survey in 1996–1997. The importance of this survey lies in the quality of the disability measure used. The measure is based upon an earlier OPCS survey of disability in 1985 in which respondents provide factual information about their condition (diagnosis) and the nature of their functional impairment (what they can and cannot do). On the basis of these responses, their level of impairment is rated by an expert panel in 13 areas of impairment. A simple calculation then places each respondent on a disability scale from one (mild) to ten (severe).[17] Kreider (1999) notes that 'questions about specific conditions are often considered more concrete and less subjective than questions about work capacity'. The HDS has been described as the most rigorous and thorough survey instrument for measuring disability and even as the 'gold standard' among disability measures.[18] The Disability Rights Movement, however, is critical of such measures precisely because the subjective assessments of the disabled themselves are not included.

Burchardt (2000), using the 1997 BHPS health status variable, reports a disability prevalence rate of 12 percent amongst the working age population. The transition patterns which can be estimated from the BHPS provide useful insights into the source of the employment disadvantage. Of those individuals of working age who acquire a disability, 17 percent lose their job within a year. This compares to 7 percent for the non-disabled population. In terms of re-entry, 4 percent of the disabled non-employed return to employment within a year. This compares to 24 percent of the non-disabled non-employed. Labour market disadvantage is thus greater at re-entry than at separation. Haardt (2006), also using the BHPS, distinguishes between poor health and very poor health. He finds that degree of impairment has an impact on exit rates for the disabled (exit rates are lower for the least impaired) but, that for re-entry, different levels of disability are broadly equal in their disadvantage.[19] These results are consistent with the results of more qualitative studies which have highlighted employers' perceptions as a key barrier in the recruitment of the disabled. Employers tend to overstate the functional restrictions of disabled job applicants in relation to the job requirements of the vacancy (see Morrell, 1990; Honey, Meager, & Williams, 1993).

Berthoud (2006), using the 1996–1997 HDS, reports a disability prevalence rate of 11.5 percent and an employment rate among the disabled of 29 percent (compared to 76 percent who are not disabled).[20] Using a logistic regression model, this study estimates the underlying probability of employment by disability and reports a 40 percent (ceteris paribus) reduction in employment chances in the presence of disability. An important finding of this study is that there is no clear dividing line between those who can and those who cannot work. Defining the disability gap as the difference between the actual employment experience of a disabled person and that which would have been experienced if disability had not caused disadvantage and plotting its distribution, Berthoud (2006) reports a smooth, symmetrical, broad and rounded hill shape.

There is a considerable literature covering deficiencies in survey definitions and the consequent measurement of disability. These deficiencies are not new to the LFS or to this study (Burchardt, 2000). Measurement error is primarily associated with inaccuracies due to self-reporting and to categorisation. Some of these sources of measurement error are discussed here, together with the consequences in terms of potential for unreliability and bias in our estimated employment probabilities.

The social incentive for non-workers to over-report disability found in a number of studies means that self-reported disability is not exogenous in the context of measuring its impact on labour market outcomes. In the United Kingdom, there is a financial incentive to non-employment by reason of disability in the form of entitlement to incapacity benefit. Theoretically endogeneity generates upward bias in the measured impact of disability on the probability of employment. However, empirically, the results of studies which address the issue of self-justification bias lack consistency. Kreider (1999), Kreider and Pepper (2007), Charles (2003) and Hotchkiss (2006) find upward bias. Campolieti (2002), Benitez-Silva, Buchinsky, Chan, Cheidvasser, and Rust (2004), Au, Crossley, and Schellhorn (2004) and Jones, Latreille, and Sloane (2006) find none. Poor health outcomes arising from non-employment (Stern, 1989) might also add to the upward bias in any measured impact although Ettner (2000) finds no such effect. We would want to include the impact of reverse causation from this source for any claimant who had been employed until the onset of impairment.

The term disability covers a heterogeneous set of conditions and impairments at different levels of severity. Questionnaire surveys impose categories which fail to capture much of this heterogeneity. Unmeasured qualitative and quantitative differences in impairment are likely to be important in determining individual employment outcomes (see Charles, 2003; Berthoud, 2006). Consider, as an example, the effect of timing of disablement on an individual's future employment prospects. We cannot distinguish in the LFS between individuals who are disabled from their early years and those who become disabled after completing their education. Those who are disabled from birth, but whose disability does not preclude them from future employment, may be better able to adapt their education and training to suit the restrictions that disability places on their employment and thus to minimise the impact of disability on their employment prospects. For the older injured claimant, the potential mismatch between the abilities that are required for the pre-injury job and the post-disablement capacity for employment may be greater. For example the skills and capabilities of a middle-aged man employed in manual work before injury will be ill suited to the clerical work for which he is physically restricted following injury (see Charles, 2003). For a given level of severity of disability, employment prospects diminish with age and with the mismatch between pre- and post-injury skill requirements. Since most personal injury claims involve injury or disease following the completion of education and training, LFS-based employment estimates will tend to understate the impact of disability on future employment.

Berthoud (2006) reports that the nature of the health condition, the type of impairment and the severity of disability all individually and collectively impact an individual's employment chances. This would explain why the measured effect of disability on employment is sensitive to the definition of disability. Rates of employment decrease according to the strictness of the definition (see Kruse & Schur, 2002, for the United States; Berthoud, 2006, for the United Kingdom and Table 1 below). As the definition becomes tighter, those with less severe impairment (and therefore better employment prospects) are progressively excluded.

Despite the difficulties in measuring disability, disability-adjusted WLE tables exist for the United States in the form of the new worklife expectancy tables (Gamboa, 1998). However, their use has been controversial (see Ciecka, Rogers, & Skoog, 2002; Skoog & Toppino, 2002; Ciecka & Skoog, 2001; Gibson & Tierney, 2000). Of particular concern is the quality of the measure of disability in the US Current Population Survey (CPS) which has been used to generate the tables. As a result of unfortunate

Table 1. Disability Prevalence and Employment Rates by Definition (%).

	Disability Prevalence	Employment Rate among Disabled	Employment Rate among Non-Disabled	Employment Rate in Population
1. Health problem or disability	27.4	57.7	80.5	74.2
2. Definition (1) and which lasts for one year	20.1	48.7	80.6	74.2
3. Definition (2) and ADL limiting	16.6	44.7	80.1	74.2
4. Definition (2) and work limiting	15.9	40.2	80.6	74.2
5. Definition (2), ADL limiting and work limiting	12.4	32.4	80.1	74.2
6. HDS 1996–1997	11.5	29.0	76.0	71.0
7. OPCS 1985	7.8	31.0	–	–

Source: Berthoud (2006); LFS, Martin, Meltzer, and Elliot (1988).

question sequencing and filtering, the sample from which disability information is collected is distorted.[21] Disability is recorded primarily from a sample selected on the basis that their employment is limited (or precluded) by ill health or disability. Those whose disability does not adversely affect their ability to work are filtered out of the sample. Prevalence rates estimated from a sample biased in this way will understate the level of disability in the population. Moreover, the impact of disability on employment effects measured from a sample selected on the basis of having disability-induced adverse employment outcomes will be overstated. There is therefore greater reliance in the United States on individually tailored testimony from 'vocational experts'. However, it is these experts' use of disability adjusted WLE which is controversial.

The quality of data used to estimate the impact of disability on employment in the United Kingdom is better than this. It does not encounter the problem of sample selection. The LFS has collected information on health and disability indicators since 1998 and provides three distinct measures of disability. The first measure is collected for the entire sample and is defined by whether or not the respondent has experienced ill health or disability for at least a year. The second measure selects from this sub-sample of the so-called 'long-term' disabled individuals who are defined as disabled in terms of the Disability Discrimination Act (DDA) 1995 – that is where disability has 'a substantial adverse effect on a respondent's ability to carry out day-to-day activities'. We call this characteristic activities-of-daily-living (ADL) limiting. Importantly, both these measures are recorded independently of employment status or employment effects. The third measure records any adverse effect of impairment on either the amount or the type of work that the respondent can undertake. We call this characteristic work limiting. Disability is defined in this study as strictly as possible within the confines of the LFS data as being both ADL limiting and work limiting, as long as this has lasted for at least a year. It is important to note that respondents who fall outside this definition of disability are not necessarily healthy. The non-disabled category includes individuals who may have some impairment which does not meet all three of the above criteria.

5. THE IMPACT OF DISABILITY AND STARTING EMPLOYMENT STATUS

We present and explain our findings both in relation to the impact of disability on future employment and the impact of an estimated lifetime of employment transitions from a given starting state. We pool three years of the spring quarter of the LFS cross-section sample (2002–2004) to comprise 191,508 individuals of working age (16–65 years for men and 16–60 years for women). Fig. 3 summarises the data in terms of the unconditional aggregate employment rates that we observe. Each sex is equally represented in the LFS samples, and both male and female samples have a similar proportion of disabled, about 12 percent. It is interesting that the rates of employment among the disabled are also roughly equal for men and women (around 30 percent), whereas there are significant differences among the non-disabled (about 10 percent higher for men than for women). The sharp reduction in employment rates for those who are disabled measured in these national data is a second indication of the inadequacy of the *Smith v. Manchester* lump sum.

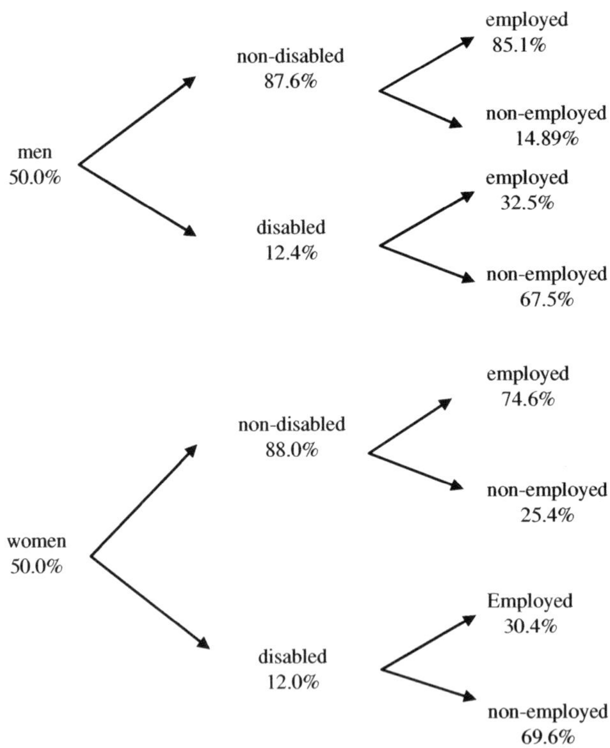

Fig. 3. Employment Outcomes by Disability in the LFS.

Table 1 illustrated the positive relationship between the breadth of the definition of disability, the population prevalence rate and the rate of employment for that group defined as disabled. The first definition is the broadest and includes the presence of a condition which gives rise to any health problem or disability. Twenty-seven percent of the working population report a long-standing health problem or disability. The second definition identifies those whose condition has lasted for at least one year. Definitions (3) through (5) become increasingly more strict so that the disability must give rise to either a limitation in ADL (3), a limitation in work activities (4) and a limitation of both ADL and work activities in (5). Just over 12 percent of the working population are defined as disabled under the strictest definition. The employment rate amongst those with any type of (long-lasting) health problem or disability is 49 percent. The employment rate amongst those whose health problem is long lasting and limits both their ADL and work activities is 32 percent.

Table 1 also facilitates comparison between disability prevalence rates and disabled employment rates across different surveys. The LFS statistics are seen to closely match those reported by Berthoud (2006) using HDS 1996/1997 data. Consistency in both disability prevalence rates and employment rates for those defined as disabled between our study and Berthoud (2006) provides some level of confirmation that the strict version of the LFS disability variable does not exaggerate either the population prevalence of disability or the adverse impact of disability on employment.[22] The outlying result in Table 1 is the disability prevalence rate in the 1985 OPCS survey. While a small part of the difference may be down to under-reporting in the 1985 survey (see Grundy, Ahlburg, Ali, Breeze, & Sloggett, 1999), the remainder is due to some combination of increased impairment, increased disability and increased reporting of both (see Burchardt, 2000; Berthoud, 2007).

In order to establish the extent to which conditioning on starting employment status makes a difference to the future time spent in employment (as opposed to non-employment), we compare lifetime employment rates at different ages. A similar simulation exercise was undertaken by Schieren (1993) and Ciecka (1994) for comparing periods of loss calculated under different assumptions and methods for the United States. In both cases, calculations are undertaken for the non-disabled and employed population. Table 2 compares single-figure lifetime employment rates at different ages using simple age-specific average employment rates and those conditioned on a particular starting employment status using the LFS data. Each is disaggregated according to disability status and, where appropriate, starting

Table 2. Lifetime Employment Rates.

Age	Unconditional Non-Disabled	Unconditional Disabled	Conditional Non-Disabled Employed	Conditional Non-Disabled Non-Employed	Conditional Disabled Employed	Conditional Disabled Non-Employed
20	0.881	0.390	0.901	0.854	0.399	0.327
30	0.899	0.375	0.909	0.842	0.453	0.292
40	0.884	0.364	0.897	0.788	0.487	0.214
50	0.840	0.326	0.866	0.674	0.544	0.122
55	0.790	0.338	0.859	0.400	0.600	0.084

Notes: Lifetime employment rate is calculated as the proportion of remaining working life in employment/remaining working life where both numerator and denominator are discounted for survival and for early receipt.

employment state. As anticipated, the unconditional (simple) average lies between those conditioned upon employment and non-employment starting states. As in the Schieren (1993) and Ciecka (1994) studies, the differences are modest for those up to the age of 50 years who are not disabled and whose starting status is employed. However, for older workers, for the disabled and for those starting in the non-employed state, the differences can be considerable.

5.1. Worked Example Revisited

To illustrate the consequences of using this approach, we rework the earlier example using the alternative methodology which conditions future lifetime employment rates on observed starting employment status and disability status. We use the year-by-year approach. The corresponding sums calculated under the conventional method reported in Section 2.2 are reported below in parentheses.

Pre-injury expected future earnings	+£490,807	(£553,143)
Post-injury expected future earnings	−£155,342	(£331,886)
Smith v. Manchester lump sum for disability-induced labour market disadvantage		(£30,000)
Total award	= £335,465	(£251,257)

Estimated pre-injury earnings are lower than under the previous calculation. This reflects the low actuarially determined employment risks in the Ogden Tables compared to those estimated in this study. Post-injury earnings are, however, lower than in the previous calculation. This reflects the substantial measured effect of disability on lifetime employment in the LFS. Of the £335,465 difference between pre- and post-injury earnings loss, the reduction in annual earnings accounts for £103,561, while the remaining £231,904 results from the adverse employment effects of disability. The element which reflects employment disadvantage is seven times greater than the *Smith v. Manchester* lump sum awarded under the conventional calculation.

6. APPLICATION TO 100 ADJUDICATED CASES

We have seen the impact of using the alternative method for the hypothetical 30-year-old claimant in our example. We now present our findings in relation to the impact of using this approach for the 100 actual awards adjudicated on the basis of the simple multiplier–multiplicand calculation including a *Smith v. Manchester* lump-sum adjustment for the effects of disablement. The sample of cases is broadly representative of personal injury cases that came to trial between 1990 and 1998 and which included an award for loss of earnings.[23] Over three-quarters of the claimants are men. Work-related injuries account for about one-half of all claims, followed by road traffic accidents (20 percent). The remaining cases involve claims for clinical negligence, product liability and crime.

Work-related injuries tend to be less severe and consequently result in lower levels of compensation. Since male claimants in our sample were more likely to be affected by work-related injuries, average awards are higher for female claimants. Over half the claimants were judged to have post-injury earnings capacity. This was considerably more than the 27 claimants who had actually secured employment in the period between injury and trial. For each individual, the court-determined level of earnings at the time of trial is used as a measure of base earnings.

In Table 3, estimates of loss of future earnings calculated under the two alternative methods discussed above are compared to the level of compensation awarded by the court, separately for men and women and for those judged to have post-injury earnings potential. The court award, shown in column (i), is compared first with an alternative award calculated on the basis of a lifetime of age-specific conditional employment rates, column (ii), and secondly with an alternative award calculated on the basis of a lifetime of age-specific average (unconditional) employment rates, column (iii). Where there is no post-injury earning potential, the court and

Table 3. Loss of Future Earnings: A Comparison of Court and Alternative Awards (£).

	Sample Size	(i) Court Award	(ii) Alternative Based upon Conditional Employment Rates	(iii) Alternative Based upon Unconditional Employment Rates
Total sample	100	104,268	110,870	106,510
			(1.06*)	(1.02)
With post-injury potential Earnings	55	78,238	93,040	90,241
			(1.19**)	(1.15**)
Without post-injury potential Earnings	45	136,081	138,020	125,789
			(1.01)	(0.92)
Males	78	109,296	116,600	113,110
			(1.07*)	(1.03)
Males with post-injury Potential earnings	48	77,852	94,005	90,655
			(1.21**)	(1.16**)
Males without post-injury Potential earnings	30	159,607	160,934	148,985
			(1.01)	(0.93)
Females	22	86,439	91,454	83,101
			(1.06)	(0.96)
Females with post-injury Potential earnings	7	80,890	92,450	91,010
			(1.14*)	(1.13*)
Females without post-injury Potential earnings	15	89,029	90,051	78,820
			(1.01)	(0.89)

Notes: (Ratio of estimated to actual award); difference between court award and alternative award significant at 10% (*) or 5% (**) levels.

alternative awards are reasonably close. The unconditional employment rates are lower than those in the Ogden Tables (Fifth Edition). The actuarially derived deductions for employment risks (increasingly used by the courts even before 1999) imply employment probabilities which are significantly higher than the employment probabilities used in all the alternative calculations based upon the LFS 2002–2004. This explains why the damages calculated on the basis of unconditional employment rates are less than those awarded by the courts. That the damages based upon conditional employment rates are the same reflects the combination of the lower employment rates in the LFS and the counter-balancing effect of using starting employment rates in a sub-population where employment rates exceed those in the general population.

There is a substantial and consistently positive differential between the alternative and court awards where the claimant has post-injury earnings potential. This reflects the failure of *Smith v. Manchester* awards to fully compensate claimants for future competitive disadvantage in the labour market. This is an important difference between the conventional and the alternative approaches. In contrast to an arbitrary lump-sum payment in the range of 6–24 months' post-injury earnings, the estimation of age-, disability- and employment status-specific post-injury employment risks is an integral part of the alternative calculation and the estimation is based upon empirical observation.

7. CONCLUSIONS

This paper has applied dynamic labour market modelling to predict future expected time in employment for the purpose of valuing future earnings in the United Kingdom. The model allows for disaggregation by disability and thus for the separate calculation of pre- and post-injury earnings. The purpose has been to provide greater accuracy in fulfilling the objective of the damages principle, that is financial restoration for the claimant in the calculation of damages for future loss of earnings.

Although the alternative approach represents a major improvement, there still remains the potential for bias. The difficulties arising from the measurement of disability have been covered in the main body of the chapter. We take comfort from the fact that the prevalence rate and the disability employment rate in the LFS sample match those reported by Berthoud (2006) based upon a survey in which the disability measure is widely regarded as achieving greater objectivity. It should also be noted that disability is assumed to remain unchanged from the date of measurement. Disability status is constant in the annual employment transitions because disability is defined as having lasted for at least a year. However, using age-specific transitions over the course of a year to estimate those of a lifetime ignores the possibility that a non-disabled person will become disabled during the course of that lifetime. To some extent account is taken of disability-induced employment effects later in life because the non-disabled are not necessarily healthy.[24] From Table 1, we know that there are a further 15 percent of the population who claim ill health (and 7 per cent who claim long-lasting ill health) but who do not qualify under the strict definition of disability.

The use of a two-state (employed–non-employed) model in which the non-employed category includes the inactive and the unemployed is likely to bias our employment estimates in an upward direction for the inactive non-employed and in a downward direction for the active non-employed.

Given the low incidence of unemployment within non-employment, the magnitude of any upward bias is likely to be very small. The incidence of unemployment among claimants is likely to be less than for the population generally, both pre-injury (the most common form of tortious injury occurs at work) and post-injury (the basis for any claim for loss of earnings is a significant and long-lasting disability which suggests non-employment due to inactivity), so the downward bias will impact on very few cases.

Perhaps, the most critical assumption made in these calculations is that the employment prospects of someone now aged, say, 30 years, who was in employment one year ago and is still in employment, need not be the same as that faced in 15 years time by someone who is currently aged 15 years. Controlling for future cohort effects is beyond the capacity of an economist. For guidance in this, we must indeed look to Lord Oliver's prophets and astrologers.

However, our proposed methodology includes the impact of disability and current employment status and is preferable to one which does not. We demonstrate in a worked example, and in the application of the alternative method to a set of 100 adjudicated cases, that both make a difference to the level of compensation. We recognise that the long-term future employment risks of a heterogeneous workforce cannot be fully described by means of a few variables (i.e. age, sex, starting economic state and disability) that are measured at a single point in time. Our purpose, however, is to provide a more accurate starting point. The intention is that the courts may deviate from this starting point according to the particular characteristics and circumstances of individual cases which are not measured in our estimates.

NOTES

1. England, Britain and the United Kingdom are used interchangeably in this chapter. In constitutional terms the courts in England and Wales are bound by English Law. In practice for the determination of quantum in personal injury, the courts in Scotland and Ireland (North and South) follow (but are not bound by) the English approach.

2. The following comments of Oliver LJ capture the general sentiment amongst the judiciary towards financial evidence of a predictive nature 'as a method of providing a reliable guide to individual behaviour patterns, or to future economic and political events, the predictions of an actuary can be only a little more likely to be accurate (and will almost certainly be less entertaining) than those of an astrologer'. In *Auty v. NCB* [1985] 1 WLR 784 at 800H and later as Lord Oliver, 'The exercise upon which one is to embark is inherently unscientific ... but to assess the

probability of future political economic and fiscal policies requires not the services of an actuary or an accountant but those of a prophet', in *Hodgeson v. Trapp* [1989] 1 AC 833.

3. 1994 2 AC 350.

4. 1999 1 AC 345.

5. The Lord Chancellor set out his reasons for the determination of the discount rate on 27 July 2001. The discount rate is intended to reflect the yield on Index-Linked Government Stock (ILGS). In the 12 years from 1996, the yield on ILGS has been below 2.5 percent in all but three months in 2001. It is currently (2008) at about 1 percent.

6. These cases were collected in 1999–2000 as part of an ESRC-funded research project. The case material was made available to us by a number of UK law firms where each case included an award for damages for loss of future earnings, information on pre-injury earnings, occupation, work history, nature of disability, age, ethnic background, education, region of residence and residual earnings capacity. The results were first reported in Lewis, McNabb, Robinson, and Wass (2002, 2003).

7. Discounts for employment risks are disaggregated by sex, age, occupation, location and level of economic activity. They average around 5 percent. This level of discount has generally been regarded as too low.

8. Scarmen LJ in *Smith v. Manchester* [1974] 17 KIRI CA.

9. It has been described thus by Lord Justice Stephenson in *Moeliker v. a Reyrolle & Co Ltd* [1976] I.C.R. 253.

10. Taylor LJ in *Forey v. London Buses Ltd* [1992] PIQR P48. See also Butler-Sloss LJ in *Tait v. Pearson* [1996] PIQR Q92: 'To do what judges over the years have done which is to pluck a figure from the air as best to provide an appropriate recognition that he has a financial loss for the future'.

11. See note 8 above.

12. The apparent justification for this level of award is that it should represent twice the average length of unemployment duration of an able-bodied job seeker (Ritchie, 1994). Of course this estimate ignores inactivity as a major labour market outcome for the disabled and the fact that periods of non-employment are often recurrent.

13. We acknowledge that employment status affects mortality but mortality is not recorded in the LFS. It is anticipated that differences in mortality rates over the working age range are likely to be relatively small.

14. Since we consider only discrete times for $t \geq 0$, the WLE can be approximated using the trapezium rule by the summation of the product of transition and survival probabilities with adjustments to the first and final observation.

15. The panel begins in the spring of 1992; however, disability is not included until spring 1998.

16. The questions on disability in the LFS are as follows: 'Do you have any health problems or disabilities that you expect to last for more than one year?' If yes 'Does this health problem or disability substantially limit your ability to carry out normal day-to-day activities?' 'Does this health problem limit the kind or amount of work that you can do?'

17. There are 108 questions in 13 different areas of limitation in which the respondent rates his/her ability to perform various activities. These responses are combined as follows: first most severe score +0.4 (second most severe score) +0.3

(third most severe score). This score is used to allocate respondents according to severity of disability on a scale of one to ten. Pen portraits of typical respondents at each point are provided in Appendix 1 of Burchardt (2000).

18. Thomas and Dodds (1998).

19. The entry rate for those in poor health is 72 percent lower than for those in excellent health. For those in very poor health, the entry rate is 75 percent lower.

20. In contrast to other studies, employment is defined as including full-time education but excluding part time work (less than 16 hours per week), and the sample is restricted to those between the ages of 19 and 59 years.

21. The US CPS was not designed to measure the population prevalence of disability or its impact on employment. Disability is used as a filter question to collect income data from those with a disability-induced work limitation.

22. The reported incidence of work-limiting illness also correlates well with the incidence of illness that is reported in visits by the adult population to general practitioner physicians (see Hodgeson, Jones, Elliot, & Osman, 1993).

23. This represents only a proportion of cases coming to trial, since many do not involve loss of future earnings. Moreover, only a small proportion of personal injury cases are resolved in court. However, it is those personal injury cases that do reach the courts that provide the basis for other awards settled out of court.

24. This group is only not disabled according to the strict LFS definition of disability.

ACKNOWLEDGMENT

We gratefully acknowledge the financial support of the Economic and Social Research Council (R000237393).

REFERENCES

Alter, G. C., & Becker, W. E. (1985). Estimating lost future earnings using the new worklife tables. *Monthly Labor Review, 108*(2), 39–42.

Au, D., Crossley T.F., & Schellhorn, M. (2004) *The effects of health changes and long term health on the work activity of older Canadians*. IZA Discussion Paper no. 1281. Berlin.

Baker, W. G., & Seck, M. K. (1987). *Determining economic loss in injury and wrongful death cases*. Colorado Springs, CO: Shepard's McGraw Hill.

Barnes, C. (1991). *Disabled people in Britain and discrimination: A case for anti-discrimination legislation*. London: Hurst & Co.

Becker, W., & Alter, G. (1987). The probabilities of life and work force status in the calculation of expected earnings. *Journal of Risk and Insurance* (June), 364–375.

Benitez-Silva, H., Buchinsky, M., Chan, H. M., Cheidvasser, S., & Rust, J (2004). How large is the bias in self reported disability. *Journal of Applied Econometrics, 19*, 649–670.

Berthoud, R. (2006). *The employment rates of disabled people*. Research Paper no. 298. Department for Work and Pensions.

Berthoud, R. (2007). *Work-rich and work-poor: Three decades of change*. York, UK: Joseph Rowntree Foundation.

Brookshire, M. L., & Cobb, W. (1983). The life-participation-employment approach to worklife expectancy in personal injury litigation and wrongful death cases. *For the Defense* (July), 20–25.

Brookshire, M. L, & Slesnick, F. (1997). A 1996 study of "prevailing practice" in forensic economics. *Journal of Forensic Economics*, *10*(1), 1–28.

Burchardt, T. (2000). *Enduring economic exclusion disabled people, income and work*. York, UK: Joseph Rowntree Foundation.

Butt, Z., Haberman, S., Verrall, R., & Wass, V. (2008). Calculating compensation for loss of future earnings: Estimating and using work life expectancy. *Journal of the Royal Statistical Society*, *171*(4), 1–37.

Campolieti, M. (2002). Disability and labour market participation of older men in Canada. *Labour Economics*, *9*, 405–433.

Charles, K. K. (2003). The longitudinal structure of earnings losses among work-limited workers. *Journal of Human Resources*, *38*, 618–646.

Ciecka, J. E. (1994). A survey of the structure and duration of time periods for lost earnings calculations. *Journal of Legal Economics*, *2*, 39–50.

Ciecka, J. E., & Skoog, G. R. (2001). An essay on the new worklife expectancy tables and the continuum of disability. *Journal of Forensic Economics*, *14*, 135–140.

Ciecka, J. E., Rogers, J., & Skoog, G. (2002). The new Gamboa tables: A critique. *Journal of Legal Economics* (Fall), 61–85.

Disability Rights Commission (2005). *Shaping the future of equality*.

Ettner, S. (2000). The relationship between labour market outcomes and physical and mental health: Exogenous human capital or endogenous health production? In: D. Salkever & A. Sorkin (Eds), *The economics of disability*. Stamford, CT: JAI Press Inc.

Frasca, R. R., & Winger, B. J. (1989). An investigation into the Nelson median and mean age at final separation from the labor force. *Journal of Forensic Economics*, *2*(3), 103–114.

Gamboa, A. M. (1998). *The new worklife expectancy tables for persons with and without disability by gender*. Louisville, KY: Vocational Econometrics.

Gibson, D. S., & Tierney, J. P. (2000). Disability and worklife expectancy tables: A response. *Journal of Forensic Economics*, *13*(3), 309–318.

Grundy, E., Ahlburg, D., Ali, M., Breeze, E., & Sloggett, A. (1999). *Disability in Great Britain*. DSS Research Report no. 94.

Haardt, D. (2006) *Transitions out of and back to employment among older men and women in the UK*. ISER Working Paper no. 2006-20.

Haberman, S., & Bloomfield, D. (1990). Work time lost to sickness, unemployment and stoppages: Measurement and application. *Journal of the Institute of Actuaries*, *117*, 533–578.

Hodgeson, J., Jones, J., Elliot, R., & Osman, J. (1993). *Self-reported work-related Illness*. Research Report no. 33, Health and Safety Executive, UK.

Honey, S., Meager, N., & Williams, M. (1993) *Employers attitudes towards people with disabilities*. Institute of Manpower Studies, Sussex University.

Hotchkiss, J. (2006). A closer look at the employment impact of the Americans with Disability Act. *Journal of Human Resources*, *41*, 997–1011.

Jones, M. K ., Latreille, P., & Sloane, P. (2006). Disability, gender and the British labour market. *Oxford Economic Papers*, *58*, 407–449.

Jones, S. R. J., & Riddell, C. W. (1999). The measurement of unemployment: An empirical approach. *Econometrica*, *67*(1), 147–161.
Kreider, B. (1999). Latent work, disability and reporting bias. *Journal of Human Resources*, *34*, 734–769.
Kreider, B., & Pepper, J. (2007). Disability and employment: Re-evaluating the evidence in light of reporting errors. *Journal of American Statistical Association*, *478*, 432–441.
Kruse, D., & Schur, L. (2002). Employment of people with disabilities following the ADA. *Industrial Relations*, *42*(1), 31–66.
Lewis, R., McNabb, R., Robinson, H., & Wass, V. (2002). Court awards of damages for loss of future earnings: An empirical study and an alternative method of calculation. *Journal of Law and Society*, *29*(3), 406–435.
Lewis, R., McNabb, R., Robinson, H., & Wass, V. (2003). Loss of earnings following personal injury. Do the courts adequately compensate injured parties? *The Economic Journal*, *113*, 568–584.
Luckett, N., & Craner, J. (1994). Multipliers: Are the courts being fair to claimants? *Journal of Personal Injury Litigation*, *5*, 139–146.
Martin, G. D. (1999). *Determining economic damages* (with Ted Vavoulis). Costa Mesa, CA: James Publishing.
Martin, J., Meltzer, H., & Elliot, D. (1988). *The prevalence of disability among adults*. London, UK: Her Majesty's Stationary Office.
Morrell, J. (1990) *The employment of people with disabilities: Research into the policies and practices of employers*. Research Paper no. 77. Department of Employment.
Nelson, D. (1983). The use of worklife tables in estimates of lost earnings capacity. *Monthly Labor Review*, *106*(4), 30–31.
Oliver, M. (1990). *The politics of disablement*. London: Macmillan.
Oliver, M. (1996). *Understanding disability: From theory to practice*. Basingstoke: Macmillan.
Randolf, P. (2005). Samuels v. Benning. *Journal of Personal Injury Law*, *1*, 77–87.
Richards, H. (2000). Worklife expectancies: Increment–decrement less accurate than conventional.. *Journal of Forensic Economics*, *13*, 271–289.
Ritchie, A. (1994). Smith v Manchester awards: How do courts assess loss of capacity on the labour market. *Journal of Personal Injury Litigation*, 103–107.
Romans, J. T., & Floss, F. G. (1993). The estimation of retirement age in the calculation of earnings loss. *Journal of Legal Economics*, *3*(2), 25–32.
Schieren, G. A. (1993). Median worklife, mean age at final separation, or transition probabilities to calculate expected lost earnings?. *Journal of Forensic Economics*, *7*(1), 103–108.
Skoog, G., & Ciecka, J. M. (2004). Reconsidering and extending the conventional/demographic and LPE models: The *LPd* and *LPi* restricted Markov Models. *Journal of Forensic Economics*, *17*(1), 47–94.
Skoog, G. R., & Toppino, D. (2002). The new worklife expectancy tables' critique: A rejoinder. *Journal of Forensic Economics*, *15*, 81–97.
Smith, S. J. (1982). New worklife estimates reflect changing profile of labor force. *Monthly Labor Review*, *105*(3), 15–20.
Smith, S. J. (1983). Using the appropriate worklife estimate in court proceedings. *Monthly Labor Review*, *106*(10), 31–32.
Smith, S. J. (1985). Estimating lost future earnings using the new worklife tables: A comment. *Monthly Labor Review*, *108*(2), 42.

Stern, S. (1989). Measuring the effects of disability on labor force participation. *Journal of Human Resources*, *24*, 361–395.

Thomas R., & Dodds, J. (1998). Survey measurement of disability and identification of disabled persons in the private household population ONS. In: *Disability and care: Questions and answers considered, Conference Proceedings* 15 June, London.

Thornton, R. J., & Ward, J. (1999). The economist in tort litigation. *Journal of Economic Perspectives*, *13*(2), 101–112.

ESTIMATING AND USING WORK LIFE EXPECTANCY IN THE UNITED KINGDOM

Zoltan Butt, Steven Haberman,
Richard Verrall and Victoria Wass

1. INTRODUCTION

The approach to the determination of damages for loss of future earnings in Britain is by means of a simple formula in which an annual loss (the multiplicand) is multiplied by a discounted work life expectancy (WLE – the multiplier) to produce a lump sum, the capitalised value of which is intended to provide an 'assumed annuity' equivalent to the annual loss. The discounted WLE is calculated with reference to actuarially determined figures which are published in the Ogden Tables. The Ogden Tables provide a set of statistical tables with explanatory notes for use in personal injury and fatal accident cases. These tables are collated by an inter-disciplinary working party comprising lawyers, accountants and actuaries, including the Government Actuary. Their purpose is to provide lawyers in England and Wales with the information that will enable them to undertake the calculation of a future pecuniary loss without recourse to evidence from financial experts. As such it is a requirement that the tables and procedures be readily comprehensible to lawyers.[1]

Personal Injury and Wrongful Death Damages Calculations: Transatlantic Dialogue
Contemporary Studies in Economic and Financial Analysis, Volume 91, 103–134

ISSN: 1569-3759/doi:10.1108/S1569-3759(2009)0000091008

In Chapter 4, two major deficiencies in this approach to the calculation of future loss of earnings were identified and their implications for the determination of damages explored. First, although the Ogden Tables have as their subject the WLEs of individuals whose working lives have been disrupted by injury, guidance on how such effects might be measured and compensated has never been offered. The WLEs are disaggregated by sex and age group but not by disability status. In cases where the claimant has residual earning capacity following a disabling injury, the conventional approach is to use the same multiplier that is used to calculate pre-injury projected earnings for the calculation of post-injury residual earnings. As discussed in the previous chapter, compensation for the impact of disability on employment is awarded by means of an additional lump sum payment (referred to as a *Smith v. Manchester* payment). This approach has been criticised within the profession as being arbitrary in both application and calculation. It was argued in Chapter 4 that such an approach routinely and substantially undervalued the post-injury earnings for claimants with post-injury earning capacity.

The second shortcoming concerns the econometric approach to the estimation of working lifetime employment risks. In the UK tort system, employment risks are expressed as reduction factors (RFs) which convert an individual's life expectancy up to retirement age (as contained in the various tables of the Ogden Tables) into a WLE. These measures of employment risk were calculated using simple age-specific averages from labour market data from the 1970s and 1980s (see Haberman & Bloomfield, 1990). Both the information and the estimation techniques were out of date by the turn of the century. In Chapter 4, the authors proposed an alternative approach which addressed both of the above deficiencies. However, their approach did not use the multiplier–multiplicand calculation. Rather, it was based on a stream of annual earnings estimates, each of which was reduced by an annual age-based employment status-dependent employment risk. This difference in approach was to prove a major obstacle to implementation.

2. BACKGROUND

This chapter is the sequel to Chapter 4. It describes the events which followed the initial publication of the findings reported in Chapter 4 in relation to the systematic under-compensation of claimants who sustained continuing and residual impairment but who remained medically capable of work (first published in Lewis, McNabb, Robinson, & Wass, 2002a). The approach proposed in Chapter 4 was simple and accessible. It had been shown to make a substantial difference to the level of compensation for future loss of earnings. It had been widely disseminated in the academic literature,[2] the practitioner press[3] and even on national radio.[4] Yet it failed to make any impact on the way in which the courts in the United Kingdom determined the level of damages. The courts continued to proceed along established lines applying the same multiplier to the pre- and post-injury annual earnings and to make a subsequent ad hoc adjustment to cover any disability-induced labour market disadvantage. Research that indicated that the courts were failing to deliver on the long-established legal principle of full and adequate compensation was completely ignored. The reason for this was that the courts, at the highest form of legal authority, the House of Lords, had recently (in 1999) endorsed the use of the multiplier–multiplicand formula in the context of calculating a future loss, and also the Ogden Tables as a means of parameterising that formula. It was the universal view within the legal profession that it was undesirable to step outside what had recently become an accepted standard legal practice in favour of what appeared to be a very different alternative.

By good fortune, the Cardiff-based research (Lewis et al., 2002a; Lewis, McNabb, & Wass, 2002b, 2002c) had come to the attention of one of the members of the Ogden Working Party in 2003. Coincidentally, the Ogden Working Party was planning to re-estimate the employment-risks RFs which feed into the WLEs for a future edition of the Ogden Tables (the sixth edition). The RFs allowing for employment risks had not been re-estimated since the beginning of the 1990s. They had been re-published in the fifth edition in 2004, even though they were widely regarded as inaccurate (see the preface to the fifth edition).[5] At the invitation of the Government Actuary, three of the authors of this chapter had undertaken to re-estimate the pre-injury RFs for the forthcoming sixth edition of the Ogden Tables. The re-estimation was to be based on observed labour market transitions and projections over a working lifetime using a Markov model. The sixth edition of the Ogden Tables, and the revised RFs therein, were to provide the critical opportunity to incorporate an adapted version of the alternative methodology for calculating compensation for the impact of disablement developed in Chapter 4 within the existing and accepted approach for calculating future loss of earnings, the multiplier–multiplicand calculation.

Over the course of the next two years, a new set of RFs and an adapted method of calculation, which explicitly makes allowance for the effects of disability on employment within the multiplier–multiplicand calculation, were developed. In November 2006 both were approved by the Ogden

Working Party and were incorporated into the sixth edition of the Ogden Tables which was published in May 2007. This chapter describes the study which underlies the four new tables (Tables A–D in the sixth edition of the Ogden Tables and reproduced in the appendix to this chapter – Tables A1 to A4) of RFs disaggregated by sex, age, starting employment status, disability status and educational achievement. The new RFs have provided the cornerstone for a major change in the way that damages are calculated for a claimant whose injury is sufficient to affect her or his employment prospects but is not so detrimental so as to preclude her or him from working altogether.

We use an increment–decrement Markov model to condition future employment prospects on starting employment status. The importance of starting employment status in the context of the loss of future earnings calculation was raised in Chapter 4. Most claimants are employed (E) prior to injury and most are non-employed (NE) at the time of trial or settlement. In Section 3, we provide some historical details on Markov chain modelling with a particular focus on the application of such models to labour market behaviour. In Section 4, we describe the model, the data and the estimation methods which form the basis of the revised RFs. Our results take the form of a set of average WLEs and employment-risks RFs measured separately by sex, age, starting employment status, disability status and educational achievement. These are presented in Section 5. We introduce educational achievement as an additional level of disaggregation in an attempt to capture the effects of skill level on employment prospects. This latter variable replaces region of residence and industrial sector, which were used as key factors in determining employment in the previous editions of the Ogden Tables. It is a consistent finding in both the United Kingdom and the United States that education confers positive returns in respect of employment chances and earnings for the disabled. If disability is a negative form of human capital (Berthoud, 2006), then the presence of transferable skills appears to provide an important counter-balance. Our findings indicate that, on average, the disabled are less well-educated than the non-disabled and that the returns to education are substantially greater for the disabled than for the non-disabled. In this respect, we believe that our findings have policy implications well beyond the measurement of damages.

The Ogden Tables, and the incorporation of the new RFs, are described in Section 6. In producing a simple methodology suitable for routine application by non-experts, there is an inevitable compromise to the precision of estimates on an individual case basis. In recognising some of the limits imposed, both by the method of calculation and the data upon which the RFs are founded, we describe the new WLEs as a 'starting point' from which a judge can apply discretion according to the particular circumstances of the case (Butt, Haberman, Verrall, & Wass, 2008). This view is also endorsed by the Ogden Working Party, as the following extract demonstrates:

> The suggestions which follow are intended as a 'ready reckoner' which provides an initial adjustment to the multipliers ... such a ready reckoner cannot take into account all circumstances and it may be appropriate to argue for higher or lower adjustments in particular cases. (Ogden Tables, 6th ed., para 32)

Our objective was to provide a method of calculation which not only offers a better starting point over the existing approach but also retains transparency and accessibility to non-statisticians, and in particular to lawyers. Any new approach needs to be capable of routine application (again by lawyers) without recourse to financial expertise. It is in this context that the usefulness and shortcomings of the new method of calculation should be viewed.

The new approach was published for the first time in the sixth edition of the Ogden Tables in May 2007. At the time of this writing, we have almost two years of court decisions. While the courts appear to have accepted and applied the new method of calculation, they have struggled with their use of discretion. In this context, a case example in Section 7 illustrates their difficulty.

3. MULTISTATE MARKOV CHAIN MODELLING

The methods and models used to analyse the data and to estimate the updated WLEs and RFs are based on the theory of Markov chains. A Markov chain is a random process which describes transitions between different states and which evolves through time in accordance with pre-determined rates of transition between states. It is an extremely powerful theory that has been extensively studied by mathematicians and statisticians and has been applied to a wide variety of problems. The basic assumption made in standard Markov chain theory is that what happens in the future depends only on the current state, and not on any previous history. In the context of WLEs, this means that future employment prospects depend only on whether a person is employed or not at present: the previous history is not taken into account. While we know that previous employment history is an important determinant of future employment, the chances of leaving a state of unemployment is duration dependent (see Narendranathan & Stewart, 1993; Arulampalam, Booth, & Taylor, 2000; Haile, 2004), therefore, there are still very good reasons for using a Markov approach.

First, data requirements are minimal in a Markov process. All that is needed is information about the current state (e.g. employed) at the start of each time period (quarter) and whether a transition to a different state is made during each time period. In order to investigate longer-term employment effects, much more information would have to be used about the history of transitions between states. Although some unemployment duration information is available in the Labour Force Survey (LFS), beyond a year's duration this information is incomplete. Second, the analysis would be greatly complicated, as would be the implementation of the formula which is currently designed in order that the calculation can be undertaken by lawyers. Finally, it is not clear that the estimates which are needed for the Ogden Tables, which present broad group averages rather than individualised predictions, would be greatly affected if the data on employment history were included.

In the remainder of this section, we summarise the background on Markov models which are applied to the quarterly LFS panel data to investigate the cohort-based labour force dynamics of the population. The aim of the analysis using these models is to map the flows of labour force cohorts between the different economic states (E and NE) by means of transition rates. We do this separately according to a dichotomous disability status variable and a five-level educational attainment variable. In the next section, we describe the mathematical framework that we have applied in order to estimate a lifetime measure of employment outcomes.

According to Pitacco (1995), the fundamentals of the multistate life-table analysis in a Markov chains framework were formulated during the eighteenth century by Bernoulli (1766) in his study of smallpox mortality model in a two-state discrete-time setup. This was later extended by Pierre de Laplace to the continuous-time case. However, it was not until the beginning of the twentieth century that the model was interpreted and solved in a concise mathematical form with significant contributions from Hamza (1900) and Du Pasquier (1912, 1913). The next significant development in application of the model came about in the 1970s with the widespread availability of electronic computing to solve the demanding matrix calculations. By the end of the twentieth century, the use of this modelling approach in actuarial, demographic and econometric applications had become the norm in almost any type of life-contingency analysis. These advances have allowed significant developments with the ease with which

Markov chains methodology can be applied, with important contributions from authors such as Hoem (1972, 1977), Heckman and Singer (1985), Jones (1994, 1997) and Haberman and Pitacco (1999).

It is customary in the United States to make use of WLE predictions for the purposes of damages calculations, and this has rapidly evolved since the US Bureau of Labor Statistics (BLS) first adopted the 'relative-frequency' approach due to Smith (1982) and which was based on a two-state Markov process.[6] Smith (1986) subsequently extended this modelling strategy further by including the effects of additional factors related to race and education. Although the BLS no longer publishes work life tables, many valuable contributions have followed which have explored additional aspects of the methodology and provided updated WLE figures based on new Current Population Survey (CPS) data, and include a series of papers by Ciecka, Donley, and Goldman (Ciecka, Donley, and Goldman, 1995, 1997, 2001). Richards (1999) makes use of a two-state increment–decrement model to recalculate the WLE conditional on starting economic state. Richards (2000) reports some empirical inconsistencies of the Markov chain methods in comparison to the 'conventional' approach in the United States.

In a more recent development in the US literature, Millimet, Nieswiadomy, Ryu, and Slottje (2003) find the relative-frequency approach to estimation inadequate to account for the effects of additional factors and propose the use of an alternative modelling framework. The authors estimate the weighted average of the individual transition probabilities calculated from a linear model of the log-odds ratio. Furthermore, the authors question the validity of the BLS two-state approach (where the employed and unemployed are grouped together in a single 'active' state) and re-estimate the WLEs in a more traditional econometric setup formed by employed, unemployed and inactive states. In this updated modelling framework, they find that the unemployed labour market outcomes are closer to the inactive for low-level education attainment (i.e. disadvantaged group), while they are similar to those for the employed only in the case of higher levels of educational attainment.

In comparison to the United States, there has been little interest within the UK economics profession in the modelling and measurement of lifetime employment outcomes. Rather, the focus has been primarily on investigating the incidence and duration of unemployment for particular segments of the population (usually disadvantaged): see, for example, Narendranathan and Stewart (1993), Stewart and Swaffield (1999), Arulampalam et al. (2000). The tort system requires statistically reliable estimates of employment over a lifetime, and Haberman and Bloomfield (1990) provided detailed lifetime employment-risks RF estimates for England and Wales using a mix of data from the 1970s and 1980s. Some 12 years later, advocating an improved methodology of loss of earnings estimation approach, Lewis et al. (Lewis et al., 2002a; Lewis, McNabb, Robinson, & Wass, 2003) calculated working-age transition probabilities using a Markov chain model. While the purpose of the Lewis et al. study was not directly the estimation of WLEs (nor RFs), they nevertheless demonstrated the merits of a systematic econometric approach of measuring lifetime employment outcome, and of the use of Markov chains modelling.

4. DATA AND METHODOLOGY

The employment-risks RFs are estimated from the application of a Markov chains model to the quarterly LFS panel data. In this section, we present the particular modelling framework alongside details of the labour market data.

The empirical estimation is based on 20 quarters of the LFS (1998–2003), a continuous sample survey administered and published by the UK Office for National Statistics (ONS). The LFS collects information on an extensive set of individual labour force characteristics and outcomes from a rotating sample of around 60,000 representative households. These households include roughly 140,000 individuals of working age. Each quarterly cross-sectional sample is formed by five separate waves (cohorts) of approximately equal number of respondents. Each household takes part in the survey for just over a year and is re-interviewed during this period five times at approximately quarterly (13 weeks) intervals. By merging the matched sections of consecutive cross-sectional samples, the ONS constructs five-quarter quasi-longitudinal LFS datasets, each providing a one-year observation window into the labour market experience of the UK labour force.

The Markov chains model makes use of observations on the timing and number of movements between transient labour market states to predict, over the course of a working lifetime, the likely time spent in a particular state. In the approach considered in Chapter 4, a transition is recorded over a one-year period if, according to the respondent's recollection of his or her employment status one year ago, there is a change from the current state. This source of information is inherently prone to measurement error due to poor recall. Here, we make use of the recorded transitions between employment and non-employment which are measured quarterly in the LFS quasi-panel.

The model is disaggregated by age, sex and a number of socio-economic factors that were expected to have a strong impact on future employment risks. Some of the effects that were considered in the early analysis and which have traditionally been part of the damages calculations (industrial sector, region of residence, level of aggregate economic activity) were included as covariates. We experimented with further disaggregation using additional factors identified in the more recent labour economics literature as being key determinants of employment, such as disability and educational attainment.

Current employment state (INECACA) is recorded in the LFS using the International Labour Office (ILO) 29-category classification of different types of activity and inactivity. Owing to small sample sizes when disaggregated by sex, age, disability status, educational achievement and starting employment state, these multiple categories indicating various forms of economic activity (categories 1–5) and inactivity (6–29) are aggregated into two transient states: employed (1–3) and non-employed (4–29). (Table 1 of Butt et al. (2008) reports the full classification and distribution of the LFS variable INECACA.) In common with most studies of the effects of disability, we adopt the employment/non-employment dichotomy rather than one which divides according to activity and inactivity. The alternative categorisations are distinguished only by the location of the unemployed who are both active and non-employed. Arguably, the unemployed ought to form a separate category but, at less than 4 per cent of the working population, their low prevalence rate makes separate modelling difficult.

The LFS has collected information on health indicators since 1998 and provides two compound measures of long-standing (minimum of one year) disability.[7] The first measure refers to the adverse effect of impairment on either the amount or the type of work that can be undertaken. The second is defined in the terms of the Disability Discrimination Act of 1995 as 'having a substantial adverse effect of the respondent's ability to carry out day-to-day activities'. The disability variable (D or ND) is the key factor which distinguishes between the pre- and post-injury positions of the claimant. Disability is defined in the sixth edition of the Ogden Tables where the respondent satisfies all three of the following criteria:

1. Impairment must be long term (over a year).
2. Its effects must substantially adversely affect ability to carry out day-to-day activities (ADL-limiting) (same as DDA 1995).

3. Its effects must adversely affect the amount or the type of work that can be undertaken (work-limiting).

Respondents who fall outside this definition, the non-disabled, are not necessarily healthy. They may have some impairment but one which does not qualify under the above definition.

Educational attainment is used as a proxy for skills and is measured in the LFS as HIQUAL, the highest qualification achieved. We use a five-level categorisation in which HD represents degree or higher, D represents higher education below degree, A represents A-level or equivalent professional qualifications, GE represents GCSE levels A–C or equivalent, and O represents other or no qualifications (see Butt et al., 2008, for further details).

There are a total of 203,966 working-age respondents in the pooled LFS sample made up of approximately 11,000 participants in each longitudinal dataset. Table 1 reports observed prevalence rates (%) by sex, disability status, employment status and educational attainment.

There are roughly equal numbers of disabled men and disabled women. However, there is an 11 percentage point difference between the employment rate of non-disabled men and women (87 and 76 per cent, respectively). Interestingly, this reduces to just 1 percentage point for

Table 1. Prevalence Rates (%) by Sex, Disability Status and Highest Educational Attainment.

Gender	Disability Status	Economic State	Highest Educational Attainment				
			HD	D	A	GE	O
M (49.8)	D (12.9)	E (32.1)	3.4	2.2	10.8	5.0	10.7
		NE (67.9)	3.0	2.6	17.7	6.4	38.2
	ND (87.1)	E (86.9)	15.9	7.8	28.3	15.2	19.9
		NE (13.1)	1.4	0.8	3.3	3.0	4.5
F (50.2)	D (12.2)	E (30.7)	3.5	3.8	4.9	7.8	10.7
		NE (69.3)	2.2	4.0	6.6	12.6	43.9
	ND (87.8)	E (76.2)	11.7	9.2	13.2	22.3	19.7
		NE (23.8)	1.8	1.4	3.6	6.9	10.2

Note: The figures in parentheses represent the relative prevalence rates of the respective subgroups.

Source: LFS 1998–2003 quarterly panel data.

disabled men and women (32 and 31 per cent, respectively). The distribution of working-age individuals across employment outcomes and education levels is markedly different between the disabled and the non-disabled. For the disabled and non-employed, there is a high prevalence of low educational achievement. Higher levels of educational attainment are associated with greater labour market success, especially for the disabled.

We describe here the methodology applied in this study to generate the RFs from the simple transitions data recorded in the LFS. The multiple state increment–decrement labour market model that we use is illustrated schematically in Fig. 1. Mathematically, we make use of a $N = 2{+}1$ Markov process $\{S(x) = s{:}x \geq 0\}$ in a continuous-time setting specified by exact age x. The model is defined by two transient (alive) economic states (employed and non-employed) and an absorbing state corresponding to the risk of pre-retirement mortality. Given that the mortality hazard rates are not estimated directly from the available labour force data, we simply refer to this setting as a two-state model. The model is stratified with respect to age, sex, education and disability status.

Within these settings, the empirical estimation of the current model proceeds using the transition intensity approach in an age-specific framework. This approach is more robust than the direct estimation described in Chapter 4 because it makes use of superior data. As explained in section 1.8 of Haberman and Pitacco (1999), we can account for the time-varying feature of the underlying process while still maintaining the simplicity of constant transition intensities by adopting an approximating stepwise

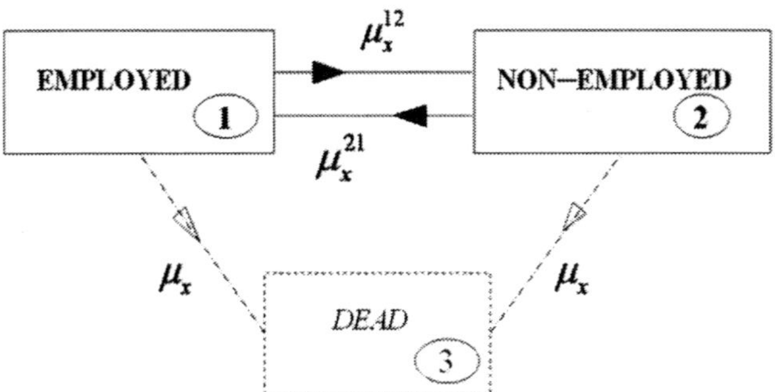

Fig. 1. Two (+1) State Econometric Model with Transition Intensity Approach Estimation Method.

function approach. Intuitively, this involves breaking down the working lifespan into single years defined by consecutive exact age intervals $(x,x+1)$ and estimating age-specific transition intensities, μ_x^{ij}, between the economic states i and j, given by the following ratio:

$$\mu_x^{ij} = \frac{n_x^{ij}}{E_x^i} \qquad \forall\, i \neq j \tag{1}$$

where n_x^{ij} and E_x^i represent the number of transitions between states i and j and the total time at risk in the starting state i across all individuals of age x, respectively.

The methodology is constrained by a number of simplifying assumptions with varying degrees of plausibility. Perhaps the most problematic assumption is that the transition intensities do not depend on the duration in the current state (as can be seen in Eq. (1)). This assumption is not supported in empirical studies of unemployment (see Narendranathan & Stewart, 1993; Arulampalam et al., 2000; Haile, 2004). However, accurate duration data beyond one year are not available in the LFS. Furthermore, as argued above, we believe that the difficulties of applying a duration-dependent model would preclude its use in the present context.

In a further, though less heroic, restriction, we assume that the respondents face the same force of mortality irrespective of their current economic status, although we do account for differences with respect to age and gender. This restriction on the model is prompted by the absence of mortality reporting in the LFS. However, we believe that this simplification has only a negligible effect on the WLEs, given that, for the working-age range, the mortality hazard rate is relatively small in comparison to the other transition intensities in the model.[8] It is trivial then to demonstrate mathematically that we can restrict the analytical treatment of the estimation in Fig. 1 to the transient states only and allow for the effects of risk of early mortality at the final stage, without contravening the fundamentals of the modelling framework.

Making use of the individual working-life paths contained in the longitudinal LFS data, we can determine exactly the quarterly transitions (n_x^{ij}) between any two states i and j that occurred during each age interval $(x,x+1)$. However, there is not sufficient information regarding the exact timing of the transitions, and hence we can only approximate the total time at risk in a given state i. Assuming that both the transition times and the dates of birth of the participants are evenly distributed in the survey, we can adjust the census method (see Benjamin & Pollard, 1980) to the current framework, as follows:

$$E_x^i = \int_0^1 l_{x+t}^i \, dt = \frac{1}{2}\sum_{k=0}^{K-1}\left(l_x^i(k) + l_x^i(k+1)\right) \times (\Delta t)_k$$
$$= \frac{0.25}{2}\sum_{k=0}^{4}\left(l_x^i(k) + l_x^i(k+1)\right) \tag{2}$$

where l_{x+t}^i is the total number of lives in state i at current age x+t , while $l_x^i(k)$ represents the total number of lives of age x (last birthday) in state i at the kth observation point. Note that in Eq. (2) we make use of the trapezium rule of approximation assuming that we have quarterly spaced observation points (i.e. $K = 5$ and $\Delta t = 0.25$). Also, we assume that we can safely overlook the effect of multiple (unobserved) transitions that could take place between two consecutive interviews for some individuals in the sample.

Thus, making use of Eqs. (1) and (2), we can calculate the crude transition intensities at each working age for the pooled LFS sample. In line with common actuarial practice, in order to eliminate random variation we further smooth the crude rates using cubic *B*-splines. Also, re-estimation by smoothing might be required in the case of particular combinations of the explanatory factors, which result in empty data cells due to the extensive segmentation of the original dataset (e.g. the disabled with higher education group). Nevertheless, we have found that, when comparing the WLE (RF) calculated from the smoothed and crude rates, the differences are negligible.[9]

For computational convenience, we express the age-specific transition intensities and the corresponding transition probabilities between states 1 and 2 in matrix forms, as follows:

$$M_x = \begin{bmatrix} -\mu_x^{12} & \mu_x^{12} \\ \mu_x^{21} & -\mu_x^{21} \end{bmatrix} \quad P_x = P_x(t=1) = \begin{bmatrix} p_x^{11} & p_x^{12} \\ p_x^{21} & p_x^{22} \end{bmatrix} \tag{3}$$

where we note that the 'occupancy' force in state i equals the negative of the total forces of 'decrement' (see section 1.4 of Haberman & Pitacco, 1999). Thus, assuming constant transition intensities (M_x) over each exact year of age (x,x+1), we have the result that the corresponding yearly probability matrix, conditional on being alive at age x, is given by the following matrix exponential:

$$P_x = \exp(M_x) = A_x \exp\left(\begin{bmatrix} d_{x,1} & 0 \\ 0 & d_{x,2} \end{bmatrix}\right) A_x^{-1} \tag{4}$$

where the diagonal matrix is formed by the eigenvalues of M_x, while A_x is a matrix formed by the corresponding eigenvectors. Then, the transition matrix over any number of integer years $t(1, 2, \ldots)$, conditional on being alive at age x, is given by the matrix product over all ages up to $x+t$, as follows:

$$P_x(t) = P_x \times P_{x+1} \times P_{x+2} \times \cdots P_{x+t-1} = \prod_{k=0}^{t-1} P_{x+k} \tag{5}$$

where the components p_{x+t}^{ij} of $P_x(t)$ can be interpreted as the proportion of people who in t years time will be in state j ($S_{x+t} = j$) based on their initial state i ($S_x = i$) occupied at age x.

In this way, the increment–decrement Markov chains model allows the measurement of age-specific transition probabilities between the two economic states. Aggregated over a lifetime, these form the basis of the WLE. The WLE is a measure that is determined, subject to a few simplifying assumptions, by the age-by-age probability of being in employment as observed across a population. The WLE is a summary statistic that gives the total number of years a person, on average, is likely to spend employed throughout his or her remaining working life, conditional on the starting economic state. In the exercise presented here, it is disaggregated by age, starting employment status, sex, disability status and educational achievement.

In general, the expected future time until the final pension age, t_p, that a person of age x might spend in a given economic state, conditional on his or her starting employment status can be expressed in the following work life matrix form:

$$W_{x:\overline{t_p - x}|} = \left\| w^{ij}_{x:\overline{t_p - x}|} \right\| = \int_0^{t_p - x} P_x(t)dt \tag{6}$$

where i and j represent the starting state and the target state, respectively. Then, in order to allow also for the risk of early mortality (dependent on age and gender), we can augment Eq. (6) by the probability of survival over the current interval $(x,\ x+t)$, denoted by $p_x(t)$, as follows:

$$W_{x:\overline{t_p - x|}} = \int_0^{t_p - x} P_x(t) p_x(t)\, dt \tag{7}$$

which can be shown to be equivalent to using the $N = 2{+}1$ state model, represented in Fig. 1, with an equal mortality hazard rate (μ_x) from the two transient economic states. We make use of the age-specific survival probabilities given in the UK Interim Life Table for 1999–2001 for the choice of $p_x(t)$. In the context of compensation for loss of earnings, only the first column components of the work life matrix ($W_{x:\overline{t_p-x|}}$) of Eq. (7) are relevant, as these represent the WLE in the employed state, conditional on the starting economic state. Given that we only consider discrete future working years, we can approximate Eq. (7) numerically using the trapezium rule, which in the case of employed state ($j = 1$) can be written as

$$w^i_{x:\overline{t_p-x|}} = \sum_{t=1}^{t_p-x-1} p_x^{i1}(t) p_x(t) + \frac{p_x^{i1}(0)p_x(0) + p_x^{i1}(t_p - x)p_x(t_p - x)}{2} \tag{8}$$

where the boundary conditions are specified by $p_x^{11}(0) = 1$, $p_x^{21}(0) = 0$ and $p_x(0) = 1$.[10]

In general, from the point of view of damages calculations, Eq. (8) gives the empirical estimates of the future number of years over which loss of earnings occurs. These reflect the overall labour market risks and also the risk of pre-retirement mortality. In order to compensate for the early receipt of all future streams of lost earnings in a form of a single lump sum, we need to discount the WLE estimates of Eq. (8) for the future real rate of return r, on the basis that the lump sum should generate a risk-free investment return. Hence, we can write:

$$w^i_{x:\overline{t_p-x|}}(v) = \sum_{t=1}^{t_p-x-1} p_x^{i1}(t) p_x(t) v^t + \frac{p_x^{i1}(0) + p_x^{i1}(t_p - x)p_x(t_p - x)v^{t_p-x}}{2} \tag{9}$$

where $v = 1/1 + r$. In June 2001, the Lord Chancellor set the discount rate for use in damages calculation in the United Kingdom at 2.5 per cent.[11] Thus, in this study we make use of $r = 2.5$ per cent (i.e. $v \approx 0.97561$).

Finally, for practical considerations, the discounted WLE can be expressed relative to the discounted life expectancy up to the retirement age, which we have referred to as the employment-risks RF, and this is given by

$$k_x^i(v) = \frac{w^i_{x:\overline{t_p - x|}}(v)}{\ddot{a}_{x:\overline{t_p - x|}}} = \frac{w^{i1}_{x:\overline{t_p - x|}}(v)}{w^{i1}_{x:\overline{t_p - x|}}(v) + w^{i2}_{x:\overline{t_p - x|}}(v)} \tag{10}$$

where $\ddot{a}_{x:\overline{t_p - x|}}$ is the discounted value of an annuity of £1 per annum paid up to the retirement age t_p. Note that this comprises the discounted WLE in the two transient economic states. The RF, $k_x^i(v)$, is easy to understand and easy to work with. It provides an intuitive standardised measure of lifetime labour market risk and is readily applied to the reported discounted life expectancies to retirement age in the various tables in the Ogden Tables to make appropriate adjustments for the effects of additional factors and personal circumstances.

5. RESULTS: NEW EMPLOYMENT-RISKS REDUCTION FACTORS

Table 2 summarises the pooled LFS data in terms of exposure times and prevalence rates for men and women across the two main economic states (E and NE) expressed separately by disability status. For the disabled workforce (panel (a) of Table 2), employment rates are distributed fairly evenly across the working-age range for both sexes so that women experience prevalence rates in employment of just above 30 per cent for the most part of their working lives, with a fall from the age of 50 years. There is very little recovery in employment rates after the years of child care for disabled women. Employment rates for disabled males are a little higher than those of disabled females, though even during the most productive years (from mid-20s to mid-40s) they do not rise beyond 40 per cent.

The prevalence rates in the employed state for the non-disabled population (shown in panel (b) of Table 2) are substantially higher and, in contrast to the disabled workforce, they are characterised by variations with respect to age. We observe prevalence rates in employment that are around double the size of those of disabled workers, and the typical inverted 'U' shape of employment rates is evident for both men and women. There is a 20 percentage point difference in employment rates for men and women at younger ages (twenties and thirties), clearly reflecting the impact of maternal responsibilities on participation rates. From the age of 40 years, this difference reduces to around 10 percentage points.

Table 2. Exposure Times (Person-Years) by Age and Disability and Corresponding Prevalence Rates (%) across Two Economic States (E and NE).

Age Range	Males			Females		
	Exposure	Economic States PR		Exposure	Economic States PR	
	(p-years)	E (%)	NE (%)	(p-years)	E (%)	NE (%)
(a) *Disabled*						
(15,20]	322	28.9	71.1	267	35.1	64.9
(20,25]	262	31.9	68.1	329	35.6	64.4
(25,30]	417	40.8	59.2	560	30.7	69.3
(30,35]	645	40.3	59.7	907	31.3	68.7
(35,40]	890	39.7	60.3	1163	33.1	66.9
(40,45]	989	40.2	59.8	1407	32.9	67.1
(45,50]	1368	34.8	65.2	1721	30.4	69.6
(50,55]	1965	30.6	69.4	2510	25.4	74.6
(55,60]	2330	23.0	77.0	2199	16.3	83.7
(60,65]	2472	12.7	87.3			
(b) *Non-Disabled*						
(15,20]	7967	60.2	39.8	7482	60.7	39.3
(20,25]	4931	86.7	13.3	5334	73.7	26.3
(25,30]	6995	93.3	6.7	8657	74.7	25.3
(30,35]	10101	94.7	5.3	12251	74.6	25.4
(35,40]	11362	94.8	5.2	13230	79.2	20.8
(40,45]	10768	94.9	5.1	11510	83.8	16.2
(45,50]	10053	94.9	5.1	10571	85.5	14.5
(50,55]	10421	92.1	7.9	10746	80.8	19.2
(55,60]	7700	82.8	17.2	7184	65.2	34.8
(60,65]	5292	59.6	40.4			

Source: LFS 1998–2003 quarterly panel data.

It is the transition rates between the two economic states that form the foundation of the WLE. In Fig. 2, we present smoothed age-specific transition hazard rates by starting status, disability and sex. Looking first at the left panel (a), which displays E to NE transitions (out of employment), it can be seen that the transition intensities to the NE state are broadly similar by sex and by disability, though they are consistently slightly higher for the disabled (D). In contrast, in the right panel (b), which displays the NE to E transitions (re-entries into employment), the difference by disability status is marked, as is the difference between men and women who are both non-disabled. This analysis clearly identifies the low intensity of re-entry from a

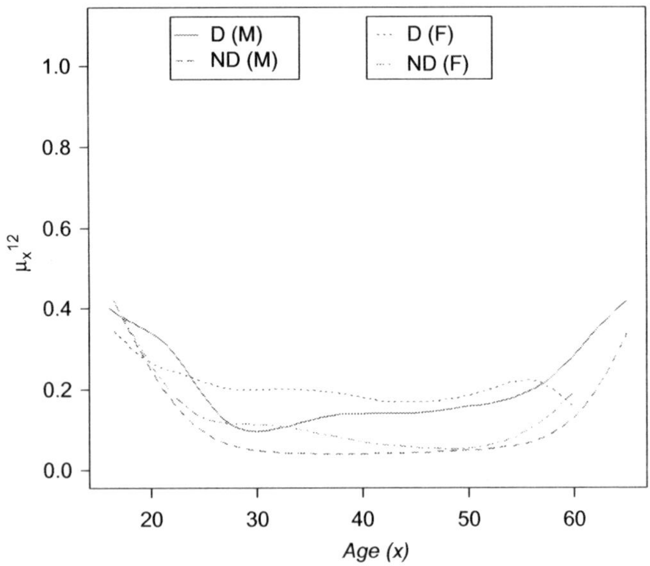

a) Smoothed E to NE rates from LFS 1998 - 2003

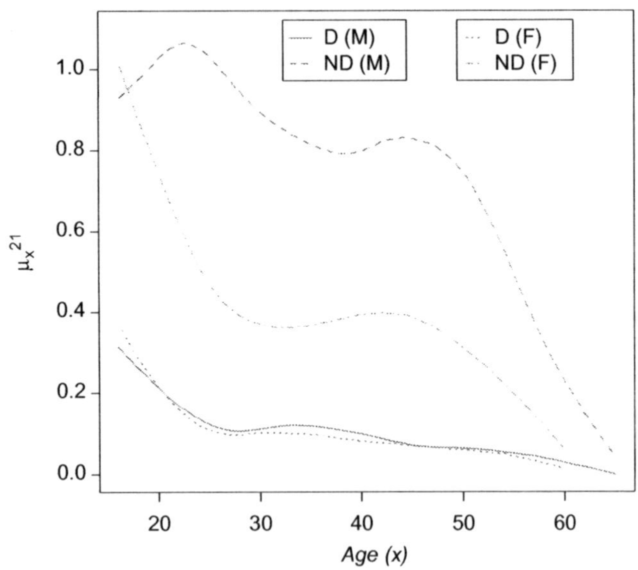

b) Smoothed NE to E rates from LFS 1998 - 2003

Fig. 2. Smoothed Age-Specific Transition Hazard Rates between Employment (E) and Non-Employment (NE) by Sex (M and F) and Disability Status (D and ND).

state of NE as the key source of labour market disadvantage for the disabled.

These findings are broadly consistent with Burchardt (2000), using the British Household Panel Survey (for 1997), who reports that 17 per cent of those who acquire a disability while at work exit within a year, compared to 7 per cent who remain non-disabled. Of the disabled who find work, 33 per cent exit within a year compared to 20 per cent of the non-disabled. The discrepancy in transition rates between non-employment and employment by disability status is much greater. The hazard rate for re-entry into employment within a year for the disabled is 4 per cent compared to 24 per cent for the non-disabled.

The effects of disability on employment transitions are seen to be cumulative and long-lasting in the age-specific RFs (discounted at a 2.5 per cent p.a. real rate of interest) which are illustrated in Figs. 3 (males) and 4 (females).[12] The graphs in Figs. 3 and 4 represent the lifetime employment-risks RFs for each combination of characteristics used to disaggregate the RFs. For reference, each graph also shows the overall age-specific RFs of the sub-group without the effect of education.

The RF is the proportion of a life expectancy to retirement that is likely to be spent in employment (see Eq. (10)). It includes both the risk of pre-retirement death and the risk of non-employment. For non-disabled men, their level of education has little impact on their employment risks and therefore on the WLE. The same is true for a starting state of non-employment prior to the age of 50 years. In contrast, disability is associated with a large increase in employment risks and a large reduction in the WLE. Interestingly, the impacts of both educational attainment and starting employment status on employment risks are much greater for disabled men. A disabled 40-year-old man with a job (E) and a degree (HD) is likely to spend 60 per cent of his remaining working life in employment compared to 40 per cent for his unqualified (O) counterpart. The non-disabled equivalents are 90 and 88 per cent. A starting state of non-employment (NE) reduces the likely working lifetime for the disabled 40-year-old graduate to 41 per cent and for the unqualified to 17 per cent. The non-disabled equivalents are 84 and 79 per cent, respectively.

RFs estimated for women in Fig. 4 display the same broad patterns in relation to age, education, employment status and disability as those observed for men in Fig. 3 (see notes to Fig. 3).

As expected, the effects of child care are evident in lower RFs prior to the age of 40 years for females. In addition, the effects of education and starting employment state are greater for women than for men in both the

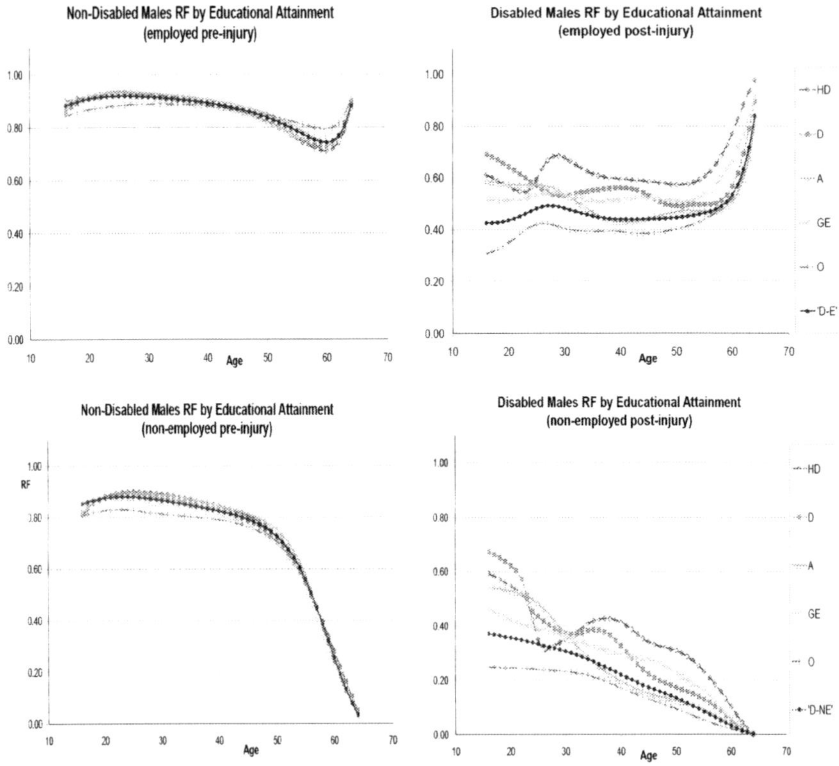

Key:

D-E/D-NE– Average excluding education variable;
HD – degree or higher; D – higher education below degree;
A – A level or equivalent;
GE – GCSE A-C or equivalent; O – other or no qualifications.

Fig. 3. Male Age-specific Employment-Risks RFs by Employment Status, Disability Status and Educational Attainment (LFS 1998–2003 with 2.5% p.a. Discount Rate).

non-disabled (ND) and disabled (D) states. A disabled 40-year-old woman with a job and a degree is likely to spend 67 per cent of her remaining working life in employment compared to 36 per cent for her unqualified counterpart. The non-disabled equivalents are 89 and 79 per cent. A starting state of non-employment (NE) reduces the likely working lifetime for the disabled 40-year-old graduate to 51 per cent and for the unqualified to

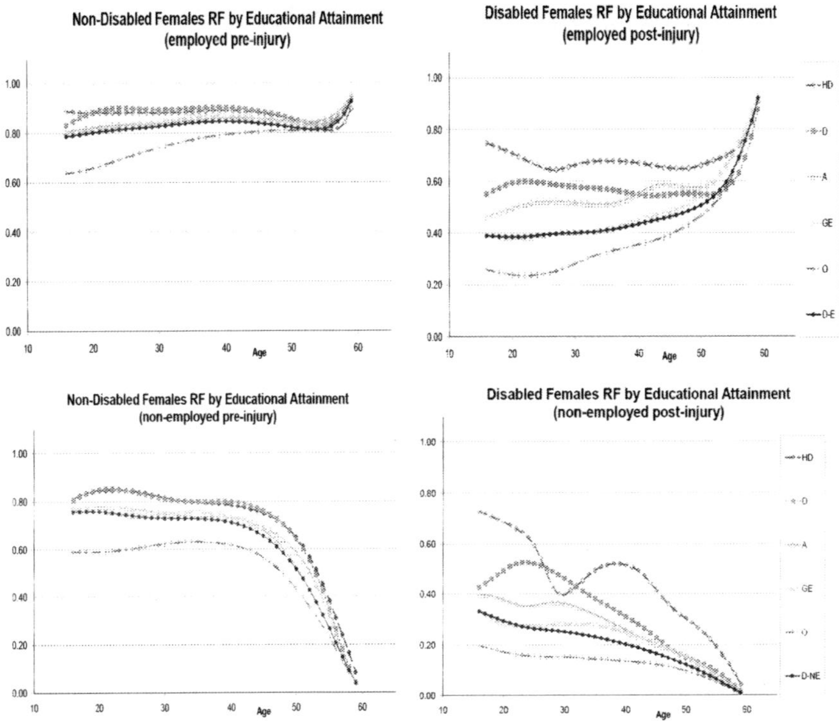

Key:

D-E/D-NE – Average excluding education variable;
HD – degree or higher; D – higher education below degree;
A – A level or equivalent;
GE – GCSE A-C or equivalent; O – other or no qualifications.

Fig. 4. Female Age-Specific Employment-Risks RFs by Employment Status, Disability Status and Educational Attainment (LFS 1998–2003 with 2.5% p.a. Discount Rate).

13 per cent. The non-disabled equivalents are 78 and 61 per cent, respectively.

Differential employment risks are measured over a lifetime and are measured as RFs for use by lawyers who, when calculating a claim for future loss of earnings, consult the Ogden Tables. Both the calculation and the Ogden Tables are discussed in Sections 6 and 7.

6. THE SIXTH EDITION OF THE OGDEN TABLES

While the use of the Ogden Tables in the UK courts is imposed by formal legislation and case law, the tables themselves do not represent the direct force of law (Trusted, 2007). Rather, their purpose is to provide useful, impartial guidance to lawyers in the calculation of a future loss with a view to providing both sides with a degree of consistency and certainty and avoiding the need for costly and complicated expert financial evidence. Therefore, it is for lawyers and policymakers to decide what information is required and how and when to use the information.

The sixth edition of the Ogden Tables follows the format of previous editions in 1984, 1994, 1998, 2000 and 2004. There is a short introduction which highlights changes from previous editions. Section A describes the application of the main body of the publication, and Tables 1–28 relate to the mortality risks over the working-age range. Section B describes the application of the RFs reported in Tables A–D, which seek to capture non-mortality (labour market) risks described in Section 5. Subsequent sections provide examples and formulae and details of the method of application where the accident results in death.

There are a number of key departures in the sixth edition approach to calculating damages from the previous versions of the Ogden Tables. The new RFs (in Tables A–D contained within Section B) are now disaggregated, in addition to by sex and age, also by disability status, employment status and three broad classes of educational attainment.[13] These are reproduced in the appendix to this chapter. Further, pre- and post-injury future earnings are now calculated separately making use of disability-adjusted RFs. It is the difference between pre- and post-injury earnings which gives the estimated future loss of earnings.

The RFs tabulated in the appendix are based on those graphed in Figs. 3 and 4 and described in Section 5 with additional grouping for age and educational attainment. The tabulated form is used by lawyers in the calculation of loss of future earnings. The RF is applied to the discounted life expectancy to retirement age estimates tabulated in Tables 1–28 of the Ogden Tables. This calculation is illustrated in Section 7.

The RFs for employment risks are averages for broadly defined groups. Their purpose is guidance rather than prediction. As a group average they will inevitably be imprecise for any particular claimant due to the impact of unmeasured employment-related characteristics. In the light of this potential for imprecision, there is a role for discretionary adjustment on the part of the courts. In the following section, we describe a case in which the court applied its discretion and set damages based on an adjusted RF.

7. AN EARLY APPLICATION OF THE SIXTH EDITION OGDEN TABLES EMPLOYMENT-RISKS REDUCTION FACTORS

In one of the first cases to be adjudicated on the basis of the new 'Ogden Six' approach and estimates, the courts have embraced their powers of discretion. We provide, as an example, the details of this case. Here the RF, which is adjusted for disability, is viewed as an extreme rather than as an average. Since the claimant's employment prospects were considered to be better than the extreme case, the courts set them at a point midway between the pre-injury (ND) and post-injury (D) published RFs. The resulting award was more or less equivalent to that which would have been made under the conventional method, using a *Smith v. Manchester* award equivalent to 24 months of post-injury earnings.

In *Conner v. Bradman* [2007][14] a large discretionary adjustment was applied to the post-injury multiplier. Mr Conner was 51 years old at the time of trial. He suffered injury to his knee when his motor bike was hit by a car. It was agreed that he would suffer permanent weakness and instability at the knee joint. Consequently, he was found to qualify as disabled within the meaning of the Disability Discrimination Act 1995. At the time of trial, Mr Conner was employed in his pre-injury job as an auto-fitter. It was agreed that the effects of his injury would preclude him from his pre-injury employment within a year. Prior to injury, Mr Conner had had a second source of earnings from work as a taxi driver and, from a medical view point, he was considered able to continue in this employment post-injury.

The basic multiplier for a 51-year-old retiring at 65 years of age is 11.40 (Table 9, Ogden Tables, Sixth Edition). On a strict application, the pre-injury RF is 0.82 (Table A) and the post-injury RF is 0.49 (Table B). Using the court-determined multiplicands the calculation is as follows:

$$113,796 = (20,327 \times 11.40 \times 0.82) - (13,645 \times 11.40 \times 0.49)$$

However, on the court's interpretation, the claimant's injury was considered to be relatively modest and the RF of 0.49 was adjusted upwards to 0.655, the mid-point between 0.49 (D) and 0.82 (ND).

The actual award based on discretionary adjustment to the RFs is calculated as follows:

$$88,130 = (20,327 \times 11.40 \times 0.82) - (13,645 \times 11.40 \times 0.655)$$

In fact, the actual award is comparable with that which would have been achieved under the old methodology in which the pre-injury multiplier was applied to post-injury earnings and the additional employment risks arising from disability were compensated by means of a *Smith v. Manchester* lump sum award, based upon 24 months of additional non-employment (see Chapter 4). This calculation is as follows:

$$89,753 = (20,327 - 13,645) \times (11.40 \times 0.82) + (13,645 \times 2)$$

The range of RFs associated with a variety of different characteristics (including E and NE, D and ND, and low, mid and high levels of qualifications) as they apply to a 51-year-old man is illustrated in Fig. 5.

The court's decision to raise the disabled RF from 0.49 to 0.66 is based on either a misunderstanding of the RF as a peer group average or the belief that the impact of disability for the claimant is less than is measured in the LFS because this claimant (or perhaps claimants generally) are different from the LFS disabled. In relation to the first point, the potential

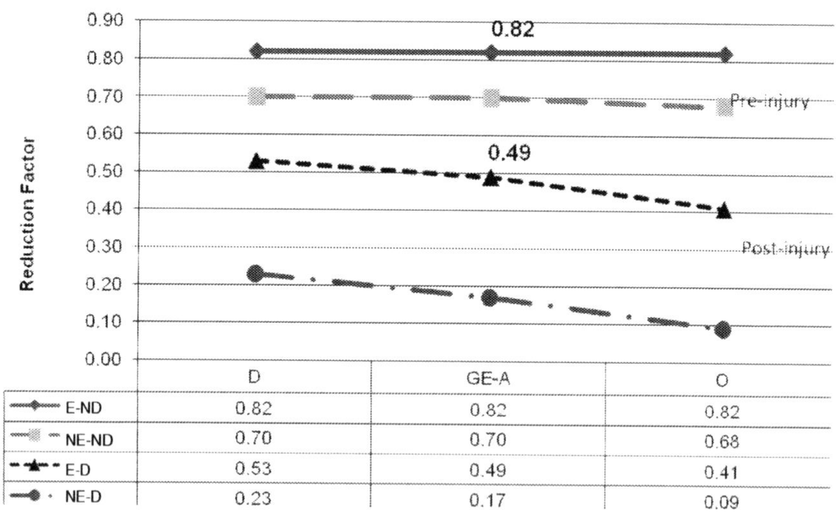

Fig. 5. Reduction Factors for a 51-Year-Old Man by Disability Status and Educational Achievement.

misunderstanding, the average RF includes adjustment for those factors which we can measure and include in the estimate and which, when we do, have the greatest impact on the employment outcome. To the extent that severity of disability affects starting employment status, this is included in the RF. A more extensive account of the reasoning on this point can be found in Wass (2008). It should be noted that if the claimant had not been employed (because, amongst other things, he was more severely disabled), the RF would have been 0.17.

The second point relates to potential imprecision and/or bias in the RFs. We readily acknowledge that the lifetime employment risks of a heterogeneous workforce cannot be fully described by means of series of transitions between two basic economic states which account only for sex, age, disability and level of education. Imprecision is inevitable when an individual outcome is determined on the basis of a group average. Imprecision refers to the deviation between the data point for the individual and the group average (where the average is correct for the population). The potential for bias is more important and refers to circumstances where the group average, based on the LFS data, is incorrect as an average for claimants. We consider two possible circumstances which might give rise to such bias.

The disabled RFs are population estimates, but claimants make up only a small proportion of the disabled population. The legitimacy of applying RFs for the LFS-disabled to claimants rests upon the assumption that there are no unmeasured differences between claimants and the disabled population which affect employment outcomes. The presence of such unmeasured employment-affecting variables which are differently distributed across claimants and the disabled population gives rise to omitted variable bias. We identify two omitted variables which are potential sources of bias: severity of disability and historical non-employment. If claimants are less severely disabled than the LFS-disabled and if severity of disability matters for future employment, then the RFs based on the LFS-disabled will overstate the employment disadvantage arising from disability for claimants. Similarly if claimants have less historical non-employment and if they would have had less historical non-employment even had they been disabled (or they will now have less non-employment), then the RFs based on the LFS-disabled will overstate the employment disadvantage arising from disability for claimants.

A direct comparison between disabled claimants and the LFS-disabled is not possible since the former cannot be separately identified in the LFS. Even if we could identify claimants, we have no measure of severity of disability on which to base a comparison. However, the definition of disability is the same in the LFS as it is under the law. There is perhaps a slightly higher threshold for claimants than for the LFS-disabled since any condition is likely to be investigated by at least two physicians and any impairment must be sufficient to justify the costs and risks of litigation.

Although claimants cannot be identified in the LFS, in the spring quarter of the LFS in 2002 additional questions were asked in relation to the different causes of disability. From these responses we find that 17 per cent of disabled men of working age report that they have been disabled from birth, 47 per cent report disability from a medical cause and 36 per cent report an injury or work-related disability or illness. It is this latter group, who comprise around a third of the working-age disabled, who most closely resemble disabled claimants. If we link cause of disability to the average employment rate for each group, we find a 27 per cent employment rate for those disabled through a medical cause and a 34 per cent employment rate for those disabled from birth, through injury or through a work-related disease. The difference in employment rates by cause of disability is relatively low, 7 percentage points, and is much lower than differences measured across age groups and education groups and by disability status itself.

It could be argued that there is more and longer inactivity in the LFS than amongst claimants. It was noted in Lewis et al. (2002a) that workplace injuries account for the greatest proportion of personal injury claims. The LFS does not include information on historical non-employment. To the extent that non-employment is duration dependent, the information contained in current employment status is incomplete. If historical non-employment is less for a disabled claimant than it is for the disabled in the LFS, then the RFs are biased downwards. While the future likelihood of non-employment increases as its history increases, the relationship is non-linear, reducing over time. For the disabled non-employed, a year out of work appears to mark an important threshold after which future employment prospects remain low but fairly constant (see Burchardt, 2000). With this one-year anniversary in mind, Burchardt's (2000) results based on within year transitions reported earlier would suggest that any bias might be expected to be low.

8. CONCLUSIONS

Our purpose was to estimate employment outcomes in a dynamic framework that incorporates the effects of disability and educational attainment and to do so in an efficient and transparent manner. This we achieved through the application of Markov chains modelling to labour force movements observed in the quarterly panel LFS data. As a result we were able to calculate WLEs and RFs conditional on the starting economic state of the claimant and to disaggregate our estimates by sex, age, disability status and educational achievement. The joint modelling of the effects of disability, educational attainment and starting economic state allows us to differentiate between pre- and post-injury states. Since we demonstrate in this study that these variables have an important impact on employment outcomes, such a development constitutes a decisive improvement over the pre-existing method of damages calculations which did not formally account for any of these factors.

We are mindful, nevertheless, that potential for bias and imprecision remains, that the lifetime employment risks of a heterogeneous workforce cannot be fully described by the means of simple two-period labour market dynamics between two basic economic states disaggregated only by sex, age, disability status and educational attainment.

In relation to the presence of imprecision, the courts have demonstrated a taste for the use of discretion in relation to the RFs. If this continues, they may need further guidance on the magnitude of such discretionary adjustments away from the average RF. In this regard, we look to important developments in the US forensic economics literature in which the average RF is treated as a random variable whose distribution can be estimated through simulation techniques. In the meantime, the magnitude of any discretionary adjustment from the average might be gauged with reference to the impact of level of qualification for this claimant in the disabled state. If the claimant had had a higher level of qualification, his opportunities for employment would have extended to include a wide range of non-manual occupations. The impact of such a qualification would have been to raise the RF from 0.49 to 0.53. This is a much smaller range of discretion than that used by the court in *Conner v. Bradman*.

NOTES

1. The position is described rather more crudely by Sir Michael Ogden QC (the first chair of the Ogden Working Party) in the preface to the first edition (1984), 'We must make sure that they [the tables and explanatory notes] are readily comprehensible. We must assume the most stupid circuit judge in the country and before him are the two most stupid advocates. All three must be able to understand what we are saying.'

2. Lewis et al. (2002a, 2003).
3. Lewis et al. (2002b, 2002c).
4. BBC Radio Five 18 December 2002 (see Wass, 2002).
5. Paragraph 25 contains a 'health warning' due to 'certain inaccuracies [that] have been noted in the figures used in tables A, B and C for contingencies other than mortality'.
6. According to Krueger (2004) this research was predated by the Schoen and Woodrow 1980 WLE estimates based on a similar increment–decrement Markov chain method applied to 1972/73 CPS data.
7. Disability is a derived variable, and the LFS algorithm which defines its derivation is reproduced in Appendix B of Butt et al. (2008).
8. In practical terms, the courts can account for increased mortality rate by choosing reduced base multipliers (term certain) when prompted by significant medical evidence.
9. That is, it is possible to simply consider the transition intensities equal to 0 wherever $n_x^{ij} = 0$ and/or $E_x^i = 0$ without significantly affecting the overall estimates of the WLE and RF.
10. Butt, Haberman, and Verrall (2006) give a generalized matrix form to Eq. (8).
11. "Setting the Discount Rate – The Lord Chancellor's Reasons" dated 27 July 2001. See also note 5 of Chapter 4.
12. Full numerical results of age-specific disability-adjusted WLEs and RFs, along with corresponding standard errors, are published in Butt et al. (2008). In addition, average adjustments for education effects for broad age ranges are also given here. Detailed numerical values of the disability- and education-adjusted RFs (presented in Figs. 3 and 4) are available at request from the authors.
13. The number of educational categories is reduced to 3 in the Ogden Tables in order to reduce the tables of RFs.
14. EWHC 2789 (QB).

ACKNOWLEDGMENTS

We are grateful for the financial support towards this research from the Economic and Social Research Council (Grant RES-000-22-0883) and the additional contribution from the Institute and Faculty of Actuaries.

REFERENCES

Arulampalam, W., Booth, A., & Taylor, M. (2000). Unemployment persistence. *Oxford Economic Papers*, *52*, 24–50.

Benjamin, B., & Pollard, J. H. (1980). *The analysis of mortality and other actuarial statistics*. London: Heinemann.

Bernoulli, D. (1766). Essai d'une nouvelle analyse de la mortalité causée par la petite vérole, et des avantages de l'inoculation pour la prévenir, Hist. Acad. Roy. Sci., Année MDCCLX, Mémoires, pp. 1–45.

Burchardt, T. (2000). The dynamics of being disabled. *Journal of Social Policy*, *29*(4), 645–668.

Butt, Z., Haberman, S., & Verrall, R. (2006). *The impact of dynamic multi-state measurement of worklife expectancy on the loss of earnings multipliers in England and Wales*. Working Paper No. 2. Cass Business School, London, UK.

Butt, Z., Haberman, S., Verrall, R., & Wass, V. (2008). Calculating compensation for loss of future earnings: Estimating and using work life expectancy. *Journal of the Royal Statistical Society, Series A*, *171*(4), 763–800.

Ciecka, J. E., Donley, T., & Goldman, J. (1995). A Markov process model of worklife expectancies based on labor market activity in 1992–93. *Journal of Legal Economics*, *5*(3), 17–41.

Ciecka, J. E., Donley, T., & Goldman, J. (1997). Regarding median years to retirement and worklife expectancy. *Journal of Forensic Economics*, *10*(3), 297–310.

Ciecka, J. E., Donley, T., & Goldman, J. (2001). A Markov process model of worklife expectancies by educational attainment based on labor market activity in 1997–98. *Journal of Legal Economics*, *10*(3), 1–22.

Du Pasquier, L. G. (1912). Mathematische Theorie der Invaliditätsversicherung. *Mitteil. Verein. Schweizer Versicherungsmath*, *7*, 1–7.

Du Pasquier, L. G. (1913). Mathematische Theorie der Invaliditätsversicherung. *Mitteil. Verein. Schweizer Versicherungsmath*, *8*, 1–153.

Haberman, S., & Bloomfield, D. (1990). Work time lost to sickness, unemployment and stoppages: Measurement and application. *Journal of the Institute of Actuaries*, *117*, 533–595.

Haberman, S., & Pitacco, E. (1999). *Actuarial models for disability insurance*. Boca Raton, FL: Chapman & Hall/CRC.

Haile, G. A. (2004). *Re-employment hazard of displaced German workers: Evidence from the GSOEP*. Working Paper No. 2004/037. Lancaster University Management School, Lancaster, UK.

Hamza, E. (1900). Note sur la théorie mathématique de l'assurance contre le risque d'invalidité d'origine morbide, sénile ou accidentelle. In: Transactions of the 3rd International Congress of Actuaries, Paris, pp. 154–203.

Heckman, J., & Singer, B. (1985). *Longitudinal analysis of labor market data*. Cambridge: Cambridge University Press.

Hoem, J. M. (1972). Inhomogeneous semi-Markov processes, select actuarial tables, and duration dependence in demography. In: T. N. E. Greville (Ed.), *Population Dynamics* (pp. 251–296). London: Academic Press.

Hoem, J. M. (1977). A Markov chain model of working life tables. *Scandinavian Actuarial Journal*, 1–20.

Jones, B. L. (1994). Actuarial calculations using a Markov model. *Transactions of the Society of Actuaries*, *46*, 227–250.

Jones, B. L. (1997). Methods for the analysis of CCRC data. *North American Actuarial Journal*, *1*(2), 40–54.

Krueger, K. V. (2004). Tables of inter-year labor force status of the U.S. population (1998–2004) to operate the Markov model of worklife expectancy. *Journal of Forensic Economics*, *17*(3), 313–382.

Lewis, R., McNabb, R., Robinson, H., & Wass, V. (2002a). Court awards of damages for loss of future earnings: An empirical study and an alternative method of calculation. *Journal of Law and Society*, *29*, 406–435.

Lewis, R., McNabb, R., Robinson, H., & Wass, V. (2003). Loss of earnings following personal injury: Do the courts adequately compensate injured parties? *Economic Journal*, *113*(491), 568–584.

Lewis, R., McNabb, R., & Wass, V. (2002b). A new way to assess damages for loss of future earnings. *New Law Journal*, *152*, 1042–1043.

Lewis, R., McNabb, R., & Wass, V. (2002c). Methods for calculating damages for loss of future earnings. *Journal of Personal Injury Law*, *2*, 151–165.

Millimet, D. L., Nieswiadomy, M., Ryu, H., & Slottje, D. (2003). Estimating worklife expectancy: An econometric approach. *Journal of Econometrics*, *113*, 83–113.

Narendranathan, W., & Stewart, M. B. (1993). How does the benefit effect vary as unemployment spells lengthen? *Journal of Applied Econometrics*, *8*, 361–381.

Pitacco, E. (1995). Actuarial models for pricing disability benefits: Towards a unifying approach. *Insurance: Mathematics and Economics*, *16*, 39–62.

Richards, H. (1999). *Life and worklife expectancies*. Tucson, AZ: Lawyers and Judges Publishing Company.

Richards, H. (2000). Worklife expectancies: Increment-decrement less accurate than conventional. *Journal of Forensic Economics*, *13*(2), 271–289.

Smith, S. J. (1982). New worklife estimates reflect changing profile of labor force. *Monthly Labor Review*, *105*(3), 15–20.

Smith, S. J. (1986). Worklife estimates: effects of race and education. Bureau of Labor Statistics Bulletin, 2254. US Department of Labor.

Stewart, M., & Swaffield, J. (1999). Low pay dynamics and transition probabilities. *Economica*, *66*, 23–42.

Trusted, H. (2007). The sixth edition of the ogden tables. *Journal of Personal Injury Law*, *3*, 262–268.

Wass, V. (2002). Under-compensation of injured claimants in UK. Interview on BBC Radio Five, 18 December.

Wass, V. (2008). Discretion in the application of the new ogden six multipliers. The case of Conner v Bradman and Company. *Journal of Personal Injury Law*, *2*, 155–164.

APPENDIX. REDUCTION FACTORS, OGDEN TABLES SIXTH EDITION (FROM SECTION B, CONTINGENCIES OTHER THAN MORTALITY, PARAGRAPH 42)

Table A1. Loss of Earnings to Pension Age 65 (Males Not Disabled).

Age at Trial	Employed			Non-Employed		
	Qualification			Qualification		
	High	Mid	Low	High	Mid	Low
16–19	0.90	0.90	0.85	0.85	0.85	0.82
20–24	0.92	0.92	0.87	0.89	0.88	0.83
25–29	0.93	0.92	0.89	0.89	0.88	0.82
30–34	0.92	0.91	0.89	0.87	0.86	0.81
35–39	0.90	0.90	0.89	0.85	0.84	0.80
40–44	0.88	0.88	0.88	0.82	0.81	0.78
45–49	0.86	0.86	0.86	0.77	0.77	0.74
50	0.83	0.83	0.83	0.72	0.72	0.70
51	0.82	0.82	0.82	0.70	0.70	0.68
52	0.81	0.81	0.81	0.67	0.67	0.66
53	0.80	0.80	0.80	0.63	0.63	0.63
54	0.79	0.79	0.79	0.59	0.59	0.59

Table A2. Loss of Earnings to Pension Age 65 (Males Disabled).

Age at Trial	Employed			Non-Employed		
	Qualification			Qualification		
	High	Mid	Low	High	Mid	Low
16–19	0.61	0.55	0.32	0.61	0.49	0.25
20–24	0.61	0.55	0.38	0.53	0.46	0.24
25–29	0.60	0.54	0.42	0.48	0.41	0.24
30–34	0.59	0.52	0.40	0.43	0.34	0.23
35–39	0.58	0.48	0.39	0.38	0.28	0.20
40–44	0.57	0.48	0.39	0.33	0.23	0.15
45–49	0.55	0.48	0.39	0.26	0.20	0.11
50	0.53	0.49	0.40	0.24	0.18	0.10
51	0.53	0.49	0.41	0.23	0.17	0.09
52	0.54	0.49	0.41	0.22	0.16	0.08
53	0.54	0.49	0.42	0.21	0.15	0.07
54	0.54	0.50	0.43	0.20	0.14	0.06

Table A3. Loss of Earnings to Pension Age 60 (Females Not Disabled).

Age at Trial	Employed			Non-Employed		
	Qualification			Qualification		
	High	Mid	Low	High	Mid	Low
16–19	0.87	0.81	0.64	0.84	0.77	0.59
20–24	0.89	0.82	0.68	0.84	0.76	0.60
25–29	0.89	0.84	0.72	0.83	0.75	0.61
30–34	0.89	0.85	0.75	0.81	0.75	0.63
35–39	0.89	0.86	0.78	0.80	0.74	0.63
40–44	0.89	0.86	0.80	0.78	0.72	0.60
45–49	0.87	0.85	0.81	0.72	0.64	0.52
50	0.86	0.84	0.81	0.64	0.55	0.43
51	0.85	0.84	0.81	0.60	0.51	0.40
52	0.84	0.84	0.81	0.56	0.46	0.36
53	0.83	0.83	0.81	0.50	0.41	0.32
54	0.83	0.83	0.82	0.44	0.35	0.27

Table A4. Loss of Earnings to Pension Age 60 (Females Disabled).

Age at Trial	Employed			Non-Employed		
	Qualification			Qualification		
	High	Mid	Low	High	Mid	Low
16–19	0.65	0.43	0.25	0.58	0.35	0.19
20–24	0.64	0.44	0.25	0.58	0.33	0.17
25–29	0.63	0.45	0.25	0.50	0.32	0.16
30–34	0.62	0.46	0.30	0.44	0.31	0.15
35–39	0.61	0.48	0.34	0.42	0.28	0.14
40–44	0.60	0.51	0.38	0.38	0.23	0.13
45–49	0.60	0.54	0.42	0.28	0.18	0.11
50	0.60	0.56	0.47	0.23	0.15	0.10
51	0.61	0.58	0.49	0.21	0.14	0.09
52	0.61	0.60	0.51	0.20	0.13	0.08
53	0.62	0.62	0.54	0.18	0.11	0.07
54	0.63	0.66	0.57	0.16	0.09	0.06

MARKOV WORK LIFE TABLE RESEARCH IN THE UNITED STATES

Gary R. Skoog and James E. Ciecka

1. INTRODUCTION

Prior to 1982, work life tables in the United States could be viewed as the labor force counterpart of life tables. Most work in this area emanated from the US Bureau of Labor Statistics (BLS) and was based on the assumptions that men entered and left the labor force only once in their lives and women only entered and left the labor force as a result of a change in their marital or parental status. The work life model for men especially was demographic in nature since departure from the labor force was akin to death in a life table in the sense that labor force reentry was not possible, just as reentry into a life table cannot occur after death. We now refer to this type of construct as the *conventional model* of work life. Tables produced by Fullerton and Byrne (1976), using data from 1970, illustrate this approach to work life expectancy (WLE).

The BLS broke away from the conventional model in 1982 and 1986 (US Bureau of Labor Statistics, 1982, 1986) when it published work life tables based on a *Markov process*, or *Increment–Decrement model*. In Bulletin 2135, the BLS viewed both men and women as "entering and leaving the labor market repeatedly during their lifetimes, with nearly all participating

Personal Injury and Wrongful Death Damages Calculations: Transatlantic Dialogue
Contemporary Studies in Economic and Financial Analysis, Volume 91, 135–158

ISSN: 1569-3759/doi:10.1108/S1569-3759(2009)0000091009

for some period during their lives." Tables were based on gender, age, initial labor force status (i.e., initially active in the labor force, inactive, and a blend of the two), and either educational attainment or race. Bulletin 2135, based on 1977 data, contained the BLS's first Markov work life table, but it also contained the most complete exposition of the conventional model, as well as some WLEs computed with the conventional model. The 1986 table in Bulletin 2254, based on 1979–1980 data, was the last BLS or other US government agency prepared WLE table; it contained only Markov process–generated tables. Others (primarily Ciecka, Donley, & Goldman, 2000; Skoog & Ciecka, 2001a, 2001b; Millimet, Nieswiadomy, Ryu, & Slottje, 2003; Krueger, 2004) have produced updated WLE tables with essentially the same method as pioneered by the BLS in its 1882 and 1986 bulletins.

A relatively small minority of forensic economists have used the *LPE model* of labor market activity. In this model, one multiplies L (probability of survival) by P (probability of participating in the labor force) and by E (probability of employment). The LP part of this model is, in effect, another alternative to the conventional model and the Markov model of work life. We discuss relations among the Markov, conventional, and LPE models in Section 2. Section 3 contains a discussion of the most recent Markov process–related work in the United States. Section 4 presents the theory and an example of an occupational-specific WLE table. Section 5 contains a brief comparison between US and UK work life–related research. We conclude with some ideas for future research in Section 6.

2. MARKOV, CONVENTIONAL, AND LPE MODELS

Transition probabilities comprise the primitive terms in a Markov process model. We let ${}^{m}p_x^n$ denote the probability that a person in state m at age x will be in state n at age $x+1$ where $m = \{a, i\}$ and $n = \{a, i, d\}$ and where a stands for active in the labor force, i for inactive, and d for the death state. We assume

$$\begin{aligned} {}^{a}p_x^a + {}^{a}p_x^i + {}^{a}p_x^d &= 1 \\ {}^{i}p_x^a + {}^{i}p_x^i + {}^{i}p_x^d &= 1 \end{aligned} \tag{1}$$

and that the transition to state d does not depend on being active or inactive, i.e., ${}^{a}p_x^d = {}^{i}p_x^d = {}^{\bullet}p_x^d$. Let ${}^{a}l_x$ and ${}^{i}l_x$ denote the number of actives and inactives at age x in a specific group (usually defined by gender, education, and initial labor force status). The magnitudes of ${}^{a}l_x$and ${}^{i}l_x$ correspond to the active and inactive portions of a population if we desire WLE regardless of initial state. If instead we desire work life for initial actives, let ${}^{a}l_x$ equal a radix value (usually taken to be 100,000) and set ${}^{i}l_x = 0$. Conversely, for work life for initial inactives, set ${}^{a}l_x = 0$ and ${}^{i}l_x = 100,000$. The Markov process model utilizes the recursions in

$$\begin{aligned} {}^{a}l_{x+1} &= {}^{a}p_x^{a\,a}l_x + {}^{i}p_x^{a\,i}l_x \\ {}^{i}l_{x+1} &= {}^{a}p_x^{i\,a}l_x + {}^{i}p_x^{i\,i}l_x \end{aligned} \tag{2}$$

If transitions occur uniformly throughout the year between age x and $x+1$, then

$$L_x^a = .5({}^{a}l_x + {}^{a}l_{x+1}) \tag{3}$$

captures person-years of activity between ages x and $x+1$. WLE without regard to initial labor force status at age x becomes

$$\bullet e_x^a = \sum_{j=x}^{\mathrm{TA}-1} \frac{L_j^a}{({}^{a}l_x + {}^{i}l_x)} \tag{4a}$$

where TA denotes the youngest age at which everyone in the population has died. Using ${}^{a}l_x = 100,000$ and ${}^{i}l_x = 0$ in Eq. (2), work life for initial actives is obtained as follows:

$${}^{a}e_x^a = \sum_{j=x}^{\mathrm{TA}-1} \frac{L_j^a}{{}^{a}l_x} \tag{4b}$$

Using ${}^{a}l_x = 0$ and ${}^{i}l_x = 100,000$ in Eq. (2), work life for initial inactives is obtained as follows:

$${}^{i}e_x^a = \sum_{j=x}^{\mathrm{TA}-1} \frac{L_j^a}{{}^{i}l_x} \tag{4c}$$

The Markov model places no restrictions of transition probabilities beyond being nonnegative and fulfilling Eq. (1). However, Skoog and Ciecka (2004b) have shown that both the conventional model and the LP part of the LPE model are in fact Markov models themselves but with additional restrictions imposed on transition probabilities. To see this, let l_x denote the number of people alive at age x, let $L_x = .5(l_x + l_{x+1})$ be the average number alive between ages x and $x+1$, and let pp_x denote the labor force participation rate at age x. Then the conventional model requires

$$\begin{aligned} {}^{a}p_{x}^{a} &= \left(\frac{L_{x+1}}{L_{x}}\right) \\ {}^{a}p_{x}^{i} &= 0 \\ {}^{i}p_{x}^{a} &= \left(\frac{L_{x+1}}{L_{x}}\right)\left(\frac{(pp_{x+1} - pp_{x})}{(1 - pp_{x})}\right) \\ {}^{i}p_{x}^{i} &= \left(\frac{L_{x+1}}{L_{x}}\right)\left(1 - \frac{(pp_{x+1} - pp_{x})}{(1 - pp_{x})}\right) \end{aligned} \tag{5a}$$

before the age of peak labor force participation, and it requires

$$\begin{aligned} {}^{a}p_{x}^{a} &= \left(\frac{L_{x+1}}{L_{x}}\right)\left(\frac{pp_{x+1}}{pp_{x}}\right) \\ {}^{a}p_{x}^{i} &= \left(\frac{L_{x+1}}{L_{x}}\right)\left(1 - \frac{pp_{x+1}}{pp_{x}}\right) \\ {}^{i}p_{x}^{a} &= 0 \\ {}^{i}p_{x}^{i} &= \left(\frac{L_{x+1}}{L_{x}}\right) \end{aligned} \tag{5b}$$

beyond the age of postpeak labor force participation.[1]

The LP part of the LPE model requires

$$\begin{aligned} {}^{a}p_{x}^{a} = {}^{i}p_{x}^{a} &= \left(\frac{L_{x+1}}{L_{x}}\right)pp_{x} \\ {}^{a}p_{x}^{i} = {}^{i}p_{x}^{i} &= \left(\frac{L_{x+1}}{L_{x}}\right)(1 - pp_{x}) \end{aligned} \tag{6}$$

These extremely restrictive assumptions make little sense. For example, the conventional model for men requires that nobody leaves the labor force for any reason other than death (i.e., ${}^{a}p_{x}^{i} = 0$) prior to peak labor force participation that occurs at about age 34, and it completely disallows labor force entry after the age of peak labor force participation (i.e., ${}^{i}p_{x}^{a} = 0$). The LPE model does not recognize that labor force status at age x tells us anything whatsoever about status at age $x + 1$ (i.e., ${}^{a}p_{x}^{a} = {}^{i}p_{x}^{a}$ and ${}^{a}p_{x}^{i} = {}^{i}p_{x}^{i}$). These severe restrictions are wrong on their face and certainly are disconfirmed by estimates of transition probabilities (see Krueger, 2004 for estimates of transition probabilities that show that these assumptions are wrong).

The BLS properly abandoned the conventional model in Bulletin 2135 in favor of the more general Markov model, here summarized by Eqs. (1)–(4c). This model, without the restrictive assumptions in Eqs. (5a) through (5c), dominates the conventional and the LPE models theoretically, empirically, and in use. Skoog and Ciecka (2004b) conclude that "... there is every reason to embrace the Markov model until it too is dominated by a superior model." In what follows, the term *Markov model* refers to the unrestricted version that is free of the assumptions in Eqs. (5a), (5b), and (6) even though the conventional model and the LPE model are, strictly speaking, Markov models themselves.

3. MARKOV WORK LIFE TABLE RESEARCH IN THE UNITED STATES

Prior to 2001, the primary object of Markov model work, as with the conventional model, was to produce a single expected value, WLE, given a person's gender, age, initial labor force status, and either education or race. Skoog and Ciecka (2001a, 2001b, 2002, 2003) were able to capture the Markov model's probabilistic implications by viewing years of activity (YA) and years to final labor force separation (YFS) as random variables. This allowed them to determine entire probability mass functions (pmf's) for YA and YFS and move beyond the study of expectations. To explain this approach, let $\mathrm{YA}_{x,m}$ denote the years-of-activity random variable with $p_{\mathrm{YA}}(x, m, y)$ being the probability that a person who is in state m at exact age x will accumulate $\mathrm{YA}_{x,m} = y$ years of labor force activity in the future. In a similar vein, let $\mathrm{YFS}_{x,m}$ denote the years-to-final-separation random variable where $p_{\mathrm{YFS}}(x, m, y)$ represents the probability that a person who is in state m at exact age x makes a final separation from the labor force in $\mathrm{YFS}_{x,m} = y$ years. YA and YFS differ in that the former only counts time in the labor force; the latter counts all time, including inactive time, prior to final departure from the labor force.

The YA and YFS probability mass functions with midperiod transitions for initial actives and inactives are specified below by the combination of global conditions, boundary conditions, and main recursions. With pmf's in hand, measurement of labor market activity was not limited to expected values (like WLE); other measures of central tendency such as properly computed medians (often used for final labor force separation in the case of YFS) and modes could be computed. Measures of dispersion and shape like the standard deviation, skewness, and kurtosis can be computed as well. In addition, probability intervals of various sizes can be calculated. The 50% probability interval may be of particular importance since it corresponds to the idea of accuracy to within a reasonable degree of economic certainty, a critical concept when providing expert testimony. In short, we know the entire probability distribution implied by the Markov model given gender, age, initial labor force status, and education. Skoog and Ciecka provided 24 tables for YA and another 24 tables for YFS characteristics – for six education groups for two initial labor force states for each gender. Tables 1 and 2, for initially active men with a high school diploma only, illustrate the most important characteristics captured by the pmf's.[2] A separate pmf underlies every row in Tables 1 and 2 and in all of 24 tables published by Skoog and Ciecka. As an illustration, Figs. 1 and 2 show pmf's for 30-year-old initially active men with high school diploma only. In Table 1, initially active 30-year-old men have a WLE of 28.26 years, and a median and mode of 28.90 and 30.50, respectively, with a distribution that is slightly skewed to the left (skewness coefficient of –.66) and a bit leptokurtic (kurtosis coefficient of 3.60). The standard deviation of YA is 8.36 years, implying a coefficient of variation of approximately .30. The smallest interval containing 50% of the probability is 26.50 years on the low side and 35.28 years on the high side, whereas the interquartile range is from 23.17 to 33.35 years. The interval which excludes 10% of the probability in each tail of the

Table 1. Skoog/Ciecka Years of Activity Characteristics for Initially Active Men with a High School Diploma Only.

Age	WLE						Minimal 50% PI					
	Mean	Median	Mode	SD	SK	KU	Low	High	25th%	75%	10%	90%
30	28.26	28.90	30.50	8.36	−0.66	3.60	26.50	35.28	23.17	33.35	16.49	37.27
31	27.40	28.01	29.50	8.25	−0.63	3.52	25.50	34.20	22.33	32.43	15.73	36.33
32	26.55	27.11	28.50	8.14	−0.60	3.45	24.50	33.13	21.50	31.50	15.00	35.39
33	25.71	26.22	27.50	8.02	−0.56	3.39	23.50	32.05	20.67	30.58	14.28	34.45
34	24.86	25.33	27.50	7.90	−0.53	3.32	23.03	31.50	19.84	29.66	13.57	33.51
35	24.02	24.45	26.50	7.78	−0.50	3.26	22.11	30.50	19.01	28.74	12.85	32.59
36	23.18	23.56	25.50	7.66	−0.46	3.20	21.21	29.50	18.20	27.82	12.15	31.66
37	22.35	22.67	24.50	7.53	−0.42	3.15	20.31	28.50	17.40	26.90	11.49	30.73
38	21.53	21.78	23.50	7.40	−0.39	3.10	19.41	27.50	16.61	25.99	10.82	29.80
39	20.71	20.90	22.50	7.26	−0.35	3.06	18.50	26.47	15.82	25.07	10.18	28.88
40	19.89	20.02	21.50	7.12	−0.31	3.02	17.64	25.50	15.04	24.16	9.57	27.95

Source: Skoog and Ciecka (2001b).

Table 2. Skoog/Ciecka Years to Final Separation Characteristics for Initially Active Men with a High School Diploma Only.

Age	YFSE						Minimal 50% PI					
	Mean	Median	Mode	SD	SK	KU	Low	High	25th%	75%	10%	90%
30	33.69	33.47	33.50	10.37	−0.42	3.70	28.50	38.94	28.09	39.54	20.00	45.95
31	32.76	32.49	32.50	10.27	−0.38	3.63	27.50	37.91	27.14	38.55	19.18	44.96
32	31.83	31.52	31.50	10.16	−0.34	3.57	26.50	36.87	26.19	37.57	18.37	43.97
33	30.91	30.54	30.50	10.05	−0.30	3.50	25.50	35.83	25.24	36.59	17.56	42.99
34	29.98	29.56	29.50	9.95	−0.26	3.44	24.50	34.80	24.30	35.61	16.76	42.00
35	29.06	28.59	28.50	9.84	−0.22	3.39	23.50	33.76	23.36	34.64	15.96	41.01
36	28.14	27.62	27.50	9.73	−0.18	3.33	22.50	32.71	22.42	33.66	15.17	40.03
37	27.23	26.64	26.50	9.62	−0.14	3.28	21.50	31.67	21.49	32.68	14.39	39.04
38	26.31	25.67	25.50	9.51	−0.09	3.24	20.50	30.62	20.55	31.71	13.61	38.06
39	25.40	24.71	24.50	9.40	−0.05	3.19	19.50	29.57	19.61	30.74	12.84	37.08
40	24.50	23.74	23.50	9.29	−0.01	3.15	18.50	28.52	18.67	29.76	12.08	36.10

Source: Skoog and Ciecka (2003), with permission from National Association Forensic Economics.

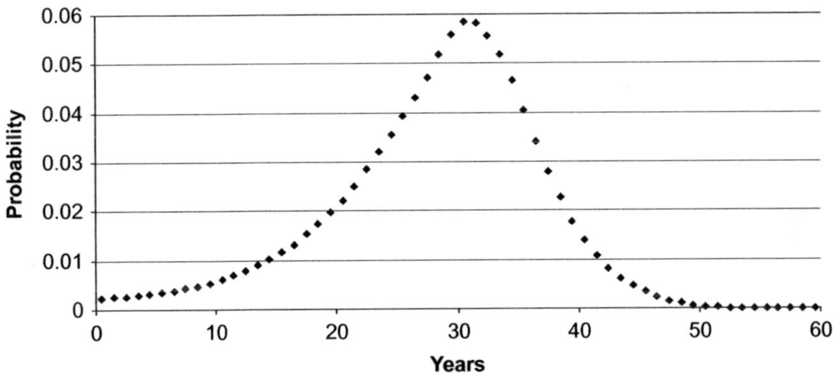

Fig. 1. PMF for Years of Activity for Initially Active 30-Year-Old Men with High School Diploma Only.

distribution ranges from 16.49 to 37.27 years. From Table 2, we know that initially active 30-year-old men with only a high school education have an average of 33.69 years until final separation from the labor force, approximately 5.4 years more than WLE. The remainder of the age-30 row gives the other characteristics of years to final separation as Table 1 does for years of labor force activity.

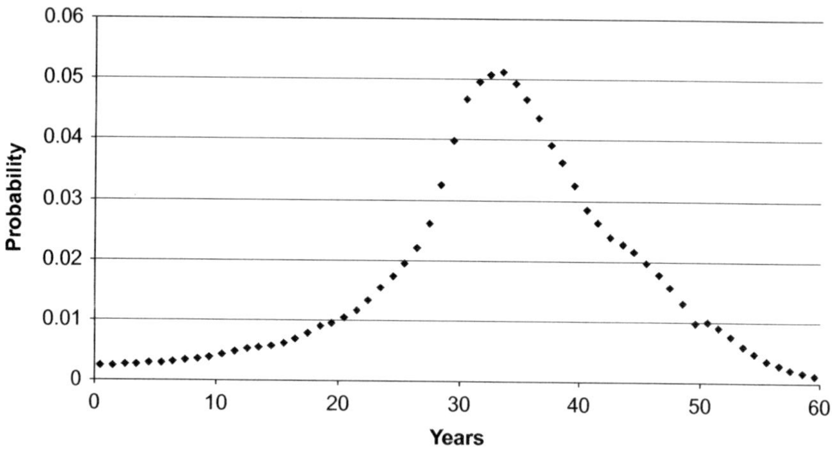

Fig. 2. PMF for Years to Final Labor Force Separation for Initially Active 30-Year-Old Men with High School Diploma Only.

Global Conditions for Random Variables RV∈{YA,YFS} with Midpoint Transitions

$$p_{\mathrm{RV}}(x,a,y) = p_{\mathrm{RV}}(x,i,y) = 0 \quad \text{if } y<0 \text{ or } y>\mathrm{TA}-x-.5$$

$$p_{\mathrm{RV}}(\mathrm{TA},a,0) = p_{\mathrm{RV}}(\mathrm{TA},i,0) = 1$$

$${}^{a}p_x^d = {}^{i}p_x^d = 1 \quad \text{for} \quad x \geq \mathrm{TA}-1$$

YA Probability Mass Functions for $\mathrm{YA}_{x,m} = y$ for $m \in \{a,i\}$ with Midpoint Transitions

Boundary Conditions

$$p_{\mathrm{YA}}(x,a,0) = 0$$

$$p_{\mathrm{YA}}(x,a,.5) = {}^{a}p_x^d + {}^{a}p_x^i p_{\mathrm{YA}}(x+1,i,0)$$

$$p_{\mathrm{YA}}(x,i,0) = {}^{i}p_x^{d} + {}^{i}p_x^{i}p_{\mathrm{YA}}(x+1,i,0)$$

for $x = \mathrm{BA},\ldots,\mathrm{TA}-1$

Main Recursions

$$p_{\mathrm{YA}}(x,a,y) = {}^{a}p_x^{a}p_{\mathrm{YA}}(x+1,a,y-1) + {}^{a}p_x^{i}p_{\mathrm{YA}}(x+1,i,y-.5),$$
$$y = 1.5, 2.5, 3.5, \ldots, \mathrm{TA}-x-.5$$

$$p_{\mathrm{YA}}(x,i,y) = {}^{i}p_x^{a}p_{\mathrm{YA}}(x+1,a,y-.5) + {}^{i}p_x^{i}p_{\mathrm{YA}}(x+1,i,y),$$
$$y = 1, 2, 3, \ldots, \mathrm{TA}-x-.5$$

for $x = \mathrm{BA},\ldots,\mathrm{TA}-1$

YFS Probability Mass Functions for $\mathrm{YFS}_{x,m} = y$ for $m \in \{a,i\}$ with Midpoint Transitions

Boundary Conditions

$$p_{\mathrm{YFS}}(x,a,y) = 0, \quad y = 0, 1, 2, 3, \ldots, \mathrm{TA}-1$$

$$p_{\mathrm{YFS}}(x,i,y) = 0, \quad y = .5, 1, 2, 3, \ldots, \mathrm{TA}-1$$

$$p_{\mathrm{YFS}}(x,a,.5) = {}^{a}p_x^{d} + {}^{a}p_x^{i}p_{\mathrm{YFS}}(x+1,i,0)$$

$$p_{\mathrm{YFS}}(x,i,0) = {}^{i}p_x^{d} + {}^{i}p_x^{i}p_{\mathrm{YFS}}(x+1,i,0)$$

for $x = \mathrm{BA},\ldots,\mathrm{TA}-1$

Main Recursions

$$p_{\mathrm{YFS}}(x,a,y) = {}^{a}p_x^{a}p_{\mathrm{YFS}}(x+1,a,y-1) + {}^{a}p_x^{i}p_{\mathrm{YFS}}(x+1,i,y-1)$$

$$p_{\mathrm{YFS}}(x,i,y) = {}^{i}p_x^{a}p_{\mathrm{YFS}}(x+1,a,y-1) + {}^{i}p_x^{i}p_{\mathrm{YFS}}(x+1,i,y-1)$$

for $x = \mathrm{BA},\ldots,\mathrm{TA}-1$ and $y = 1.5, 2.5, 3.5,\ldots, \mathrm{TA}-x-.5$

Skoog and Ciecka (2004b) also bootstrapped estimates of standard errors for WLE and other characteristics illustrated in Table 1. Bootstrapped standard errors refer to WLE expectancy itself and other YA characteristics due to sampling error, whereas the standard deviations illustrated in Table 1 refer to intrinsic variation in YA in the population itself. Bootstrap standard errors are much smaller than the standard deviations in Table 1. The former give us information about the accuracy of estimates of WLE (and other characteristics), whereas the latter refer to the range of years of labor market activity. Table 3, for all initially active men, illustrates bootstrapped standard errors. The bootstrap standard error for WLE is .20 years for initially active 30-year-old men in Table 3. That is, the sampling error is much smaller than the standard deviation of YA itself, which was found to be 8.36 years in Table 1.

Millimet, Nieswiadomy, Ryu, and Slottje (MNRS, 2003) use data from 1992 to 2000 to estimate WLEs using the BLS approach to a Markov process outlined above, and they also estimate parametric models of transition probabilities using logit functions. Referring to the BLS and logit approaches, they indicate that "[f]or both males and females the work life expectancies are extremely close … at all education and age levels." MNRS also estimate a multinomial logit function that they use to get work life estimates for those initially employed, unemployed, and inactive. They have two main conclusions: (1) for both men and women with less than a high school education, work life estimates for the unemployed are closer to work life estimates for inactives than for those employed and (2) as education increases, work life estimates for the unemployed approach work life estimates for employed people. Table 4 illustrates their work life tables for employed, unemployed, and inactive men.[3] The standard errors for WLE initially active men with only high school education are about the same size as the bootstrap standard errors reported by Skoog and Ciecka (see Table 3) but much smaller than the standard deviations of years of population activity in Table 1.

Krueger (2004) published WLEs by age, gender, labor force status, and education using 1998–2004 data. Table 5 illustrates some of Krueger's results.[4] Krueger's WLEs are quite close to those reported by Skoog and Ciecka (compare WLEs in Table 1 with the active column in Table 5). Krueger also provided counts of people in initial active and inactive states and the numbers that moved from one state to another by age, gender, and education. This information enables anyone to compute transition probabilities that are basic to a Markov process. Besides being current, Krueger, as other researchers, utilized the *Current Population Survey*, the

Table 3. Skoog/Ciecka Bootstrap Estimates of the Mean and Standard Deviation of Years of Activity Characteristics for Initially Active Men, Regardless of Education.

Age	Bootstrap Mean of WLE	Bootstrap SD of WLE	Bootstrap Mean of Median	Bootstrap SD of Median	Bootstrap Mean of Mode	Bootstrap SD of Mode
30	29.35	0.20	29.97	0.20	31.77	0.84
31	28.48	0.20	29.05	0.20	30.82	0.85
32	27.61	0.19	28.14	0.20	29.88	0.86
33	26.75	0.19	27.23	0.20	28.92	0.87
34	25.89	0.19	26.32	0.20	27.97	0.87
35	25.03	0.19	25.41	0.20	27.03	0.88
36	24.17	0.19	24.50	0.20	26.07	0.88
37	23.32	0.19	23.59	0.19	25.11	0.88
38	22.47	0.19	22.68	0.19	24.15	0.89
39	21.62	0.19	21.78	0.19	23.18	0.89
40	20.77	0.19	20.87	0.19	22.22	0.90

Age	Bootstrap Mean of SD	Bootstrap SD of SD	Bootstrap Mean of Skewness	Bootstrap SD of Skewness	Bootstrap Mean of Kurtosis	Bootstrap SD of Kurtosis
30	8.19	0.10	−0.81	0.04	4.02	0.10
31	8.08	0.10	−0.78	0.04	3.92	0.10
32	7.96	0.10	−0.74	0.04	3.83	0.10
33	7.84	0.10	−0.70	0.04	3.74	0.09
34	7.72	0.10	−0.66	0.04	3.65	0.09
35	7.59	0.10	−0.62	0.04	3.57	0.08
36	7.46	0.10	−0.58	0.04	3.49	0.08
37	7.33	0.10	−0.54	0.04	3.41	0.08
38	7.20	0.10	−0.49	0.04	3.34	0.07
39	7.07	0.10	−0.45	0.04	3.27	0.07
40	6.94	0.10	−0.40	0.04	3.20	0.07

Age	Bootstrap Mean of 25th%	Bootstrap SD of 25th Percentile	Bootstrap Mean of 75th%	Bootstrap SD of 75th Percentile	Bootstrap Mean of 10th%	Bootstrap SD of 10th Percentile	Bootstrap Mean of 90th%	Bootstrap SD of 90th Percentile
30	24.69	0.25	34.27	0.21	18.11	0.32	38.04	0.25
31	23.82	0.25	33.33	0.21	17.35	0.32	37.09	0.24
32	22.95	0.25	32.40	0.21	16.60	0.31	36.15	0.24
33	22.10	0.25	31.46	0.21	15.85	0.31	35.20	0.24
34	21.25	0.25	30.52	0.21	15.13	0.30	34.25	0.24
35	20.40	0.24	29.59	0.21	14.41	0.30	33.31	0.24
36	19.55	0.24	28.65	0.21	13.69	0.29	32.36	0.24
37	18.71	0.24	27.72	0.21	12.99	0.29	31.41	0.25
38	17.87	0.23	26.79	0.21	12.29	0.29	30.46	0.25
39	17.03	0.24	25.85	0.21	11.60	0.28	29.52	0.25
40	16.21	0.24	24.92	0.21	10.93	0.27	28.57	0.25

Source: Skoog and Ciecka (2004a), with permission from National Association of Forensic Economics.

Table 4. Millimet/Nieswiadomy/Ryu/Slottje Work Life Expectancies and Standard Errors for Initially Active Men with High School Diploma Only.

Age	WLE	Standard Error
30	29.477	.267
31	28.606	.266
32	27.735	.264
33	26.862	.263
34	25.989	.262
35	25.112	.261
36	24.240	.259
37	23.370	.258
38	22.504	.256
39	21.641	.254
40	20.782	.252

Source: Millimet, Nieswiadomy, Ryu, and Slottje (2003).

Table 5. Krueger's Work Life Expectancies for Initially Active, Inactive, and All Men with a High School Diploma Only.

Age	All	Inactive	Active
30	28.46	26.35	28.64
31	27.63	25.46	27.77
32	26.74	24.55	26.91
33	25.88	23.72	26.05
34	25.01	22.83	25.20
35	24.10	21.72	24.34
36	23.24	20.75	23.48
37	22.43	19.87	22.63
38	21.52	18.88	21.77
39	20.69	17.92	20.93
40	19.80	16.88	20.09

Source: Krueger (2004), with permission from National Association of Forensic Economics.

same data used by the BLS to compile labor statistics. Among other attributes, his dataset replicates US participation rates reported by the BLS, which gives users a high degree of confidence in his transition probabilities. Forensic economists can use Krueger's WLEs directly from his tables, but the transition probabilities themselves allow users to compute all of the individual terms in Eqs. (4a)–(4c). These terms, when summed, comprise

WLE. However, each individual term may be of interest when calculating the present value of lost earnings because successive individual terms are subject to greater discounting. For example, using Eq. (4b), individual terms are $L_x^a/{}^a l_x, L_{x+1}^a/{}^a l_x, \ldots, L_{\mathrm{TA}-1}^a/{}^a l_x$ with present values of $(L_x^a/{}^a l_x)(1+r)^{-.5}, (L_{x+1}^a/{}^a l_x)(1+r)^{-1.5}, \ldots, (L_{\mathrm{TA}-1}^a/{}^a l_x)(1+r)^{-(\mathrm{TA}-x-.5)}$ for lost earnings of one dollar at ages x, $x+1, \ldots$, TA–1 using r for the net discount rate and assuming midperiod receipt of earnings.[5] Krueger also announced his intention to make transition probabilities available on a rolling 10-year basis. His most currently available data covers the period 1998–2007.

Krueger, Skoog, and Ciecka (2006) calculated WLEs for full-time and part-time workers based on the Markov model. This research provides the first estimates of the percentage of work life spent in full-time activity and part-time activity. It also shows differences in work life for those initially in full-time activity and part-time work. The underlying Markov theory resembles Eqs. (1)–(4c). Using *ft*, *pt*, and *i* for full time, part time, and inactive, respectively, we have

$$\begin{aligned} {}^{ft}p_x^{ft} + {}^{ft}p_x^{pt} + {}^{ft}p_x^{i} + {}^{ft}p_x^{d} &= 1 \\ {}^{pt}p_x^{ft} + {}^{pt}p_x^{pt} + {}^{pt}p_x^{i} + {}^{pt}p_x^{d} &= 1 \\ {}^{i}p_x^{ft} + {}^{i}p_x^{pt} + {}^{i}p_x^{i} + {}^{i}p_x^{d} &= 1 \end{aligned} \tag{7}$$

The left superscript indicates beginning period status at age x, and the right superscript indicates the status at the end of the period. We assume that ${}^{ft}p_x^d = {}^{pt}p_x^d = {}^{i}p_x^d = {}^{\bullet}p_x^d$, i.e., the probability of dying is independent of labor force status. If one wishes WLE conditional upon an initial status, say full-time, set ${}^{ft}l_x$ to 100,000, and ${}^{pt}l_x = 0$ and ${}^{i}l_x = 0$ to start the recursions in Eq. (8) and calculate the number of persons in the statuses on the left-hand sides at age $x+1$:

$$\begin{aligned} {}^{ft}l_{x+1} &= {}^{ft}p_x^{ft}\,{}^{ft}l_x + {}^{pt}p_x^{ft}\,{}^{pt}l_x + {}^{i}p_x^{ft}\,{}^{i}l_x \\ {}^{pt}l_{x+1} &= {}^{ft}p_x^{pt}\,{}^{ft}l_x + {}^{pt}p_x^{pt}\,{}^{pt}l_x + {}^{i}p_x^{pt}\,{}^{i}l_x \\ {}^{i}l_{x+1} &= {}^{ft}p_x^{i}\,{}^{ft}l_x + {}^{pt}p_x^{i}\,{}^{pt}l_x + {}^{i}p_x^{i}\,{}^{i}l_x \end{aligned} \tag{8}$$

Define

$${}^{ft}L_x = .5({}^{ft}l_x + {}^{ft}l_{x+1}) \tag{9}$$

as the person-years spent in the full-time state, and calculate

$$ {}^{ft}e_x^{ft} = \sum_{j=x}^{j=\text{TA}-1} \frac{{}^{ft}L_j}{{}^{ft}l_x} \tag{10} $$

as the WLE of years in the full-time state (the upper right ft superscript) having started in the ft state (the upper left superscript) for a person exact age x.

To count time in the part-time state, but again starting in the full-time state, we compute

$$ {}^{pt}L_x = .5({}^{pt}l_x + {}^{pt}l_{x+1}) \tag{11} $$

as the person-years spent in the part-time activity. We calculate the WLE of part-time years, starting full time, as

$$ {}^{ft}e_x^{pt} = \sum_{j=x}^{j=\text{TA}-1} \frac{{}^{pt}L_j}{{}^{ft}l_x} \tag{12} $$

In this way, overall WLE from the full-time state is defined by the sum of the time in the active states, full-time and part-time, as

$$ {}^{ft}e_x^{a} \equiv {}^{ft}e_x^{ft} + {}^{ft}e_x^{pt} \tag{13} $$

Had we begun in the part-time state, we would have started Eq. (8) with ${}^{ft}l_x = 0$, ${}^{pt}l_x = 100,000$, and ${}^{i}l_x = 0$ and calculated ${}^{pt}e_x^{ft}$ and ${}^{pt}e_x^{pt}$. If inactivity had been the initial state, we would have assumed ${}^{ft}l_x = 0$, ${}^{pt}l_x = 0$, and ${}^{i}l_x = 100,000$ and calculated ${}^{i}e_x^{ft}$ and ${}^{i}e_x^{pt}$.

Table 6 illustrates some Krueger/Skoog/Ciecka results for part-time/full-time activity for males with high school diploma only. For example, consider 30-year-old males who are employed full time. The expected number of years in future part-time work is 2.12 years, and the expected time in full-time activity is 26.53 years. Total expected labor force time would be 28.65 years ($=2.12+26.53$), and approximately .93 ($=26.53/28.65$) of labor force activity would be in the full-time state (see the last column of Table 6).

In a recent paper, Skoog and Ciecka (2008) presented estimates of the mean and other distributional characteristics of the present value random variable evaluated at several net discount rates. This research contains the first tabulations of the mean, median, standard deviation, skewness, kurtosis, and probability intervals for present value functions at various

Table 6. Krueger/Skoog/Ciecka Full-time and Part-time Expectancies for Males with High School Diploma Only.

Age	Years of NILF				Years Part-time				Years Full-time				Years in the Labor Force				Portion Years Full-time			
	Beginning State				Beginning State				Beginning State				Beginning State				Beginning State			
	All	NILF	PT	FT	All	NILF	PT	FT	All	NILF	PT	FT	All	NILF	PT	FT	All	NILF	PT	FT
30	17.86	20.03	17.97	17.66	2.16	2.22	3.05	2.12	26.30	24.07	25.30	26.53	28.46	26.29	28.35	28.66	0.92	0.92	0.89	0.93
31	17.74	19.97	18.16	17.58	2.13	2.18	2.87	2.09	25.51	23.23	24.35	25.71	27.64	25.41	27.22	27.80	0.92	0.91	0.89	0.92
32	17.71	19.93	18.13	17.51	2.10	2.14	2.95	2.06	24.63	22.38	23.36	24.88	26.74	24.52	26.31	26.94	0.92	0.91	0.89	0.92
33	17.63	19.82	17.88	17.44	2.09	2.09	3.03	2.04	23.78	21.60	22.60	24.03	25.87	23.69	25.63	26.07	0.92	0.91	0.88	0.92
34	17.57	19.78	17.76	17.36	2.05	2.07	3.01	2.02	22.96	20.73	21.81	23.19	25.01	22.80	24.82	25.21	0.92	0.91	0.88	0.92
35	17.55	19.97	17.83	17.29	2.02	2.06	2.90	1.99	22.08	19.61	20.92	22.36	24.10	21.67	23.82	24.35	0.92	0.90	0.88	0.92
36	17.48	20.03	17.70	17.22	2.00	2.05	2.80	1.96	21.24	18.64	20.23	21.53	23.24	20.69	23.02	23.50	0.91	0.90	0.88	0.92
37	17.37	19.99	17.62	17.15	1.97	2.02	2.82	1.93	20.46	17.79	19.35	20.71	22.43	19.81	22.17	22.64	0.91	0.90	0.87	0.91
38	17.36	20.05	17.69	17.08	1.94	2.00	2.83	1.91	19.57	16.82	18.35	19.88	21.52	18.82	21.18	21.79	0.91	0.89	0.87	0.91
39	17.27	20.11	17.66	17.01	1.92	2.01	2.81	1.88	18.77	15.84	17.49	19.07	20.69	17.85	20.30	20.95	0.91	0.89	0.86	0.91
40	17.25	20.24	17.54	16.94	1.90	1.99	2.82	1.86	17.89	14.82	16.69	18.25	19.80	16.81	19.51	20.11	0.90	0.88	0.86	0.91

Note: NILF, not in labor force; FT, full time; PT, part time.
Source: Krueger, Skoog, and Ciecka (2006), with permission from National Association of Forensic Economics.

net discount rates. Table 7 shows these characteristics for 30-year-old men, regardless of education, at net discount rates of 0, .005, .01, .0125, .0150, .0175, .02, .025, .03, .035, and .04. The row with the net discount rate of zero gives WLE and the distributional characteristics of years of labor force activity for men age 30. The table shows negative skewness at all net discount rates, with the median exceeding the mean present value. Standard deviations vary inversely with discount rates, and probability intervals tighten (e.g., see the interquartile range) as net discount rates increase. The Ogden tables, discussed in Section 5, contain expected present values at the legally mandated rate of 2.5% in Great Britain. However, none of the distributional characteristics in Table 7 have been estimated for the present value random variable in any previous work in the United States or elsewhere.

4. OCCUPATION-SPECIFIC WORK LIVES

In most applications, forensic economists assume, implicitly or explicitly, that all future work life will be in the occupation used to determine the earnings base. While this is reasonable in many applications, we know that this would not be a good assumption for workers in some occupations. For example, professional baseball and football players do not continue in these occupations as would be suggested by the WLE table for the overall relevant population. While many such persons may continue in their sport in a related role, such as a coach, scout, or announcer, the time spent in competitive play is drastically shorter than the years dictated by one of the population work life tables, and competent forensic economists would adjust their estimates accordingly. However, there are less obvious situations, such as railroad workers (shorter work lives than average) and forensic economists (likely longer work lives than average). Because reliable occupation- or industry-specific data and technically trained economists, statisticians, demographers, or actuaries are needed to produce such tables on a case-by-case basis, there are relatively few such tables currently available.

Skoog and Ciecka (2006a) used multiple decrement theory, known as competing risks in biometrics, to estimate WLEs and other distributional characteristics of railroad workers. The Bureau of the Actuary of the US Railroad Retirement Board collects data for all US railroad workers. In this theory, transitions into railroad work are disallowed, but death, disability, retirement, or withdrawal (to another occupation or out of the labor

Table 7. Skoog/Ciecka Characteristics of Present Value Probability Mass Functions for Initially Active Men, Regardless of Education.

Age	Net Discount Rate	Expected Present Value	Median Present Value	Standard Deviation of Present Value	Skewness of Present Value	Kurtosis of Present Value	10th Percentile Present Value	25th Percentile Present Value	75th Percentile Present Value	90th Percentile Present Value
30	0.0000	30.00	31.50	8.08	−0.69	3.91	19.50	25.50	35.50	39.50
30	0.0050	27.54	28.44	7.07	−0.81	4.14	18.42	23.90	32.38	35.41
30	0.0100	25.37	26.31	6.22	−0.93	4.40	17.25	22.28	29.58	31.98
30	0.0125	24.38	25.39	5.85	−0.99	4.55	16.67	21.49	28.28	30.60
30	0.0150	23.45	24.48	5.50	−1.05	4.70	16.17	20.73	27.06	29.30
30	0.0175	22.58	23.57	5.19	−1.11	4.86	15.82	19.98	25.96	28.08
30	0.0200	21.75	22.69	4.89	−1.17	5.02	15.45	19.41	24.99	26.94
30	0.0250	20.23	21.08	4.38	−1.27	5.36	14.58	18.23	23.22	24.81
30	0.0300	18.88	19.68	3.93	−1.38	5.72	13.73	17.09	21.59	22.90
30	0.0350	17.66	18.50	3.55	−1.48	6.09	13.14	16.11	20.10	21.21
30	0.0400	16.57	17.35	3.22	−1.57	6.47	12.44	15.24	18.75	19.69

Note: Krueger's (2004) transition probabilities were used for all males until age 80 and active-to-active and inactive-to-active transition probabilities were gradually diminished to zero as age approached 111.
Source: Skoog and Ciecka (2008), with permission from National Association of Forensic Economics.

force) cause members to leave the occupation. They use the following notation:

x denotes exact age;

ω denotes the youngest age for which the probability of being active in the railroad industry is zero;

s denotes years of railroad service, here $s = 0, \ldots, x - 17$;

$q'^{(1)}_{x}$ denotes the mortality rate between age x and $x+1$ (this is the net rate of mortality),

$q^{(2)}_{x,s}$ denotes the probability of a railroad disability retirement between x and $x+1$ given s years of service;

$q^{(3)}_{x,s}$ denotes the probability of a railroad age retirement between x and $x+1$ given s years of service;

$q^{(4)}_{x,s}$ denotes the probability of withdrawal from railroad work between x and $x+1$ given s years of service;

$q^{(1)}_{x} = q'^{(1)}_{x}[1 - .5(q^{(2)}_{x,s} + q^{(3)}_{x,s} + q^{(4)}_{x,s})]$, $q^{(1)}_{x}$ denotes mortality probability;

$WLE^{CR}_{x,s}$ denotes competing risks railroad WLE for an individual at age x with s years of railroad service under the assumption of mortality, disability, age retirement, and withdrawal as the competing risks.

The probability that a railroad worker age x with s years of service in railroad work will remain in the railroad industry at age $x+1$ is

$$_{1}p_{x,s} = 1 - (q^{(1)}_{x} + q^{(2)}_{x,s} + q^{(3)}_{x,s} + q^{(4)}_{x,s}) \tag{14}$$

The probability of continuing as a railroad worker is defined recursively by

$$\begin{gathered} _{i+1}p_{x,s} = {}_{i}p_{x,s}[1 - (q^{(1)}_{x+i} + q^{(2)}_{x+i,s+i} + q^{(3)}_{x+i,s+i} + q^{(4)}_{x+i,s+i})] \\ \text{where} \quad i = 1, \ldots, \omega - x - 1 \quad \text{and} \quad {}_{\omega-x}p_{x,s} = 0 \end{gathered} \tag{15}$$

The pmf for future years of railroad work YA for a person age x with s service years in the competing risks (CR) model consists of the boundary condition and a main recursion in

$$\begin{gathered} \text{Boundary Condition: } p^{\text{CR}}_{\text{YA}}(x, s, .5) = 1 - {}_{1}p_{x,s} \\ \text{Main Recursion: } p^{\text{CR}}_{\text{YA}}(x, s, y) = {}_{y-.5}p_{x,s} - {}_{y+.5}p_{x,s} \\ y = 1.5, 2.5, \ldots, \omega - x - .5 \end{gathered} \tag{16}$$

Table 8 illustrates railroad WLEs and standard deviations (see the column entitled New CR Expectancy and the column immediately to its right) computed with Eqs. (14)–(16) for railroad workers ages 30, 35, and 40 with various years of service. The column in Table 8, entitled Old AAR-Type Expectancy, contains WLEs when withdrawals $q_{x,s}^{(4)}$ are excluded from Eqs. (14)–(16). This column resembles work previously published by the Association of American Railroads. One immediately notices the striking difference in work lives between the new and old estimates reflecting the importance of withdrawals from railroad work. Finally, the last two columns of Table 8 show Increment–Decrement model WLEs and standard deviations that reflect the special 30 year/age 60 retirement provisions enjoyed by railroad workers. This is a hybrid model that allows for entry and egress until age 60 but disallows reentry into railroad work after age 60.[6]

Skoog and Ciecka (2009) presented a paper that calculated work lives of position players in major league baseball. The model was the first to move beyond a first-order discrete state Markov model to a second-order model, allowing next year's state to depend on the states not only in this period but also in the previous period. The data problem is solved because information on the playing careers of baseball players is publicly available in the United States.

Table 8. Work Life Expectancies of Railroad Workers Utilizing Competing Risk (CR) Theory and the Increment–Decrement Model.

Age	Service Years	New CR Expectancy	Standard Deviation	Old AAR-Type Expectancy	ID Expectancy	Standard Deviation
30	0	14.21	12.03	27.05	28.81	6.58
30	5	18.51	11.34	26.62	26.71	5.52
30	10	20.20	10.74	26.20	26.71	5.52
35	0	13.68	11.46	24.92	24.49	6.53
35	5	16.55	9.26	22.31	24.04	5.92
35	10	17.72	8.67	21.87	22.24	5.04
35	15	18.43	8.22	21.45	22.24	5.04
40	0	12.18	9.81	20.84	20.35	6.10
40	5	15.52	8.82	20.31	20.06	6.10
40	10	14.83	6.89	17.66	19.61	5.45
40	15	15.13	6.60	17.21	17.80	4.53
40	20	15.21	6.57	16.84	17.80	4.53

Source: Skoog and Ciecka (2006a), with permission from National Association of Forensic Economics.

5. COMPARISON OF MARKOV WORK LIFE TABLE RESEARCH IN THE UNITED STATES AND UNITED KINGDOM

We take the paper by Butt, Haberman, Verrall, and Wass (BHVW, 2008), based on 1998–2003 data, to be the standard for Markov work life research in the United Kingdom. That paper is an important contribution to the literature and rightfully focuses on a Markov process model embedded in Ogden-type tables. When comparing their work with US research, the main differences occur in regard to the information embedded into WLE. In the United Kingdom, several variables are incorporated into WLE that usually are kept separate in the United States.

In the United States, WLE typically refers to time in the labor force, whether working or looking for work. BHVW use the term more restrictively to denote time spent working – time spent unemployed being excluded from WLE. Both constructs have merit. On the one hand, we recognize that earnings and fringe benefits flow from actual work time rather than time in unemployment, and losses due to personal injury and wrongful death should capture foregone earnings and benefits. Therefore, BHVW's usage seems appropriate in personal injury and wrongful death matters. On the other hand, the US concept of WLE has merit as well. Consider a person with a work and earnings history encompassing several years. The effects of unemployment on earnings will then be incorporated into that individual's earnings base (BHVW's multiplicand), and no additional adjustment for unemployment would be required or desirable for that person. When including only employed time in WLE, one must be careful to not double count the effects of unemployment: once in a plaintiff's base earnings and a second time embedded in WLE. To avoid double counting the effects of unemployment, the forensic economist may have to "gross up" the earnings base to a full-employment equivalent before applying a BHVW-type WLE (their multiplier) that already has been diminished by the probability of unemployment.

In BHVW's construct, WLE is a present value. It would be similar to computing the present value of each term in Eqs. (4a), (4b), or (4c) and then summing all terms. This is not commonly done in the United States where WLE consists of undiscounted labor force time. The US convention potentially creates a "front loading" problem and overestimates of lost earnings (Skoog & Ciecka, 2006b). This problem is avoided in BHVW's construct of work life that focuses on present value, the ultimate object of interest for compensation purposes. However, a specific net discount rate

(2.5%) is embedded in WLE as calculated by BHVW. If, for whatever reason, a forensic economist wanted to use another discount rate, the BHVW-type WLE would have to be recomputed.

BHVW report standard errors for their WLEs. This is important because it enables users to better judge accuracy and formulate ranges within which loss estimates should lie. Similar standard errors have been computed using the US notion of WLE. In addition, standard errors have also been computed for the median, mode, standard deviation, skewness, kurtosis, and various percentile points for the US version of WLE (Skoog & Ciecka, 2004b).

BHVW incorporate disability into their WLEs. In the United States, a vocational expert often presents courtroom testimony integrated with work of a forensic economist in personal injury matters. Vocational experts are replaced in the BHVM tables by average employment experience of disabled people in the UK database. However useful this might be if only a "rough and ready" multiplier is deemed sufficient, the use of such averages generally is avoided in the United States where vocational experts assess the plaintiff for type of work and ability to hold competitive employment, postaccident. They take into account the unique qualities of the injured party – the effects of his education, training, occupation, and transferable skills. Rather than determine that a large statistical group might retain some fraction of its former capacity when disabled, a more individual analysis is undertaken. In considering transferable skills and acknowledging that the vast heterogeneity in the disabled population gives little guidance for "disabled" individuals, it is concluded that, if the injured plaintiff can hold a job postaccident and absent specific medical evidence to the contrary, economic losses are likely to be reflected in lower earnings (multiplicand) in the postaccident job rather than in lowered WLE. For example, the employment experience of "disabled" coal miners from a particular musculoskeletal injury has virtually nothing to say about what the prospective employment experience would be for an injured plaintiff schoolteacher suffering an adult onset brachial plexus injury, who further has a duty to mitigate damages by working if possible. The illusion of precision in using disability data often adds noise rather than signal, and can in fact create damages where none exists. For example, by declaring a person disabled who is earning the same amount in the same job postaccident, a statistically irrelevant lowered work life spuriously assigns damages where none may exist.

Finally, UK work life research deals only with WLE (the mean of additional years of labor force activity) whereas work in the United States has dealt with probability distributions of YA and its characteristics, including WLE.

6. POSSIBLE FUTURE RESEARCH

Future WLE-related research will likely progress along several fronts.

(1) Tables will be updated. New tables probably will be based on Krueger's 1998–2008 transition probabilities.
(2) Updated tables will likely contain more refined educational groups. For example, those with a formal high school education may be separated from GED holders. New educational groups may include only those with PhDs and other more advanced educational attainments.
(3) Expected present values of active time, as well as other distributional characteristics of the present value random variable, may be computed for a range of net discount rates.
(4) More parametric functions may be estimated and used to calculate WLE and other labor force variables.
(5) New tables and/or parametric functions may include variables like race and the impact of both race and education.
(6) We may improve on the Markov model itself, which is a discrete state autoregressive process of order one, since transition probabilities depend on a person's current labor force state but not on the path of labor force states that led to that state. An autoregressive model of order two would incorporate information on a person's current state and previous state. So, for example, a person being active at age x–1 and active at age x may lead to a different transition probability of being in a certain state at age $x+1$ than for the case of a person who was inactive at age x–1 and active at age x.

NOTES

1. Monotonicity conditions also must be fulfilled in order to get sensible estimates of transition probabilities. In Eq. (5a), ${}^{i}p_x^a$ would be negative if $pp_{x+1} < pp_x$ for ages x and $x+1$ prior to peak labor force participation. Similarly, estimated ${}^{a}p_x^i$ would be negative in Eq. (5b) if $pp_{x+1} > pp_x$ for postpeak participation rates. Since probabilities cannot be negative, the model could not be used if estimated participation rates implied negative transition probabilities.

2. Only ages 30–40 are shown. Complete sets of tables begin at ages 16, 18, 22, and 26, depending on educational attainment, through age 75.

3. Depending on educational attainment, MNRS tables start at ages 16, 17, or 21 and end at age 85.

4. Krueger supplies 10 transit tables by gender and education that can be used to compute transition probabilities. He also gives WLEs by gender and education for initial actives, inactives, and without regard to initial status. Tables begin at ages 17, 18, or 20 depending on education and run through age 75.

5. See Skoog and Ciecka (2006b) for an alternative approach that computes the present value of lost earnings using WLE and then corrects for front loading by using a set of nomograms for net discount rates of .01, .02, .03, and .04.

6. See Skoog and Ciecka (1998, 2006c) for additional estimates of Old AAR-Type expectancies and Markov process expectancies for railroad workers.

REFERENCES

Butt, Z., Haberman, S., Verrall, R., & Wass, V. (2008). Calculating compensation for loss of future earnings: Estimating and using work life expectancy. *Journal of the Royal Statistical Society, Series A, 171*(4), 763–805.

Ciecka, J., Donley, T., & Goldman, J. (2000). A Markov Process Model of work-life expectancies based on labor market activity in 1997–98. *Journal of Legal Economics, 9*(3), 33–66.

Fullerton, H., Byrne, N., & James J. (1976). *Length of working life for men and women, 1970*. Special Labor Force Report 187. US Bureau of Labor Statistics.

Krueger, K. (2004). Tables of inter-year labor force status of the U.S. population (1998–2004) to operate the Markov Model of worklife expectancy. *Journal of Forensic Economics, 17*(3), 313–381.

Krueger, K., Skoog, G. R., & Ciecka, J. E. (2006). Worklife in a Markov Model with full-time and part-time activity. *Journal of Forensic Economics, 19*(1), 61–87.

Millimet, D. L., Nieswiadomy, M., Ryu, H., & Slottje, D. (2003). Estimating worklife expectancy: An econometric approach. *Journal of Econometrics, 113*, 83–113.

Skoog, G. R., & Ciecka, J. E. (1998). Worklife expectancies of railroad workers. *Journal of Forensic Economics, 11*(3), 237–252.

Skoog, G. R., & Ciecka, J. E. (2001a). The Markov (Increment–Decrement) Model of labor force activity: New results beyond worklife expectancies. *Journal of Legal Economics, 11*(1), 1–21.

Skoog, G. R., & Ciecka, J. E. (2001b). The Markov (Increment–Decrement) Model of labor force activity: Extended tables of central tendency, variation, and probability intervals. *Journal of Legal Economics, 11*(1), 23–87.

Skoog, G. R., & Ciecka, J. E. (2002). Probability mass functions for labor market activity induced by the Markov (Increment–Decrement) Model of labor force activity. *Economics Letters, 77*, 425–431.

Skoog, G. R., & Ciecka, J. E. (2003). Probability mass functions for years to final separation from the labor force induced by the Markov Model. *Journal of Forensic Economics, 16*(1), 49–84.

Skoog, G. R., & Ciecka, J. E. (2004a). Reconsidering and extending the conventional/demographic and *PLE* models: The *LPd* and *LPi* restricted Markov modes. *Journal of Forensic Economics, 17*(10), 47–94.

Skoog, G. R., & Ciecka, J. E. (2004b). Parameter uncertainty in the estimation of the Markov Model of labor force activity: Known error rates satisfying Daubert. *Litigation Economics Review*, *6*(2), 1–27.

Skoog, G. R., & Ciecka, J. E. (2006a). Worklife expectancy via competing risks/multiple decrement theory with an application to railroad workers. *Journal of Forensic Economics*, *19*(3), 243–260.

Skoog, G. R., & Ciecka, J. E. (2006b). Allocation of worklife expectancy and the analysis of front and uniform loading with nomograms. *Journal of Forensic Economics*, *19*(3), 261–296.

Skoog, G. R., & Ciecka, J. E. (2006c). Markov Model worklife expectancies and association of American railroads type worklife expectancies of railroad workers based on the *Twenty-Second Actuarial Valuation* of the US Railroad Retirement Board. *The Earnings Analyst*, *8*, 13–25.

Skoog, G.R., & Ciecka, J.E. (2008). Present value recursions and tables. Paper presented at Allied Social Sciences Association meetings, New Orleans.

Skoog, G.R., & Ciecka, J.E. (2009). An autoregressive model of order two of worklife expectancies and other labor force characteristics with an application to major league baseball. Paper presented at Allied Social Sciences Association meetings, San Francisco

US Bureau of Labor Statistics. (1982). *Tables of Working Life: The Increment–Decrement Model.* Bulletin 2135.

US Bureau of Labor Statistics. (1986). *Worklife Estimates: Effects of Race and Education.* Bulletin 2254.

PERIODICAL PAYMENTS AWARDS AND THE TRANSFER OF RISK

Richard Cropper and Victoria Wass

1. BACKGROUND AND INTRODUCTION

The traditional method of compensation for a future continuing loss in UK tort law has always been by means of a lump-sum payment.[1] The lump sum is calculated by means of a simple formula in which a net annual sum (the multiplicand) is multiplied by a factor (the multiplier) that takes into account early receipt by a rate of discount periodically set by the Lord Chancellor (at 2.5 percent since June 2001). The resulting sum provides a 'rough and ready' estimate of the capital sum that, if invested to achieve a real net rate of return of 2.5 percent, will fund the estimated annual loss over the expected period of that loss. The operation of this formula in the calculation of damages for loss of future earnings was demonstrated in previous chapters (4) and (5) of this volume.

Whilst a lump-sum payment offers a once-and-for-all payment, and a clean break is often attractive to both sides, it has long been recognised that this form of award is unsatisfactory in its ability to deliver on the restitution objective of damages. Future continuing losses and expenditures are experienced by the claimant as just that; continuing annual sums. The chances that the capital sum determined to produce these annual payments will be the correct one is very close to zero. Other than by chance, claimants do not die on the date predicted and investments do not deliver an ex post

Personal Injury and Wrongful Death Damages Calculations: Transatlantic Dialogue
Contemporary Studies in Economic and Financial Analysis, Volume 91, 159–191

ISSN: 1569-3759/doi:10.1108/S1569-3759(2009)0000091010

real net rate of return of exactly 2.5 percent. As Lord Scarman noted in the case of *Lim Po Choo* (1979)[2], 'There is really only one certainty: the future will prove the award to be either too high or too low'. If the party who bears the risk associated with these uncertainties is risk averse, such risks comprise a net cost ex ante. Under a lump-sum form of award, the burden of risk lies wholly with the claimant. This is both unjust and inefficient. On equitable grounds, it is the tortfeasor who ought to bear the risk. On efficiency grounds, it is likely that the tortfeasor is less risk averse than is the claimant and also better able to manage the risk – for example through access to reinsurance markets or pooling.

Twenty years ago an alternative form of award, the structured settlement, was imported from the United States as a means of converting a lump sum into a lifetime income stream (Lewis, 1994). The first structured settlement achieved judicial approval in 1989.[3] Despite the deficiencies of the lump-sum form of award and the added benefit that the income stream under a structured settlement was free of tax liability, structures were never widely used (Lewis, 1994; Lush, 2005). The reasons for the low take-up of structured settlements are explored later in this chapter. The issue of the low take-up of structures in the context of the unsatisfactory nature of the alternative (the lump sum) was raised by the House of Lords in *Wells v. Wells* (1999)[4] and this prompted a period of consultation.[5] The result of this consultation was an amendment to the Damages Act of 1996 (in the Courts Bill 2003), which was to come into law as the Court Act in April 2005.

This statutory amendment to the Damages Act of 1996 profoundly changed the way in which damages for a future loss are assessed and the discretion of the parties over the form of award. This new approach to settling claims has been described as 'the most fundamental change in 150 years in the quantification of bodily injury claims involving continuing loss' (London International Insurance and Re-Insurance Market Association, 2003). Its purpose was to increase the incidence of awards made by means of continuing periodical payments rather than as a lump sum in order to 'ensure that injured people receive compensation to which they are entitled for as long as it is needed without the worry of the award running out if they happen to live longer than expected' (Lord Chancellor's Department [LCD], 2002a).

To emphasise the break with the past, the terminology was changed from a structured settlement to a periodical payment. The approach to the method of assessment is reversed from the backward-looking, top-down focus on financial redress under the lump-sum method (and the old structured settlement) towards a bottom-up evaluation of provision for the claimant's ongoing future needs. Assessment of the annual sum is based on the needs of the claimant, and it is for the compensator to provide the necessary sum and to provide it with security for the future. This focus on meeting the future needs of the claimant is a clear departure from the conventional approach of seeking financial restoration (see Lewis, 2007). A second major departure concerns the priority given to the preferences of the parties and the court in deciding the form of award. Judicial discretion, while taking into account the needs of the claimant, now takes precedence over the preferences of the parties. In short, the judge has the power to impose on each or both of the parties damages in the form of periodical payments.

One issue which was left unresolved by the legislation, but which was raised in advance of it in the report of the Master of the Rolls' Working Party (2002), was the means by which the real value of the annual payments was to be maintained over time. Section 2 subsection (8) of the amended Damages Act 1996 identifies the Retail Price Index (RPI) as the default measure of indexation, but at subsection (9) the court was given the powers to 'disapply' the default or to 'modify' its effects where, according to the Explanatory Notes to the Courts Act (2003), 'circumstances make it appropriate to do so' (para. 354). The Government anticipated indexation according to the RPI was clearly set out by Baroness Scotland (of the LCD):

> We expect that, as now, periodical payments will be linked to the retail prices index in the great majority of cases. (House of Lords Official Report, 19 May 2003)

The circumstances for departure were not made explicit and were not thought to occur with any frequency:

> ... the court will depart from it only where the particular circumstances of the case make it appropriate. That position is parallel with that of the discount rate, which effectively incorporates the retail prices index in calculating the future loss element of lump-sums. (Baroness Scotland, House of Lords Official Report, 19 May 2003)

There have in fact been no cases involving a UK-based claimant where a departure from the discount rate, set either under *Wells* or by the Lord Chancellor, has been considered appropriate by the higher courts.[6]

Consequently, in April 2005 it seemed that, as with the majority of structured settlements before them, periodical payments were likely to be linked to the RPI. The vast majority of continuing future losses relates to earnings rather than the goods and services, and historically UK earnings inflation has exceeded price inflation (by an average difference of 2 percent per annum over the last 40 years). It was therefore unlikely that the application of the RPI as a means to up-rate periodical payments would accurately reflect the actual increase in the claimant's costs over time. The issue of indexation was clearly going to be of considerable importance to the uptake of periodical payments and, according to Lewis (2007), to the future of the tort system itself. Three years of litigation on this issue followed the legislation and culminated in a decision at the Court of Appeal in January 2008 that increases in care costs are primarily driven by the growth in the earnings of the carers and that a periodical payment in respect of future care costs would be more appropriately up-rated by a measure of occupational earnings than by the RPI.

This chapter outlines the evidence presented in court which provided the foundation for this policy reversal. Both authors were called to give evidence for the claimant, and it was the claimant's case which was to prevail. The chapter is organised as follows. Initially we examine the nature and incidence of risk under the lump-sum award. Dissatisfaction with the lump sum is driven by the undue burden of risk that is placed upon the claimant. We then consider the early annuity-based structured settlement in which two risks, uncertain investment returns and uncertain life expectancy, are transferred to a Life Office or a government department. This proved to be an unsatisfactory alternative and take-up was low. One of the two parties had to pay to avoid the risks and, given that such awards could only be achieved by consent, this invariably meant that the cost would fall on the claimant. In paying the premium to avoid the risk, the claimant would be left with insufficient funds to meet his/her lifetime needs. It is against this impasse that we examine the new form of periodical payment. This was intended to replace the old-style structured settlement and to be a viable and attractive alternative to the lump-sum award. The two key points of departure under this new form of award are that assessment of the annual sum is based upon the claimant's needs or losses and not upon annuity rates, and that it is the court, and not the parties, which ultimately determines the form of award. On the defendant side, the legislation provides for insurers to self-fund from reserves, subject to security of future payments, thus avoiding the need for the defendant to purchase an annuity. The one risk not addressed in the legislation is the indexation risk – the risk that the growth in the claimant's expenses or losses might increase at a rate above that of the annual payments. This issue was to become pivotal in determining the success or failure of periodical payments. It was settled in litigation that immediately followed the implementation of the legislation.

2. THE RISK TO THE CLAIMANT IN A LUMP-SUM AWARD

2.1. The Lump-Sum Award

The history behind the development of lump-sum damages has been adequately covered in many previous texts (see,e.g. *McGregor on Damages* in McGregor, 2007). It is the aim of any form of award of damages to provide for the claimant's anticipated annual needs (as a result of the negligence) for life and to provide a degree of flexibility in order to cope with any unforeseen changes to those needs. In the calculation of a conventional lump-sum award of damages, it is assumed that the claimant's needs are to be met out of the interest achieved upon the capital sum and the original capital itself, such that the capital sum is exhausted upon death.

This is only achieved with precision where (i) the claimant's life expectancy is correctly anticipated; (ii) the investment achieves a return of 2.5 percent per annum net of inflation, taxation and management charges and (iii) the claimant's losses or expenses increase in line with the net investment returns over time. Herein lies the disadvantage of the lump-sum form of award for the claimant. Life expectancy, investment returns and differential rates of inflation are all uncertain. The lump-sum form of award creates three major risks, that of investment, indexation and mortality. All of these are borne by the claimant. Each is considered in more detail below.

2.2. Investment Risk

In setting the discount rate at 2.5 percent, the Lord Chancellor considered it likely that the yield on index-linked gilts (the benchmark 'risk-free' asset) would rise in the future, and that, in reality, claimants would be advised to invest in 'a mixed-portfolio in which any investment risk would be managed so as to be very low'.[7] With any investment there is an element of risk – its value can move quite sharply over short periods of time, and can go down as well as up. Of course with investment risk comes investment opportunity, the opportunity to invest the damages in a manner to achieve more than a 2.5 percent real net return. Past performance indicates that equities will outperform other types of investment over the longer term. Whether or not a conventional lump sum will achieve this goal will depend on what the claimant is prepared to invest in and how these investments perform over time. As was recognised by the House of Lords in *Wells v. Wells*, the claimant is not in the position of the ordinary investor:

> The plaintiffs are not in the same happy position. They are not "ordinary investors" in the sense that they can wait for long-term recovery, remembering that it was not until 1989 that equity prices regained their old pre-1972 level in real terms. For they need the income, and a portion of their capital, every year to meet their current cost of care. A plaintiff who invested the whole of his award in equities in 1972 would have found that their real value had fallen by 41 percent in 1973 and by a further 62 percent in 1974. The real value of the income on his equities had also fallen.
>
> So it does not follow that a prudent investment for the ordinary investor is a prudent investment for the plaintiffs. Equities may well prove the best long-term investment. But their volatility over the short term creates a serious risk. This risk was well understood by the experts. Indeed Mr. Coonan conceded that if you are investing so as to meet a plaintiff's needs over a period of five years, or even 10 years, it would be foolish to invest in equities. But that concession, properly made as it was on the evidence, is fatal to the defendants' case. For as Mr. Purchas pointed out in reply, every long period starts with a short period. If there is a substantial fall in equities in the first five or 10 years, during which the plaintiff will have had to call on part of his capital to meet his needs, and will have had to realise that part of his capital in a depressed market, the depleted fund may never recover.

The opportunity of doing better with a conventional lump sum is often cited as an advantage of a conventional lump sum. It is the authors' experience that claimants feel little comfort when strong investment returns mean that they have done better than expected because future returns may not be as good. The problem for the claimant is that s/he cannot go without care when investment returns are poor. Over consumption of capital is the result. If the claimant never has the future certainty of return to allow her/him to benefit from a period of strong investment returns, such a period will benefit only the claimant's estate.

Taxation will also affect the net return on an investment. There are no taxation breaks given to investment returns derived from a conventional lump-sum award of damages in the United Kingdom.[8] From a taxation viewpoint, the Inland Revenue treats the award in the same way as a lottery win. The effects of taxation are uncertain and depend on factors which change for a given award over time, including taxation allowances, taxation bands and taxation rates, and between awards depending on the size of the award (the impact of taxation will be higher the larger the award) and the nature of the investment plan (income and capital gains are taxed in different way and at different levels).

2.3. Indexation Risk

The discount rate also assumes that the cost of meeting the claimant's future needs increases in line with the RPI.[9] The fact that most future losses are earnings based, and earnings have historically increased faster than prices, means that this is unlikely. The assumption that the growth in the RPI reflects the growth in the claimant's spending will be considered in greater detail later in this chapter; however, The Master of the Rolls' Working Party (2002) identified the issue in the following terms:

> A multiplier which is derived from assumptions as to investment performance … may be vulnerable to future movements in interest rates and [it] assumes that the cost of provision of services and the specialised needs that the seriously injured may require will rise in accordance with the RPI rather than the National Average Earnings Index, or at some other rate. (para. 15)

2.4. Mortality Risk[10]

What is the chance that, even with the benefit of the best medical and statistical expertise, the court will precisely calculate the date of death of the claimant? In the event that the claimant lives longer than the court's calculation, there will be under-compensation unless the performance of the investment has been sufficient to compensate. Whilst the over-compensation caused by premature death may well be an issue for the defendant, it is of no benefit to the claimant. Therefore, from the claimant's perspective, mortality risk is a no-win situation.

Calculating the probability of dying in any one year is not the easiest concept and, as each year has its own probability, the court would be faced with a fairly large array of numbers that would, on their own, mean little. Therefore, these concepts and figures are summarised into one number – the future life expectancy, which is defined as the average expected future lifetime for an individual. This life expectancy is determined by considering standard probabilities of dying, derived from population life tables, which in turn are derived from national census data. The improbability of living to one's average life expectancy can be illustrated by considering a simple example. The life expectancy of a 40-year-old female, according to UK population data, is 47 years; however, the probability that a 40-year-old female will die at the exact age of 87 is just 3 percent.

The population life table includes estimates of the future, which are by nature uncertain. Past experience that has been observed between the last two censuses is used as a guide to the future. But it is only a guide. Two adjustments are made. First, as time progresses the tables become more out of date. Therefore, between censuses, interim life tables are derived based on expected changes since the last census was analysed. Secondly, and this is UK practice and not, the authors understand, US practice, assumptions may be made about improvements in mortality experience into the future.[11] It has been observed that people are living longer, and it is felt in the United Kingdom that it would be unwise not to plan for that trend to continue. The UK tables assume, for example that if a 30-year-old female survives 10 years into the future then her life expectancy at that time, when she will be 40 years old, will not be 47 but 48 years. However sophisticated the estimation procedure, the estimate is very likely to be wrong.

There are further uncertainties to consider in the case of an impaired life expectancy. Assume that the court has decided that the 40-year-old female does not have a normal life expectancy (of 47 years) but that her life expectancy has been reduced to 25 years. Two possibilities arise immediately. In the first, we assume that she will certainly live for 25 years and no longer. If this assumption is adopted, multipliers are available where a loss is to be paid for a certain term. This would give rise to a lifetime multiplier of 18.65 using the normal discount rate of 2.5 percent. This is unsupportable in an actuarial sense. However, since it is easy, convenient and well understood by the courts, it is the method most often used. It does lead to some problems of interpretation when losses for a limited period (say loss of earnings) are required.

An alternative approach is to look at the mortality tables and note that a 62-year-old female has a life expectancy of 25 years, assume that the claimant will experience the mortality of a 62-year old and use the multipliers appropriate for such a person. The lifetime multiplier would then be 17.98. This is more supportable actuarially, but is perhaps less easy to understand and certainly less easy to use when losses for a limited period are assessed. In this case, and assuming that the claimant would have retired in 20 years time at the age of 60, we will need a multiplier for loss of earnings for a 62-year old retiring in 20 years time at the age of 82.[12]

Method 1 gives a multiplier for a lifetime loss greater than that for method 2. This will be true for all ages and both sexes. Method 2 may or may not be more 'correct'. That will depend on whether the mortality experience of the claimant is more or less similar to that of a standard 62-year old.

If the courts restrict themselves to one of these two options, sharing the advantage that they are based on published tables of multipliers, then they are constrained by the format of the tables. Alternatively, it is possible to construct a customised mortality table for the claimant using further alternative means. Whilst this gives the court flexibility and greater scope to take into account of the opinions of the expert witnesses, it clearly leads to greater argument on appropriateness and subjectivity. It is important to remember that all of these options are likely to give rise to a different lifetime multiplier, and only hindsight will reveal which, if any, was even close to being right.

2.5. Summary of Risks

The lump-sum award creates three risks, each of which falls squarely on the shoulders of the claimant. As evidenced by the report of The Master of the Rolls' Working Party (2002), it is the inherent nature of these risks, together with the magnitude of the potential inaccuracy of the award, which lie at the heart of the judiciary's dissatisfaction with the lump sum as a form of award to meet continuing losses.

> The one thing which is certain about a once and for all lump-sum award in respect of future loss is that it will inevitably either over-compensate or under-compensate. This will happen particularly where the claimant survives beyond the life expectancy estimated at the time of trial, or alternatively dies earlier. It will frequently be the case in practice that there is over-compensation in six figure sums, or, correspondingly, that a combination of increased life expectancy, the cost of care, and (it may be) the cost of new but necessary medical treatments is such that the sum needed exceeds anything that might have been awarded at the date of trial. (para. 12)

and

> … of the features we have identified that of accuracy is the most important. We are concerned that a consequence of a system of once and for all lump-sum awards is that there will be under- or over-compensation (in some cases considerable) and particularly concerned that a proportion of claimants whose life expectancy is uncertain, and who need significant continuing care, might be left with significant uncompensated need. It adds to our concern that this is likely to occur later in life when the consequences will be particularly hard to manage. It is also of concern that appreciation of this may give rise to excessive prudence and under expenditure in earlier years. (para. 21)

We are reminded in Lewis (2007) that it is the claimant who bears the burden of uncertainty: 'The enormous responsibility for safeguarding the future that it imposes upon a claimant makes it a very worrying means of obtaining compensation'. The Master of the Rolls' Working Party (2002) concludes that 'we prefer a system that is better able to meet future needs as and when they arise' (at para. 21). In the next section, we consider the extent to which an annual settlement structured out of a lump sum fulfils this objective.

3. THE STRUCTURED SETTLEMENT

Although it had always been open for the parties to agree that a claim be met by way of periodical payments,[13] structured settlements, as we know them today, can be traced back to 14 July 1989 and the case of *Kelly v. Dawes*.[14] At that time, structured settlements were simply 'life-impaired purchase life annuities' that were purchased by a defendant to reinsure against obligations made to a claimant as set out in an agreement. The agreement allowed for payment of the damages as a combination of a lump sum and a stream of tax-free payments that were guaranteed for the lifetime of the claimant. For reasons clearly set out in the case of *Burke v. Tower Hamlets Health Authority*,[15] this arrangement could only be implemented with the agreement of both parties.

Prior to the Finance Act 1995, damages received under a structured settlement relied on common law for exemption from tax (*Dott v. Brown*).[16] The Finance Act 1995 provided a statutory exemption from income tax to income from a structured settlement. A year later, further legislative refinements allowed the defendant to purchase a structured settlement annuity on behalf of the claimant and for the provider of the structured settlement annuity to be able to make payments gross and direct to the claimant.[17]

In the same year, the Damages Act 1996 gave enhanced (100 percent) protection to the claimant with a structured settlement annuity in the event of the insolvency of the provider and broadened to all public sector bodies the provisions first contained in the National Health Service (NHS) (Residual Liabilities) Act 1996,[18] allowing the same level of protection to self-funded structured settlements. This meant that governmental bodies could self-fund structured settlements rather than having to purchase or provide an annuity in order to benefit from the 100 percent protection.

Despite all this facilitating and encouraging legislation, and the gross deficiencies in the only alternative, the lump sum, the early-style structured settlement failed to establish itself as an alternative form of award in the United Kingdom. The court had no power to impose a structured settlement, and it was rarely in the interests of both parties to consent to one. In order to obtain the consent of the defendant, the cost of the structured settlement (to the defendant) had to be less, or at least no greater, than the cost of the claim on a conventional lump-sum basis. This would only apply if the Life Office were to take a much more pessimistic view of the claimant's life expectancy than the court or the claimant was willing to carry the additional cost of the periodical payments. The first scenario was relatively rare. In terms of the second, the cost to the claimant of transferring the mortality and investment risks to an insurer is a heavy one. This is illustrated in Table 1 of multipliers implied by quotations from four Life Offices in the structured settlement market in September 2003.[19] Where the structured settlement was to be self-funded, for example where the defendant was a department of the government, it would often only offer to match the terms available in the market.

A claimant aged 30 at the time of settlement, who has no loss of life expectancy, makes a claim based upon a conventional multiplier of 28.22.[20] The conventional claim assumes a real net return of 2.5 percent per annum for life. Therefore, assuming an annual loss of £10,000.00 per annum, the claimant is entitled to a conventional lump sum of £282,200.00. If the same claimant wants periodical payments of £10,000.00 per annum, tax free, RPI linked and guaranteed for life, the cost from the cheapest provider in the market at that time, Windsor Life, would be £341,300.00. The cost from Scottish Widows would be £463,000.00. For the cost of the settlement to be no greater, the claimant would have to accept a lower level of income. From Windsor Life s/he would get £8,268.39 per annum instead of £10,000.00 per annum, and from Scottish Widows s/he would get £6,095.03 per annum.

Under this top-down approach, in which an annual settlement is structured out of a conventionally determined lump sum, the claimant pays a very high price for transferring the mortality and investment risk to the

Table 1. Structured Settlement Equivalent Conventional Multipliers[a].

Male Aged …	Full Life Conventional Multiplier	Windsor Life Equivalent Conventional Multiplier	NFU Mutual Equivalent Conventional Multiplier	Standard Life Equivalent Conventional Multiplier	Scottish Widows Equivalent Conventional Multiplier
20	30.74	37.49	38.14	62.31	52.63
25	29.56	35.98	36.04	57.45	49.50
30	28.22	34.13	33.78	52.60	46.30
35	26.68	32.00	31.33	47.65	42.74
40	24.93	29.63	28.71	42.63	39.22

[a]PFP Limited, figures provided by the named Life Offices.

Life Office. The vast majority of claimants simply could not afford to forgo so much of their annual payment in order to buy the certainty of receiving it. Already reduced annual payments would be further eroded over time since most structured settlement were RPI linked which, as we will explore below, would not have been sufficient to maintain the real value of earning-based expenditures.[21]

This fundamental shortcoming of a structured settlement is aptly summarised by the parents of a claimant who required life-long care, as quoted in *The Times* (24 February 2001):

> Anxious to ensure that the compensation would provide specialist care and support for Sarah throughout her lifetime, the Manns first investigated structured settlements, designed for such cases. Based around an index-linked annuity, these settlements provide a guaranteed income for life, and significant tax advantages. But although they offer peace of mind, plummeting annuity rates – down by about 40 percent in the past three years – mean that they are providing poor returns.
>
> . . .
>
> As Mr. Mann says: "As soon as anything happens to me and my wife, it's going to cost Sarah a lot of money. The income generated by a structured settlement would not cover that – full stop".
>
> . . .
>
> It has left the family to bear an awful burden of uncertainty. Already in their late 50s, Mr. and Mrs. Mann are particularly concerned about the financial difficulties Sarah could face after their deaths. Mr. Mann says: "We're always very, very aware that it's not our money that we're investing, it's Sarah's money. It does put a great strain on you." He adds: "If a structured settlement were viable, we'd go for that every time because it's safe, and you haven't got the risk. It would be a damn sight easier on the whole family because there's a guaranteed income that we could rely on for ever." To try to compensate, the couple are tightening the purse strings while they can look after their daughter.[22]

4. PERIODICAL PAYMENTS: A NEW FORM OF AWARD

Under the structured settlement approach, the courts had no power to impose, and it was rarely in the interest of both parties to agree to one. Consequently they were rarely used. The impetus for change at governmental level was first recorded in the Lord Chancellor's Department (LCD) Consultation Paper (2000). This was followed up with the second LCD

Consultation Paper in 2002a. This latter invited comments/responses from interested parties. Responses were invited by June 2002, and a summary/analysis thereof was published in LCD (2002b) in November.

The title of the second report was a clear indication as to where government policy was aimed. As Baroness Scotland said at the time:

> I consider there is a need to move towards a culture where periodical payments are seen as a natural way of paying personal injury damages for significant future financial loss. While either party can insist on a lump-sum, that culture will not develop. Our proposals will encourage the use of periodical payments in appropriate cases and should help to ensure that injured people receive the compensation to which they are entitled for as long as it is needed.[23]

The third report (LCD, 2002b) revealed that the majority of respondents to the consultation paper (which included a mix of insurers, legal and medical practitioners and public bodies) agreed with the government that the courts should have the power to order periodical payments without consent.

This groundswell of support for the periodical payment form of award was also in evidence in the conclusions of Department of Constitutional Affairs (DCA) (2002), also produced in November. In addition to addressing the concerns of the judiciary over the unfair and inefficient incidence of risk, the report reveals the potential financial benefits to the exchequer arising from cash flow benefits to the NHS and other public sector departments. Both Lewis (2007) and Bevan, Huckle, and Ellis (2007) identify this latter as underpinning the government's interest in and commitment to the reform of the lump-sum award.

> The NHS would achieve a significant improvement in its cash flow situation … .
>
> Significant real economic benefits would arise from a transfer of the risk of providing the compensation from individual investment portfolios to the State. Individual risk-averse injured people would achieve a lower real rate of return on lump-sum investment than the 3.5% Treasury Discount Rate that the NHS uses to evaluate the real cost of periodical payments. (DCA, 2002, para. 51)

4.1. The Benefits to the NHS

The anticipated benefits to the NHS relied upon the method used to calculate the relative costs of alternative forms of award. This calculation is known as the value for money report (VFM). The precise terms and assumptions adopted in the VFM report are closely guarded, but the overall outcome of the NHS's policy in respect of periodical payments was summarised in the cases of *YM v. Gloucestershire Hospitals NHS Foundation Trust and Secretary of State for Health* (2006)[24] and *Kanu v. King's College Hospital Trust and Secretary of State for Health* (2006),[25] where Mr Justice Forbes stated:

> In paragraphs 12 to 14 of his witness statement, Mr. Walker [Chief Executive of the NHS Litigation Authority] gave a short history of periodical payments in claims involving the NHS and pointed out that the NHSLA has always encouraged and supported the resolution of cases through "*self funded annual/periodic payments.*" As Mr Walker observed, the benefit to the Department of Health and the NHS of such arrangements is "*the cash flow value of retaining the lump-sum and replacing it with an annual stream of payments into the future.*" It is also the NHSLA's view that this method can offer the most sensible and positive way of resolving claims from the perspective of the injured individual for the term of his or her life. (para. 20)

4.2. Security of Payments

Section 2(3) of the Damages Act 1996 sets out that the courts can only make a periodical payments order in cases where it is satisfied that the continuity of the payments is 'reasonably secure'. Reasonable security is defined under Section 2(4) of the Damages Act, as set out below:

> For the purpose of subsection (3) the continuity of payment under an order is reasonably secure if (a) it is protected by a guarantee given under section 6 of the Schedule to this Act; (b) it is protected by a scheme under section 213 of the Financial Services and Markets Act 2000 (compensation) (whether or not as modified by section 4 of this Act); or (c) the source of payment is a government or health service body.

In essence, in the event that the defendant was to cease to exist, the periodical payments will be met in full by a statutory body. Whilst the legislation does not cover every defendant in every case, the vast majority of cases are covered into the future.[26] This means that most insurers could now self-fund periodical payments in the same way as the governmental bodies had done for some period of time.

What significantly separates the governmental departments from insurers in respect of self-funding periodical payments is that, unlike insurers, governmental departments are not required to hold a financial reserve for the liability. Whilst the accounts of the government departments do show a liability, no corresponding assets are held to match it (as future expenditure will be met out of future tax revenues). Insurers on the other hand are required by the Financial Services Authority to hold adequate reserves in order to meet the liability to a third party under the original contract of insurance.

In the event that the defendant is not covered under Section 2(4), the only available means of providing automatically reasonably secure periodical payment is by way of an annuity issued by a Life Office in the United Kingdom who is covered by the Financial Services Compensation Scheme.[27]

5. PERIODICAL PAYMENTS: A NEW BEGINNING OR ANOTHER DEAD DUCK?

Since the implementation of the Courts Act 2003 on 1 April 2005, the courts have had the power to make periodical payments orders for damages for 'future pecuniary loss' in personal injury cases pursuant to section 2(1) of the Damages Act 1996.[28] In every suitable case since 1 April 2005, the courts have been directed that they 'shall consider whether to make' a periodical payments order by section 2(1)(b) of the Damages Act 1996. Within three weeks of the courts being given the power to impose periodical payments on either or both parties, Mitting J. did so at trial where both parties had indicated that they preferred a conventional lump-sum settlement.[29] In accordance with what appeared to be the intention of the Act, the court ordered that these periodical payments were to be linked to the RPI.

It was thus clear that the courts were prepared to use their new-found 'revolutionary' powers. However, it was not clear that such a form of award was in the claimant's best interest if the measure used to up-rate the periodical payments (the RPI) was almost certain to escalate at a rate that would mean that the earnings-based need would not be met in full over time. The inevitable shortfall in the annual payment was recognised by the court in a subsequent case in which the trial judge refused to impose an award by means of an RPI-linked periodical payment:

> ... while the provision of periodical payments would provide a measure of security to the Claimant in this case, there is a high degree of likelihood that if they are calculated by reference to RPI they will not meet the actual cost of care and that the shortfall would be very substantial. (*A v. B Health Authority* (2006). (para. 24)[30]

Moreover

> It is also significant that the shortfall in the ability of periodical payments to meet actual care costs would be apparent from the first anniversary of the award. Even if RPI and the rate of increase of actual care rates were to converge in future, because periodical payments would be assessed by applying RPI to the payment in the preceding period, the

> shortfall in periodical payments would come entrenched and would continue notwithstanding the fact that RPI and the actual rates of increase in care costs had come into line. (para. 23)

This decision clearly identifies the incompatibility between the principle of full and adequate compensation (the 100 percent principle) on the one hand and RPI-linked annual payments to meet an earnings-based expenditure on the other. The court in this case clearly felt bound by the 100 percent principle.

In neither of the cases above did the court hear evidence on the issue of indexation, since both claimants had sought a lump sum. The issue of indexation in relation to care costs was brought before the courts for the first time in the case of *Flora v. Wakom (Heathrow) Ltd* (2005).[31] This proved to be a critical case, even though the evidence on indexation was never heard. The defendant, and its insurer, attempted to strike out an attempt by the claimant to produce evidence in respect of indexation. The defendant relied upon the words of the government ministers when debating this issue in parliament (see Baroness Scotland, House of Lords, 19 May 2003) and on the decisions in two cases in which differential inflation rates, between care costs and the RPI, had been raised as an issue for the court to consider. These two cases, *Warriner v. Warriner* (2002)[32] and *Cooke v. Bristol United Health Care Trust* (2004),[33] in different ways sought to persuade the courts to apply a lower discount rate (and a higher multiplier) in the determination of a lump sum for future care to account for differential rates of inflation. The Court of Appeal found against both claimants and, in settling the rate of discount at 2.5 percent, also settled the concept of RPI inflation as the universal measure in the determination of a lump-sum award.

However, in the case of *Flora*, the court at first instance, and subsequently the Court of Appeal, found in favour of admitting evidence in relation to relative inflation rates. The judgment of Lord Justice Brooke firmly rejects the relevance of the *Warriner* and *Cooke* decisions (both lump-sum awards) on the basis that periodical payments represent a new and distinctive form of award:

> This brief summary of the recent history of the discount rate used for the purpose of calculating lump-sum awards for future pecuniary loss is sufficient to show that an award of a lump-sum is entirely different in character from an award of periodical payments as a mechanism for compensating for such loss .... (para. 27)[34]

> The fact that these two quite different mechanisms now sit side by side in the same Act of Parliament does not in my judgment mean that the problems that infected the operation of the one should be allowed to infect the operation of the other. (para. 28)[35]

As in the decision in *A v. B Health Authority* above, the incompatibility between the 100 percent principle and under-indexation is resolved in favour of the 100 percent principle.

> There is nothing in the statute to indicate that in implementing s 2 of the 1996 Act (as substituted) Parliament intended the courts to depart from what Lord Steyn described in *Wells v Wells* at pp 382H-383B as the "100% principle," namely that a victim of a tort was entitled to be compensated as nearly as possible in full for all pecuniary losses. (see also paras. 18–19)
>
> For this reason I reject the argument that in enacting s 2(8) and 2(9) of the 1996 Act Parliament must be taken to have intended to provide compensation lower than that which would be awarded through adherence to the 100% principle if a periodical payments order was to be made. (para. 28)[36]

The Court of Appeal predicted that, as we were now dealing with a different statutory provision:

> ... it is likely that there will be a number of trials at which the expert evidence on each side can be thoroughly tested. A group of appeals will then be brought to this court to enable it to give definitive guidance in the light of the findings of fact made by a number of trial judges. The armies of experts will then be able to strike their tents and return to the offices or academic groves from which they came. (para. 33)[37]

This is indeed what transpired, and the following section describes in outline some of the evidences presented for the claimants in four trials which were to form the basket of cases subsequently heard in the Court of Appeal.[38] The resolution of the indexation issue in these cases would determine the viability of periodical payments as a new form of award.

6. THE INDEXATION OF CARE COSTS

The argument over indexation had care costs as its exclusive focus. It was this element of the claim that was the subject of the appeal in each of the four cases. In each case, the claimant was catastrophically damaged, unable to manage his or her own financial affairs and had long but uncertain life expectancies. In each case, the other major future loss, the earnings element of the claim, was capitalised in order to purchase adapted accommodation.

6.1. Care Cost Inflation in a Lump-Sum Award

We have seen that, in the context of a lump-sum payment, the concept of inflation is incorporated in the setting of a discount rate to reflect the real rate of return arising from the investment of the capital sum, that is the rate of return net of price inflation as measured by the RPI. The cost of a care plan comprises very largely the earnings of the people who provide the care. For the United Kingdom, earnings, including those of carers, have historically increased faster than have prices, and by a significant margin (see Table 3 below). That the RPI is therefore likely to be an inadequate means of inflation proofing the claimant's ongoing care costs was first brought before the courts in the context of a lump sum in the cases of *Warriner* and *Cooke*. The Court of Appeal found against both claimants, and in settling the rate of discount at 2.5 percent also settled the concept of RPI linkage, at least in the determination of a lump sum. However, in the context of a periodical payment, in return for certainty over annual payments, the opportunity to achieve a rate of return to meet an above-RPI inflation rate is not available. It is in this sense that 'an award of a lump sum is entirely different in character from an award of periodical payments as a mechanism for compensating for such loss' (*Flora v. Wakom*).

The arguments for and against indexation according to the RPI were rehearsed in the legal press as the legislation was enacted. Hogg (2004) demonstrated that historically aggregate earnings (as measured by the New Earnings Survey, NES), care costs (as measured by NHS Pay Cost Index (PCI)) and carers' earnings (as measured by British Nursing Association (BNA) rates of pay for carers) have all increased faster than have prices. Norris (2005), in a reply to Hogg (2004), raised a number of objections to indexation to anything other than the RPI including the absence of an alternative reliable series, the unwieldy prospect of identifying and applying an individually matched series to each of the different heads of damages and also the potentially considerable cost to society of higher awards for damages (what later came to be known as the distributive justice argument).

6.2. The Case Against the RPI

Since care costs primarily comprise the earnings of carers, and because historically earnings inflation has exceeded price inflation, a periodical payment which seeks to compensate the claimant for future expenditure on care, and which is increased on the basis of a prices index, will almost certainly fail to keep pace with the increase in that expenditure over time. Moreover, the shortfall will be a cumulative one. The impact of this cumulative shortfall is demonstrated in the much publicised case of Charlie Beattie, whose annuity for future care costs under a structured settlement order was linked to the RPI and had increased by 35 percent between 1992 and 2004.[39] His care costs had increased by 60 percent, which is roughly in line with the Average Earnings Index (AEI) and, as a consequence of inappropriate indexation, Mr Beattie was unable to afford the care package that he needed. This same effect is demonstrated in appendix over a 45-year period from 1963 to 2007 (45 years would be more typical of a lifetime of expenditure on care for a claimant aged under 30 years). An annual payment of £10 thousand in 1963 indexed to the RPI would have risen to just under £150 thousand in 2007. If the salary-based costs of care had risen according to the growth in the AEI, these would have risen to just under £333 thousand in 2007. The annual shortfall in 2007 would have been £183 thousand. If the salary-based costs of care had increased by the AEI, then an RPI-linked annual sum would only meet 45 percent of the annual cost after 45 years. It is this shortfall that, together with the absence of any investment opportunity to cover it, forms the prima facie case for an alternative to the RPI as a means of up-rating care costs, a measure based on either earnings or on care costs.

6.3. An Alternative Measure

The Damages Act identifies the RPI as the default measure for the escalation of an annual payment. The RPI is well known, widely used (including in the up-rating of annuities, pensions and state benefits) and generally accepted as a reliable measure of UK price inflation. Any alternative measure must be evaluated in comparison to the RPI and found to be the better choice. The following criteria were established by the trail judge in *RH v. United Bristol Healthcare NHS Trust* (2007)[40] (para. 71), and endorsed by the Court of Appeal (at para. 75), as the criteria on which any comparison should be based:

(i) precision–accuracy of match to type and level of expenditure,
(ii) authority of collector,
(iii) statistical reliability,
(iv) accessibility,
(v) consistency over time past,

(vi) reproducibility in the future,
(vii) simplicity and consistency in application.

The target expenditure that the measure seeks to match is the cost of the care plan. In each care plan within the basket, the earnings of the carers accounted for upwards of 80 percent of the annual cost. The type of care required is of a social nature (communication, stimulation and interaction) rather than a medical nature. The injured claimant is living at home, and the team of carers is to be directly employed by the household. The recommended care is of a complex nature due to the catastrophic nature of the injury, which resulted in severe physical and intellectual impairment, and which requires a relatively high degree of skill and experience on the part of the carers. This is reflected in the hourly earnings rates of the carers which is around £9.50 per hour for weekday daytime hours in 2007 compared to a median level of earnings for this occupational group as reported in the Annual Survey of Hours and Earnings (ASHE) of this year of £7.53.

The RPI achieves simplicity and consistency but at the expense of precision. It lacks precision partly because it measures average price inflation across a variety of households which experience very different rates of inflation (see Bootle, 2006) and partly because it relates to the purchase of goods and services in household consumption and is a poor match for the purchase of labour in the household production of care services. The typical household does not purchase care. This is reflected in the weight attached to home care fees within the RPI basket, which is around 1 in 1,000.

There are a number of indices used to measure inflation in the health care sector in the United Kingdom, though none that relate to the increasing costs of a care plan. The most widely used is the hospital and community health services (HCHS) pay and price index, which is a measure of medical treatment cost within the NHS. It is produced by the Department of Health and is used to up-rate the tariff for the recovery of NHS costs from an insurer for injuries incurred in road traffic accidents. This index is calculated as a weighted average of two separate indices, one for pay costs in the NHS, the PCI, and the other a price index based upon health service costs, the HSCI. Given the predominance of labour costs in the care plans, the PCI is potentially a useful measure. However, within the NHS employment structure upon which the PCI is calculated, highly paid professional groups (hospital managers and doctors) are over-represented as compared to a home-based care plan. Furthermore, the NHS is not a major employer of carers.

Give that earnings account for a disproportionate amount of care costs, earnings measures are considered as replacements for the RPI. There is no exact measure of earnings for each individual claimant's basket of carers, so a raft of more general earnings series is considered. Each can be usefully distinguished according to level of disaggregation, whether or not they are 'official', that is collected and published by, or on behalf of, a government department, and whether they measure pay settlements or actual earnings.

Table 2 summarises the relevant characteristics of five alternative measures based upon earnings that were considered as potential candidates for the indexation of care costs.

The AEI is attractive because it is the companion earnings series to the RPI. It is updated annually on a similar basis to the RPI (e.g. regarding re-weighting), and it is available with the same frequency, that is monthly, quarterly and annually. The growth in the mean is recorded as an index. The AEI (as with the RPI) is compiled with the purpose of measuring inflation, and therefore consistency in the data over time is given greater priority than

Table 2. Comparison of Five Alternative Measures.

Pay Cost Index (PCI)	Aggregate (across occupations) measure of labour costs in the NHS. Collected from an official source. Lacks precision to care costs. May not continue in a consistent form.
Average Earnings Index (AEI)	Aggregate measure of earnings growth from an official source. Used by Government as the key indicator of inflationary pressure in labour market. Simple to apply. Measured as an index that is based upon mean level of earnings. No disaggregation. Long established (1963), consistent and likely to continue.
Annual Survey of Hours and Earnings (ASHE)	Annual 0.8 percent sample survey of all PAYE employees from an official source. Precision achieved through disaggregation to four-digit occupational group for carers and choice of 11 point estimates across the occupational earnings distribution. Occupational classifications change every 10 years to reflect changes in the composition of the workforce with dual classification in crossover years.
National Joint Council (NJC) pay settlement	Pay settlement data from non-official source. Although disaggregated to carers, it lacks precision to care plans because jobs and pay rates in public sector care are different. No guarantee of continuity. Excludes pay drift.
British Nursing Association (BNA) pay rates	Recommended pay rates in UK's largest employment agency for carers. Disaggregated by region. Non official. No continuity. Series stops in 2005.

in a series produced from a repeated cross section where the primary purpose is the comparison of earnings levels for different categories of employees at a particular point in time. However, the AEI is an aggregate measure with no close relationship to the earnings of carers. Carers comprise a small proportion of the working population (around 2.5 percent of employees), and carers employed by private households would not form part of the AEI sampling frame that has a minimum threshold for company size of 25 employees. The distribution of aggregate earnings is asymmetrical, and the mean is a poor measure of its central location, and likewise of its growth. Given the increasing skewness of earnings, average earnings are now officially measured at the median rather than the mean (ONS, 2006). The mean level of hourly earnings in 2007 was £13.36, above that for carers. Like the RPI, the AEI is strong on simplicity and consistency, but rather weak in terms of precision of match to the target expenditure.

The ASHE is a nationally representative survey of earnings conducted by the ONS. Estimates are published annually in November for a survey point in April and include 11 points across the earnings distribution (deciles and quartiles). ASHE disaggregates earnings to the level of the four-digit occupational group where 6115 relates to 'Care Assistants and Home Carers'. This category includes a variety of job titles within the care sector, and includes carers employed in the public sector and in institutional settings as well as private sector home carers. However, occupation is defined in terms of a common set of core tasks that are those found in most care packages.[41] The range of earnings within the occupational group primarily reflects different qualifications, skills, experience, responsibilities and type of care (see Incomes Data Services (IDS), 2006). A precise match to the care plan is achieved by linking the recommended wage rate to the nearest published percentile estimate in the occupational earnings distribution. ASHE is a cross-section survey that is repeated annually. Consistency in methods over time is less of a priority than in a survey whose purpose is to produce an index. This is particularly relevant to an occupational earnings measure since occupations are reclassified at regular intervals.[42] However, the ONS has recently committed to produce a dual set of estimates in years where methods change and did so in 2006 when certain coding activities were automated.

The BNA is the dominant labour agency in the nursing and care sector in the United Kingdom. The BNA has published rates of pay for nurses and carers by category of carer, region and times of the day and week. These have historically provided reference pay rates for carers used by personal injury lawyers in the preparation of the schedule of loss. These are recommended pay rates rather than actual earnings, they are from an unofficial source and there is no guarantee of continuity. Indeed from 2006 the BNA ceased to supply carers, and their successor organisation does not publish recommended rates of pay for commercial reasons.

A substantial minority of carers is directly employed by local authorities, and their pay is negotiated annually under public sector pay bargaining machinery called the National Joint Council Salaries Agreement for Local Authorities (NJC). The effects of national collective bargaining are likely to extend beyond carers in public sector employment to those employed by medium and large organisations – in particular, employment agencies specialising in care and residential care homes. Pay setting uses a spine-based approach in which a particular grade of staff is assigned to a particular spine point, point 8 for home-based carers, and a pay settlement increase is negotiated annually for this point. Both the rates of pay and pay increases are published annually. The NJC is of uncertain duration since local authorities are increasingly contracting out of national collective bargaining in the care sector and contracting out of direct care provision altogether. Precision of match is also uncertain since both the NJC hourly pay rate and the growth in the pay rate are substantially lower than the pay rate for the privately purchased domiciliary care recommended in the basket of cases and general measures of carers' earnings in both the public and private sectors (see Table 3). The former may reflect differences in the skills and abilities of the carers in the local authority sector, differences in the type of work undertaken and/or differences in the terms and conditions of employment. The latter is accounted for by 'pay drift'. This is the term used to describe the difference between pay settlement inflation and earnings inflation. Its relevance, or otherwise, to the future cost of the claimant's care plan was to become a key issue in the selection of the alternative measure.

6.4. Pay Drift

Pay drift is defined as the difference between wage settlement inflation and earnings inflation. In recent years, 1998–2004, annual earnings growth measured by pay settlement data was between 1 and 1.5 percent lower than the annual growth in earnings measured by the AEI (Miller, 2005). The gap is accounted for primarily by changes in workforce composition but pay progression, net promotion, interim market adjustments and pay restructuring all play a role. Compositional change at the aggregate level refers to a change in the employment structure at the occupational or industrial level.

Table 3. Earnings and Earnings Growth 1997–2006.

		Hourly Earnings in 2006 (£)	Average Growth in Nominal Earnings 1997–2006 (%)	Average Growth in Real Earnings 1997–2006 (%)
1	PCI[a]	(Index)	6.01	3.45
2	AEI	(Index)	4.26	1.65
3	ASHE 70 (6115)	8.27	4.79	2.15
4	ASHE 80 (6115)	9.14	4.82	2.37
5	ASHE 90 (6115)	10.58	4.64	2.19
6	BNA rates[a]	7.83	7.84	5.13
7	NJC rates	6.43	3.21	0.79
8	RPI total	(Index)	2.58	

Notes: BNA and NJC weekday daytime hours. An expanded form of this table is available in Wass (2007).
Source: ONS, Department of Health.
[a]2005 data.

Such changes can bring about a change in the aggregate average wage even though the average wages measured within constituent groups are unchanged. So, for example a shift in employment towards the more highly skilled (and highly paid) occupations would cause the aggregate average wage to increase even though the average wages measured for each occupational group, including the highly skilled, had not changed. In the care market, compositional change refers to the upward shift in the mix in roles, skills and qualifications that has been observed over the course of the last decade. This reflects increasing professionalisation in the care sector. As an example, legislation in the form of the Care Standards Act 2000 requires organisations that employ carers to ensure that at least 50 percent of them are qualified to level 2 under the scheme of National Vocational Qualifications (NVQ-2). The consequences are readily observed in above-settlement increases in earnings growth in the care sector.

The relevance of compositional change to the indexation of care costs depends upon whether or not the claimant's care plan should be allowed to move with an increase in the nation's living standards, including any increase in expectations about care provision. If not, then the claimant will always be able to afford the care plan that was determined at the time of trial but will be excluded from any future improvements if they are more costly to provide.

The arguments for and against the inclusion of pay drift in an indexation measure mirror those more commonly versed in the debate over the measurement of the poverty line. Relative measures involve a link to earnings; absolute measures are linked to prices. The poverty threshold in the United Kingdom is the line drawn at 60 percent of the median level of earnings. It is a relative measure that seeks to ensure that poor households keep up with the wider community as living standards rise. A poverty line fixed in relation to the purchase of a particular basket of goods is maintained over time by a linkage to price inflation. The household whose income is determined by the level of an absolute poverty line will fall behind its peers whose income increases in relation to earnings, although it will continue to be able to purchase the original basket of goods. The provision and delivery of care has changed vastly over the last 20 years. It has also become more expensive. A claimant (like Charlie Beattie, whose case is discussed above) whose care plan was determined 20 years ago and which had been increased by price inflation could not afford contemporary standards of care.

In the fourth 'appeal bundle' case, *RH v. Bristol United Health Care NHS Trust* (2007), the court adopted a practical, as opposed to moral, approach to this issue in the use of an extreme example in which care becomes a graduate profession during the claimant's lifetime. The claimant would then be unable to recruit unqualified carers at all, and he would be unable to employ qualified carers for the hours that he needs. On this basis, the lower court in RH, and subsequently the Court of Appeal, decided that the 100 percent principle required that care costs need to be up-rated by an earnings measure, which includes the effects of pay drift:

> We are concerned with measuring the *actual*, not the theoretical, costs of care; and, as Mackay J pungently observed at paragraph 66 of *RH*, people, including the claimants, pay money and not rates. It is therefore a recommendation, and not a detriment, that an index captures pay drift. As Mackay J put it in paragraph 69 of *RH*, "It is a virtue which lead[s] to accuracy and an improved chance of achieving the 100% principle of compensation". (para. 69)

6.5. Some Empirical Evidence

Real and nominal growth rates for each of the alternative measures for the period 1997–2006 are reported in Table 3 below. From an empirical perspective, the choice of measure is important. In general terms, earnings growth has exceeded prices growth by 1.65 percent per annum (row 2, column 3). The earnings growth in the care sector (rows 3–6) has been significantly above the average at over 2 percent per annum. This primarily reflects the effects of compositional change and the Care Standards Act. The effects of pay drift are apparent from the differential between the growth in the NJC rate (row 7) and the growth in the earnings measures. Pay inflation in the health care sector has exceeded that in the social care and in the economy more generally. The cause is predominantly compositional change brought about by an ongoing programme of professionalisation under the NHS Agenda for Change.

6.6. Choice of Earnings Measure

Avoiding non-official series and their uncertain authority and continuity, and including the effects of pay drift, leaves a choice between AEI and a particular percentile of ASHE 6115. The choice between the two depends on the relative importance attached to precision on the one hand and simplicity and consistency on the other. Disaggregation to the level of occupational pay in ASHE 6115 achieves greater precision and sensitivity to the impact of occupation-specific labour market conditions (labour shortage or surplus) and occupation-specific labour market reforms. These have proved to be important over the last 10 years. The trade-off is additional complexity (and scope for argument and error) when dealing with annual earnings statistics and the effects of methodological changes. The advantage of AEI lies in its simplicity and consistency over time. The disadvantage is the greater scope for the effects of compositional change and the absence of a close match to carers' earnings.

The lower courts all selected ASHE 6115 at the relevant percentile. The trial judge in *Thompstone*[43] noted the following deficiencies in the AEI:

> The most serious disadvantage of the AEI as a measure is the systematic over-compensation that is likely to result from its use. I accept that the potential over-compensation is likely to be considerably less than the under-compensation that would result from use of the RPI. Nevertheless, I find that, over a period of years, the extent of the over-compensation is likely to be significant. (para. 140)
>
> The AEI has other disadvantages. It is an aggregate measure covering all occupational groups, including those with high earnings. Its earnings data include additional payments which would not be received by home carers of the type employed by the Claimant. It is not a measure which would be sensitive to changes specific to the care market. All these features cause me to conclude that, despite the attraction of its simplicity of use, the AEI will not necessarily be a reliable and accurate indicator of the growth in carers' earnings and that it would not, therefore, be a suitable alternative to the RPI. (para. 141)

The trial judge in RH detailed the advantages of ASHE 6115:

> I return to the criteria against which the measure should be judged [as reproduced at paragraphs 56 and 75 of this judgment]. First and foremost I regard 6115 as the most accurate match to the target expenditure; it is of undoubted authority, coming from the ONS; it is statistically reliable as all agree, with tight CVs; it is freely accessible, albeit with a time lag problem which I believe can be overcome; it is consistent over time past, although it does not go back beyond 1997, not a serious flaw in my view; it is reproducible in the future. (para. 87)

The Court of Appeal concurred, giving final judgment on the issue of indexation on 17 January 2008:

> We hope that as a result of these proceedings the National Health Service, and other defendants in proceedings that involve catastrophic injury, will now accept that the appropriateness of indexation on the basis of ASHE 6115 has been established after an exhaustive review of all the possible objections to its use, both in itself and as applied to the recovery of costs of care and case management. It will not be appropriate to re-open that issue in any future proceedings unless the defendant can produce evidence and argument significantly different from, and more persuasive than, that which has been deployed in the present cases. Judges should not hesitate to strike out any defences that do not meet that requirement. (para. 100)

6.7. Workability: The Application of ASHE 6115

Whilst it is clear that the courts were attracted by the precision offered by ASHE 6115, they also had to consider simplicity of application and workability. In this respect, the ASHE statistics present a number of challenges: (i) the data are collected annually (in April of each year) rather than monthly; (ii) statistics are first published in the October/November of the same year but these are provisional and subject to revision in the final release in October/November the following year; (iii) occupational categories are subject to reclassification every 10 years and (iv) continuous methodological improvements give rise to potential discontinuity in the series.

The claimant's advisers were charged with overcoming these difficulties and assisting with ease of application and understanding. All these were achieved through a model Schedule to the Periodical Payment Order which received approval in 104 cases in the High Court on 2 December 2008 with the following proviso from Sir Christopher Holland:[44]

> It goes without saying that these Schedules do no more than offer practitioners a precedent for adaptation to meet the particular nature of an award of damages – that

> said, the terms represent the best current expertise and departure from such in case of any future draft Order will have to be justified in order to secure approval from the Court. (para. 8)

It has since become clear that government bodies and insurers alike have accepted the workability of ASHE 6115 and have established mechanisms in order to comply with the requirements of the orders in terms of making payments and calculating future increases. Moreover, in the present uncertain financial climate, the number of periodical payment orders is increasing dramatically and is fast becoming the default option for the future care and case management elements of the claim.

7. SUMMARY AND CONCLUSION

The shortcomings of conventional lump-sum awards for future loss in catastrophic personal injury damages are clear. Assumptions have to be made today about the future, assumptions that must hold, or the damages will either prove to be too much or too little. Error is virtually certain. The direction and magnitude of the error will depend upon the outcome of the following unknowns: future investment returns (after taxation and above inflation); future levels of inflation; future taxation rates; future taxation regimes; the claimant's actual future needs; the escalation in cost of providing for those future needs and, finally, the claimant's actual life expectancy.

Under the lump-sum award, the consequences of error fall in full on the claimant, the party to the action who is the least able to bear them and the least qualified to avoid them. As noted by The Master of the Rolls' Working Party (2002):

> A claimant may fear that the lump-sum award may run out and accordingly may be overcautious in investing and in spending the sums on his reasonable needs. Conversely a claimant may dissipate the award and may require State Benefits to provide for minimum standards after the award is spent. (para. 19)

Periodical payments do not remove any of these uncertainties, but they do transfer the risk associated with many of them from the claimant to the tortfeasor where, for reasons of equity and efficiency, they ought more properly to lie. The claimant is left with the risk that the medical condition may alter, leading to the need for more care. However, the investment and mortality risks are effectively transferred and, on the assumption that the measure applied to up-rate the periodical payments is an accurate match for the cost of the ongoing need that has to be met, the claimant is provided with real financially certainty and security that will allow him/her the peace of mind to spend this year's periodical payment on his/her care needs, safe in the knowledge that there will be another payment made next year and every year for life thereafter.

The indexation decision was critical to this outcome and to the future of periodical payments as a viable alternative to the conventional lump-sum award. Many have noted that over the last year, the growth in ASHE 6115 has been at or below the rate of the RPI inflation and that, therefore, claimants would have been better off with the RPI. Whilst this is likely to be unsustainable as a trend, it misses the point. For the authors, at least, it was never a question as to which measure will provide 'more' for the claimant. Rather, it was about making sure that the periodical payments would be sufficient. On the basis that ASHE 6115 reflects earnings growth in the care sector, including the claimant's care plan, then whatever level of earnings growth is recorded (including zero real growth), it will be enough to meet the increase in this year's care costs. In this sense, appropriately indexed periodical payments really do 'better meet the needs of the claimant as and when they arise' (Master of the Rolls' Working Party, 2002).

NOTES

1. This has never been a right at common law.
2. [1979] 2 All ER 910.
3. *Kelly v. Dawes* (1990) Times, 27 September QBD.
4. [1999] 1 AC 345.
5. See LCD (2000), LCD (2002a), LCD (2002b), DCA (2002), Master of the Rolls' Working Party (2002).
6. There have been just two cases at first instance where the discount rate was reduced as a result of 'exceptional circumstances'. Both cases involved Dutch nationals injured whilst in the United Kingdom but who were resident in the Netherlands. *Biesheuvel v. Birrel* (1999) P1QR. Q40 compromised following the first instance judgment. Exceptionality was overturned by the Court of Appeal in *Van Oudenhoven v. Griffin Inns Limited* QBENF 2000/0102/A2.
7. For reasons set out in 'Setting the Discount Rate – The Lord Chancellor's Reasons' dated 27 July 2001.
8. In the Republic of Ireland, for example taxation can be reclaimed on gains realised on a lump-sum personal injury claim in order to provide for personal care.
9. This is inferred from the reasons given by the House of Lords in *Well v. Wells* to set the discount rate in line with an assumed "no risk" investment return produced by the three-year average return on Index-Linked Government Stocks (ILGS), the return of which increases by reference to the RPI. However, in setting the discount rate at 2.5

percent, the Lord Chancellor abandoned this sole measure, noting that claimants were investing in part in real assets (such as equities). One might consider that, due to the fact that many of the claimant's needs were almost certain to increase at a rate above the RPI, although he had been compensated on the basis of a 'no risk' assumption, investment risk still had to be taken in order to match earnings-related needs.

10. The authors are grateful to Anthony Carus for his contribution to this part of the chapter.

11. This has created issues in transposing US data, which is recognised as being largest pool of life expectancy data, for use in the UK courts.

12. This combination is not tabulated in the published tables so requires individual consideration by an actuary.

13. *Metcalfe v. London Passenger Transport Board* (1938) 2 All ER 352.

14. (1990) *Times*, 27 September.

15. (1989) *Times*, 10 August, [1989] CLY 1201.

16. [1936] 1 All E.R. 543, 154 LT 484, 80 Sol Jo 245, CA.

17. Finance Act 1996.

18. Which has now been repealed and replaced with the Health Act 2006.

19. None of the above providers will currently provide quotations in the open market. There is presently only one provider of suitable annuities, namely AIG Life.

20. Ogden IV, Table 19, 2.5 percent discount rate, Ogden V had yet to be released when this data was collected.

21. Both Windsor Life and the NFU Mutual did offer life-impaired structured settlement annuities on a with-profits basis for a limited time between 1999 and 2002. Such annuities are no longer offered by any life office. Rather than being linked to the RPI, these annuities increased by way of an annual bonus rate that reflected the return achieved on the company's with-profits fund. Once the bonus had been added, it would not be taken away (in the event of a fall in the value of the fund). This was the first attempt to link structured settlements to a measure that would produce long-term real escalation.

22. Money section (page 1).

23. http://www.lawyerslegal.co.uk/news-content.cfm/Article/82671/Results-Of-Consultation-On-Peridocal.html

24. EWHC 820 (QB).

25. EWHC 820 (QB).

26. The Medical Protection Society, The Medical and Dental Defence Union of Scotland and the Medical Defence Union (for cases prior to January 2005) are not covered. Policies issued by Lloyds Syndicates prior to 1 January 2004 are also potentially not covered, although it has been suggested that the Motor Insurers' Bureau will be the insurer of last resort in such cases. Foreign insurers are not automatically covered.

27. The Motor Insurers' Bureau (MIB) has satisfied the courts that due to its quasi-governmental role and link with European legislation, it is reasonably secure to self-fund periodical payments, under Section 2(5) of the Damages Act 1996, even though it does not meet the requirements of Section 2(4).

28. The Courts do not have the same power in relation to past loss or general damages. However, under section 2(2) of the Damages Act 1996, with the parties' consent the courts may make a periodical payments order for any damages. The

power to order periodical payments without the consent of the parties applies in all cases that had not been finalised on 1 April 2005. Provisions on the making of variable orders for periodical payments only applied in cases where proceedings were issued on or after the date of implementation.

29. *Godbald v. Mahmood* (2005) EWHC 1002 (QB).
30. EWHC 2833 (Admin).
31. [2005] EWHC 2882 (QB).
32. [2002] EWCA Civ 81 [2003] 3 All ER 447.
33. [2004] 1 All ER 797.
34. *Flora v. Wakom (Heathrow) Ltd.* (2006) EWCA Civ 1103.
35. *Flora v. Wakom (Heathrow) Ltd.* (2006) EWCA Civ 1103.
36. *Flora v. Wakom (Heathrow) Ltd.* (2006) EWCA Civ 1103.
37. *Flora v. Wakom (Heathrow) Ltd.* (2006) EWCA Civ 1103.
38. *Thompstone v. Tameside and Glossop Acute Health Service NHS Trust* (2006) EWHC 2904 (QB); *Corbett v. South Yorkshire* SHA March 28 2007; *RH v. United Bristol Healthcare NHS Trust* (2007) EWHC 1441; *De Haas v. South West London Strategic Health Authority* (2006) U20060145.
39. This case was reported by the Master of the Court of Protection in Lush, D. (2005).
40. EWHC 1441.
41. Core tasks include (i) assists residents to dress, undress, wash and bathe; (ii) serves meals to residents at table or in bed; (iii) accompanies infirm residents on outings and assists with recreational activities and (iv) undertakes light cleaning and domestic duties as required.
42. Reclassification is necessary in order to maintain representativeness to a changing employment structure.
43. (2006) EWHC 2904.
44. (2008) EWHC 2948 (QB).

ACKNOWLEDGMENT

We are grateful to Ian Gunn for his helpful comments on an earlier draft of this chapter.

REFERENCES

Bevan, N., Huckle, T., & Ellis, S. (2007). *Future loss in practice: periodical payments and lump-sums*. London: LexisNexis Butterworths.

Bootle, R. (2006). Fact and fiction about inflation. *Sunday Telegraph*, 23 July 2006.

Department of Constitutional Affairs. (2002). Regulatory impact assessment courts bill: Power to order periodical payments for future loss.

Hogg, R. (2004). Will periodical payments provide adequately for costs of care? *Journal of Personal Injury Litigation*, *4*(3), 209.

Incomes Data Services. (2006). *Pay and conditions in housing and social care.*
Lewis, R. (1994). Structured settlements: An emergent study. *13 Civil Justice Quarterly, 18*, 18–28.
Lewis, R. (2007). Judicially imposed periodical payments of damages. *Modern Law Review, 69*(3), 418–442.
London International Insurance and Re-Insurance Market Association. (2003). *Third UK bodily injury awards study*. London: International Underwriting Association of London.
Lord Chancellors Department. (2000). Damages: The discount rate and alternatives to lump-sum payments.
Lord Chancellor's Department. (2002a). *Damages for future loss: Giving the courts the power to order periodical payments for future loss and care costs in personal injury cases.* Consultation Paper 01/02.
Lord Chancellors Department. (2002b). *Analyses of the responses.* Consultation Paper (R) 01/02.
Lush, D. (2005). Damages for personal injury: Why some claimants prefer a conventional lump-sum to periodical payments. *London Law Review, 1*(2), 187.
Master of the Rolls' Working Party. (2002). Structured settlements: Report of the Master of the Rolls Working Party.
McGregor, H. (2007). *McGregor on damages: Main work and supplement* (17th Revised Edition).
Miller, S. (2005). The difference between pay settlements and earnings growth. *Labour Market Trends, 113*(2), 67–71.
Norris, W. (2005). Periodical payments: Indexation, variation, protection and practice. *Journal of Personal Injury Litigation, 5*(1), 59.
ONS. (2006). Frequently asked questions. Available at: www.statistics.gov.uk
Wass, V. (2007). The indexation of future care costs. *Journal of Personal Injury Law, 3*, 247–261.

APPENDIX

Year	Growth AEI (%)	Growth RPI (%)	Annual Expenditure (£)	Annual Payment (£)	Expenditure Covered by Payment (%)
1963			10,000.00	10,000.00	100.00
1964	7.69	2.04	10,769.23	10,203.78	94.75
1965	4.76	5.56	11,282.05	10,771.47	95.47
1966	9.09	3.58	12,307.69	11,157.21	90.65
1967	0.00	3.00	12,307.69	11,491.99	93.37
1968	8.33	4.43	13,333.33	12,001.46	90.01
1969	9.62	5.58	14,615.38	12,671.03	86.70
1970	10.53	5.57	16,153.85	13,377.00	82.81
1971	11.11	9.41	17,948.72	14,636.10	81.54

APPENDIX. (*Continued*)

Year	Growth AEI (%)	Growth RPI (%)	Annual Expenditure (£)	Annual Payment (£)	Expenditure Covered by Payment (%)
1972	12.86	6.32	20,256.41	15,560.41	76.82
1973	13.92	9.21	23,076.92	16,994.18	73.64
1974	11.11	15.16	25,641.03	19,570.60	76.33
1975	32.00	21.68	33,846.15	23,813.68	70.36
1976	18.18	18.92	40,000.00	28,318.78	70.80
1977	8.97	17.45	43,589.74	33,260.55	76.30
1978	12.94	7.94	49,230.77	35,902.47	72.93
1979	13.54	10.08	55,897.44	39,519.65	70.70
1980	21.10	21.75	67,692.31	48,114.99	71.08
1981	13.64	12.04	76,923.08	53,908.30	70.08
1982	10.67	9.41	85,128.21	58,981.08	69.29
1983	9.04	4.00	92,820.51	61,339.16	66.08
1984	5.52	5.17	97,948.72	64,512.37	65.86
1985	9.42	6.93	107,179.49	68,981.08	64.36
1986	8.37	3.05	116,153.85	71,084.43	61.20
1987	6.40	4.23	123,589.74	74,090.25	59.95
1988	8.09	3.93	133,589.74	77,001.46	57.64
1989	9.79	8.03	146,666.67	83,187.77	56.72
1990	9.44	9.45	160,512.82	91,048.03	56.72
1991	8.31	6.39	173,846.15	96,870.45	55.72
1992	6.19	4.28	184,615.38	101,018.92	54.72
1993	3.75	1.30	191,538.46	102,328.97	53.42
1994	2.95	2.56	197,179.49	104,949.05	53.23
1995	3.90	3.33	204,871.79	108,442.50	52.93
1996	3.38	2.42	211,794.87	111,062.59	52.44
1997	3.75	2.42	219,743.59	113,755.46	51.77
1998	5.83	4.03	232,564.10	118,340.61	50.89
1999	4.08	1.60	242,051.28	120,232.90	49.67
2000	4.56	2.97	253,076.92	123,799.13	48.92
2001	5.27	1.76	266,410.26	125,982.53	47.29
2002	3.85	1.50	276,666.67	127,874.82	46.22
2003	2.59	3.13	283,846.15	131,877.73	46.46
2004	4.52	2.48	296,666.67	135,152.84	45.56
2005	4.24	3.18	309,230.77	139,446.87	45.09
2006	4.06	2.56	321,794.87	143,013.10	44.44
2007	3.43	4.53	332,820.51	149,490.54	44.92

Source: ONS

THE U.S. APPROACH TO COMPUTING ECONOMIC DAMAGES DUE TO PERSONAL INJURY AND WRONGFUL DEATH

Kurt V. Krueger and Gary R. Albrecht

1. INTRODUCTION

This chapter examines the legal and scientific approaches taken in the United States for computing economic damages due to personal injury and wrongful death. The U.S. law of tort damages conforms to a general economic valuation of reduced or lost productivity due to injury under the goal of assigning tort damages optimally so that harm in the society is minimized. Today, "economic damages" are defined in every U.S. jurisdiction, and the field of forensic economics has produced a body of literature concerned with accurately measuring them.

This chapter is a general overview of the economic damages topic designed for readers without a thorough exposure to the measurement of economic damages under U.S. tort law. Readers interested in further research may refer to the "References and Bibliography" section which is organized under the major subject areas in the chapter. The chapter begins by examining the social objectives of tort damages in the United States. It is noted that state jurisdictional law can influence some of the calculations

Personal Injury and Wrongful Death Damages Calculations: Transatlantic Dialogue
Contemporary Studies in Economic and Financial Analysis, Volume 91, 193–231

ISSN: 1569-3759/doi:10.1108/S1569-3759(2009)0000091011

without changing the core economic methods of determining tort damages. The commonly accepted components of U.S. tort economic damages are then listed. This listing is followed by the generally accepted economic theories and methodologies which form the "U.S. approach" to computing economic damages. The chapter shows typical analytical steps followed in determining economic damages in the United States. At the end of the chapter is a sample personal injury case to which the U.S. approach and calculation methods are applied.

2. THE SOCIAL OBJECTIVES OF U.S. TORT DAMAGES COMPUTATION

Under U.S. civil law, the remedy offered to the victim of a tort is money paid by the tortfeasor to compensate for the damages caused. Regardless of jurisdiction, the United States relies upon the reasoning of judges or juries (the trier of the facts) to ascertain the amount of money under a universal "make-whole" principle that intends to make the tort victim as well off as if the injury had not occurred. Tort damages are assigned to three categories: general, special, and punitive. General and special damages are to restore the plaintiff to his or her former state (to make whole), while punitive damages are intended to punish a defendant who acted with malice in committing the tort. General damages are defined as those that flow as the natural, necessary, logical, and anticipated consequences of a wrongful act. For example, the consequence of legitimate personal injury must be pain, suffering, and/or the loss of the enjoyment of life, so those elements of loss are assigned to general damages. General damages are also described as any component of the loss of life or lifestyle which cannot be measured in monetary terms. Special damages, on the other hand, are those that result from the defendant's act by reason of the unique circumstances of the case. Special damages require some proof of causation resulting from the tort. When an injury forces a plaintiff to miss work, that plaintiff's loss of earnings is a special damage because not every personal injury causes a loss of earnings. All economic damages in the United States are special damages, and general damages have been referred to as simply "noneconomic damages."

To decide damages, the U.S. law encourages all forms of evidence to be presented to the trier of the facts. Whenever scientific or specialized knowledge could assist in the understanding of evidence, the U.S. courts allow expert witnesses to give their opinions regarding the issues to be ultimately decided by the trier of the facts. The court or judge qualifies the expert's testimony by way of the witness's education, training, and experience and the utilization of generally accepted theories and methods within his or her field. The trier of the facts is not bound by any expert testimony and may accord such testimony as little or as much weight as deemed appropriate. Since forensic economists have knowledge of the scientific methodologies that are generally accepted for accurately measuring pecuniary damages, they are utilized as expert witnesses by plaintiffs and defendants. In the United States, forensic economists most often testify on behalf of the plaintiff, as every U.S. jurisdiction places upon the plaintiff a burden of proof as to the best evidence of his or her damages claims. A forensic economist for the defense provides advice and/or serves as a testifying expert witness to rebut the plaintiff's expert's analysis or to calculate damages utilizing evidence offered by the defendant.

All economic damages must be expressed as a lump sum, and any loss that would have likely occurred after the date of judgment is subject to a present-value calculation. Hence, the economic study of interest rates and price inflation has shaped the methodology of complying with the legal present value requirement – again a legal subject calling for expert economic testimony. The U.S. Supreme Court recognizes that prediction of the future is affected by various probabilities and resulting jury speculations but "(t)hat juries in tort cases must routinely engage in such difficult predictions (compounded further by discounting for present value) is the price paid by the common-law approach for the finality of a one-time lump-sum judgment."[1] A goal of rigorous economic analysis in U.S. litigation is to work to minimize the error made in predictions about the future, and the U.S. approach works to provide neutral, accurate methods of computing tort economic damages.

The study of "make-whole" considerations is embedded into economics with such concepts as externalities and compensating and equivalent variations related to changes in utility and prices. The prospect of opining "make-whole" calculations is engaging to an economist versed in economic value-of-life theories, methods, and empirical research. The findings of value-of-life research based upon indirect measurement of the prices people pay in order to reduce the chance of incurring injury could be relevant to general and special tort damages; and the costs avoided or the profits obtained by a firm under a malicious creation of public harm could be relevant to punitive damages. Despite what "make-whole" information might be produced using such value-of-life theories and measurements, general economic analysis within the United States is limited to quantifying the directly measurable market values of the special damages claims of the loss of earnings and/or earning capacity, the ability to perform services, future medical expenses, and the loss of financial support due to wrongful death. The justification for the reduced emphasis on economic value-of-life empirical evidence reverts to (a) the consensus within the U.S. case law that any witness is no more expert than are jurors regarding the personal value of life; (b) the fact that, while economists using revealed preferences can rank an individual's economic enjoyment-of-life positions, there are no dollar-based data available to quantify the differences between an individual's enjoyment rankings; and (c) empirical value-of-life or profit-motivation abstractions obtained from the behavior of populations are not reliable indicators for evidence of damages in an individual case.

A well-established principle in the U.S. law of damages is that the wrongdoer is generally not entitled to have the damages for which he or she is liable reduced by proving that the plaintiff has received or will receive compensation for the loss from a collateral source. This collateral source rule flows directly from the law and the economic goal of minimizing harm by making tortfeasors responsible for all of the harm they create. While tort reform movements across U.S. jurisdictions have chipped away at the collateral source rule (and injected related issues such as the role of income taxes on lost earnings claims), jurisdictional laws have not overridden the basic economic elements of the U.S. approach; they have only added some required adjustments to them. For example, a jurisdiction might offset economic damages by the receipt of disability insurance benefits or the required payment of income taxes. The admissibility of those two considerations does not eliminate the need of a calculation of the loss of earnings or earning capacity before those deductions. Some jurisdictions also have rules regarding the method of the present value calculation, which again does not detract from its requirement in the U.S. approach.

3. ORIGINS OF GENERAL AND SPECIAL TORT DAMAGES

Legal theory addresses tort damages with economic questions such as "who pays the cost" and "for what to compensate the victim?" The U.S. Supreme Court in *Carey v. Piphus* wrote that the law provides to us a legal right to engage in our own meaningful life activities, and tort liability provides to us a broad range of damages to compensate us "fairly for injuries caused by the violation of (our) legal rights."[2] Related to the question "for what to compensate?," state and federal damage items for consideration by the trier of the facts in personal injury and wrongful death include the loss of earnings, earning capacity, services, future medical costs, and financial support, as well as life activities related to the loss of affection, aid, assistance, attention, care, comfort, companionship, consortium, disability, disfigurement, domestic duties, education, enjoyment of life, guidance, inconvenience, nurture, pain, protection, services, suffering, etc., among other items. While a plaintiff is legally entitled to such broad areas of compensable damages, the law gives little guidance on how the trier of fact should make the damages valuation. Each jurisdiction requires that the compensable items of damages must be considered in light of such economic-related productivity characteristics as the plaintiff's ability, age, character, expectation of life, habits, health, industry, intelligence, mental and physical capacity (before and after injury) with the probable increase or diminution of that ability with the lapse of time, occupation, work record, and (in wrongful death cases) the care and attention the deceased may have been expected to give his family. The U.S. Supreme Court in *Sea-land Services, Inc. v. Gaudet* stated that tort compensation rests on "the good sense and deliberate judgment" of the trier of fact and "as in all damages awards for tortious injury, insistence on mathematical precision would be illusory and the judge or juror must be allowed a fair latitude to make reasonable approximations guided by judgment and practical experience."[3] The above statement does not diminish the value of the U.S. approach with its economics focus; it simply points out that the deliberation of damages must also include other matters such as the "character" of the plaintiff, which are unable to be captured by mathematics and statistics.

The U.S. approach to computing tort damages is grounded in microeconomic theories that model the personal creation of utility or enjoyment of life through the consumption of leisure and goods. Since everyone labors to acquire goods, injury through the loss of personal productivity (1) lowers the enjoyment of life attainable during leisure hours and (2) lowers the ability to obtain money income during work hours in order to purchase goods.[4] These results are demonstrated by Krueger, Albrecht, and Ward in "the whole-time concept" of tort damages.[5] The whole-time model begins with the maximization of the enjoyment of life subject to personal budget constraints relating the value of time at leisure and the prices of market goods. When an injury causes a decrease in personal productivity, the budget constraint contracts to lower values, reducing the possibility for enjoyment of life. By comparing pre- and post-injury earning capacity, the whole-time concept allows the computation of the market dollar-based amount necessary to push the post-injury budget constraint out to its pre-injury level. However, that amount of damage compensation would still not necessarily restore the pre-injury utility or enjoyment of life. The reason is that even with additional income, the impact of the injury on productivity persists, thereby diminishing alternative leisure and consumption choices.

Since all legitimate torts are subject to general damages for the loss of enjoyment of life, the beginning values of special tort damages are the market prices of goods now unobtainable due to decreased (or eliminated) work productivity caused by the injury (or death). The loss of obtainable goods such as food, shelter, transportation, and medical care using the pre-injury expected amount of time the tort victim would have spent in the labor market is measured as the difference in pre- and post-injury earning capacity.[6] When the "goods" desired result from hours of nonmarket labor provided by a person for his or her own or family's consumption, such as a clean house or child care, those losses are measurable using the market price to replace the output from that nonmarket work. The economist can state to the trier of the facts that the U.S. approach to dollar-measurable values of special damages allows the injured person to restore the same possible set of consumption goods available to him before the injury; however, having the ability to purchase those lost goods with the money damages does not necessarily make the plaintiff whole when considering that the loss of physical productivity persists post-injury to hamper the ability to enjoy life with the consumption of those pre-injury selected goods.

Can economists say anything more about economic damages? Freidman (1982)[7] has asked "How much money would it take to compensate a blinded man?" In an attempt to restore enjoyment to the blind man through his remaining senses, the trier of the facts could attempt to decide how many gourmet meals, nice fitting clothes, or concert performances it would take to compensate for the blinding. Economists are unable to embark on such compensatory routes for two reasons. First, economists do not have methods for determining required compensating bundles of goods or for knowing how many of those goods would be necessary to reach a compensating value of pre-injury enjoyment of life. Secondly, economists discourage such expeditions recognizing that under the law of diminishing returns, eventually such goods have little value, and it would be socially inefficient to satiate the tort victim with them. Instead of focusing only on how to compensate for the loss of enjoyment of life with money, general legal and economic thought endorses providing special damages that work toward restoring the pre-injury productivity of the plaintiff. Medical experts opine on the cost of medical, psychological, and supportive care, as well as medicines and equipment which would increase the post-injury productive capabilities of the plaintiff to work or to enjoy leisure. These special damages offset some general damages, however. For example, if the plaintiff requires a wheelchair and special transportation in order to interact with the community, the costs of those items offset to some degree the general damages for the loss of enjoyment of life from not being able to interact with the community. The present value of such future life-care costs (where lifetime costs in today's dollars are specified by medical evidence) is often an integral part of the special tort damages evaluated by an economist expert witness, and methods to calculate those present values are included in the U.S. approach.

4. THEORETICAL AND METHODOLOGICAL COMPONENTS OF THE U.S. APPROACH

The U.S. approach to computing tort damages is generally limited to the damage categories of the loss of earnings and/or earning capacity, services, future medical expenses, and the loss of financial support. These damages originate from the reduction in personal productivity due to injury (or its elimination due to death). This section presents the generally accepted economic theories and methods[8] which have defined the terms and procedures used to compute economic damages in the United States. This material demonstrates that determining portions of tort damage compensation is an exercise clearly rooted in economics. The section also serves as a reference guide to the generally accepted methods taken to compute tort economic damages.

4.1. Loss of Earning Capacity and Earnings

4.1.1. Economic and Legal Definitions of Earning Capacity and Earnings

At the heart of the U.S. approach to determining economic tort damages is the concept of earning capacity. From an economist's view, an individual's *earning capacity* is equal to the amount of money one could reasonably expect to earn working at a job that fully utilizes one's abilities. An individual's *expected earnings* are the money amounts it is anticipated that will actually be earned working at a job. The extent to which the person utilizes his or her abilities in the labor market over the course of their working life determines his or her *lifetime expected earnings*.

In U.S. case law, the phrase "earning capacity" was first associated with the potential market worth of property. When property was destroyed or held in dispute, damages were assigned according to the property's potential market worth or earning capacity. Relevant to personal injury, an early appearance of the term "earning capacity" was in a 1901 U.S. Supreme Court opinion (*Texas & Pacific Railway v. Humble* (181 U.S. 57, 1901)) where the court allowed a married woman to make a claim for her own loss of earning capacity due to injury. At issue was an Arkansas court's instruction that:

> If you should find for the plaintiff, in assessing her damages you will take into consideration her age and earning capacity before and after the injury was received, as shown by the proofs, her physical condition before the injury, and her physical condition after the injury, and the nature and character of the injury she received, whether it be permanent or temporary in its nature, and find for her such sum as will fairly and reasonably compensate her therefor, including therein fair and reasonable compensation for any physical and personal pain and suffering she may have undergone as the result thereof.

The case illuminates the simultaneity of economic and noneconomic damages. First, the court instructs the trier of the facts to consider the economic damages associated with the impact of the reduced "physical condition" or productivity caused by the injury and then to consider the noneconomic damages compensating for pain and suffering.

While every state has since commented on earning capacity as a component of tort damages, a clear, early economic statement of the term was provided by the Supreme Court of Missouri in *Wolfe v. Kansas City* (334 Mo. 796, Mo. 1934):

> Capacity to labor (physically or mentally) includes the capacity to earn money, and more. Our law is that recovery may be had for an impairment of the capacity to labor, although there may be in fact no actual loss of earnings, and to be deprived of the power to work is a source of injury, independent of the pecuniary benefits that such labor may confer … .
>
> There is a distinction between the power or capacity to work and earn money and loss of time or money that one probably will lose in the future on account of physical or mental disability. Loss of time, or what one may reasonably be expected to earn in the future, comes under the head of the amount of loss of time or earnings, or the fruits or gains from the power or capability to work and earn money … .

> Compensation for incapacity to labor or work is not founded on the theory that such incapacity is merely a matter of discomfort, inconvenience or annoyance, as was said in some of the earlier cases and, for that reason, compensation as a part of the general injuries received. Inability to work is something more than a discomfort, inconvenience and annoyance. The mere inability to move about or to use a movable member of the body is a discomfort, inconvenience or annoyance. Therefore, inability to play or engage in any active diversion comes under the same head. While inability to work, mentally or physically, is a discomfort, inconvenience and annoyance, unless such inability is compensated upon the theory that it results in more than a limitation of the power or disposition to move around as one does in play, it is entirely logical to say that it is merely a discomfort, inconvenience and annoyance. However, there is quite a difference in one's loss as a result of inability to work and inability to play. The main difference between work and play is that, in the former, the activity is engaged in order to exist or live and in the latter the activity is entered into merely as a pastime. Therefore, any activity engaged in, other than play, is work or the exacting of a living from one's surroundings or environment. This, of course, includes the earning of money, which is merely a medium of exchange for work where one works for another.
>
> So the inability to work or labor, physically or mentally, is something more than discomfort, inconvenience or annoyance. It is that plus the inability to, wholly or partially earn a living, either by working for others at a wage or salary (money) or for one's self. Viewing it from this standpoint, the inability to earn money is included in the inability to work.

The above passages from the *Wolfe* case correspond to the economic theories presented in this chapter. The inability of a person to achieve his or her earning capacity is an inability to productively exist or live, while the inability to enjoy leisure is a discomfort, inconvenience, or annoyance that is compensated by general or noneconomic damages. The inability to work includes the inability to work for others at a wage or to work for one's self to exist or to live. Therefore, earning capacity is something that exists in every human being (young/old, disabled/able-bodied, unemployed/employed/retired); and when an injury impacts the ability to work, an economic tort damage exists coinciding with that harm. The U.S. approach captures these economic damages with models of the loss of earnings and/or earning capacity, the lost of ability to perform service work, future medical expenses, and the loss of financial support.

4.1.2. Theory of the Determination of Earning Capacity

Economic theory holds that a plaintiff's earning capacity at a point in time (e.g., at date of injury or death) is determined by employers who know the current abilities of the plaintiff. The generally accepted economic theory of earning capacity has its origin in the economics literature with the wage-rate[9] conditions of a profit-maximizing firm (or organization) in economic equilibrium. It is generally accepted that when a firm maximizes profits and is in equilibrium, an employee of the firm receives a wage rate, w, which is equal to the marginal revenue product of his or her labor input, MRP_L. After dissecting MRP_L, the wage-rate-determining equation becomes $w = MR \times MP_L$, which states that the wage rate is equal to the multiplicative product of marginal revenue and the marginal product of the individual's labor, which is in turn determined by the innate abilities and the human capital of the individual worker. From the marginal revenue part of the wage-rate-determining equation, since the worker has no control over market prices, the wage rate that he or she receives is influenced by factors exogenous to the quality or kind of work supplied by the worker.

4.1.3. Growth in Earning Capacity

Not only must the forensic economist in the United States forecast earning capacity at a point in time in a plaintiff's working life, it is also necessary to forecast future changes in earning capacity by age or expected employment tenure. The wage-rate-determining equation shows that through marginal revenue wages will change when prices change (inflation); and when an economist includes changes in the price level as one of the reasons for wage-rate changes, he or she is said to be studying "nominal rates" of wage-rate growth. When an economist does not include changes in price levels as one of the reasons for wage-rate changes (therefore focusing on the marginal product part of the wage-rate-determining equation), he or she is said to be studying "real rates" of wage-rate growth.

According to economic theory, the changes in an individual's marginal product of labor or productivity over time are a function of changes in innate abilities, human capital, and technological conditions. Innate abilities refer to the individual's natural mental and physical capacities that are subject to changes with age. Loss of innate ability may create negative marginal productivity growth, causing earning capacity to decline (the decline can be gradual with advancing age or immediate with the onset of a disability). Human capital, in contrast to innate abilities, refers to skills and positions acquired by individuals throughout life. The generally accepted human capital model argues that the behavior of earnings over time depends on the human capital possessed by the individual. As human capital increases, productivity, and hence earning capacity, increases. Human capital research shows that growth in human capital is greatest at younger ages and then diminishes over a worker's lifetime. To address human capital's impact on earning capacity, economists empirically analyze life-cycle earnings patterns that coincide with the theoretical models of human capital. Technological change can also result in changes in the individual's marginal product and thus changes in his or her wage rate (or earning capacity). Economists usually measure the impact on technology on wages as a part of the real growth in wages observed in secular wage trends over time.

4.1.4. Exercising Earning Capacity to Produce Earnings

The possession of an earning capacity provides the ability to achieve earnings in the labor market, and the extent to which a person utilizes his or her abilities in the labor market over the course of working life determines his or her lifetime expected earnings. The theory of labor supply is used to understand reasons for attachment to the labor force. The conventional labor supply model begins with a consumer dividing a fixed amount of allocable time, T, into hours worked in the labor market, h, and hours spent at consumption, l. Ignoring savings, the consumer with characteristics A possesses a utility function defined by the consumption of commodities, x, and hours of work, h, as $U = U(x, h, A, \varepsilon)$ where ε stands for the consumer's tastes, availability for home production, or whatever essential item that the consumer balances between work in the labor market and consumption. Income from market work depends upon hours of work h and, in the simplest case, the fixed wage rate w (or earning capacity) per unit of work. If p is the fixed per unit price of the bundle of commodities x, and if y is income independent of the labor supply decision, then the consumer's budget constraint is $px = wh+y$. The consumer is assumed to choose $x>0$ and $h\geq 0$ that maximizes utility subject to the budget constraint. At the utility maximization point, when the market's valuation of the consumer's time, w, exceeds the consumer's implicit value of his or her time when $h = 0$ (w^*, the reservation wage), then the consumer will participate in the labor force and supply a positive number of hours h of market work. Conversely, if at the margin the consumer places a greater value on an extra unit of his consumption time than does the market on his or her work time ($w^* > w$), then the consumer will not supply labor to the labor market. Earning capacity is a key component in determining lifetime labor supply. When earning capacity declines rapidly at advanced age due to declines in innate ability and/or in the value of human capital, the reservation wage quickly eclipses earning capacity and retirement occurs.

4.1.5. Lifetime Expected Earning Capacity and Expected Earnings

We have seen that generally accepted economic theory supplies the framework to evaluate an individual's lifetime expected earning capacity through his or her marginal product by age and an individual's lifetime expected earnings through his or her demand for consumption. The economic situation of a plaintiff at a point in his or her lifetime, which we call an economic "state," is caused by the various factors discussed that are specific to the plaintiff (innate ability, human capital, and choice of leisure vs. work) and by other factors that are relevant to all persons in the economy (price levels and technology). Generally, accepted economic theory includes components that anticipate transition or movement from one economic state to another over the course of a lifetime. For example, the decrease in innate ability with age (physical deterioration) decreases the individual's marginal product capability leading to a decrease in his or her earning capacity, which in turn influences his or her demand for consumption. Consumption demand controls how much labor he or she supplies to the market, which ultimately determines his or her earnings level.

In order to estimate future multiyear earning capacity and expected earnings, in the U.S. approach, economists use econometric models formed from generally accepted economic theories. Using a variety of empirical data to properly account for the variability in lifetime earnings and earning capacity, the economist describes the relationships that produce earning capacity and earnings by presenting statistics. Going back to the human capital example, economists are interested in measuring the effects of human capital on lifetime earnings. In order to describe the relationship statistically, the economist obtains observations of the earnings of similar persons with respect to age or tenure in an occupation, called the "sample." The human capital model sets forth the hypothesis of the mathematical form expected in the relationship of earnings to age or tenure. From the sample, using statistical methods the economist tests whether the mathematical form of human capital theory is observed within the sample. The economist presents an estimate of earnings resulting from the statistical relationship of age or tenure to earnings and then tests whether that relationship is reliably described by using deviations (or error rates) between the earnings in the sample and the predicted life-cycle earnings pattern. Therefore, economists use econometrics to obtain quantitative values of the relationships posited in the parameters of an economic theory and test those values for reliability as operators of economic theory.

Individuals have certain identifying characteristics (current abilities and their records of earnings and human capital attainment), and the economy possesses certain current and historical characteristics (inflation, unemployment, and the progress of technology) that together affect earning capacity. Likewise, persons of comparable characteristics over various ages (a cross section of the current population) present a relevant sample from which to draw information regarding transitions or movements in economic states over a lifetime. In order to present reliable economic information to the trier of fact regarding the expected present value of multiyear earnings losses, the economist uses econometric methods to apply all of the relevant determinants of earning capacity and earnings to appropriate samples of population data within the economy. While the detail in sampling and statistical estimation is subject to debate and variation among economists, conformity to the firm economic theories of earning capacity and expected earnings is required in all statistical studies. For example, a valid projection of earning capacity will include both human capital and innate ability analysis. An economist cannot project earning capacity based on human capital attainment over a lifetime without also considering the expected effects of the reduction in innate ability.

4.1.6. Estimating Growth and Other Economic Parameters

In order to implement any economic loss model involving projections, it is necessary to forecast variables that are exogenous to the model. Some variables are assumed to be static, and their future value is based upon current cohort values. For example, survival probabilities for a cohort group are usually assumed to be static, and forecasts are based upon recent observations of survival from the cohort group. Other variables fluctuate to the extent that a method of forecasting that takes into account a series of values over time is required. For example, the unemployment rate for a particular cohort group may change from year to year to such an extent that using only the most recent observation to forecast future amounts is not an appropriate forecasting method. In economics, forecasting methods range from complex econometric models to simple univariate time-series forecasts, also referred to as extrapolation. In this section, we briefly discuss various methods of forecasting variables with the focus on simple extrapolation methods as best suited for implementing the U.S. approach.

A goal of the U.S. approach is to present reliable economic estimates formed from existing economic and demographic information. Traditionally, complex economic forecasting models are designed for simulation exercises in order to provide information for the evaluation of government policy or near-term expectations of general macroeconomic variable values such as economic growth and inflation. Complex econometric modeling may reveal, for example, that an increased life expectancy affects individuals' decisions with regard to the accumulation of human capital and labor force participation. While the forecasts of the U.S. Centers for Disease Control point to increased life expectancy, the general U.S. approach is not designed to account for the effect that increased life expectancy may have on human capital acquisition and labor force participation in the future; they rely upon the past and present cohort situation to develop the forecast without changes in the cohort segment. For example, economic data show what the labor force participation rate of 45-year-old males with a high school education is and has been. It is beyond the forensic economist's purview to forecast changes in the labor force participation rate due to increased life expectancy. Changes over time in the cohort population's disability rates, unemployment rates, wage growth rates, medical cost growth rates, participation rates, and other variables that may be used to forecast earnings would each cause the actual value of economic loss to be above or below the model's estimate. Since *ex post* measurements of actual economic losses are not possible, an objective is to apply the U.S. approach such that the immeasurable errors would tend to offset each other.

Often the economic loss forecast period embedded into the U.S. approach is long – a 40-year forecast of an individual's earnings is not uncommon. The forecast period for wage and medical price growth rates is similar in length to demographic forecasts. Complex econometric models are generally quarterly models that forecast about eight future quarters. It is certainly not the consensus in the field of economics that a complex econometric model is capable of a more reliable long-term forecast than less complex extrapolative methods. Rather, absent an expectation of substantial structural shifts, a method "that simply extrapolates from previous outcomes may be more successful. If the economy stays on track, such extrapolative forecasts are generally accurate" (Hendray et al., 2001, p. 8). In conclusion, the goal of the U.S. approach is to present reliable economic estimates formed from existing economic and demographic information. As such, simple averages of relevant past economic information, or extrapolations, form the basis of the forecasts made by the U.S. approach. Since the trier of the facts should be made aware of qualitative information regarding the tort victim, the nature of any economic forecast and its potential variations should be information that the trier of the facts considers when evaluating the usefulness of the forensic economic evidence of damages presented.

4.2. Loss of Nonmarket Work or Services

4.2.1. Economic and Legal Definitions of Services

As previously discussed in this chapter, service losses originate from an individual's loss of nonmarket productivity due to physical harm created by a tort. A tort victim has experienced service losses when physical injury has reduced the victim's productivity in performing labor-related activities in order to exist or to live a certain lifestyle. A Missouri appellate court in the case *Larose v. Washington University* (154 S.W.3d 365, (Mo. App. 2004)) pointed out the inseparability of impaired ability to perform services with the loss of earning capacity as follows:

> Defendant also claims that the award of damages for Gail's loss of ability [was] included as future economic damage, and such damages should have been classified as noneconomic damage under Richard's loss of consortium claim instead. We disagree. As discussed above, the court in *Collier* discussed a wife's ability to recover damages for her loss of ability to perform household services. 366 S.W.2d at 500. In its discussion, the court noted that "[a]ny physical inability of a housewife to perform domestic duties must necessarily mean a physical inability to work and labor." Id. at 499. Additionally, the court acknowledged that such impairment is a compensable item of damage to the wife, and not to her husband. Id. at 500. As previously stated, the loss of ability to work has been defined as an economic damage under section 538.205. Thus, the loss of ability to perform household services, or loss of ability to work, was properly included as an economic damage, recoverable by Gail.

Such association of impairment in ability to perform services and loss of earning capacity is recognized across state and federal jurisdictions in the United States.

The motivation to work is to acquire consumption goods – labor market work produces money income to purchase goods while service work produces actual goods to consume. For example, when the good to consume is a tidy lawn, a person can work at a job to obtain money to hire the neighbor boy to cut his lawn or the person can cut his lawn himself. Basic economic theory demonstrates that when a person performs service work that has a market price less than that person's earning capacity, in addition to the good produced the person must be receiving compensating utility value. When service activities are personal in nature, such as teaching one's child to read, the teaching work might have a market price less than one's earning capacity, but the addition of bonding time with one's child is an inducement to perform that activity. While the value of joyful services such as family time are apparent, mundane tasks such as cleaning the house may have additional personal value, such as acquiring exercise, comfort in not having strangers around one's house, deferring income in order to take a vacation or saving to purchase some good, or strong disutility from labor market work. Because the performance of services clearly involves enjoyment-of-life issues, the generally accepted approach to valuing economic damages associated with reduced productivity in the ability to perform services is to measure the service activity's market replacement cost.

The Kansas Supreme Court addressed the concurrency of services and enjoyment of life during family activities in the case of *Clark v. Southwestern Greyhound Lines* (144 Kan. 344; Kan., 1936). The *Clark* case involved the plaintiff's husband bringing an action for loss of services and companionship from his injured wife. The Court wrote:

> The position taken by plaintiff would require courts and juries to distinguish between services and companionship. That is, when a dutiful wife arose in the morning and prepared breakfast for her husband, that would be services, and the husband could not maintain an action for loss of that, but while this happy couple were eating breakfast and the wife had surrendered the morning papers and during a lull in the efforts necessary to induce the children to eat their cereal she laughed at an occasional stale joke or offered a comment on some passing news of the day, that would be companionship, and the husband could maintain an action for loss of that. Then when the time came to go to the office and the wife drove the husband to work in the family car, that would be work that might be performed by a chauffeur and would be called services, and the husband could not maintain an action for loss of it. If, however, on the way down there was gay laughter and happy conversation while this happy couple planned a picnic for the evening, that would be companionship and the husband could maintain an action for the loss of that. It seems that the mere statement of the proposition is a refutation of it. The fact is that the wife owes the duty to observe the little amenities and attentions that tend to keep the matrimonial bark riding at an even keel as much as she does the duty to look after the more material tasks of the household. By way of dicta it may be said that the husband owes the same duty. They are all services as dealt with by R. S. 23-205. To hold otherwise would require the installation of a time sheet in every home and devolve upon courts and juries the impossible task of deciding where services left off and companionship began. We are loath to think that the legislature intended to place upon the courts such a task.

While the law at the time of *Clark* was different than today regarding how spouses claim damages, the case points out that enjoyment of life exists with service performance. The fact that enjoyment of life is also obtained with service activity does not eliminate the obtainable damages when physical injury causes reduced capability in performing services.

4.2.2. Determining Service Value

While we often apply feelings or special care to our service activity time, pecuniary service losses are not based on emotional activity. Service losses are valued by their market cost of obtaining productivity or work commensurate with the service tasks once performed by the tort victim at his or her pre-injury productivity level. As noted earlier, economic theory holds that a plaintiff's earning capacity at a point in time (e.g., at the date of injury or death) is determined by employers who know the productive abilities of the plaintiff. In order to value a tort victim's loss of services, the pre-injury work effort expended by the tort victim must be determined and then matched to the labor market wage associated with such output. In order to identify an appropriate market replacement cost of normal service work (cooking, cleaning, home maintenance, child care, etc.), the productivity applied to service work is assumed to be low when compared to skilled labor supply in the marketplace. For example, while a homeowner might occasionally nail down a loose board on his house, that task does not require the skills of a carpenter to complete. In order to minimize the anticipated general differential between service productivity level and for-hire labor, services are valued using labor market wage data for the lowest skilled workers whose jobs involve tasks related to service work (e.g., cooks, maids, childcare workers, trade helpers, etc.). Any unique aspects of the tort victim's ability to perform service activities is presented to the trier of the facts through evidence from persons who know the talents of the tort victim.

4.2.3. Inventorying Lost Service Time

The most common methods used to inventory lost services are through "direct questions" and "time diaries." In the direct question approach, a common service activity such as cooking is suggested by the interviewer, and the tort victim forms a recollection and determination of the total weekly time devoted to cooking before the injury and how much time is now spent cooking after the injury. Claimed lost service time includes such activities as housework, food cooking and cleanup, taking care of pets, maintaining home and vehicles, household financial management, shopping, travel for household activities, and caring for or helping household members. The time-diary approach requires respondents to record in time sequence their usual daily services activities during a week, often splitting the week into weekdays and weekends. From the responses, service-related tasks are separated from other time use. Studies that compare time-diary to direct-question data find that direct questions typically produce higher time estimates than time-diary questions, especially for activities that occur frequently. For activities that occur infrequently, direct questions produce lower time estimates, possibly because a longer period of recall is required.

An alternative approach to discovering service losses is for tort victims to rate themselves in terms of efficiency and/or output of service effort before and after the injury. Case-specific medical evidence might also be used to determine or verify the loss of productivity rating. To quantify service losses, survey data regarding hours-of-service performance of people not involved in litigation is applied to the reduced productivity rating supplied by the tort victim or presented as evidence regarding the victim's functional capacities.

The amount of services provided is a function of the situation of the individual at the particular point in time. Some aspects of the individual's situation may change in the future, and the changes may alter the amount of services provided by him or her. For example, the amount of services provided is a function of the existence of children in the household, the age of the children, and the employment status of the individual. Changes in these parameters will likely change the amount of services provided. In order to estimate the multiyear value of services provided, economists utilize models that estimate the changes in the services provided when the situation of the particular individual changes. The models are derived from data showing how services provided change with children aging, with children leaving the household, and with retirement. It is necessary to take these changes into account to accurately estimate the amount of services that would have been provided.

4.2.4. General Economic Parameters of Service Losses

Many variables that are beyond the scope of the economist using the general approach to service losses will affect the value of the services that an individual will supply. A relative wage change in the sectors that provide the household services would affect the estimations in different ways. The hours individuals devote to household activities may change due to relative wage changes between the individual's wages and the wages of those who provide the services. The relative wage change would also likely affect the value of a unit of services provided. As in earning capacity forecasts, the probability of survival and maintained productivity affects the future value of services provided. Again, these variables are assumed to be cohort determined at the point in time. Furthermore, absent an expected structural shift, simple extrapolations are used by the economist to determine service losses.

4.3. Future Medical Costs

Instead of focusing only on monetary compensation for the loss of enjoyment of life, special damages related to medical items or services can work toward restoring some of the pre-injury productivity of the plaintiff. Medical experts present testimony on the cost of medical, psychological, supportive care, medicines, and equipment which would increase the post-injury productive capabilities of the plaintiff to work or to enjoy leisure. To a degree, these special damages offset some general damages. For example, a surgery which costs $30,000 might alleviate some pain, so the $30,000 medical cost works toward reducing general damages for suffering pain. Economists do not opine on the set of medically related goods that might work toward restoring the pre-injury productivity of the plaintiff. However, economists do testify to the present value of such future life-care costs (where lifetime costs in today's dollars are specified by medical evidence).

4.4. Loss of Financial Support

4.4.1. Economic and Legal Definitions of Loss of Financial Support

Survivors' claims for the loss of financial support derive from the expected living expenses, gifts, and bequests that would have been provided to them by the decedent but for the wrongful death. The objective of the wrongful death loss computation is to calculate the present value dollar amount that, with investment, will enable the survivors to replace their economic losses incurred due to the wrongful death of their benefactor.

Within U.S. state law, wrongful death damages are usually specified by statute, and they are often referred to as the sum of lost support and lost net accumulations. For example, the Florida wrongful death statute 768.21 (5) (a) calls for damages regarding the

> (l)oss of earnings of the deceased from the date of injury to the date of death, less lost support of survivors excluding contributions in kind, with interest. Loss of the prospective net accumulations of an estate, which might reasonably have been expected but for the wrongful death, reduced to present money value, may also be recovered.

Lost support can be referred to as the present value of the expected routine payments of living expenses and gifts to the survivor by the decedent, and lost net accumulations represent the present value of what the decedent's estate would have been worth to the survivor at the time of normal death less the value of the estate at the time of death.

4.4.2. Economic Calculation of Loss of Financial Support

The methodology for the economic calculation of the loss of financial support is presented by Krueger and Albrecht (2007) beginning with a person having three assets during the time he is living: (1) stored wealth, (2) earning capacity, and (3) the monetary value of expected gifts to be provided to him or her before death. During the person's expected lifetime, he might have provided routine annual support to legal heirs, and upon the person's death the legal heirs might have inherited some portion of the person's stored wealth. Wrongful death damages of the loss of financial support are related to the loss of expected annual financial support and inheritance due to a premature death. The calculation of the loss of financial support (including potential net estate accumulations) can be reduced to a calculation of the decedent's expected lifetime earnings less his or her own personal consumption of those earnings. See Krueger and Albrecht (2007) for the mathematics of this method.

4.5. Discounting to Present Value

After a forensic economist estimates an expected multi-period loss according to the U.S. approach, the expected future stream earnings must be reduced to a present-value lump sum. Present-value lump-sum payments must comply with two legal requirements: (1) the plaintiff's damages must be paid in full and (2) the defendant must be equitably treated because the plaintiff will be able to receive a secondary stream of investment income from that portion of the lump sum that is not needed to compensate for current losses. Generally accepted economic theory anticipates the rewards and risks of investing lump sums that allow for reliable present-value calculations. Below we address the generally accepted methods regarding the discounting procedure to account for the time value of money and investment risk.

4.5.1. Discounting Formula

The formula used to calculate the amount required today, the present value, in order to compensate for an amount that would have been received in the future, the future value, is $\mathrm{PV} = \mathrm{FV}[1/(1+i)^t]$, where $\mathrm{PV} =$ the present value; $\mathrm{FV} =$ the future amount to be received in period t; $i =$ the interest rate, per time period, used for discounting; and $t =$ the number of time periods in the future until FV would be received. The term in the brackets is often referred to as the discount factor, and the interest rate, i, is often referred to as the discount rate. If there are several periods in the future where an amount would have been received, the formula is written as $\mathrm{PV} = \sum_{t=1}^{n} \mathrm{FV}_t[1/(1+i)^t]$, where $\mathrm{FV}_t =$ the future amount to be received in period t. The amount of future value, FV_t, is not necessarily the same amount at every period t. Likewise, it is not necessary that the interest rate, i, be the same for every time period t.

4.5.2. Risk Associated with Receiving the Future Value

One factor that affects the choice of the appropriate discount rate is the known probability (or risk) that is associated with receiving the future amount. The greater the probability of the future amount would have been received, the greater is the present value of the amount. Assume that an amount FV will be received with certainty in one year. Moreover, further assume that the appropriate risk-free discount rate has been determined to be i percent so that the present value is $\text{PV} = \text{FV}[1/(1+i)]$. Now assume that the amount FV will be received with the probability of η_{FV} where $0 \leq \eta_{\text{FV}} \leq 1$ so that the expected amount received is defined by $E(\text{FV}) = \text{FV} \times \eta_{\text{FV}}$. With the existence of risk, it is not appropriate to calculate the present value of FV by using the risk-free discount rate of i and amount FV. There are two equivalent methods of calculating the present value of FV when FV will be received with a probability of less than one. The first method uses the discount rate i with the expected future value $E(\text{FV})$, so that the present value is $\text{PV} = E(\text{FV})[1/(1+i)]$. The second method uses a discount rate that incorporates the probability of receiving the amount. The discount rate that incorporates the probability of receiving the amount FV is represented as, i_p, where $i_p = [(1+i)/\eta_{\text{FV}}] - 1$, then $\text{PV} = \text{FV}[1/(1+i_p)]$. There are situations when $E(\text{FV})$ and i_p are each present in the discounting problem. When $E(\text{FV})$ and i_p are independent of each other and can be separately estimated, it is appropriate to use both of their values in the discounting equation. When using both $E(\text{FV})$ and i_p in the discounting problem, the economist must articulate their independence and separable estimation; otherwise risk will be doubly counted in the resulting present value amount and the plaintiff will be undercompensated for his or her losses. In summary, if there is risk concerning the receipt of the future amount, the risk must be accounted for or else the plaintiff will be overcompensated. The risk can be accounted for either by adjusting the amount to be received to the expected amount or by adjusting the discount rate to reflect the risk (or both when independent risks exist).

4.5.3. Inflation and the Discount Rate

Amounts to be received in the future may be affected by price inflation. To show how inflation affects the choice of the discount rate, we begin with the explanation of the difference between a nominal discount rate and a real discount rate. The nominal interest rate is the observable market rate. According to the Fisher[10] equation, the nominal interest rate is a function of the real interest rate and the expected rate of inflation. For discrete growth

Table 1. U.S. Approach for Estimating Lifetime Expected Earning Capacity.

Step 1: Determine the base value of earning capacity
The base value is the beginning year or age value of earning capacity measured by (1) the individual's earnings, wage, and benefits history; or (2) matching the individual's demonstrated levels of innate ability and human capital to empirical labor market data; or (3) deferring to the expertise of a vocational specialist.

Step 2. Forecast changes in earning capacity due to individual changes
Apply an age-earnings profile to measure the changes from the base value of earning capacity due to changes in the individual's innate abilities and human capital. The age-earnings profile is calculated by matching characteristics relevant to the individual's innate ability and human capital to a cross section of age-earnings experiences of similarly situated people as measured by empirical labor market data.

Step 3. Forecast changes in earning capacity due to changes in market conditions
The individual's earning capacity changes (at a minimum) from the base period dollar level with (1) inflation and (2) increases in labor productivity due to technology. The evaluator either estimates expected future price inflation based on market expectations or ignores growth due to price inflation and discounts earnings capacity to present value using an inflation-free discount rate. The evaluator often estimates productivity by observing secular changes in the real earnings (earnings growth absent expected general price inflation) paid by employers to workers performing specific tasks.

Step 4. Additional consideration of benefits
Earning capacity is the sum of wages and the value of employer-provided benefits. The percentage mix of wages and the value of benefits summing to total compensation can differ after the base period. Also, the economic value of benefits may not be realized at the time they are earned; and the expected rate of change in wages and the value of benefits may differ due to market reasons. As a result of these expectations, the evaluator may sometimes estimate only wages under steps 1–3 and then estimate the value of employer-provided benefits separately as step 4.

Step 5. Possible consideration of income taxes
In some situations, an after-tax estimate of earning capacity is required. Annual expected income taxes are estimated in step 5 based on the earning capacity estimates determined in steps 1–3.

Step 6. Hazards preventing the individual from realizing earning capacity
After the base period, there is a non-zero expectation that an individual would be prevented from obtaining his or her earning capacity due to a variety of involuntary factors including death, the onset of disability that precludes work, and lack of access to employers (e.g., unemployment or discouragement). The evaluator estimates the probability of these hazards to the individual using cross-sectional observations of mortality, morbidity, and labor market experiences of similarly situated persons.

Step 7. Determining the boundary age of reliable estimation
Steps 2 and 6 are estimated from cross-sectional observations of persons in similar situations to that of the individual. When making economic calculations, the evaluator must consider

Table 1. *(Continued)*

the reliability of the application of the information contained within his or her samples of population data to the individual studied. While the detail in sampling and statistical estimation is subject to debate and variation, reasonable conformity to the individual is required for all statistical studies. As such, the evaluator must determine a reasonably conforming final earning capacity age level to apply to his or her estimates of an individual's expected earning capacity in order for the estimates to remain reliable.
Step 8. Discounting to present value
The completion of steps 1–7 produces a multi-period stream of expected, or risk-adjusted, earning capacity. The last step is to reduce that multi-period stream of expected earning capacity to a present-value lump sum. Since risks related to earning capacity are recognized in previous steps, expected lifetime earning capacity is generally discounted to present value using a risk-free rate associated with the currently available yields of United States Treasury securities. However, in some situations there may be justifiable risks not accounted for in steps 1–7 that require increasing the discount rate above the risk-free rate. In those cases, the economic rationale of such a rate increase must be grounded in the analysis in steps 1–7. If income taxes are considered as a part of step 5, the present-value calculation must also consider any income taxes on investment return.

rates, the function is $i = i_r + f + i_r f$, where i is the nominal interest rate, i_r the real interest rate, and f the expected rate of inflation. When discounting a future amount that changes according to the rate of inflation, the future amount can be inflated by the expected rate of inflation and then discounted by i. Conversely, the future amount, absent the expected inflation increase, can be discounted by i_r.

5. AMERICAN TORT DAMAGES MODELS

So far in this chapter, the legal and economic foundations of the U.S. approach have been presented. Using a series of tables, this next section presents the U.S. approach as a set of broad analytical steps that are used in every generally accepted scientific analysis of economic damages in the following areas: loss of lifetime earning capacity (Table 1), loss of lifetime earnings (Table 2), loss of financial support (Table 3), loss of lifetime ability to perform services (Table 4), and the present value of future medical expenses (Table 5). Each of the procedural steps in the tables draws upon the economic methodologies presented in the previous sections of this chapter.

Table 2. U.S. Approach for Estimating Lifetime Expected Earnings.

Step 1. Base earnings determination

Earnings, consisting of wages and value of employer paid benefits, are the money results of the individual's choice, in some part, to utilize his or her earning capacity in the labor market. The evaluator measures the base value of earnings in a similar manner as the base value of earning capacity shown in Table 1 (earning capacity).

Step 2. Forecast changes in earnings due to individual changes

At each age beyond the base value, assuming the continuance of the individual's base choice to utilize his or her earning capacity in the labor market (see step 6), the age-earnings profile measures the change from the base value of earnings due to changes in the individual's innate abilities and human capital. The age-earnings profile is similar to that as in step 2 of Table 1 (earning capacity).

Step 3. Changes in earnings due to changes in market conditions

The individual's earnings will change for the same market reasons as in step 3 of Table 1 (earning capacity).

Step 4. Additional consideration of benefits

Benefits may also be considered in a separate step as in step 4 of Table 1 (earning capacity).

Step 5. Possible consideration of income taxes

Income taxes are calculated as in step 5 of Table 1 (earning capacity).

Step 6. Hazards preventing the individual from having earnings

After the base period, there is a non-zero expectation that an individual would not have earnings due to a variety of voluntary and involuntary factors including the choice to work, death, the onset of disability that prevents work, and lack of access to employers (e.g., unemployment or discouragement). The evaluator estimates the probability of these hazards to the individual using cross-sectional observations of decision to work, mortality, morbidity, and labor market experiences of similarly situated persons to the individual.

Step 7. Determining the boundary age of reliable estimation

As in step 7 of Table 1 (earning capacity), the evaluator must determine a reasonably conforming final earnings age level to his or her estimates of an individual's expected earnings in order for the estimates to remain reliable. The boundary age is influenced by the age beyond which cross-sectional information from the population has high error rates due to the combined effects of (a) high risks of mortality and morbidity, (b) the small size of the population that works from which to draw earnings experience data, and (c) the large variations in the earnings and labor supply of the elderly.

Step 8. Discounting to present value

Discounting to present value is accomplished as in step 8 of Table 1 (earning capacity).

Table 3. U.S. Approach for Estimating Loss of Financial Support.

Step 1. Determine the discounted value of earnings
The evaluator measures the base value of financial support as in the base value of earnings as shown in steps 1–8 in Table 2 (earnings). Not all employment benefits may be available to survivors.

Step 2. Optional – estimate retirement income derived from employment
In situations where the decedent's retirement income is relevant as a loss to survivors, the evaluator measures the present value of the retirement income received as a benefit of employment in the same manner as he or she would in steps 1–8 in Table 2 (earnings).

Step 3. Subtract from earnings (and optionally retirement income) the present value of the decedent's personal consumption
The evaluator measures personal consumption as the amount of money that the decedent would have used for his or her own exclusive benefit had death not occurred. Personal consumption is often either measured as a percentage of the present value of earnings or measured in detail as in steps 1–8 of Table 2 (earnings).

Table 4. U.S. Approach for Estimating Lifetime Services.

Step 1. Base annual service value determination
The base value of services is the beginning point for quantifying the lifetime value of services. The evaluator estimates the base value of services by first (1) using the amount of the individual's pre-event service production or (2) matching the individual's current status to empirical data reflecting the service production of similarly situated individuals. Generally, the amount of production is measured by time units devoted to various tasks. The amount of production is then valued by placing a value on the time units or by estimating the cost of having the tasks performed. The value of time may be obtained by using occupational wage data. For example, the wage rate of a maid may be used to value the time devoted to cleaning.

Step 2. Forecast changes in earnings due to individual changes
For each age beyond the base year, the individual's situation in terms of his or her individual and household situation is forecasted. The evaluator takes into account variables such as the aging of children in the household, the status of the spouse, and the labor force status of the individual in question. The changes in the household makeup and labor force status are matched to characteristics of similarly situated individual using cross-sectional data. The changes in the value of services supplied by the particular individual are generally denominated in the dollar level associated with base value of services provided.

Step 3. Changes in earnings due to changes in market conditions
The replacement cost of services will change for the same market reasons as in step 3 of Table 1 (earning capacity).

Step 4. Additional consideration of benefits
The cost of benefits of employing workers to replace service losses may also be considered in a separate step as in step 4 of Table 1 (earning capacity).

Step 5. Hazards preventing the individual from producing services
After the base period, there is a non-zero expectation that an individual would have been prevented from producing services. For example, the onset of reduced productivity with age that would have prevented the production of services or death must be accounted for. The evaluator estimates the probability of these hazards to the individual using cross-sectional observations of mortality and morbidity. The probability is then used to obtain the expected value.

Step 6. Determining the boundary age of reliable estimation
As in step 7 of Table 1 (earning capacity), the evaluator must determine the boundary age to his or her estimates of an individual's expected service performance in order for the estimates to remain reliable. The boundary age is relevant to the same factors as earnings and earning capacity.

Step 7. Discounting to present value
Discounting to present value is accomplished as in step 8 of Table 1 (earning capacity).

Table 5. U.S. Approach for Estimating the Present Value of Future Medical Costs.

Step 1. Timing medical costs to the future periods when consumed
Future medical costs are generally supplied to the economic evaluator as current dollar amounts per future time period. The economic evaluator first schedules current dollar life-care needs to each future period as they are to be consumed.

Step 2. Changes in current medical costs due to changes in market conditions
Medical costs will change from their current cost to each future consumption date for the same market reasons as in step 3 of Table 1 (earning capacity). Instead of wage data, the evaluator studies changes in price data related to the medical need.

Step 3. Mortality hazard
After the base period, there is a non-zero expectation that an individual would not survive in order to consume the life-care need. The evaluator estimates the expected cost of future medical needs by applying a mortality hazard calculated from data regarding similarly situated individuals as the injured person.

Step 4. Discounting to present value
Discounting to present value is accomplished as in step 8 of Table 1 (earning capacity).

Table 6. Mr Smith's Parameters for Computing Lifetime Expected Earning Capacity.

Step 1. Determine the base value of earning capacity
The base value earning capacity is set to $75,000.

Step 2. Forecast changes in earning capacity due to individual changes
An age-earnings profile is calculated based upon the mean earnings of male managers in the U.S. medical care services industry.

Step 3. Forecast changes in earning capacity due to changes in market conditions
Price inflation is ignored at this step and a mid-year 1% growth in earning capacity per year is applied.

Step 4. Additional consideration of benefits
Since benefits are included in total compensation, they are not separately computed.

Step 5. Possible consideration of income taxes
The jurisdiction of the litigation case forbids the introduction of evidence of income taxes.

Step 6. Hazards preventing the individual from realizing earning capacity
A hazard is computed reflecting involuntary factors including death, the onset of disability that prevents work, and lack of access to employers (e.g., unemployment or discouragement). The data selected to compute the hazard are from males that have completed a 4-year college degree.

Step 7. Determining the boundary age of reliable estimation
The calculation of earning capacity is presented to age 67, the age Mr Smith would be qualified to receive his full social security benefits.

Step 8. Discounting to present value
A mid-year 2.5% real, inflation-free discount rate is chosen to compute present value.

Table 7. Mr Smith's Present Value of Lost Earning Capacity.

Age	Step 1	Step 2	Step 3	Step 6		Step 8	Present Value of Expected Earning Capacity ($)
	Base earning capacity ($)	Age-earnings profile	Market growth	Mortality	Risk of being unable to work	Present-value factor	
30	75,000	1.00000	1.00499	0.99939	0.98513	0.98773	73,298
31	75,000	1.04945	1.01504	0.99812	0.96650	0.96364	74,269
32	75,000	1.09709	1.02519	0.99683	0.96269	0.94014	76,104
33	75,000	1.14291	1.03544	0.99549	0.96312	0.91721	78,052
34	75,000	1.18691	1.04579	0.99407	0.96824	0.89483	80,180
35	75,000	1.22909	1.05625	0.99255	0.97333	0.87301	82,120
36	75,000	1.26946	1.06681	0.99094	0.97523	0.85172	83,603
37	75,000	1.30802	1.07748	0.98919	0.97557	0.83094	84,761
38	75,000	1.34475	1.08826	0.98729	0.97487	0.81068	85,639
39	75,000	1.37967	1.09914	0.98522	0.97195	0.79090	86,137
40	75,000	1.41277	1.11013	0.98297	0.96548	0.77161	86,137
41	75,000	1.44406	1.12123	0.98055	0.96133	0.75279	86,171
42	75,000	1.47353	1.13245	0.97792	0.95978	0.73443	86,271
43	75,000	1.50118	1.14377	0.97508	0.95912	0.71652	86,293
44	75,000	1.52702	1.15521	0.97198	0.95771	0.69904	86,092
45	75,000	1.55104	1.16676	0.96863	0.95478	0.68199	85,606
46	75,000	1.57324	1.17843	0.96498	0.95708	0.66536	85,443
47	75,000	1.59362	1.19021	0.96105	0.96003	0.64913	85,199
48	75,000	1.61219	1.20211	0.95680	0.95796	0.63330	84,372
49	75,000	1.62895	1.21413	0.95223	0.95394	0.61785	83,250
50	75,000	1.64388	1.22628	0.94728	0.94896	0.60278	81,923
51	75,000	1.65700	1.23854	0.94197	0.94504	0.58808	80,578
52	75,000	1.66831	1.25092	0.93627	0.94129	0.57374	79,141
53	75,000	1.67779	1.26343	0.93022	0.93896	0.55974	77,727
54	75,000	1.68546	1.27607	0.92379	0.93293	0.54609	75,918
55	75,000	1.69131	1.28883	0.91703	0.92874	0.53277	74,182
56	75,000	1.69535	1.30172	0.90987	0.93035	0.51978	72,825
57	75,000	1.69757	1.31473	0.90229	0.93229	0.50710	71,404
58	75,000	1.69797	1.32788	0.89410	0.93212	0.49473	69,723
59	75,000	1.69656	1.34116	0.88523	0.92575	0.48267	67,500
60	75,000	1.69333	1.35457	0.87553	0.92402	0.47089	65,536
61	75,000	1.68828	1.36812	0.86500	0.93106	0.45941	64,094
62	75,000	1.68142	1.38180	0.85352	0.94298	0.44820	62,860
63	75,000	1.67274	1.39562	0.84119	0.94601	0.43727	60,925
64	75,000	1.66224	1.40957	0.82808	0.94374	0.42661	58,586
65	75,000	1.64993	1.42367	0.81419	0.94985	0.41620	56,705
66	75,000	1.63580	1.43790	0.79932	0.95600	0.40605	54,737
							2,833,359

6. A SAMPLE PERSONAL INJURY CASE

In this section, a sample personal injury case is presented in order to demonstrate the U.S. approach to estimating personal injury tort damages of lost earning capacity and services. Assume an injured married male, Mr Smith, age 30, with two children ages 8 and 14. Mr Smith completed a college degree in the field of business, and he has worked for the past seven years at a medical services corporation. His current job title is manager of procurement. His total compensation package is worth $75,000 per year. The injury permanently prevents Mr Smith from being able to be employed in the competitive labor marketplace. He has also lost some of his ability to perform household work services for his and his family's benefit. Sample chosen parameters for each step of the U.S. approach of lifetime expected earning capacity are shown in Table 6 with the calculations shown in Table 7. Service parameters are contained in Table 8 with the calculations shown in Table 9.

Table 8. Mr Smith's Parameters for Computing Lifetime Expected Services.

Step 1. Base annual service value determination
A review of Mr Smith's service performance before and after injury reveals 15 lost weekly hours of services. Replacement costs are estimated, including legally required benefits, to be $13.00 per hour.

Step 2. Forecast changes in earnings due to individual changes
Based upon empirical data on married males that work full time with and without children in the home, when the youngest daughter is age 13–17, services are increased by 20%, and when the youngest daughter turns 18 years old, service losses are decreased by 25%. At retirement age, service losses are increased by 25%.

Step 3. Changes in service costs due to changes in market conditions
Price inflation is ignored at this step and a mid-year 0.7% growth in service cost per year is applied.

Step 4. Additional consideration of benefits
Ignored since legally required benefits are included in step 1.

Step 5. Hazards preventing the individual from producing services
A combination mortality/morbidity hazard is applied based upon morbidity statistics regarding functional capacity.

Step 6. Determining the boundary age of reliable estimation
While his life expectancy is age 80, service losses for Mr Smith are computed to age 75.

Step 7. Discounting to present value
A mid-year 2% real, inflation-free discount rate is chosen to compute present value.

Table 9. Mr Smith's Present Value of Expected Lost Services.

Age at End of Year	Steps 1 and 2		Step 3	Step 5	Step 7	Present Value of Expected Service Losses ($)
	Weekly service hours	Replacement cost of services ($)	Market growth	Mortality and morbidity	Present-value factor	
30	15	13.00	1.00349	0.99857	0.99015	10,061
31	15	13.00	1.01052	0.99557	0.97073	9,903
32	15	13.00	1.01759	0.99238	0.95170	9,745
33	15	13.00	1.02472	0.98896	0.93304	9,588
34	15	13.00	1.03189	0.98527	0.91474	9,430
35	18	13.00	1.03911	0.98134	0.89681	11,128
36	18	13.00	1.04639	0.97712	0.87922	10,938
37	18	13.00	1.05371	0.97263	0.86198	10,749
38	18	13.00	1.06109	0.96782	0.84508	10,560
39	18	13.00	1.06851	0.96271	0.82851	10,370
40	11.25	13.00	1.07599	0.95729	0.81227	6,363
41	11.25	13.00	1.08352	0.95159	0.79634	6,244
42	11.25	13.00	1.09111	0.94556	0.78072	6,126
43	11.25	13.00	1.09875	0.93921	0.76542	6,007
44	11.25	13.00	1.10644	0.93254	0.75041	5,888
45	11.25	13.00	1.11418	0.92554	0.73569	5,770
46	11.25	13.00	1.12198	0.91817	0.72127	5,651
47	11.25	13.00	1.12984	0.91048	0.70713	5,532
48	11.25	13.00	1.13775	0.90244	0.69326	5,413
49	11.25	13.00	1.14571	0.89407	0.67967	5,295
50	11.25	13.00	1.15373	0.88530	0.66634	5,176
51	11.25	13.00	1.16181	0.87618	0.65328	5,057
52	11.25	13.00	1.16994	0.86671	0.64047	4,939
53	11.25	13.00	1.17813	0.85694	0.62791	4,821
54	11.25	13.00	1.18638	0.84681	0.61560	4,703
55	11.25	13.00	1.19468	0.83640	0.60353	4,586
56	11.25	13.00	1.20304	0.82565	0.59169	4,470
57	11.25	13.00	1.21146	0.81453	0.58009	4,353
58	11.25	13.00	1.21994	0.80287	0.56872	4,236
59	11.25	13.00	1.22848	0.79065	0.55756	4,119
60	11.25	13.00	1.23708	0.77776	0.54663	4,000
61	11.25	13.00	1.24574	0.76417	0.53591	3,880
62	11.25	13.00	1.25446	0.74979	0.52541	3,758
63	11.25	13.00	1.26324	0.73477	0.51510	3,636
64	11.25	13.00	1.27209	0.71911	0.50500	3,513
65	11.25	13.00	1.28099	0.70283	0.49510	3,390
66	11.25	13.00	1.28996	0.68571	0.48539	3,265
67	18.75	13.00	1.29899	0.66782	0.47588	5,232
68	18.75	13.00	1.30808	0.64904	0.46654	5,021
69	18.75	13.00	1.31724	0.62942	0.45740	4,807

Table 9. *(Continued)*

Age at End of Year	Steps 1 and 2		Step 3	Step 5	Step 7	Present Value of Expected Service Losses ($)
	Weekly service hours	Replacement cost of services ($)	Market growth	Mortality and morbidity	Present-value factor	
70	18.75	13.00	1.32646	0.60879	0.44843	4,590
71	18.75	13.00	1.33574	0.58732	0.43964	4,372
72	18.75	13.00	1.34509	0.56486	0.43102	4,151
73	18.75	13.00	1.35451	0.54139	0.42256	3,928
74	18.75	13.00	1.36399	0.51670	0.41428	3,701
						268,464

7. CONCLUSION

This chapter has presented an examination of the scientific approach taken in the United States to compute the economic damages due to the torts of personal injury and wrongful death. The general law on tort damages presented reveals that U.S. tort damages include a damages component which directly corresponds to the economic science of studying the impact of reduced productivity on lifetime-obtainable goods and services. While we have noted a few instances of jurisdictional law, which causes economic damages to deviate from a general economic result, those jurisdictional adjustments do not override the core economic compensating mechanisms of the U.S. approach to tort damages. With a strict adherence to appropriate economic compensation, the U.S. approach to tort damages corresponds with efficient tort solutions where harm is minimized when all economic consequences are included in the monies paid by the tortfeasor to his or her victim.

NOTES

1. *Metropolitan Stevedore Co. v. Rambo*, 521 U.S. 121, 133 (1997).
2. 435 U.S. 247, 257 (1978).
3. 414 U.S. 573 (1974).
4. The same restrictions upon utility or enjoyment of life can be placed on the surviving victims of wrongful death because they are no longer able to enjoy the goods and services given to them by their decedent.
5. See Krueger (2001).

6. Suppose a tort victim loses half of his earning capacity per hour worked, and post-injury the victim doubles his pre-injury level of work to restore his income. In these types of situations, the ability to achieve a greater earning capacity existed pre-injury under the post-injury hours worked; therefore, loss is the same as comparing pre- and post-injury earning capacity during the amount of pre-injury work time.

7. David Freidman (1982). "What is 'fair compensation' for death or injury?" *International Review of Law and Economics, 2* (1), 81–93.

8. Portions of this and the next section are from Krueger (2006), and they are contained here with permission of *The Earnings Analyst.*

9. The wage rate in this context is assumed to be the total unit cost of labor that includes money wages to the worker, fringe benefits, payroll taxes, and unemployment insurance, etc. The mix of money wages and other labor costs within the total unit cost of labor is variable under the theories of wage-rate determination. In most forensic economic wage rate determination problems, economists disaggregate their empirical analysis of money wages and fringe benefits. The "unit" in "total unit cost of labor" is also variable and dependent upon the specification of the profit maximization function. The demand for labor determines the units of earning capacity (e.g., a job giving a certain level of earning capacity might be constrained in the market to eight hours per day for five days per week for 52 weeks per year). Due to market, mental, and physical constraints, a person may possess one or more levels of earning capacity. For example, within the labor market, a person might weekly supply H_1 hours of labor at C_1 level of earning capacity and also provide H_2 hours at C_2 level of earning capacity where $C_1 > C_2$. A typical example is where a person works a strenuous full-time day job for H_1 at C_1 and a light duty part-time night job for H_2 at C_2; it is unlikely that the person could work (H_1+H_2) hours per week at C_1 level of earning capacity due to limiting market, physical, and mental constraints.

10. See Fama (1976), Hirshliefer (1970), and Varian (1978). Albrecht and Moorehouse (1989) provide a detailed discussion of the distinction between continuous and discrete growth rates.

REFERENCES AND BIBLIOGRAPHY

Law and Economics Related to Tort Damages

Arlen, J. (1990). Reconsidering efficient tort rules for personal injury: The case of single activity accidents. *William and Mary Law Review, 32*, 41–103.

Arlen, J. (1992). Liability rules for physical injury when injurers as well as victims suffer losses. *Journal of Law, Economics and Organization, 8*, 411–426.

Arrow, K. (1971). Insurance, risk, and resource allocation. In: *Essays in the theory of risk-bearing*. Chicago, IL: Markham.

Arthur, W. B. (1981). The economics of risks to life. *American Economic Review, 71*, 54–64.

Bishop, W., & Sutton, J. (1986). Efficiency and justice in tort damages: The shortcomings of the pecuniary loss rule. *Journal of Legal Studies, 15*, 347–370.

Brown, J. P. (1973). Toward an economic theory of liability. *Journal of Legal Studies, 2*, 323–350.

Choi, A., & Sanchirico, C. W. (2004). Should plaintiffs win what defendants lose? Litigation stakes, litigation effort, and the benefits of decoupling. *Journal of Legal Studies, 33*, 323–354.

Conley, B. C. (1976). The value of life in the demand for safety. *American Economic Review, 66*, 45–65.

Cooter, R. D. (1982). Economic analysis of punitive damages. *Southern California Law Review, 56*, 79–101.

Cooter, R. D. (1989). Towards a market in unmatured tort claims. *Virginia Law Review, 75*, 383–412.

Cooter, R. D. (1989). Punitive damages for deterrence: When and how much? *Alabama Law Review, 40*1143 ff.

Cooter, R. D., & Porat, A. (2006). Liability externalities and mandatory choices: Should doctors pay less? *Journal of Tort Law, 1*(1)Article 2.

Kaplow, L., & Shavell, S. (1996). Accuracy in the assessment of damages. *Journal of Law and Economics, 39*, 191–210.

Karpoff, J. M., & Lott, J. R., Jr.. (1999). On the determinants and importance of punitive damage awards. *Journal of Law and Economics, 42*, 527–573.

Komesar, N. K. (1974). Toward a general theory of personal injury loss. *Journal of Legal Studies, 3*, 457–486.

Landes, W., & Posner, R. (1980). Joint and multiple torts: An economic analysis. *International Review of Law and Economics, 9*, 517–556.

Landes, W., & Posner, R. (1981). An economic theory of intentional torts. *International Review of Law and Economics, 1*, 127–154.

Landes, W., & Posner, R. (1984). Tort law as a regulatory regime for catastrophic personal injuries. *Journal of Legal Studies, 13*, 417–434.

Landes, W. M., & Posner, R. A. (1987). *The economic structure of tort law*. Cambridge, MA: Harvard University Press.

Polinsky, A. M., & Rubinfeld, D. (1996). Optimal awards and penalties when the probability of prevailing varies among plaintiffs. *RAND Journal of Economics, 27*, 269–280.

Polinsky, A. M., & Shavell, S. (1994). Should liability be based on the harm to the victim or the gain to the injurer. *Journal of Law, Economics, and Organization, 10*, 427–437.

Polinsky, A. M., & Shavell, S. (1998). Punitive damages: An economic analysis. *Harvard Law Review, 111*, 869–962.

Posner, R. A. (1972). A theory of negligence. *Journal of Legal Studies, 1*, 29–96.

Posner, R. A. (2003). *Economic analysis of law* (6th ed.). New York, NY: Aspen Publishers.

Rizzo, M. (1982). A theory of economic loss in the law of torts. *Journal of Legal Studies, 11*, 281–310.

Schwartz, G. (1986). Economic loss in American tort law: The examples of J Aire and of products liability. *San Diego Law Review, 23*, 37–78.

Shavell, S. (1979). On moral hazard and insurance. *Quarterly Journal of Economics, 93*, 541–562.

Shavell, S. (1980). Strict liability versus negligence. *Journal of Legal Studies, 9*, 463–516.

Shavell, S. (1987). *Economic analysis of accident law*. Cambridge, MA: Harvard University Press.

Van Wijck, P., & Winters, J. K. (2001). The principle of full compensation in tort law. *European Journal of Law and Economics, 11*(3), 319–332.

General Economic Methods Relevant to Forensic Economics

Akerlof, G. A., & Yellen, J. (1986). *Efficiency wage models of the labor market*. Cambridge: Cambridge University Press.

Becker, G. (1993). *Human capital, a theoretical and empirical analysis with special reference to education* (3rd ed.). Chicago, IL: University of Chicago Press.

Benninga, S., & Protopapadakis, A. (1983). Real and nominal interest rates under uncertainty: The fisher problem and the term structure. *Journal of Political Economy, 91*, 856–867.

Ben-Porath, Y. (1967). The production of human capital and the life cycle of earnings. *Journal of Political Economy, 75*, 352–365.

Cameron, S., & Heckman, J. (1998). Life cycle schooling and dynamic selection bias: Models and evidence for five cohorts of American males. *Journal of Political Economy, 106*(2), 262–333.

Cox, J. C., Ingersoll, J. E., & Ross, S. A. (1985). An intertemporal general equilibrium model of asset prices. *Econometrica, 53*, 385–408.

Duesenberry, J. (1952). *Income, saving, and the theory of consumer behavior*. Cambridge, MA: Harvard U. Press.

Dupont, D., & Sack, B. (1999). The treasury securities market: overview and recent developments. *Federal Reserve Bulletin, 85*, 785–806.

Evans, M. D. D. (1998). Real rates, expected inflation, and inflation risk premia. *Journal of Finance, 53*, 187–218.

Fama, E. F., & Gibbons, M. R. (1982). Inflation, real returns, and capital investments. *Journal of Monetary Economics, 9*, 297–323.

Fama, E., & French, K. (1993). Common risk factors in the returns on stocks and bonds. *Journal of Financial Economics, 33*, 3–56.

Fama, E., & French, K. (1995). Size and book-to-market factors in earnings and returns. *Journal of Finance, 50*, 131–155.

Fama, E. F. (1975). Short-term interest rates as predictors of inflation. *American Economic Review, 65*, 269–282.

Fama, E. F. (1976). Inflation, uncertainty and the expected returns on treasury bills. *Journal of Political Economy, 84*, 427–448.

Fama, E. F. (1990). Term structure forecasts of interest rates, inflation, and real returns. *Journal of Monetary Economics, 25*, 59–76.

Fama, E. F. (1996). Discounting under uncertainty. *Journal of Business, 69*, 415–428.

Feldstein, M. (1976). Inflation, income taxes, and the rate of interest: A theoretical analysis. *American Economic Review, 66*, 809–820.

Fishburn, P. C., & Rubinstein, A. (1982). Time preference. *International Economic Review, 23*(2), 677–694.

Fisher, I. (1930). *The theory of interest*. New York: Macmillan.

Fisher, F., & Romaine, R. C. (1990). Janis Joplin"s yearbook and the theory of damages. *Journal of Accounting, Auditing and Finance*, 145–157.

Freeman, R. (1979). The effect of demographic factors on age-earnings profiles. *Journal of Human Resources, 14*, 289–318.

Gali, J. (1992). Keeping up with the joneses: Consumption externalities, portfolio choice, and asset price. *Journal of Money, Credit, and Banking, 26*, 1–8.

Harris, M., & Holmstrom, B. (1982). A theory of wage dynamics. *Review of Economic Studies, 49*, 315–333.

Heckman, J. (1976). A life-cycle model of earnings, learning and consumption. *Journal of Political Economy*, *84*(4), 11–44.

Heckman, J., & Polachek, S. (1974). Empirical evidence on the functional form of the earnings-schooling relationship. *Journal of the American Statistical Association*, *69*, 350–354.

Heckman, J., Lochner, L., & Taber, C. (1998). Explaining wage inequality: Explorations with a dynamic general equilibrium model with heterogeneous agents. *Review of Economic Dynamics*, *1*(1), 1–52.

Hendray, D. F., & Ericsson, N. R. (2001). *Understanding economic forecasts*. The MIT Press: Cambridge, MA.

Ireland, P. N. (1996). Long-term interest rates and inflation: A Fisherian approach. Federal reserve bank of Richmond. *Economic Quarterly*, *82*, 21–36.

Keane, M., & Wolpin, K. (1997). The career decisions of young men. *Journal of Political Economy*, *105*(3), 473–522.

Killingsworth, M. (1982). 'Learning by doing' and 'investment in training': Two rival models of the life cycle. *Review of Economic Studies*, *49*, 263–271.

Knight, F. H. (1921). *Risk, uncertainty and profit*. Boston: Houghton Mifflin.

Labadie, P. (1994). The term structure of interest rates over the business cycle. *Journal of Economic Dynamics and Control*, *18*, 671–698.

Laibson, D., Repetto, A., & Tobacman, J. (1998). Self-control and saving for retirement. *Brookings Papers on Economic Activity*, *1*, 91–196.

Lazear, E. (1979). Why is there mandatory retirement? *Journal of Political Economy*, *87*, 1261–1284.

Lazear, E. (1981). Agency, earnings profiles, productivity, and hours restrictions. *American Economic Review*, *71*(3), 606–620.

Medoff, J., & Abraham, K. (1981). Are those paid more really more productive: The case of experience. *Journal of Human Resources*, *16*, 281–302.

Mincer, J. (1974). *Schooling, experience and earnings*. New York: Columbia University Press.

Moore, M. J., & Kip Viscusi, W. (1988). The quantity-adjusted value of life. *Economic Inquiry*, *26*(3), 369–388.

Murphy, K. M., & Katz, L. (1992). Changes in relative wages, 1963–1987: Supply and demand factors. *Quarterly Journal of Economics*, *107*, 992.

Neal, D. (1995). Industry-specific human capital: Evidence from displaced workers. *Journal of Labor Economics*, *13*(4), 653–677.

Parsons, D. (1974). The cost of school time, foregone earnings, and human capital formation. *Journal of Political Economy*, *82*, 251–266.

Polachek, S., & Siebert, W. (1993). *The economics of earnings*. Cambridge: Cambridge University Press.

Read, D. (2001). Is time-discounting hyperbolic or subadditive? *Journal of Risk and Uncertainty*, *23*, 5–32.

Rosen, S. (1972). Learning and experience in the labor market. *Journal of Human Resources*, *7*(3), 326–342.

Rosen, S. (1979). Substitution and the division of labour. *Economica*, *45*, 235–250.

Rosen, S. (1981). The economics of superstars. *American Economic Review*, *71*, 845–858.

Salop, S. (1979). A model of the natural rate of unemployment. *American Economic Review*, *69*, 117–125.

Samuelson, P. (1937). A note on measurement of utility. *Review of Economic Studies*, *4*, 155–161.

Tinbergen, J. (1939). Econometric business cycle research. *Review of Economic Studies*, *7*, 73–90.

Topel, R. (1991). Specific capital, mobility, and wages: Wages rise with job seniority. *Journal of Political Economy*, *99*(1), 145–176.

Varian, H. R. (1978). *Microeconomic analysis*. New York: W. W. Norton.

Viscusi, W. K., & Moore, M. J. (1989). Rates of time preference and valuation of the duration of life. *Journal of Public Economics*, *38*(3), 297–317.

Weiss, A. (1980). Job queues and layoffs in labor markets with flexible wages. *Journal of Political Economy*, *88*(3), 526–538.

Weiss, Y. (1986). The determination of life cycle earnings. In: O. Ashenfelter & R. Layard (Eds), *Handbook of Labor Economics* (Vol. 1, pp. 603–640). Amsterdam: North-Holland.

Welch, F. (1970). Education and production. *Journal of Political Economy*, *78*, 35–59.

Williams, J. (1979). Uncertainty and the accumulation of human capital over the life cycle. *Journal of Business*, *52*(4), 521–548.

Willis, R. (1986). Wage determinants: A survey and reinterpretation of human capital earnings functions. In: O. Ashenfelter & R. Layard (Eds), *Handbook of Labor Economics* (Vol. 1, pp. 525–602). Amsterdam: North-Holland.

Willis, R., & Rosen, S. (1979). Education and self-selection. *Journal of Political Economy*, *87*, 7–36.

Zarkin, G. (1985). Occupational choice: An application to the market for public school teachers. *Quarterly Journal of Economics*, *100*, 409–446.

Calculation of Economic Damages

Albrecht, G. R. (1997). Risk and damage awards: Short-term bonds vs. long-term bonds. *Journal of Legal Economics*, *7*(1, Spring/Summer), 48–54.

Albrecht, G. R. (1997). The need to use risk-free discount rates. *Journal of Legal Economics*, *7*(1, Spring/Summer), 92–95.

Albrecht, G. R., & Moorehouse, J. C. (1989). On the derivation and consistent use of growth and discount rates for future earnings. *Journal of Forensic Economics*, *2*(3), 95–102.

Anderson, G. A., & Barber, J. R. (1992). A simple procedure for computing the present value of non-annual damages. *Journal of Forensic Economics*, *6*(1), 3–6.

Anderson, G. A., & Willig, R. D. (1985). Economic theory and the present value of future lost earnings: An integration, unification, and simplification of court adopted methodologies. *University of Miami Law Review*, *39*, 723–756.

Arlen, J. (1985). An economic analysis of tort damages for wrongful death. *New York University Law Review*, *60*, 1113–1136.

Ben-Zion, B., & Reddall, R. G. (1985). Life expectancy and actuarial present values: A note to forensic economists. *Research in Law and Economics*, *7*, 160–171.

Brookshire, M., & Caruthers, S. (1995). Principles of establishing the lost earnings base. *Litigation Economics Digest*, *1*(1), 45–61.

Brookshire, M. L., & Ireland, T. R. (1994). Converting from a present value lump sum to a future payment stream. *Journal of Forensic Economics*, *7*(2), 151–157.

Brookshire, M. L., & Smith, S. V. (1990). *Economic/hedonic damages: The practice book for plaintiff and defense attorneys*. Cincinnati, OH: Anderson Publishing Company.

Brown, R. J., & Johnson, D. A. (1983). Wrongful death and personal injury: Economics and the law. *South Dakota Law Review*, *29*, 1–23.

Bruce, C. J. (1984). An efficient technique for determining the compensation of lost earnings. *Journal of Legal Studies*, *13*, 375–378.

Bruce, C. J. (1987). Measure of damages for the wrongful death of a child. *Canadian Bar Review*, *66*, 344–359.

Cahill, G. A., & Goldberg, G. F. (1993). Life insurance as an offset to economic loss in wrongful death cases: A note. *Journal of Forensic Economics*, *6*(3), 277–279.

Carter, R. A. L., & Palmer, J. P. (1991). Real rates, expected rates, and damage awards. *Journal of Legal Studies*, *20*, 439–462.

Ciecka, J. E. (1994). A survey of the structure and duration of time periods for lost earnings calculations. *Journal of Forensic Economics*, *4*(2), 39–50.

Coyne, T. J. (1982). Present value of future earnings: A sensible alternative to simplistic methodologies. *Insurance Counsel Journal*, *49*(1), 25–31.

Depperschmidt, T. O. (1994). Unintended consequences and perverse effects in forensic economic award calculations. *Journal of Legal Economics*, *4*, 65–72.

Dulaney, R. A. (1991). "Estimating decedents" consumption expenditures in wrongful death actions: Some refinements. *Journal Legal of Economics*, *1*(2), 94–98.

Durham, S. E. (1993). The correct value of social security contributions in personal injury and wrongful death settlements: A comment. *Journal of Forensic Economics*, *6*(2), 151–152.

Fischer, C. C. (1994). The valuation of household production: Divorce, wrongful injury and death litigation. *American Journal of Economics and Sociology*, *53*, 187–201.

Fitzgerald, P., & Krueger, K. V. (2006). Tort remedy in the law versus economic restitution for personal injury and wrongful death. *The Earnings Analyst*, *VIII*.

Horner, S., & Slesnick, F. (1999). The valuation of earning capacity: Definition, measurement, and evidence. *Journal of Forensic Economics*, *12*(1), 13–32.

Ireland, T. (2007). Valuing advice, counsel and companionship between parents and adult children. *The Earnings Analyst*, *9*, 35–61.

Ireland, T., et al. (1998). *Expert economic testimony: Reference guides for judges and attorneys*. Tucson, AZ: Lawyers & Judges Publishing, Co.

Jennings, W. P., & Phillips, M. G. (1989). Risk as a discount rate determinant in wrongful death and injury cases. *Journal of Risk and Insurance*, *56*(1), 122–127.

Jones, D. D. (1990). Choosing a discount rate for future losses in wrongful death and injury cases. *Journal of Risk and Insurance*, *57*(1), 137–140.

Kidner, R., & Richards, K. (1974). Compensation to dependents of accident victims. *Economic Journal*, *84*, 130–142.

King, E. M., & Smith, J. P. (1988). *Computing economic loss in cases of wrongful death*. Santa Monica, CA: Rand Institute for Civil Justice.

King, E. M., & Smith, J. P. (1988). *Economic loss and compensation in aviation accidents*. Santa Monica, CA: Rand Institute for Civil Justice.

Knoll, M. S. (1996). A primer on prejudgment interest. *Texas Law Review*, *75*, 293–374.

Krueger, K. V. (2008). Personal consumption by husbands and wives. *Journal of Forensic Economics*, *20*(1), 15–30.

Krueger, K. V. (2004). Tables of inter-year labor force status of the U.S. population (1998–2004) usable in operating the Markov model of worklife expectancy. *Journal of Forensic Economics*, *17*(3), 313–381.

Krueger, K. V., & Albrecht, G. R. (2007). A review of the economic foundations of earnings and discounting theories used in forensic economics. *The Earnings Analyst*, *IX*, 1–34.

Krueger, K. V., & Albrecht, G. R. (2008). The present value of lost financial support due to wrongful death. *Journal of Legal Economics*, *15*(1), 35–42.

Krueger, K. V., Skoog, G., & Ciecka, J. (2006). Worklife in a Markov model with full-time and part-time activity, with Gary Skoog and Jim Ciecka. *Journal of Forensic Economics*, *19*(1), 61–82.

Krueger, K. V., Ward, J. O., & Albrecht, G. R. (2001). Introduction to the whole-time concept. *Journal of Forensic Economics*, *14*(1), 3–8.

Lewis, W. C. (1992). The rationale and quantitative evidence for the personal consumption offset in wrongful death actions. *Journal of Legal Economics*, *2*(2), 1–18.

Martin, G. (2008). *Determining economic damages*. Santa Ana, CA: James Publishing Company.

Pacey, P. L. (1985). Measures of economic loss in the wrongful death of a child. *Colorado Lawyer*, *14*, 392–402.

Piette, M. J., & Thornton, J. R. (1994). Using new labor force participation rates when computing economic damage and loss: A methodological note. *Journal of Legal Economics*, *4*(2), 81–88.

Plummer, J. L. (1995). The cost of substitute consumption activities: A better alternative than hedonic damages. *Journal of Forensic Economics*, *8*(2), 159–165.

Rogers, W. B., Fayissa, B., & Balch, B. W. (1991). Variations in the economic estimation of personal injury and wrongful death claims. *Journal of Legal Economics*, *1*(1), 81–88.

Schieren, G. A. (1994). On using minimum-cost portfolios to determine present value. *Journal of Legal Economics*, *4*(1), 47–59.

Skoog, G., & Ciecka, J. (2001). A Markov (increment-decrement) model of labor force activity: Extended tables of central tendency, variation, and probability intervals. *Journal of Legal Economics*, *11*(1, Spring/Summer), 23–87.

Skoog, G., & Ciecka, J. (2003). Probability mass functions for years to final separation from the labor force induced by the Markov model. *Journal of Forensic Economics*, *16*(1, Winter), 51–86.

Tinari, F. D. (1998). Household services: Toward a more comprehensive measure. *Journal of Forensic Economics*, *11*(3), 253–265.

Trout, R. R., & Foster, C. B. (1993). Estimating a decedent's consumption in wrongful death cases. *Journal of Forensic Economics*, *6*(2), 135–150.

Ward, J. O., & Olson, G. W. (1986). Forensic economics: The development and outlook for the field. *Journal of Forensic Economics*, *1*(1).

Yandell, D. (1991). The value of lost future earnings: Methodology, the discount rate, and economic theory. *Journal Legal Economics*, *1*(3), 54–67.

Yunker, K. K. (1994). Addressing the real problems for law and economics of factoring interest rates, earnings growth and inflation into awards for lost future earnings. *University of Pittsburgh Law Review*, *56*, 1–106.

Role of Income Taxes

Alberts, R. J., Clauretie, T. M., & Jameson, M. (1994). Ordinary and reverse tax effect in personal injury and wrongful death cases. *Journal of Forensic Economics*, *7*(3), 245–266.

Albrecht, G. R. (1994). Modeling taxes in personal injury and wrongful death award calculations. *Journal of Forensic Economics*, *7*(3), 239–243.
Bell, E. B., & Taub, A. J. (1994). An analysis of alternative methods of calculating tax-adjusted awards. *Journal of Forensic Economics*, *7*(3), 267–274.
Blackburn, J. W. (1989). Taxation of personal injury damages: Recommendations for reform. *Tennessee Law Review*, *56*, 661–691.
Brady, D., Brookshire, M., & Cobb, W. (1985). The development and solution of a tax-adjusted model for personal injury awards: A response. *Journal of Risk and Insurance*, *52*, 520–521.
Brush, B. C., & Breeden, C. H. (1994). Income taxes and economic damages. *Journal of Legal Economics*, *4*(2), 51–63.
Burke, J. F., & Rosen, H. S. (1983). Taxes and compensation for lost earnings: A comment. *Journal of Legal Studies*, *12*, 195–200.
Creedy, J. (1988). Taxation and compensation to dependents of accident victims. *International Review of Law and Economics*, *8*, 85–95.
Markowski, E. P., & Cross, E. M. (1991). Determination of tax-adjusted lost income awards`. *Journal of Legal Economics*, *1*(1), 11–18.
Markowski, E. P., & Cross, E. M. (1991). Determination of tax-adjusted lost income awards: Reply. *Journal Legal Economics*, *1*(3), 103–104.
Rea, S. (1990). Taxation, the standard of care and damage awards. *International Review of Law and Economics*, *10*, 285–292.
Schieren, G. A. (1994). Taxes and present value awards for wrongful death. *Journal of Forensic Economics*, *7*(3), 293–304.

Noneconomic/Hedonic Damages

Albrecht, G. R. (1994). The application of the hedonic damages concept to wrongful death and personal injury litigation. *Journal of Forensic Economics*, *7*(2), 143–150.
Ashenfelter, O. (2006). *Measuring the value of a statistical life: Problems and prospects*. IZA Discussion Paper Series no. 1911.
Bagenstos, S. R., & Schlanger, M. (2007). Hedonic damages, hedonic adaptation, and disability. *Vanderbilt Law Review*, *59*, 101–153.
Becker, W. E., & Stout, R. A. (1992). The utility of death and wrongful death compensation. *Journal of Forensic Economics*, *5*, 197–208.
Berla, E. P., Brookshire, W., & Smith, S. V. (1990). Hedonic damages and personal injury: A conceptual approach. *Journal of Forensic Economics*, *3*(1), 1–8.
Broome, J. (1978). Trying to value a life. *Journal of Public Economics*, *9*, 91–100.
Buchanan, J. M., & Faith, R. L. (1979). Trying again to value a life. *Journal of Public Economics*, *12*, 245–248.
Fraser, C. D. (1984). What is 'fair compensation' for death or injury? A note. *International Review of Law and Economics*, *4*, 83–88.
Friedman, D. (1982). What is 'fair compensation' for death or injury? *International Review of Law and Economics*, *2*, 81–93.
Gilbert, R. F. (1994). The application of hedonic models to personal injury litigation. *Journal of Legal Economics*, *4*(3), 13–26.

Havrilesky, T. (1993). The misapplication of the hedonic damages concept to wrongful death and personal injury litigation. *Journal of Forensic Economics*, *6*(2), 93–98.

Havrilesky, T. (1995). The persistent misapplication of the 'hedonic damages' concept to wrongful death and personal injury litigation. *Journal of Forensic Economics*, *8*(1), 49–54.

Ireland, T. R. (1993). The meaning of 'hedonic damages' in tort litigation. *Journal of Forensic Economics*, *4*(2), 99–104.

Ireland, T. R. (1995). The application of the hedonic damages concept to wrongful death and personal injury litigation: A comment. *Journal of Forensic Economics*, *8*(1), 93–94.

Ireland, T. R., & Rodgers, J. D. (1993). Hedonic damages in wrongful death/survival actions: Equitable compensation or optimal life protection? *Journal of Forensic Economics*, 343 ff.

Ireland, T. R., & Ward, J. O. (Eds). (1998). *The new hedonics primer for economist and attorneys*. Tucson, AZ: Lawyers and Judges Publishing Co.

Kornhauser, L. A. (1990). The value of life. *Cleveland State Law Review*, *38*, 209–230.

Miller, T. R. (1990). The plausible range for the value of life – Red herrings among the mackerel. *Journal of Forensic Economics*, *3*(3), 17–40.

Mishan, E. J. (1981). The value of trying to value life. *Journal of Public Economics*, *15*, 133–137.

Smith, S. V. (1990). Hedonic damages in the courtroom setting – A bridge over troubled waters. *Journal of Forensic Economics*, *3*, 41–49.

Viscusi, W. K. (1990). The value of life: Has voodoo economics come to the courts? *Journal of Forensic Economics*, *3*(1), 1–15.

PRINCIPLES OF COMPENSATION FOR INJURY AND WRONGFUL DEATH IN IRELAND

Shane Whelan

1. INTRODUCTION

Compensation for personal injury in Ireland is based on the principle that the wronged party should be restored to the position that he or she was in prior to the action of the other (restitution in integrum). Compensation must be in a single lump sum for both past and future loss, with no further redress even if losses subsequently arise that were unknown at the time of the trial.

It is, of course, often impossible to right the wrong with a cash payment so the application of the simple principle requires delicate consideration, which not only reflects the circumstances of the case but also reflects broader cultural mores.[1] The latter is, of course, most apparent in the award of punitive or exemplary damages and, perhaps, even in the apportionment of liability. Accordingly, tort law in Ireland has diverged from many other territorial jurisdictions that adopt the same principle, so now the practice of assessing damages in Ireland is different on many points. We summarise the application of the principle in Ireland by referring to statutes and landmark precedents (from which the interested reader can explore the underlying rationale). However the focus in this chapter is on how damages in Ireland

Personal Injury and Wrongful Death Damages Calculations: Transatlantic Dialogue
Contemporary Studies in Economic and Financial Analysis, Volume 91, 233–254

ISSN: 1569-3759/doi:10.1108/S1569-3759(2009)0000091012

are computed, highlighting those assumptions to which the quantum of damages is most sensitive and those that are most contestable.

A report by the Law Reform Commission of Ireland (1996) gives a comprehensive review of the current system of awarding damages, together with its rationale and how it compares internationally. The report recommended no change to the way awards of damages are calculated,[2] but recommends provision be made for (a) an interim award of damages where liability is admitted and (b) for structured settlements when both parties agree. In the event, these provisions have not, as yet, been made.[3] While there have been other changes to the system in Ireland over the last decade or so (which we treat below), the single lump sum settlement remains the only method to extinguish the wrong.

1.1. Components of the Lump Sum

The lump sum is often sub-divided into general damages and special damages or other categories helpful to assess the overall loss. However, such sub-divisions are only notional and simply help to arrive at the result: it is the overall quantum that must be judged by the Irish court as fair compensation.[4] This reflects the obvious fact that the loss cannot in general be decomposed into a purely mathematical problem as it is contingent on too many factors, many of which are non-monetary and some, though monetary in nature, are not possible (as yet) to model in a satisfactory manner to arrive at a lump sum of equivalent value.

The trial is often conducted in the natural way of, after establishing liability, breaking down the different aspects of the wrong to the plaintiff and determining the remedy for that wrong. The damage may be divided into pecuniary loss and non-pecuniary loss. Non-pecuniary loss includes redress for pain and suffering, expectation of life curtailed and quality of life impaired. In addition, there is a long precedent of punitive and exemplary damages in Irish courts, and a more recent one of restitutionary damages,[5] where the plaintiff's sense of injury (or indeed that of the law) is aggravated by the manner or motive behind the actions of the defendant. The practice of Irish courts in this latter area is summarised and discussed in the Report of Law Reform Commission of Ireland (2000), which allowed that such aggravated, exemplary or restitutionary damages are best left as a matter for common law and its evolution in the courts.

Compensation for non-pecuniary loss clearly depends on the details of each case. We narrow the scope of this overview to how Irish courts determine the lump sum compensation for monetary loss. As determining the loss to the date of the trial is often a straightforward accounting matter, we narrow our focus further to how the lump sum compensation is estimated for future loss.

Note that the actual lump sum award is treated as a capital receipt that is not subject to tax in the hands of the recipient. However, any proceeds derived from the lump sum – by way of income or capital gain – are taxed in the normal way for all but one class of plaintiff.[6]

2. BRIEF HISTORY OF ACTUARIES AS EXPERT WITNESSES IN IRELAND

Actuaries advise the Irish courts on the assessment of the capital value of future financial loss. The role of the actuary has long been valued by the Irish courts, best put in a Supreme Court judgement in 1968:

> It has been decided by this court in many cases that where there is a substantial element of future loss of earnings involved with any claim the evidence of an Actuary is not merely desirable but necessary. It is immaterial whether the prospective loss is in respect of a long period and whether the period has already commenced or whether it will arise at some stage in the future. The appropriate Actuarial evidence is necessary in all these cases to enable the Jury to arrive at a reasonably accurate mathematical computation of the present value of the actual loss which they find will be incurred.
>
> – Quoted from Segrave-Daly (1998)

Professional guidance for actuaries engaged in litigation in Ireland[7] requires the actuary to assist the court by giving impartial advice ‘that is not modified to suit the exigencies of litigation’ and confine his/her evidence to matters lying within his/her expertise and experience. Given the requirement for the actuary to assist the court, not primarily the party who engaged his/her services, it might seem odd that it is usual for both sides to put forward their own independent actuarial evidence. However, the briefing of the actuary by either side is generally not complete; therefore, actuarial evidence is based on different premises of the circumstances in the case. It is not uncommon for the actuaries of both parties to meet (perhaps on direction by the court) to determine the matters that remain in dispute on the capitalisation of the loss. The matters on which opinions differ, be they either factual matters or the assumptions adopted by either expert, can then be identified and brought back to the client or the court.

Actuaries, of course, do not possess a reliable crystal ball to foretell the future. However, they do have a statutory role in advising on the management of institutions that offer benefits in the long-term future contingent on survival (e.g. life assurance companies, friendly societies, pension funds), and the financial soundness of these institutions has no doubt reassured the judiciary of their expertise in this area. However, while the reputation of the profession was not unhelpful, it was individual actuaries – and no more than a handful in the early days – whose evidence impressed the courts and forged for the profession a dominant role in assessing future financial loss.

One of the actuaries pioneering this role of expert witness in the Irish courts was Brian S. Reddin. Due to his reputation in this regard, he was the nominated member by the Faculty of Actuaries on the original (UK) Ogden Committee. The Ogden Committee produced their first report and actuarial tables in 1984 to assist in assessing damages in Great Britain.[8] The key recommendation of the Ogden Committee was that the rate of discount applied to discount future pecuniary loss (that rises with inflation) should be the market-determined real yield on index-linked stock guaranteed by the government at the time. This approach was unanimously agreed by the committee, who went as far as claiming that 'the reasoning which leads to such figures could not be faulted'.[9] That reasoning was the basis on which actuarial advice was given to the Irish courts at that time. The 'Ogden tables', of course, eventually proved influential in England when the approach was endorsed by the House of Lords.[10] However, back in 1984, the actuarial evidence was neither common nor highly regarded in the UK courts, or as Lord Justice Oliver put it at the time:

> As a method of providing a reliable guide to individual behaviour patterns or future economic and political events, the predictions of an actuary could be only a little more likely to be accurate (and would be certainly less entertaining) than those of an astrologer.
>
> *Auty and Others v. National Coal Board* (1984) 1 WLR 784

Overall, it can be said that, ceteris paribus, the award in respect of future financial loss tended to be lower in the United Kingdom than Ireland before the adoption of the actuarial approach encapsulated in the Ogden tables.

A good summary of the practice of assessing damages in UK courts at the time is given in Owen and Shier (1986) and Martin et al. (1997), and a contrast with the system in Ireland is given in Section 2 of the Report of Law Reform Commission of Ireland (1996). The evolution of actuarial practice on the assessment of damages in Ireland can be traced through Segrave-Daly (1974, 1998) and Delany (1990).

One would imagine that the UK and Irish methods of valuing future pecuniary loss are now identical, as they are informed by the same actuarial principles summarised in the Ogden tables. However, both jurisdictions have departed from the reasoning 'that could not be faulted' to a degree that is material to the size of the award computed. In the United Kingdom, the Lord Chancellor under powers conferred on his office by Section 1 of the Damages Act 1996 prescribed a rate of 2.5% as the rate of discount to apply in putting a present value of future pecuniary loss in injury cases since June 2001,[11] which thereby broke the link with the real yields on index-linked stock.[12] In Ireland, the market in index-linked securities failed to develop from the early 1980s. With no freely traded market in such securities, it is not possible to estimate satisfactorily the secure real yield obtainable from time to time or, materially, manage the risk involved in investing the lump sum award to replicate the lost real cash flows in the future. In short, there are no freely traded securities in Ireland to match the inflation-linked loss of many plaintiffs, so determining the fair quantum of award is considerably more uncertain. Despite petitions from, inter alia, the Society of Actuaries in Ireland, the Irish government has failed to issue index-linked bonds as part of its funding programme to help the very large number of investors manage the risks in achieving a secure real return in the future – from successful plaintiffs to pension savers and others. These, less than ideal developments, have influenced how damages have come to be assessed in Ireland.

3. ACTUARIAL TECHNIQUES APPLIED IN THE ASSESSMENT OF DAMAGES

Damages for future monetary loss are generally computed using a 'multiplicand' and a 'multiplier', with the initial quantum of loss found by multiplying the two figures. The multiplicand is the estimated monthly (or weekly or annual) loss and the multiplier is the capitalised value of a monthly (or weekly or annual) loss of €1. If expected losses are dependent on different contingencies, reoccur at different frequencies, or increase at different rates, then separate multipliers are computed for each category of loss and the overall capitalised amount is the sum of their products.

3.1. The Multiplicand

In an injury case, the monetary loss would include loss of earnings and perquisites of employment, loss of pension benefits, additional health care and living expenses arising from injury. The onus is on the plaintiff to take reasonable measures to minimise the loss by, say, finding suitable alternative employment. Accordingly, the calculation is not strictly made on the actual loss but on the loss when minimised. This is qualified somewhat further as an Irish statute[13] stipulates that the hypothecated 'loss' or better, the multiplicand, is not to be reduced by the proceeds of a contract of insurance or, in certain circumstances, by social insurance benefits payable, as a result of the wrongful action (presumably on the justification that plaintiffs provided for these latter benefits themselves).

Sometimes precision is impossible in determining the loss sustained, such as the future loss of earnings for a child incapacitated by an accident long before his or her career path is clear. Even in these cases, the Irish courts generally impute a loss of earnings from when the child could have been expected to enter the workforce, to be capitalised with a suitable multiplier. The loss of earnings and other losses determined above are all net of income tax, social insurance contributions, or any other deductions that would have been payable by the plaintiff. The offsets are similarly the net receipts in the hand of the plaintiff.[14]

An interesting issue arises if the plaintiff's life expectancy has been curtailed as a result of the injury. In that case, medical expenses and other losses are estimated on the basis of the plaintiff's current life expectancy but the loss of earnings calculation is based on the pre-injury life expectancy. The reasoning behind this approach was explained in the precedent set by the Supreme Court in 1966:[15]

> In my opinion the period or the length of time by which the expectation of life has been reduced must also be taken into account, though of course, for that particular period the sum to be considered would not be the gross loss of wages for the period but the surplus, if any, after providing for what it would have cost to live during those years if he had not had the accident.
>
> – Justice Walsh's judgement in *Doherty v. Bowater Mills Ltd* quoted in Delany (1990)

For wrongful death, a member of the extended family who is dependent on the deceased can sue for remedy for loss of financial support or services, less any gains accruing as a result of the premature death.[16] The actuarial principles are thus very similar to the injury case, but now due allowance must be made for both the mortality of the dependant and the deceased, were it not for the wrongful death (with the latter assumed from the time of death rather than the time of trial). It is often a matter of some practical difficulty to assess the reasonable pecuniary loss suffered as a result of the wrongful death – for example when the deceased is a mother of young children.

3.2. The Multiplier

The multiplier to be applied to the multiplicand is to capitalise the loss of a €1 per month (or other frequency of the loss) over the total period of the loss. To calculate the multiplier the actuary must make assumptions on

(i) The probability that each future payment is made. This typically requires assumptions on the mortality rates for the plaintiff, but it could involve other contingencies.
(ii) The amount by which the net loss of €1 in present day terms might increase by the time of payment. This assessment, in turn, typically requires assumptions on the general level of future inflation, the general level of real salary increases (that is salary increases above inflation) and the probability that the salary level of the plaintiff might have changed other than by the general level as a result of, say, promotion.
(iii) The rate of discount that must be applied to each future payment so that its present day value is determined.
(iv) The rate and manner of taxation of income and capital gains in the future, both to determine the net future loss and the net proceeds from investing the compensating lump sum to replicate those net future losses.
(v) Other assumptions, such as investment expenses, and loss ceasing on contingencies other than death or reaching a certain age (such as on marriage).

When all the above assumptions are made, it is a straightforward computation to determine the appropriate multiplier to apply to the multiplicand.

We treat in turn the key considerations in setting the assumptions required ((i)–(v)) under the following headings: *Mortality*, *Discount Rate* (taking in (ii) and (iii)), *Taxation* and *Other*. In the discussion we highlight the sensitivity of the multiplier to the assumptions.

3.3. Mortality

Mortality rates have declined markedly over the world in the twentieth century. In the case of Ireland, life expectancy at birth was 49.3 years for males and 49.6 years for females in 1900–1902, but by the close of the century life expectancies had increased to 75.1 years for Irish males and 80.3 years for females (Central Statistics Office, 2004). Accordingly, the rate of increase of life expectancies averaged 0.26 years for males and 0.30 years for females with the passage of each calendar year over the twentieth century. Mortality improvements over the last century were not, of course, uniform over either calendar year or year of age. At the start of the last century mortality improvements were more pronounced at the earlier ages with little or no improvements discernible at higher ages. As the century progressed, improvements were evidenced at all ages and most especially at the older ages in the last decades (Whelan, 2008).

Up until recently, the UK actuarial profession issued mortality tables that incorporated an allowance for future mortality improvements, but this practice has ceased since 2000 because of dramatic declines in mortality rates and the consequent very significant uncertainty inherent in any single projection. To date, actuaries in Ireland do not explicitly allow for future mortality improvements in calculating the multiplier. Instead, they either make an implicit allowance for it, by basing their calculations on a mortality table that is believed to have rates lighter than believed appropriate for the individual in question,[17] or ignore it altogether (i.e. assume no mortality improvements in the future).[18]

Given the recent accelerating improvements observed in mortality rates, especially at advanced ages, it is of interest to examine how sensitive the multiplier is to projected improvements. To do this we compare how the multiplier changes (a) when it is based on the most recent Irish population mortality experience (Central Statistics Office, 2004) and (b) when it is based on the projected mortality rates used in the official forecasts of the population and labour force in Ireland (Central Statistics Office, 2008; Whelan, 2008). It should be noted that the official mortality forecasts require a separate mortality table for each age and gender as mortality rates are forecast to reduce by different rates depending on sex, age in calendar year 2005 and projected year since 2005. Fig. 1 summarizes how mortality rates in Ireland are forecast to fall from the rates observed in a three-year period centred in calendar year 2005. The multipliers at different ages and discount rates are set out in the appendix. Table 1 summarizes the financial significance of allowing for future mortality improvements. It is clear that it makes little difference for annuities terminating at age 65 years, given the already low probability of dying before that age. However, for life annuities the effect is material – being more material with increasing age of claimant, with a lower discount rate employed and for males than females. So allowing for mortality improvements is especially significant when valuing retirement benefits foregone or other anticipated losses at advanced ages.

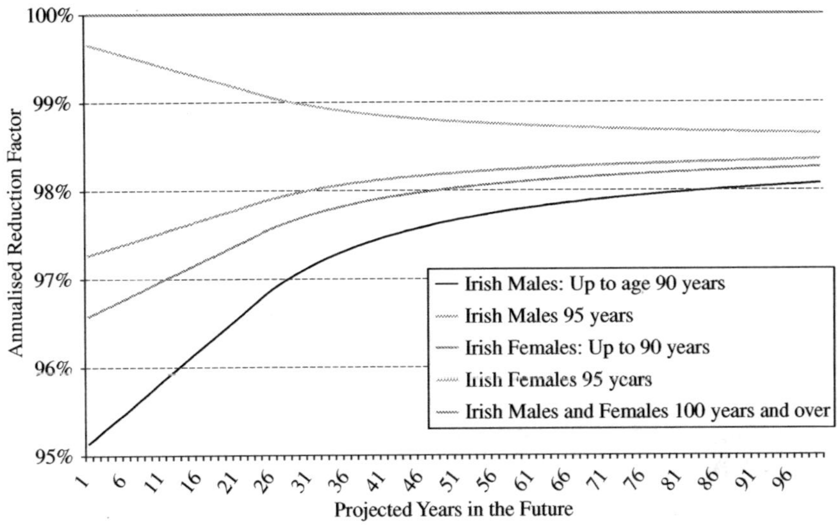

Fig. 1. Mortality Reduction Factors (Annualised) for Each Age, Years Forecast from Calendar Year 2005 and Gender, Used in Official Population Projections of Ireland.

Table 1. Percentage Increase in Multiplier for Loss of One Unit per Annum, When Allowance is Made for Future Mortality Improvements.

Gender	From Age (years)	Discount Rate 0%		Discount Rate 2%		Discount Rate 4%	
		Annuity to 65	Annuity for Life	Annuity qto 65	Annuity for Life	Annuity to 65	Annuity for Life
Males	25	2%	25%	2%	13%	1%	7%
	45	2%	30%	2%	19%	2%	13%
	65	–	37%	–	29%	–	23%
	85	–	36%	–	33%	–	31%
Females	25	1%	17%	1%	9%	1%	4%
	45	1%	20%	1%	13%	1%	8%
	65	–	23%	–	18%	–	14%
	85	–	18%	–	17%	–	16%

Of course, forecasting mortality improvements is more an art than a science; and any projection, including the official forecasts, are little more than educated guesses. However, the very long history of improvements and their continuing trend suggest that some allowance should be made, and the official projections are as reasonable to use as any other.

3.4. The Discount Rate

Irish actuaries subscribe to a market-consistent valuation principle that can be summarised as follows: *If there exists a freely traded asset whose proceeds exactly reproduce the pecuniary loss, then the market price of the replicating asset gives the value of the claim.* This principle is essentially equivalent to the 'Law of One Price' of economists or the Non-Arbitrage Principle of financial economists.

Suppose that the plaintiff's loss is a series of future inflation-linked payments that can be replicated by a portfolio of state guaranteed index-linked bonds, then the above principle says that the market value of the portfolio of bonds gives the size of the compensatory lump sum. This solution not only derives a value for the loss, but also gives a method to invest the lump sum to restore the plaintiff's lost pecuniary cash flows. As noted earlier, this is the principle underlying how the Ogden Committee recommended that its tables be employed.

The principle has the pre-condition that such assets are 'freely tradeable'. This might be rephrased as saying that the market price is set between a willing buyer and a willing seller, both possessed of all relevant information. A more practical interpretation is that the market price is a realistic guide to the price one can actually buy or sell the security at, in reasonable volumes, within a reasonable timeframe. For if the latter is the case, then any expert opining to the court that the plaintiff should receive more (or less) than the amount so determined is saying that such an index-linked portfolio should be bought (respectively, sold) and the portfolio recommended by the expert be sold (respectively, bought) which would give, on the expert's opinion, a profit. In fact, if such profits can be made, then in theory profits of any magnitude could be obtained from the market by repeating the above trade indefinitely. This logic could be used to undermine the testimony.

In Ireland, unlike the United Kingdom, the United States and many other regions, there is no freely traded market in index-linked bonds. However, since 1998 the French government has issued some bonds with payments linked to French inflation and some bonds with payments linked to eurozone inflation (excluding tobacco). As Ireland has been part of the eurozone since its establishment at the end of 1999, the Irish plaintiff can consider investing in French index-linked bonds with no currency risk. The risk with such an investment is how French or eurozone inflation might differ from Irish inflation in the future.

Studies of inflation levels in different regions with the same currency suggest that inflation rates do not differ significantly over time. By way of

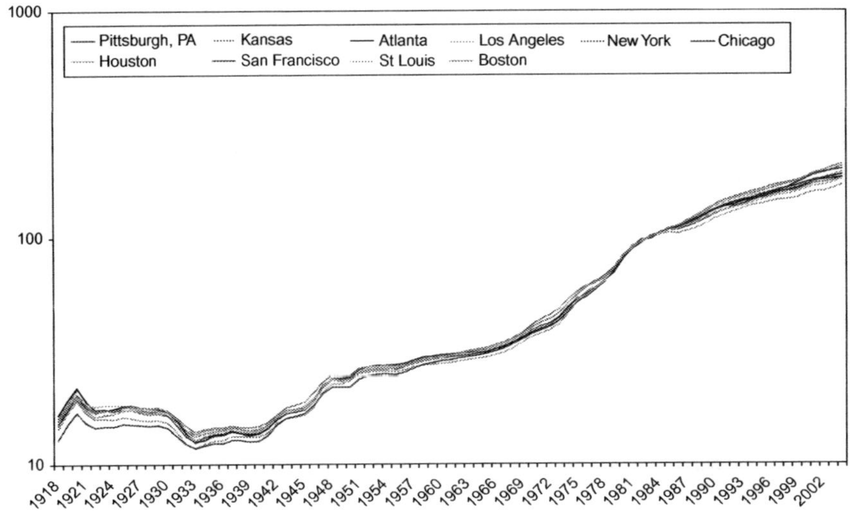

Fig. 2. Inflation Indices from Ten US Cities, 1918–2004 [log scale]. *Source:* US Department of Labor.

illustration, Fig. 2 plots the inflation indices in a selection of ten US cities for a period of almost nine decades. It is difficult to tell the lines in the graph apart – showing that the inflation experience is very similar. In fact, the difference in the annualised inflation rate from the highest to the lowest is only 0.4%.[19]

It can, I believe, be reasonably maintained that over the longer term the average inflation rates within the countries of the eurozone should be reasonably close. Furthermore, over such long periods it is not obvious which region would have higher or lower rates of inflation. Accordingly, investing in French (or other sovereign eurobloc) index-linked stock to match Irish inflation-linked cash flows does involve an element of risk, but the risk is not that significant. Arguably, such an investment strategy is the optimum strategy of all possible strategies in the sense that it minimises the risk in replicating the lost cash flows. Accordingly, the real yield on French (or other sovereign eurobloc) index-linked bonds of suitable term can be used as the real discount rate to apply to future inflation-linked losses in Ireland to estimate the lump sum.

Another argument (though somewhat looser) is to suggest that now that a worldwide market has developed in index-linked bonds, we can observe the market's expectation of real returns over different terms from low-risk

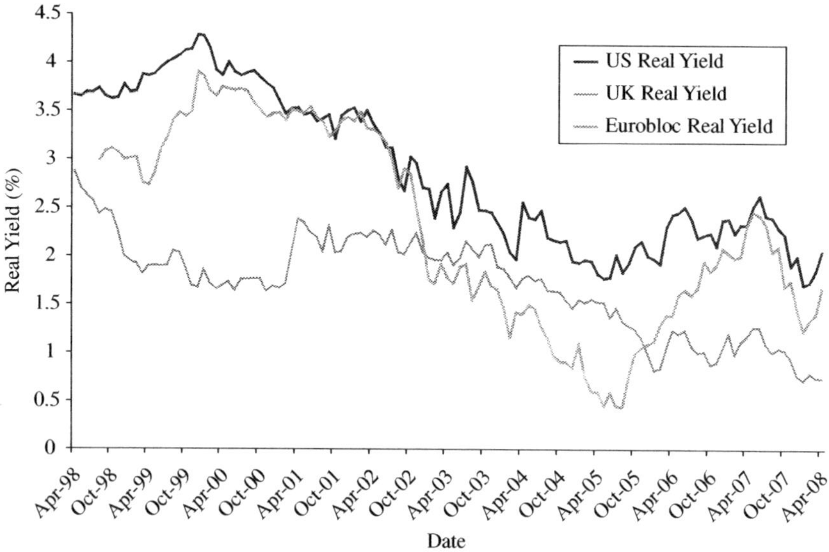

Fig. 3. Real Yields on State-Guaranteed US, UK and Eurobloc Bonds, April 1998 to April 2008.

investments. As an Irish plaintiff must invest in such capital markets, we can use observed real yields from time to time to inform real return expectations. This requires that we pay attention to real yields in different currencies, not just for the euro. Fig. 3 sets out the real yield on sovereign guaranteed index-linked bonds in three major currencies over the last decade.

The real yields are not identical and have been apart by as much as a full 2 percentage points in late 1999/early 2000 when UK rates were comparatively low. The average real yield rate over the decade was 2.9% in the United States, 1.7% in the United Kingdom and 2.3% in the Eurobloc (9.7 years). These considerations suggest that a real yield in the range of 2% to 3% seems reasonable over the last decade.

Over the last two decades, the Irish courts have generally opted for a real rate of interest of 4%, but more recently a rate of 3 percentage points above inflation has been settled upon since April 2002,[20] which was coincidentally close to the real yield on French index-linked bonds at that time. Other jurisdictions tend to settle on different real rates of return with, for instance, the real rate prescribed for use in courts in England and Wales set at the lower rate of 2(1/2)% since June 2001, as previously mentioned. Should these rates be updated to reflect more recent developments in index-linked markets, then we can expect them to be somewhat lower based on the arguments above and Fig. 3. At the time of this writing, real yields are about 2.5% in the Eurobloc, 3.0% in the United States, 1.3% in the United Kingdom, 2.6% in Canada and 2.0% in Sweden.[21]

The current precedent of using a real rate of return of 3% for use in discounting was set in Ireland back in April 2002, but not by reference to the real yield on French or other index-linked bonds. In that case of *Luke Boyne v. Bus Átha Cliath and James McGrath*,[22] Justice Finnegan (President of the High Court) ruled that as there were no index-linked stocks available in this jurisdiction, a prudent investor would invest in a mixed portfolio of higher risk equities and lower risk gilts. He acknowledged that the portfolio mix between these two asset classes would depend on the particular circumstances of the case but held, for the plaintiff Mr Boyne, that a portfolio consisting of 70% in equities and 30% in gilts was prudent and would reasonably mitigate the damages. On the basis of evidence presented, he judged that the real rate of return on such a portfolio would be 3%.

Of course, it is difficult to estimate the real return from a portfolio of risky assets – otherwise the investment would not be termed 'risky'. Table 2 summarises the annualised real returns to local investors delivered by the different markets over a period of 101 years from 1900 on, with particular attention to those markets on which Irish investors tend to focus.

The table suggests that 3% is not unreasonable, but neither would 4% or 4.5% be. It must also be borne in mind that the real returns crucially depend on when the original investment was made (in the table at the start of 1900) and when encashed (in the table at the end of 2000). There is a very large variation in the returns for other periods. The crux of the issue is that the proceeds of a risky portfolio are not transparent, and experts can differ in their estimates of likely real returns by a margin that is very material when used to quantify the lump sum.[23] Accordingly, the better approach is probably the one identified earlier that identifies the least-risky strategy to replicate the desired cash flows and then estimates the market value of that portfolio.

Note that our considerations so far have been on the best approach to identify the real return when the lost cash flows rise in line with consumer price inflation. Typically, a large component of future monetary loss, whether in an injury or fatal case, is in respect of loss earnings (or replacement services or medical care). The general level of earnings rise in line with general salary inflation, not general price inflation. Over the last century and longer, wages have risen faster than inflation, a key factor leading to the dramatic rise of living standards of workers over time. Fig. 4

Table 2. Annualised Real Returns on Major Markets and Inflation (Local Currency), 101 Years Ending 31 December 2000.

Market	Equity (% p.a.)	Bonds (% p.a.)	Cash (% p.a.)	Portfolio of 70% Equities/30% Bonds (% p.a.)	Inflation (% p.a.)
Ireland	4.7	1.0	0.7	3.6	4.5
United Kingdom	5.8	1.3	1.0	4.5	4.1
United States	6.7	1.6	0.9	5.2	3.2
Japan	4.5	−1.6	−2.0	2.7	7.6
Netherlands	5.8	1.1	0.7	4.4	3.0
Germany	3.6	−2.2	−0.6	1.9	5.1
France	3.8	−1.0	−3.3	2.4	7.9
Italy	2.7	−2.2	−4.1	1.2	9.1
Spain	3.6	1.2	0.4	2.9	6.1

Sources: Data taken from Tables 4-1 and 5-1 in Dimson, Marsh, and Staunton (2002) and, for Ireland, from Whelan (2002). Data for Germany exclude the two-year hyperinflationary period of 1922–1923. If this episode were to be included, then German inflation would rise at an annualised rate of about 34%, cash returns would fall to −19% real p.a. bond returns to −8.5%, and equities to 4.5% real p.a. (Dimson, Marsh, & Staunton, 2000).

shows the year-on-year change in the minimum hourly rate of carpenters in Ireland compared with year-on-year inflation, while Table 3 summarises the annualised increase in wages above inflation over periods to the end of calendar year 2000.

The table confirms the reasonably stable relationship, with wage increases being on average 1–2 percentage points per annum above inflation over the long term. We can conclude from this analysis that if allowance is to be made for increases in line with wage increases rather than with consumer price inflation, then the discount rate should be of the order of 1–2 percentage points per annum lower. Many projections of the Irish economy assume salaries will tend to rise by 2% real per annum over the long term (Pensions Board, 2005, 2006), presumably incorporating a further modest increase due to skill enhancement with experience. A reduction in the discount rate of 2 percentage points anywhere in the range of 0% to 4% increases the lump sum by about 40% for a 25-year-old (male or female) and by about 20% for a 45-year-old, for a regular loss up to age 65 years. Irish actuaries will allow for increases on a promotional scale if that is deemed reasonable but do not typically allow for a general level of wage escalation above price inflation.

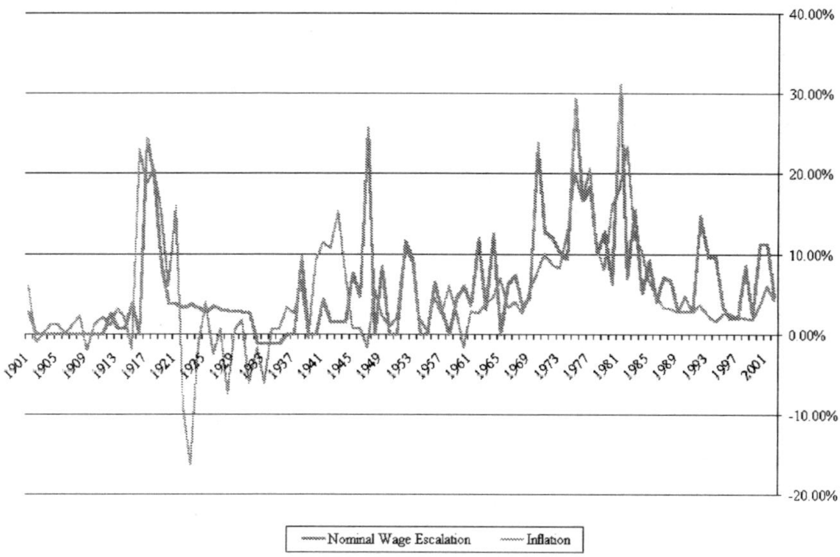

Fig. 4. Nominal Wage Escalation (Carpenters) and Inflation in Ireland, Year-on-Year over Twentieth Century.

Table 3. Summary Statistics on Real Irish Wage Rates (Carpenters), Periods Ending Year End 2000.

Years Ending 2000	Nominal Wage Increase (%)	Real Wage Increase (%)	Of Real Wage Increase			
			Average (%)	SD (%)	Min. (%)	Max. (%)
25	7.9	1.7	1.8	5.5	−13.2	10.9
50	8.1	1.7	1.8	5.1	−13.2	15.1
75	6.4	1.3	1.5	6.2	−13.2	27.9
100	5.7	1.1	1.3	6.5	−18.7	27.9
Since start 1900	5.6	1.0	1.2	6.5	−18.7	27.9

Source: See Whelan (2002).

3.5. Taxation

The calculations of the actuary, which are no doubt mathematically precise, assume, *inter alia*, that, for the lifetime of the plaintiff (something over 50 years) the current rates of taxation will be maintained for the entire period....

– Judgement of Griffin J. of Supreme Court, *Griffiths v. Von Raaj* (1985) ILRM 582.

The loss to the plaintiff is the estimated net loss of tax, social insurance and other deductions. The proceeds of the lump sum are subject to tax in the normal way on both income and capital gains.[24] Accordingly, the actuary needs to assume future tax rates, or future average tax rates, over the term of the loss. No clear precedent has as yet been set by the courts in Ireland on an acceptable approach. Irish actuaries typically assume that the real burden of tax and other deductions will remain the same as their current levels and base their calculations on current rates (following a judgement in English law).[25] That is, actuaries estimate the ratio of net income to gross income at the current time and assume that the ratio will remain unaltered into the future. On this basis, an estimate of the future net loss can be made.

To make allowance for tax on the investment income of the lump sum, the actuary will first estimate the lump sum at a real discount rate that makes no allowance for such tax. As noted earlier, the real discount currently used is 3% per annum. The annual income tax payable on the interest of the lump sum is estimated (i.e. income tax payable on 3% of lump sum, given the other assumed income of the plaintiff) and so the net real income derived from the interest on the lump sum is determined. The ratio of the net real interest income to the lump sum gives the net real interest rate – a figure of 3% or less at the current time. The multiplier is now recalculated using a discount rate set equal to the net real rate: this (higher) multiplier is the appropriate one to use to allow for tax on investment income.

Note that the approach to estimating the future net loss to the plaintiff on the one hand and the approach to calculating the multiplier to allow for future income tax on the interest proceeds on the other are mutually consistent. If a different level of income tax is deemed appropriate in estimating the future net loss, then the same rate should be used in estimating the appropriate multiplier. If tax rates different from the current ruling rates are used, then net future loss will be higher or lower, but the appropriate revised multiplier will move in the opposite direction – will be lower or higher.

Assumptions on the level and manner of taxation in the future are necessary to make, as the Irish courts have determined that the net future loss is to be made good from the net future proceeds of the lump sum. The quantum of damages is sensitive to the assumptions made in this regard, but there is little justification for, and therefore little confidence in, any particular set of assumptions. The actuary, without giving an opinion, makes a pragmatic assumption so the figures can be computed, highlights the assumptions underlying the figures and is willing to provide figures on any alternative basis preferred by the court. Few would disagree with the Law

Reform Commission of Ireland (1996) when it states that 'the position as regards estimating future income tax rates is still uncertain' (paragraph 2.46).

3.6. Other Contingencies

The actuary's calculations are based on an oversimplification of the plaintiff's financial future. Typically, allowance is made only for mortality and interest, and the calculations do not 'take into account any risk of unemployment, redundancy, illness, accident or the like. It assumes that the Plaintiff, if uninjured, would have continued to work, week in week out, until retirement and would have in effect guaranteed employment at a constantly increasing annual rate of wages until retirement or prior death'.[26] We can add to the list many other possibilities not modelled – a change in retirement age in the future, change of occupation, medical advances in the future so incapacity from the injury is reduced, etc.

Accordingly, the actuarial evidence is only a guideline to the court. In view of the factors ignored, the court will typically make a deduction from the quantum calculated by the actuary to allow for these other possibilities, the deduction known as the 'Reddy v. Bates discount'. The extent of the discount depends on many factors particular to the case (e.g. level of overtime earnings and industry sector of employment)[27] so that the overall quantum of damages is judged fair compensation.

4. CONCLUSION

Actuaries in Ireland have come to be regarded over many decades as necessary to help the courts quantify the capitalised value of future pecuniary loss in injury and fatal accident cases and, through the Ogden tables, have influenced developments in the United Kingdom. The actuary employs a relatively straightforward approach that emphasises the key assumptions to which the quantum of damages is particularly sensitive. He outlines how the uncertainties inherent in estimating a lump sum for future pecuniary loss can be quantified and the risks managed. More sophisticated models are simply not warranted as they would detract from the more financially significant decisions the court must make.

There has been change over the last few decades to how damages are assessed in Ireland, change designed on the whole to reduce the cost of the awards. Two decades ago, juries were abolished in High Court actions in respect of personal injury or wrongful death.[28] The Personal Injury Assessment Board (now known as the Injuries Board) was established in 2004 to provide a quicker and less expensive alternative to the assessment of compensation for personal injuries arising either in the workplace, as a result of a motor accident, or due to a public liability accident. Claimants are required to first take their case to the Injuries Board, which applies a document-based system (rather than the court's adversarial system) to arrive at an assessment of the fair compensation. The principles on which compensation for future loss are computed are the same as those on which the courts operate – outlined earlier – and, if necessary, an actuarial report will be commissioned. Claimants or defendants are, of course, not obliged to accept the assessment of the Board, being free to appeal their case to the courts, but in practice the award recommended by the Board is accepted in the majority of cases. Some, including a Professor of Law at Trinity College Dublin, have argued that such developments, in reaction to the previous compensation culture, have now gone too far and 'tort law is now in a state of crisis' (Binchy, 2004).

However, over the years there has been little change to the way the lump sum is calculated by actuaries. Two initiatives have reduced the award in certain cases – the move to make certain social insurance payments deducible from the claim[29] and, in certain circumstances when the claims can be very high, making tax-free the investment proceeds of the lump sum. Neither of these developments could reasonably be described as leading to crisis. But, of course, the cost of justice in Ireland is not only the quantum of damages to the plaintiff. Legal costs and experts fees add another 46% on average to the cost of a claim in Ireland.[30]

NOTES

1. An extensive series of Irish law texts survive dating from the seventh to the eighth centuries, which reflect a very ancient Indo-European social system with remarkable similarities to traditional Hindu law (Byrne, 1994). This legal system, known as the Brehon laws, assigned each person an 'honour price' (literally, 'the price of his face') depending on his or her rank. Recompense for any offence against the person was judged relative to the victim's honour price. There was a very extensive list of injuries (which included satire and refusal of hospitality as well as physical injury) and corresponding fines – six alone for damage to teeth. For instance, a small facial wound required a milch cow as compensation if the victim was a lord or a fleece if the victim was an apprentice (Kelly, 1988, see pp. 8–9, 129–135). These laws are believed to have continued in use in Ireland until the start of the seventeenth century, with their end usually dated to the Flight of the Earls in 1607.

From that time, the English law system was in use, modified and developed since Ireland's independence from 1922 when justice could again reflect cultural differences.

2. See paragraph 16.69.

3. The delay in implementing the recommendations suggests that the insurance industry, a politically powerful lobby group, is not unhappy with the closure afforded by the current system and, perhaps, indicates a belief that a structured settlement would not lead to an appreciably lower cost of claim.

4. *Reddy v. Bates* (1984) ILRM 197.

5. Restitutionary damages may be defined as a monetary remedy that is measured according to the gain to the defendant, rather than the loss to the plaintiff.

6. The income from the lump sum is exempt from income tax if the plaintiff is permanently and totally incapable of maintaining himself and such income is the main income (Section 5 of Finance Act, 1990).

7. Society of Actuaries in Ireland (2008), Guidance Note 24 (ROI).

8. The Ogden tables are now in their sixth edition, having been updated and extended in 1994, 1998, 2000, 2004 and 2007.

9. Introduction to the first edition of Ogden tables (or strictly, *Actuarial Tables with Explanatory Notes for Use in Personal Injury and Fatal Accident Cases*. London: Government Actuary's Department, HMSO).

10. *Wells v. Wells* (1999) AC 345.

11. The Damages (Personal Injury) Order 2001, SI 2001/2301.

12. The Lord Chancellor's reasoning for fixing the rate at 2.5% (very close to the real yield on index-linked government stock prevailing at that time) is summarised in *Setting the Discount Rate: Lord Chancellor's Reasons* (27 July 2001). One of the reasons was 'the fact that yields in index-linked government stock appear to be artificially low'.

13. Section 2 of the Civil Liability (Amendment) Act, 1964; Social Welfare Consolidation Act 1993.

14. *Cooke v. Walsh* (1984) ILRM 208.

15. Strictly, the plaintiff in an injury case is being compensated for an impairment of his or her ability to earn, which may be estimated as the capitalised value of a lost income stream (Justice Barr in *Phelan v. Coillte Teoranta* (1993) 1 IR 18).

16. Redress for wrongful death are taken under the Civil Liability Act, 1961.

17. For example, by basing their calculations on the mortality rates of insured lives rather than population mortality rates.

18. More recent editions of the Ogden tables make explicit allowance for mortality improvements, using the mortality rates from the latest available population projection by the UK Government Actuary's Department. Earlier editions of the Ogden tables did not make any allowance for improvements, either explicitly or implicitly, as the mortality assumed was simply the latest population mortality rates available.

19. Another example is inflation in Ireland and the United Kingdom over the period from the political independence of Ireland at the end of 1921 to the breaking of the fixed exchange rate in early 1979. Over the period the accumulated difference was less than 7%, or, equivalently, averaged less than 0.2% per annum. This remarkably similar inflation experience was recorded despite our different standards of living, our different consumption preferences and our differing taxation regimes.

20. *Luke Boyne v. Bus Atha Cliath & James McGrath*, April 2002, No. 2000/12133 p.
21. From *Financial Times*, 18 November 2008.
22. For a concise summary of the case, see Hall (2002).
23. For a discussion on the range of expert opinion on the real return from equities and bonds over the long term, see the Appendix in Whelan (2007).
24. Except for a very restricted class of plaintiffs – see earlier.
25. *British Transport Commission v. Gourley* (1955) UKHL 4, 3 All ER 796.
26. From judgement of Justice Griffin in *Reddy v. Bates* (1984) ILRM 197.
27. The discount would, coincidentally, generally be within the broad range estimated for such contingencies in the sixth edition of the Ogden tables.
28. Courts Act, 1988.
29. See Law Reform Commission of Ireland (2002).
30. From website of the Personal Injury Assessment Board, www.injuriesboard.ie. This assessment is supported by Healy (2002).

ACKNOWLEDGMENTS

I thank all those who participated in the discussion of an earlier draft of the paper read to the Society of Actuaries in Ireland on 18th November 2008, especially John Byrne, Joe Byrne, Pete Byrne, Brendan Lynch and Rodney Smythe. This paper is dedicated to the memory of Brian S. Reddin, FFA, FSAI, who introduced me to the actuarial profession, was my inspirational mentor and later friend. Time to complete this research was facilitated by a Government of Ireland Research Fellowship from the Irish Research Council for the Humanities and Social Science.

REFERENCES

Binchy, W. (2004). Recent developments in the law of torts. *Judicial Studies Institute Journal, 4*(1), 8–78.

Byrne, F. J. (1994). Early Irish society: 1st–9th centuries. In: T. W. Moody & F. X. Martin (Eds), *The course of Irish history*. Dublin: Mercier Press.

Central Statistics Office (Ireland). (2004). *Irish life table 14*. Dublin, Ireland: The Government Stationery Office.

Central Statistics Office (Ireland). (2008). *Population and labour force projections: 2011–2041*. Dublin, Ireland: The Government Stationery Office.

Delany, R. P. (1990). *The role of the actuary in the assessment of damages in personal and fatal injury claims*. Unpublished paper read to the Society of Actuaries in Ireland (November).

Dimson, E., Marsh, P., & Staunton, M. (2000). *The millennium book: A century of investment returns* (128 pp.). London: ABN-Amro & London Business School.

Dimson, E., Marsh, P., & Staunton, M. (2002). *Triumph of the optimists*. New Jersey: Princeton University Press.

Hall, E. (2002). Personal injury judgement: Luke Boyne v. bus Átha Cliath and James McGrath. *Law Society Gazette* (December), 42–45.

Healy, P. (2002). Profit and other controversial issues in motor insurance. *Irish Banking Review* (Winter), 2–13.

Kelly, F. (1988). *A guide to early Irish law*. Dublin: School of Celtic Studies, Dublin Institute for Advanced Studies.

Law Reform Commission of Ireland. (1996). *Report on personal injuries: Periodic payments and structured settlements*.

Law Reform Commission of Ireland. (2000). *Report on aggravated, exemplary and restitutionary damages*.

Law Reform Commission of Ireland. (2002). *Report on Section 2 of the civil liability (amendment) Act, 1964: The deductibility of collateral benefits from awards of damages*.

Lord Chancellor's Department (UK). (2001). *Setting the discount rate: Lord chancellor's reasons*. (27th July).

Martin, A. C., Beardmore, J. W., Gallop, A. P., Kennedy, P. G., McKenzie, J. L., Owen, R., Patel, C. C., Pettengell, C. T., & Wright, P. W. (1997). *Damages: Personal injury awards*. London, UK: Institute and Faculty of Actuaries.

Ogden Report. (1984–2007). *Actuarial tables for use in personal injury and fatal accident cases*. 1–6th ed. London: Government Actuary's Department, HMSO.

Owen, R., & Shier, P. S. (1986). The actuary in damages cases – expert witness or court astrologer? *Journal of the Institute of Actuaries Students' Society* (29), 53–93.

Pensions Board. (2005). *National pensions review*. Dublin 2: The Pensions Board.

Pensions Board. (2006). *Special savings for retirement*. Dublin 2: The Pensions Board.

Segrave-Daly, P. (1974). *Problems in valuing death and injury claims*. Unpublished paper read to the Society of Actuaries in Ireland (March).

Segrave-Daly, P. (1998). *The actuary in Irish litigation work*. Unpublished paper read to the Society of Actuaries in Ireland (February).

Society of Actuaries in Ireland. (2008). *The actuary as expert witness*. Guidance Note GN24 (ROI).

Whelan, S. F. (2002). *Prudent pension planning*. Dublin: Hibernian Investment Managers.

Whelan, S. F. (2007). Valuing Ireland's pension system. *Quarterly Economic Commentary, Economic and Social Research Institute (of Ireland)* (Summer), 55–80.

Whelan, S. F. (2008). Projecting population mortality for Ireland. Forthcoming in the *Journal of the Statistical and Social Inquiry Society of Ireland*, XXXVII 37, and available at www.ssisi.ie

APPENDIX

Table A1. Multiplier for Loss of One Unit per Annum, Based on ILT 14 Males and Females.

Gender	From Age (years)	Discount Rate 0%		Discount Rate 2%		Discount Rate 4%	
		Annuity to 65	Annuity for Life	Annuity to 65	Annuity for Life	Annuity to 65	Annuity for Life
Males	25	38.32	51.25	26.69	31.57	19.64	21.55
	45	19.06	32.33	15.80	23.25	13.32	17.61
	65	–	15.36	–	12.81	–	10.89
	85	–	4.61	–	4.29	–	4.02
Females	25	39.06	56.01	27.11	33.34	19.89	22.27
	45	19.41	36.59	16.07	25.45	13.52	18.8
	65	–	18.74	–	15.19	–	12.62
	85	–	5.81	–	5.34	–	4.93

Table A2. Multiplier for Loss of One Unit per Annum, Based on Cohort Projected Population Mortality from 2008.

Gender	From Age (years)	Discount Rate 0%		Discount Rate 2%		Discount Rate 4%	
		Annuity to 65	Annuity for Life	Annuity to 65	Annuity for Life	Annuity to 65	Annuity for Life
Males	25	39.26	63.98	27.20	35.69	19.93	23.00
	45	19.47	41.93	16.11	27.75	13.55	19.84
	65	–	21.04	–	16.55	–	13.43
	85	–	6.27	–	5.72	–	5.26
Females	25	39.51	65.71	27.35	36.31	20.03	23.25
	45	19.60	43.74	16.21	28.64	13.62	20.31
	65	–	22.99	–	17.91	–	14.41
	85	–	6.85	–	6.23	–	5.7

DOING AWAY WITH INEQUALITY IN LOSS OF ENJOYMENT OF LIFE☆

Giovanni Comandé

1. INTRODUCTION

The United States and European countries have for a long time affirmed non-pecuniary loss as a proper title of damages. On both sides of the Atlantic in the preceding decades, we have witnessed an escalation in the monetary amounts awarded for the non-pecuniary component of damages in cases of personal injury.[1] As a result of this escalation, the countries referred to have embarked on a shrill debate in trying to decipher a definition of their concrete notions of non-pecuniary damages[2] and on their awarding methods.[3]

In the United States, the expression "pain and suffering" often subsumes all damages for non-pecuniary loss,[4] even though its technical meaning itself involves more with the restricted connotation of moral and physical suffering. On the contrary, loss of enjoyment of life could be defined as a material modification of the capacity to enjoy life as distinguished both from the loss of earning capacity, as well as from pain and suffering.[5]

Broadly speaking, in our view[6] noneconomic damages for personal injury are essentially an attempt to offer compensation for "limitations on the

☆This article was previously selected for *Opinio Juris in Comparatione*, Vol. 1, 2009, paper no. 2. URL: http://lider-lab.sssup.it/joomla/opinio-juris

Personal Injury and Wrongful Death Damages Calculations: Transatlantic Dialogue
Contemporary Studies in Economic and Financial Analysis, Volume 91, 255–275

ISSN: 1569-3759/doi:10.1108/S1569-3759(2009)0000091013

person's life created by the injury."[7] However, this attempt at pinpointing the role of noneconomic damages has resulted in a distinction within the domain of traditional non-pecuniary loss, that is, between loss of enjoyment of life[8] and pain and suffering. These two types of damage redress diverse, intangible losses[9] in personal injury cases. The latter (pain and suffering) attempts to restore entirely subjective noneconomic damages for intangible loss, while the former (loss of enjoyment of life) relies upon an "objective"[10] basis for evaluation: the existence of an ascertainable medical condition.[11] In several jurisdictions – especially the European ones – this outlined distinction echoes the constitutional choice of protecting health and bodily integrity as a reaffirmed social value (e.g., in Italy or Germany) which deserves tort damages compensation in order to grant a minimum level of protection.[12]

No such clear reference to the constitutional protection of health exists in the United States in awarding damages for non-pecuniary loss. What is clearly evident, however, is a distinct trend to identify and distinguish between pain and suffering (as subjectively perceived *pretium doloris*) and loss of enjoyment of life as an "objective" component in non-pecuniary damages – damages that Europeans would probably qualify as compensation for lost health and bodily integrity as such.[13] Indeed, European jurisdictions have more openly opted for a clear differentiation between pain and suffering (with the sole purpose of compensating mental–moral suffering) and loss of enjoyment of life (as a means to redress health and bodily integrity accompanying physical injury or indeed purely emotional harm generating an illness). This trend is indeed discernable (albeit faintly) in the United States; however, it is certainly far from uniform across the American jurisdictions.[14]

With the doubtless existence and increasing role of non-pecuniary damages, both in Europe and the United States, set out, we now turn to the main objective of this chapter: to offer a quick overview of the awarding systems for non-pecuniary loss in Europe. Alongside this, it is intended to highlight the potential benefits, an adoption (or adaption) of one of the various European systems by the United States would realize, in particular for the assessment of loss of enjoyment of life. It is important to stress from the outset that such a maneuver would not subtract from the traditional tort feature of individualized justice but alternatively would serve better both horizontal and vertical equality.[15]

In Section 2, we will briefly discuss the evolution and actual state of the art of the awarding methods for loss of enjoyment of life in four European countries, thereby obtaining some challenging suggestions for the American experience. Finally, in Section 3, we will discuss how the European solutions can be adapted to fit the American system while simultaneously promoting individualized justice and more predictability in the awarding system for loss of enjoyment of life.

2. AWARDING NON-PECUNIARY LOSS IN EUROPE

A study of non-pecuniary loss in Europe unfolds an assortment of names and definitions for non-pecuniary damages: *smartengeld*, pain and suffering, *préjudice corporel*, *préjudice d'agrément*, *daño corporal*, *daño moral*, *danno alla salute*, *Schmerzensgeld*, *danno morale*.[16] In European jurisdictions, they stem from the same inspiring principles which guide legal protection in general.[17] In all jurisdictions, we discover a quest to avoid unjustified variations within levels of injury seriousness, fulfilling the principle of horizontal justice. Equally, a will to avert divergences in the amounts awarded for the duration of the injury can be discerned, effectuating the principles of vertical justice. The equality principle is therefore the point of convergence and goes hand in hand with the search for individual justice in the courtroom. As mentioned, several European countries distinguish – at least de facto – between damage to health and bodily integrity and mere psychological alterations or subjective predispositions resulting from a personal injury. The first, damage to health and bodily integrity, amounting to documented illnesses and disabilities assessable by medical experts, is awarded under notions similar to loss of enjoyment of life. Mere psychological alterations, amounting to transient sufferings such as anger or temporary stress, are awarded under titles easily incorporated into the notion of pain and suffering as moral suffering. Yet often European systems award a global sum encompassing both losses.

Considering the above, all European awarding systems[18] depend on medical description or evidence in evaluating objective noneconomic damages.[19] Medical evaluation is critical in offering an "objective" description and a uniform estimation of loss of enjoyment of life. In general terms, in Europe, once obtained, the medical description is affiliated to a monetary *barème* (i.e., a system of standardization using scheduling) based upon age and confirmed permanent disability expressed either in percentage permanent impairment (in France and Italy) or by descriptive tables (in United Kingdom and Germany). These aids offer to judges the basic parameters within which respect of the equality principle should be obtained.

With this bedrock of commonalities laid out, we must turn to the differences that exist between the examined jurisdictions of which insight is essential in relation to their applicability in the United States.

2.1. The English Common-Law Approach to Intangible Loss

A useful starting point for our comparative analysis is the English experience. This system has dramatically changed since the Court of Appeal began the process of monitoring awards[20] and setting standardized compensation amounts according to their findings. These efforts have produced brackets of values to be utilized by the courts in computing damages. This method simplifies the calculation process, attains consistency in the outcome of cases, and also aids predictability, useful both in promoting settlements and in maintaining insurability.

In practice, in assessing pain and suffering and loss of amenity of life, this approach permits trial judges and the Court of Appeal to consider the severity of the injury and to equate it with an amount within the brackets. These amounts (within the brackets) are deduced from precedents on quantum and are currently produced and periodically published by the Judicial Studies Board.[21] Amounts are updated in accordance with both inflation and new increasing/decreasing trends.[22]

It is rather intuitive that standardization ensued leading to reliable tables of values based on the relative seriousness of different injuries. The guidelines and the cases referred to in them offer at least a starting point for any case.[23] Yet these guidelines are not a fixed tariff, nor are they binding even where injuries are comparatively uniform and physically very similar. Indeed, the court will have to assess damages with regard to the actual claimant, meaning that it will have to consider her injury and its impact on her life according to her age (though decisions rarely mention age expressly), the severity, and permanence of her injury. The key to the evolution of the system lies in the fact that an explanation as regards to the actual amount awarded is required. Thus, only where insufficient reasoning is supplied can the Court of Appeal intervene.[24]

The described system necessitates a significant body of case law detailing the facts of and the reasons for the decision, a sustained policy decision, easy accessibility to the information for all the stakeholders, and a sufficient degree of itemization of the awarded damages.[25] All the elements required to borrow from the experience of the United Kingdom are present in the United States: the only requirement is that juries are given access to information on previous awards. Note also that itemization has been introduced in the Great Britain tradition and indeed in some American jurisdictions as well.[26]

2.2. German Tables and Descriptions

Germany, being a civil-law country, strikingly enough has developed a system, comparable to the British one, to assist in awarding loss of enjoyment of life accompanying damage to health and bodily integrity. However, contrary to English lawyers, German jurists may only refer to private compilations reciting cases and amounts awarded for noneconomic damages (so-called *Schmerzensgeldtabellen*).

Accordingly, German practice created an indicative system of scheduling to assess non-pecuniary damages (*Schmerzensgeld*) in personal injury cases. As in the United Kingdom, trial courts' discretionary decisions on compensation are reviewed on appeal for their reasonableness according to the relevant circumstances of the case.[27] Indeed, the individual circumstances of each case remain decisive, but they are pigeonholed in uniform patterns emerging from practice. Indeed, the *Schmerzensgeldtabellen* [28] describe the injury suffered by the victim and the amounts awarded according to claimant's request in an ever-growing set of actual cases decided by courts.

Overall, the German model offers information more structured and complex than the English one.[29] It is perhaps more functional in relation to practitioner use. In fact, there are diverse publications of *Schmerzensgeldtabellen* which offer collections indexed in different ways (e.g., according to the kind of impairment suffered or on the global sum awarded) and offering both a description of the case and the specific arguments used by the parties and the judges.

2.3. The Franco-Italian Approach to Scheduling

The use of "objective" factors in the evaluation of loss of enjoyment of life is common to other jurisdictions. In the Franco-Italian model, medical *baremes* in conjunction with monetary schedules are used by courts. Often monetary scheduling and models are elaborated by courts or by scholars but always with reliance upon previous decisions.[30] This is important to note, since Italy and France are civil-law countries; but in relation to tort law, the evolution of their legal systems, and especially for the awarding of damages, case law has always played a significant role comparable to that of a judge-made law legal system.

The French equivalent[31] of loss of enjoyment of life is named *préjudice physiologique (ou déficit physiologique ou déficit fonctionnel)*. *Préjudice physiologique* compensates the victim for the permanent reduction of physical, psychological, or intellectual functions. The medical expert describes and subsequently expresses, in percentage points, the loss suffered by the victim. The percentage is decided by reference to authoritative disability scorings.[32] As in some German *Schmerzensgeldtabellen*, the disability scorings group decisions by disabilities.

As in the other experiences considered in this chapter, none of the medical scoring tables have official character, though they are, so to speak, "appreciated" by the French Supreme Court. Indeed, in all examined countries, medical scorings tables have gained their authoritative role in the judicial arena by their scientific reputation.

Usually both the parties to a case and the court itself appoint their own medical expert, and the judges then assign a percentage value to the plaintiff's disability according to the evaluation provided by the medical experts. This percentage value is then multiplied by the monetary value currently assigned by the court itself for claimants in similar circumstances. Courts create their own tables of monetary values, which decrease according to age and increase according to the disability rate. In summary, courts, by multiplying the victim's disability rate expressed in percentage points by the corresponding monetary value, obtain the monetary damages award.[33]

Another important factor to note is that France courts update the monetary value assigned to a particular disability to reflect both inflation and different perceptions of the complained non-pecuniary loss.[34] Subsequently, any alterations find acceptance at the Court of Appeal level.

2.4 A Search for a Synthesis: The Italian Evolution

The French model has been adopted and developed by the Italian judiciary and scholars. The system is used for awarding the so-called *danno alla salute* or *danno biologico*, which we assimilate with loss of enjoyment of life. Indeed, the Italian judiciary by way of judicial interpretation has distinguished loss of enjoyment of life (*danno alla salute*) from pain and suffering (*danno morale*). Compensation for the former should ensue even though damage to health and bodily integrity neither reduced the ability to generate earnings nor caused pain and suffering[35] because *danno alla salute* is "a first, essential, priority compensation that conditions every other one."[36] According to the Italian Constitutional Court, damages for *danno alla salute* are compensatory and health "cannot suffer limits to the compensation for damage done to it."[37]

It is important to stress this last consideration because it emphasizes the compensatory nature of awards for loss of enjoyment of life/*danno alla salute*. It is undeniable that a lost limb cannot literally be fully restored by any amount of money. However, social perception visualizes the award of damages as capable of making the victim whole.[38] Consequently, the use of indicative scheduling must be seen as an instrument used to obtain equal treatment, not as means to reduce compensation or individual justice.

Similarly to France, the Italian awarding method finds its uniformity by carrying out a medical evaluation of the psychophysical disability and, with reference to consistent monetary guidelines, developed once more from an examination of prior awards. Again, corresponding to the French system, a medical evaluation, based upon reputed scientific and practitioners' publications, assigns to the permanent disability a percentage value. The court thereupon allocates a monetary value to this percentage value and multiplies the value by the percentage value. Needless to say, the Court's discretion remains absolute in defining the final monetary value of each percentage value according to its previous awards. The judicial assessment of the disability is the responsibility of the court in any given case, its correspondence to a severity percentage, medical evidence being the leading guide.[39]

In summary, courts in the European countries examined developed local tables of monetary values from their previous case evaluations and now use them together with scientific medical scorings to award objective noneconomic damages (*danno alla salute* and *préjudice physiologique*, loss of enjoyment of life). Local tables enable a reflection of the "local" social perception of the amount of money required to consider the victim whole. Strange as it might seem, those amounts might vary, and indeed vary significantly, from one Italian (or French) region to another, as is probably the case in various American court districts. This somewhat awkward result illustrates once again that the European scheduling mechanisms are not a way of curtailing victims' rights but are rather a means to improve and govern the awarding of non-pecuniary loss. Indeed, medical scoring tables and monetary values used in Europe at the very least grant the sharing and distribution of information among all the stakeholders in personal injury cases.

In principle, it would be possible to develop a single-scheduling system capable of serving horizontal and vertical justice. This notion could be realized by projecting the monetary value of the permanent impairment, defined by each court, into a conceptual uniform grid[40] which would reflect the actual perception of the relationship between different types of loss of enjoyment of life as awarded in case law and as described by medical expertise. Indeed, Italian judges developed a system in which an indicative monetary value is assigned to the percentage values of permanent impairment illustrated by medical experts. Those monetary values translate the described impairment into a final amount of money, which reflects (it is assumed) the local socially accepted valuation of loss of enjoyment of life. Of course, a perfect system would require a methodology uniform to all courts.[41] Nevertheless, even a disparate approach is capable of affording predictability to the system and higher levels of horizontal and vertical equality in a given jurisdiction. Indeed, the monetary scheduling tables developed in France and Italy function simply by multiplying the value of the relevant point for each age/degree of disability combination by the *basic monetary award* decided by each court. This system of calculating damages is utilized only if an amount has not already been established by averaging previous awards. Every different amount of the basic monetary award decided in a given jurisdiction respects principles of vertical and horizontal equality.

2.5 Judicial Scheduling the European Way

The awarding methods we have briefly described have improved vertical justice (among lesser and greater injuries) and horizontal justice (among similar personal injuries). Moreover, these awarding systems do not transform the personal injury victim into a faceless number but instead permit, along with a uniform base of monetary parameters, the delivery of better horizontal justice. This can be said with confidence, since the monetary values are indicative and susceptible to equitable adjustment, according to the specific case before the court. These awarding methods allow different injuries to be treated in different ways and similar injuries to be treated alike, always taking into consideration their individual and distinctive aspects. These results are mainly achieved by legal systems on a jurisdictional level. A vision of achievement of the same on a national level would indeed be ideal.

Where tables of monetary values have been developed, evidence of the personalization of awards is clear. The first avenue of personalization is offered by the combination of age and disability in the schedule. The second one allows for the adaption of these results depending on the facts of the case.

Medical–legal evaluations of psychophysical disabilities provide the basis for uniformity in the awarding process. These evaluations offer objective parameters and measurability while establishing homogeneous grounds for the evaluation of damages based on an examination of disabilities from past case law. The equitable power of each judge is safeguarded. She can adjust the objective measurement to the peculiarities of the case, and the creationctive evaluation is her choice.

The joint effort of the judiciary and of experts (legal, medical, and economic) has produced descriptiveimentation has made objective non-pecuniary damages easier to ascertain and assess.

With the European situation outlined, we now turn to the question whether or not a similar process of assessing damages could be initiated in the United States.

3. EMPOWERING THE AMERICAN JUDICIARY SYSTEM USING EUROPEAN INSIGHTS

Italy, France, Germany, and the United Kingdom, by their processes of systemization, tend to reach similar results. Within the civil-law and common-law traditions considered, the basis for the assessment of damages for non-pecuniary loss relies on preceding cases on quantum, which set out the sum of money awarded and a description of the medically ascertainable condition suffered.[42] The two European models briefly described have been coined by the "disability schedule and value table" model and the "precedent model."[43] A process of hybridization of the diverse models could result in an array of variations, useful for different American jurisdictions. In practice, however, the two models have diverse functionalities. As Rogers states, "The French or Italian lawyer, having obtained medical evidence which places the injury at the relevant level of disability in terms of points, then turns to the relevant 'value' table to convert that into a sum of money. The English lawyer, having obtained evidence on the nature and effects of the injury, then tends to regard it in 'descriptive' terms and goes to the standard sources of specialist material reporting court awards, to look for something similar."[44]

When considering application in the United States, each model presents hurdles. Though the disability schedule and value table approach would appear the simplest to implement, it would most probably result in competing expert views. This would most certainly arise in deciphering where on the matrix a particular disability should be allotted. Indeed, problems may also arise in relation to the accuracy of the scoring.

With this said, we suggest that these methods can easily function in every country in evaluating those noneconomic damages for which an objective criterion for establishing and measuring them is possible. Indeed, through medical expertise we can objectively ascertain and score noneconomic damages for bodily and health impairment that we have compared to loss of enjoyment of life.

Drawing on the Anglo-German (use of descriptive tables)[45] and on the Franco-Italian (adoption of scoring percentages), the American system can achieve standardization and a more equalitarian use of resources for calculating simply by profiting more from available information. Indeed, when information is collected and shared, it becomes a theoretical starting point for evaluation both in and out of the courtroom. The information sharing process does not threaten the individualized justice which tort law promises. In fact, the search for clear guidelines reduces vertical and horizontal inequality, since it enables judges to justify their departure from the guidelines.[46]

3.1. Learning the Lesson and ...

It is absolutely clear that the combination of reasonable predictability with the tailored assessment of damages is possible, tackling simultaneously the problem of uncertainty and justice (both vertical and horizontal). European legal systems, as shown, attain this either by using leading cases on *quantum* or building upon scientific tables. Both options contribute information about past evaluations relative to both the litigating parties and the courts. Moreover, each system conserves ample discretion for decision makers (judges, juries, and claim adjusters) in determining the amount of damages. Also important to note is that both systems allow for the adaption of the collated information (in the descriptive tables or in the scoring ones) to the case at hand. Every mentioned method requires rational justifications if departure from the previous decisions occurs. The case has to be actually distinguished to avoid review on appeal.[47] Except for the United Kingdom, the European systems discussed in this article are not based on fully binding precedents, but, once elaborated in a meaningful way, they offer a preliminary informative framework that can be used repeatedly leading to higher certainty in predicting the possible award of a given case.

No statutory intervention was required in Europe nor is it called for if implementation of any of the European insights were to occur in the United States. Special verdicts, for example, can be used to supply juries with the required information on values[48] without subtracting from the essence of case-by-case assessment of trial by jury. Simultaneously, every judicial discretion would be circumscribed by the requirement to justify awards which depart from the precedents on quantum. We understand that this is a significative departure from routine practice in American courts. Clearly, the describing or scheduling guidelines cannot be binding for the jury in situations where they arrive at a contrasting evaluation based on the evidence presented to it. Nevertheless, a review process is already in force; and although the jury would *not* justify the award explicitly, no attorney would appeal a decision that was actually based on clear evidence and obviously well founded. After all, *additur* and *remittitur* are based on the evidence of the case at trial.

The European experiences certainly demonstrate that rationalizing the awarding system for loss of enjoyment of life without taking away victims' rights and judicial powers is not a mythical chimera. In fact, it introduces rationality by supplying information and also has the potential to increase the possibilities for settlement which would correspondingly reduce litigation.

European examples suggest that no limit to the discretion of the judicial system is required to foster these goals. The only requirement is the transformation of the judicial process into a better-informed process.

The American legal system can reach results similar to the European ones by relying on the presence of a capable objective basis for loss of enjoyment of life (a description in medical terms) and its assessability in personal injury cases using medical scoring or descriptive tables. This is indeed feasible, and evidence suggests that the wheels for its implementation have already been set in motion.[49]

3.2. … Doing It the American Way

Our basic assumption here is that (1) informing juries and judges about previous verdicts and (2) letting them use disability scheduling as they occasionally do at present[50] would serve vertical and horizontal justice at least within the specific jurisdictions. Moreover, it would continue to allow determining the value of damages either according to previous decisions or by their own evaluation.

Drawing from Europe, courts could create a reference scale for the case at hand, defining both their scheduling and monetary values by relying on factors such as age and severity of the injury.[51] It would not require statutory intervention and could be both adopted and adapted without necessarily imposing monetary scheduling on judges and juries.

Indeed, section 905 of the Restatement (Second) of Torts already indicates the severity of the injury, its permanence, and the age of the plaintiff as predictors of award size,[52] similar to jury instructions which often stipulate the severity of injury as a crucial element in awarding noneconomic damages.[53] Moreover, "severity of injury scales" is already readily available to litigants and courts.[54]

Another aid to the adoption or adaption process of European experiences is that itemized verdict forms are used in several states,[55] making it easier to introduce the itemization of damages, which in any case is useful in reviewing awards on appeal.

Reference to previous monetary awards could receive legitimization again by precedents;[56] and data on awards from a specific date onward can be collected on a court-by-court level if the goal is to offer equal treatment within a single jurisdiction.

The critique that previous awards could restate noneconomic damages that are hardly deemed as correct can be refuted based on the fact that, even if previous awards are absolutely incorrect, a minimum level of credibility in the judicial system must be accepted to confer on the American system a basic adhesion to principles of justice.[57]

All sorts of criticisms can be poised against the European insights we have described so far. Indeed, they are not perfect – perfection is unattainable while something is evolving. European databases and reporting systems have not developed simultaneously nor without biases or errors. Nevertheless, it seems undeniable that building upon the European approaches can bring invaluable stability and predictability to the legal system in the United States. Initial discrepancies regarding costs of implementation and errors would be ironed out through the lengthy process of incremental steps made of trial and error which would undoubtedly play a part in the integration process in the American system.

4. AS A CONCLUSION: DOING INDIVIDUAL JUSTICE AND RETAINING JUDICIAL "DISCRETION"

In the course of adapting European insights to the American specifications, courts and scholars can develop several modifications to their original prototypes. Indeed, each described European experience is more nuanced than it appears in this article. For instance, almost every Italian or French court has developed its own schedule of monetary values for the percentage of permanent impairment medically assessed. Similarly, to offer one more example, each American court can easily develop its own monetary schedule by searching its own records and drawing from its own awarding experiences. Indeed, every jury could establish before hearing the case (ex ante) the monetary values to be allocated to the permanent impairment causing loss of enjoyment of life based on medical description. This approach would also diminish the risk of repeating erroneous decisions at scales larger than a single jurisdiction/decision. Each court could incorporate in its instruction to the jury a description of the methodology which charters the main attributes of a case or the proposed awarding methods might become a presentation tool for lawyers, already permissible in some jurisdictions.[58] After hearing the case, the jury still has the opportunity to adapt the monetary value (which is selected ex ante or from a national, state, or local schedule) to the facts of the case. In any case, all parties would have debated the case according to shared rules and information, framing the evidence brought by the parties in a clear structure.

While safeguarding the jury's independence, the use of guidelines "European style" would help the review process, conducted by the appellate courts or the trial judge, perhaps even better than the usual *remittitur/additur* standards, enabling the court to consider the legitimate evidential factors that evoked the specific jury verdict.

The more the elaboration and application of the awarding technique are suited to a particular court, the easier will be the periodic revision of them to reflect the changes in social perception[59] and in the justified departures from the guidelines. This is so because it would closely reflect the jury sentiment as an expression of the community perception of the appropriate award for loss of enjoyment of life. Nevertheless, to serve on a larger scale horizontal and vertical equality, it would be advisable to reach a state or, at least, multiple jurisdiction uniform approach. Yet, European jurisdictions as well are struggling in search of more uniform monetary evaluations even if at the national level, the awarding methodology is sufficiently shared and agreed upon.

In short, what the European insight suggests is the development of a shared methodology aiming at guaranteeing that similar loss of enjoyment of life, medically ascertainable, receives more similar treatment, even if the monetary value attached to each case would still be relatively different.

Trying to use European experiences would at least bring more consistency in striving for individual justice and retaining judicial "discretion." Consistency and equality would result along with several beneficial "side effects"[60] that make it worth trying to pursue. One must bear in mind the proverb: change hurts, but stagnation kills.[61]

NOTES

1. In this sense, see Giovanni Comandé, *Risarcimento del Danno alla Persona e Alternative Istituzionali*, Torino, Giappichelli, 1999, 3–45; Damages for Personal Injuries: A European Perspective 1 (Frederick J. Holding & Peter Kaye, Eds., 1993); A. Geerts et al., Compensation for Bodily Harm: A Comparative Study 95-98 (1977); Werner Pfenningtorf and Donald G. Gifford, A Comparative Study of Liability Law and Compensation Schemes in Ten Countries and the United States 9–14, 77, 155–57 (1991); Victor E. Schwartz and Leah Lorber, *Twisting the Purpose of Pain and Suffering Awards: Turning Compensation into "Punishment"*, 54 S.C. L. Rev. 47, 64 (2002). *But see* Mark Geistfeld, *Placing a Price on Pain and Suffering: A Method for Helping Juries Determine Tort Damages for Nonmonetary Injuries*, 83 Cal. L. Rev. 775, 777 (1995). Of course, recognition of non-pecuniary damages as a proper title of damages does not preclude this expansive trend from having experienced both misuses and abuses or, at least, misunderstandings. *See generally* Peter W. Huber, Liability: The Legal Revolution and Its Consequences (1988); Walter K.Olson, The Litigation Explosion (1991).

2. For a much more detailed clarification, see Giovanni Comandé, *Risarcimento del Danno alla Persona e Alternative Istituzionali*, Torino, Giappichelli, 1999, 3ff; ID. *Le non pecuniary losses in common law*, in *Rivista di diritto Civile*, 1993, I, p. 453ff. *See also* N. K. Komesar, *Toward a General Theory of Personal Injury Loss*, 3 J. Legal Stud. 457, 459 (1974). For further commentary on these same issues, see P.S. Atiyah, *Personal Injuries in the Twenty-First Century: Thinking the Unthinkable*, *in* Wrongs and Remedies in the Twenty-First Century, (Peter Birks, Ed., 1996); P. S. Atiyah, The Damages Lottery (1997) p. 138 (criticizing the U.K. tort system sharply). For a survey of different theories and policies on non economic damages, see Bruce Chapman, *Wrongdoing, Welfare, and Damages: Recovery for Non-Pecuniary Loss in Corrective Justice*, *in* Philosophical Foundations of Tort Law 409 (David G. Owen, Ed., 1995).

3. For a wider account of the state of the art and of the debate see Stephen D. Sugarman, *Pain and Suffering: Comparative Law Perspective*, 55 DePaul Law

Review, 399 (2005 Clifford Symposium); Giovanni Comandé, *Towards a Global Model for Adjudicating Personal Injury Damages: Bridging Europe and the United States*, 19 Temple International & Comparative Law Journal, no. 2, 2005, 241ff. For a critical perspective on awarding pain and suffering, see *Paul v. Niemeyer, Awards for Pain and Suffering: The Irrational Centerpiece of Our Tort System*, 90 Va. L. Rev. 1401, 1401 (2004), who argues that awarding damages for pain and suffering "without rational criteria for measuring [them undermines] the tort law's rationality and predictability," and advocates legislative intervention.

4. Dan B. Dobbs, Handbook on the Law of Remedies, Damages for Personal Injury (2nd ed. 1993), § 8.1; Restatement (Second) of Torts § 924 (1977). For further commentary on pain and suffering awards and notions, see Peter A. Bell, *The Bell Tolls: Toward Full Tort Recovery for Psychic Injury*, 36 U. Fla. L. Rev. 333 (1984); Mark A. Cohen, *Pain, Suffering, and Jury Awards: A Study of the Cost of Crime to Victims*, 22 Law & Soc'y Rev. 537 (1988); Stanley Ingber, *Rethinking Intangible Injuries: A Focus on Remedy,* 73 Cal. L. Rev. 772 (1985); Peter N. Kalionzes, Case Notes, *Infant Pain and Suffering: The Valuation Dilemma,* 1 Pepp. L. Rev. 102 (1973); David W. Leebron, *Final Moments: Damages for Pain and Suffering Prior to Death*, 64 N.Y.U. L. Rev. 256 (1989); Jeffrey O'Connell and Rita J. Simon, *Payment for Pain & Suffering: Who Wants What, When & Why?*, 1972 U. Ill. Legal F. 1; Cornelius J. Peck, *Compensation for Pain: A Reappraisal in Light of New Medical Evidence,* 72 Mich. L. Rev. 1355 (1974); Margaret A. Somerville, *Pain and Suffering at Interfaces of Medicine and Law,* 36 U. Toronto L.J. 286 (1986); Neil Vidmar and Jeffrey J. Rice, *Assessments of Noneconomic Damage Awards in Medical Negligence: A Comparison of Jurors with Legal Professionals,* 78 Iowa L. Rev. 883 (1993); William Zelermyer, *Damages for Pain and Suffering*, 6 Syracuse L. Rev. 27, 31 (1954) (suggesting that the only jury guide-posts in its task of assessing damages for these matters are common sense and sound judgment).

5. Sometimes the expression hedonic damages is used to signify the compensation for limitations "on the injured person's ability to participate in and derive pleasure from the normal activities of daily life, or for the individual's inability to pursue his talents, recreational interests, hobbies, or avocations." See *Boan v. Blackwell*, 541 S.E.2d 242, 244 (S.C. 2001).

6. Giovanni Comandé, *Towards a Global Model for Adjudicating Personal Injury Damages: Bridging Europe and the United States*, 19 Temple International & Comparative Law Journal, no. 2, 2005, 241ff.

7. *McDougald v. Garber*, 536 N.E.2d 372, 379 (N.Y. 1989) (Titone, J., dissenting) (citing *Thompson v. Nat'l R.R. Passenger Corp*., 621 F.2d 814, 824 (6th Cir. 1980)).

8. For commentary on the problem of awarding damages for loss of enjoyment of life, also known as "hedonic" damages, see, among others, R. Cramer, Comment, *Loss of Enjoyment of Life as a Separate Element of Damages,* 12 Pac. L.J. 965, 972 (1981); Stephen J. Fearon, *Hedonic Damages: A Separate Element in Tort Recoveries?* 56 Def. Couns. J. 436 (1989); Eric L. Kriftcher, Comment, *Establishing Recovery for Loss of Enjoyment of Life Apart From Conscious Pain and Suffering*: *McDougald v. Garber*, 62 St. John's L. Rev. 332 (1988); Paul E. Marth, Comment, *Loss of Enjoyment of Life: Should It Be a Compensable Element of Personal Injury Damages?*, 11 Wake Forest L. Rev. 459 (1975); Ronald J. Mishkin, Comment, *Loss of Enjoyment of Life as an Element of Damages*, 73 Dick. L. Rev. 639 (1969); Carel

J.J.M. Stolker, *The Unconscious Plaintiff: Consciousness as a Prerequisite for Compensation for Non-Pecuniary Loss*, 39 Int'l & Comp. L.Q. 82 (1990).

9. Such a distinction in the American tort system has already been acknowledged. *See, e.g.*, Annotation, *Loss of Enjoyment of Life as a Distinct Element or Factor in Awarding Damages for Bodily Injury*, 34 A.L.R. 4th 293 (1984); R. Cramer, Comment, *Loss of Enjoyment of Life as a Separate Element of Damages*, 12 PAC. L.J. 965 (1981), p. 972.

10. As already distinguished, "objective" means "existing independently of perception or an individual's conceptions" as opposed to "distorted by emotion or personal bias."

11. As per Lord Justice O'Connor in *Housecroft v. Burnett*, 1 All E.R. 332, 337 (1986), "The human condition is so infinitely variable that it is impossible to set a tariff, but some injuries are more susceptible to some uniformity in compensation than others."

12. See for instance Corte di Cassazione 8827 8828/2003 in *Danno e responsabilità*, 2003, 816, con note di F. D. Busnelli, *Chiaroscuri d'estate. La Corte di Cassazione e il danno alla persona*, 826; G. Ponzanelli, *Ricomposizione dell'universo non patrimoniale: le scelte della Corte di Cassazione*, 829.

13. Giovanni Comandé, *Le non pecuniary losses in common law*, in *Rivista di diritto Civile*, 1993, I, p. 453.

14. Giovanni Comandé, *Towards a Global Model for Adjudicating Personal Injury Damages: Bridging Europe and the United States*, 19 Temple International & Comparative Law Journal, no. 2, 2005, 241ff.

15. For further references on the actual distinction and its perfect fit in the American system see Giovanni Comandé, *Towards a Global Model for Adjudicating Personal Injury Damages: Bridging Europe and the United States*, 19 Temple International & Comparative Law Journal, no. 2, 2005, 241ff.

16. For information on several European Community member States, see generally W. V. Horton Rogers, *Comparative Report*, in Damages for Non-Pecuniary Loss in a Comparative Perspective 246 (W. V. Horton Rogers, Ed., 2001), pp. 245–296; Bernard A. Koch and Helmut Koziol, *Comparative Analysis*, in Compensation for Personal Injury in a Comparative Perspective 407, 419–434 (Bernard A. Koch & Helmut Koziol, Eds., 2003); and Giovanni Comandé, *Risarcimento del Danno alla Persona e Alternative Istituzionali*, Torino, Giappichelli, 1999, pp. 17–45.

17. Busnelli, Francesco D., *Il danno alla salute; un'esperienza italiana; un modello per l' Europa?, Responsabilità civile e previdenza*, 2000, fasc. 4–5, pp. 851–867.

18. From now on we will be referring exclusively to methods of evaluating loss of enjoyment of life as damages to health as such as opposed to pain and suffering in the sense of *pretium doloris*.

19. See generally, W. V. Horton Rogers, *Comparative Report*, in Damages for Non-Pecuniary Loss in a Comparative Perspective 246 (W. V. Horton Rogers, Ed., 2001), pp. 268–275 (stressing the different systemic impact of medical evidence in several European countries).

20. Roughly after World War II. See, e.g., *Ward v. James*, [1966] 1 Q.B. 273, 299–300 (U.K.). The background idea in this assessment of evolution is clearly summarized in *Wright v. British Rys. Bd.*, [1983] 2 A.C. 773, 784-85 (H.L.) (U.K.).

21. The Civil and Family Committee of the Judicial Studies Board is in charge of the guidelines. *See generally* Judicial Studies Board, http://www.jsboard.co.uk. For the guidelines, see Judicial Studies Board, Guidelines for the Assessment of General Damages in Personal Injury Cases (6th ed. 2002). These Guidelines are not in themselves law, but are regarded with the respect accorded to the writings of any specialist legal author. See *Arafa v. Potter* [1994] P.I.Q.R. 73, 79. See also David A. Kemp et al., The Quantum of Damages in Personal Injury and Fatal Accident Claims (4th ed. 2000) (using a thirteen category classification system based on both the area and severity of the injury, with subcategories for more specific parts of the body); John Munkman, Damages for Personal Injury and Death 130 (10th ed. 1996) (18-category classification system based on both the area and severity of the injury, with subcategories for specific parts of the body and more specific types of injuries).

22. For instance, after a consultation paper in 1996, the English Law Reform Commission issued a report in 1999 urging the "Court of Appeal and/or the House of Lords, using their existing powers to lay down guidelines as to quantum in the course of personal injury litigation" and to adopt recommendations for increasing non-pecuniary loss awards. The Law Comm'n, Damages For Personal Injury: Non-Pecuniary Loss 5 (1999), http://www.lawcom.gov.uk/docs/lc257.pdf, p. 7. The invitation was answered by in *Heil v. Rankin*, [2000] 3 All E.R. 138 (C.A.) (Eng.); *see* Richard Lewis, Increasing the Price of Pain: Damages, the Law Commission and *Heil v. Rankin*, 64 Mod. L. Rev., 100 (2001).

23. See W. V. Horton Rogers, *Comparative Report*, in Damages for Non-Pecuniary Loss in a Comparative Perspective 246 (W. V. Horton Rogers, Ed., 2001).

24. For an updated description L. Di Bona De Sarzana, *L'evoluzione del modello inglese: il ruolo della Court of Appeal nel controllo dei valori liquidati e le Guidelines dello Judicial Studies Board.*, in La Valutazione delle Macropermanenti: Profili Pratici e di Comparazione (Giovanni Comandé & Ranieri Domenici, Eds.) ETS, 2005, 97.

25. See W. V. Horton Rogers, *Comparative Report*, in Damages for Non-Pecuniary Loss in a Comparative Perspective 246 (W. V. Horton Rogers, Ed., 2001), pp. 276.

26. See also James F. Blumstein, Randall R. Bovbjerg, and Frank A. Sloan, *Beyond Tort Reform: Developing Better Tools for Assessing Damages for Personal Injury*, 8 Yale J. on Reg. 171, 179–180 (1991).

27. See, e.g., Ulrich Magnus, *Schadensersatz für Körperverletzung in Deutschland*, Compensation for Personal Injury in a Comparative Perspective (Bernard A. Koch & Helmut Koziol, Eds., 2003), pp. 148–176.

28. There are several publications available on the market. *See, e.g.*, Susanne Hacks, Ameli Ring and Peter Böhm, *Schmerzensgeldbeträge* (2004); Lothar Jaeger and Jan Luckey, *Schmerzengeld* (2003); Walter Hampfing and Ärztliche Fehler, *Schmerzensgeldtabellen* (1989).

29. See S. Wünsch, *Il modello tedesco delle Schmerzensgeldtabellen*, in La Valutazione delle Macropermanenti: Profili Pratici e di Comparazione (Giovanni Comandé & Ranieri Domenici, Eds.) ETS, 2005, 85.

30. Note that in several European jurisdictions courts usually appoint their own impartial experts.

31. For information on the French experience of awarding damages for personal injuries, see Christophe Radé and Laurent Bloch, *La Réparation du Dommage Corporel en France*, Compensation for Personal Injury in a Comparative Perspective (Bernard A. Koch & Helmut Koziol, Eds., 2003), pp. 101–104.

32. This list of medical scoring points sets a rate for disabilities, by recommending either a specific rate or a scale of rates for each of them *See* in general S. Galand-Carval, *France*, in Damages for Non-Pecuniary Loss in a Comparative Perspective (W. V. Horton Rogers, Ed., 2001), p. 90. Galand-Carval also argues that along with objective parameters, medical experts have an important role in measuring the so-called "personal temporary incapacity" (*l'incapacité traumatique temporaire à caractère personnel*). *Id.* p. 89.

33. It is noteworthy to remark that the uniform descriptions of health impairments developed by medical scientists and monetary value tables based upon precedent decisions were developed by judges and scholars intending them as not binding. Indeed they should not be binding according to the French Supreme Court. *See* Cass., 2e civ., February 1, 1995, Bull. civ. II, no. 42.

34. See. Suzanne S. Galand-Carval, *France*, in Damages for Non-Pecuniary Loss in a Comparative Perspective (W. V. Horton Rogers, Ed., 2001), p. 101. Note also that damages for disfigurement and physical pain are assessed according to schedules calculated with reference to previous awards, and judges indicate the lowest, highest and dominant awards of the past year for each of the several scale degrees.

35. See Cass., 6 June 1981, no. 3675, in *La Valutazione del Danno Alla Salute* 398 (M. Bargagna & F. D. Busnelli, Eds., 1995). In this work, most of the leading decisions on personal injury damages can be found as an appendix, in addition to other materials and commentary from members of the research group on Danno Alla Salute of Pisa under the auspices of the Italian National Research Council. See also *Rapporto Sullo Stato Della Giurisprudenza in Materia di Danno Alla Salute* (M. Bargagna & F. D. Busnelli, Eds., 1996) (analyzing over 1,000 decisions).

36. Corte Cost., 14 July 1986, no. 184, Foro It. I 1986, I, 2053 with commentary by Giulio. Ponzanelli, *La Corte Costituzionale, il Danno Non Patrimoniale e il Danno Alla Salute*.

37. Corte Cost., 14 July 1986, no. 184, Foro It. 1986, I, 2053 with commentary by Giulio Ponzanelli, *La Corte Costituzionale, il Danno Non Patrimoniale e il Danno Alla Salute*.

38. Wright, [1983] 2 A.C. p. 777: "Any figure at which the assessor of damages arrives cannot be other than artificial and, if the aim is that justice meted out to all litigants should be even-handed instead of depending on idiosyncrasies of the assessor … the figure must be 'basically a conventional figure derived from experience and from awards in comparable cases." (per Lord Diplock); see also *Rushton v. Nat'l Coal Bd.* [1953] 1 Q.B. 495, 502 (U.K.), stating:

> The only way … in which one can achieve anything approaching a uniform standard is by considering cases which have come before the courts in the pasts and seeing what amounts were awarded in circumstances so far as may be comparable with the case which the court has to decide.

39. Indeed, the Italian Constitutional Court expressly fostered: "a criterion fulfilling both the need for basic monetary uniformity and [the need] for elasticity

and flexibility to adjust awards to reflect the actual effects of the ascertained disablement on activities of daily life." See Corte cost., 14 July 1986, no. 184, Foro It. 1986, I, 2067. While the manuscript was in production, four important decisions of the Italian Supreme Court have confirmed the Italian awarding system for non-pecuniary losses, stressing the need for a personalized award which can be based on the described tables but should not forgive personalization of awards. See Giovanni Comandé, *"Comare formica", il danno non patrimoniale, le Sezioni Unite e gli operatori del diritto*, in "Il danno non patrimoniale. Guida commentata alle decisioni delle S.U., 11 novembre, nn26972/3/4/5", Giuffré Editore 2009.

40. Further information and references available in Giovanni Comandé, *Towards A Global Model For Adjudicating Personal Injury Damages: Bridging Europe And The United States*, 19 Temple International & Comparative Law Journal, no. 2, 2005, 241ff.

41. As proposed in G. Turchetti, *Gli sviluppi dello studio sulla determinazione del valore monetario base del punto di invalidità, in* Rapporto Sullo Stato Della Giurisprudenza in Materia di Danno Alla Salute (M. Bargagna & F. D. Busnelli, Eds., 1996).

42. See generally David Baldus, John C. MacQueen, M. D., and George Woodworth, *Improving Judicial Oversight of Jury Damages Assessments: A Proposal for the Comparative Additur/Remittitur Review of Awards for Nonpecuniary Harms and Punitive Damages*, 80 Iowa L. Rev. 1109 (1995); Randall R. Bovbjerg, Frank A. Sloan, and James F. Blumstein, *Valuing Life and Limb in Tort: Scheduling "Pain and Suffering*, 83 Nw. U. L. Rev. 908 (1989).

43. See W. V. Horton Rogers, *Comparative Report*, in Damages for Non-Pecuniary Loss in a Comparative Perspective 246 (W. V. Horton Rogers, Ed., 2001), p. 274.

44. See W. V. Horton Rogers, *Comparative Report*, in Damages for Non-Pecuniary Loss in a Comparative Perspective 246 (W. V. Horton Rogers, Ed., 2001), pp. 274–275.

45. Moreover, the Charter of Fundamental Rights of the European Union now strongly supports health, although this document has political value only. *See* Charter of Fundamental Rights of the European Union, December 18, 2000, 2000 O.J. (C 364) 1.

46. The argument is not novel. *See* James F. Blumstein, Randall R. Bovbjerg, and Frank A. Sloan, *Beyond Tort Reform: Developing Better Tools for Assessing Damages for Personal Injury*, 8 Yale J. On Reg. 171 (1991), p. 179, "An unexplained outlier should constitute a prima facie case for either remittitur or additur by the trial judge or an appellate holding of inadequacy or excessiveness of the judgment."

47. Similar standards do exist in the United States. See, e.g., *Steinke v. Beach Bungee, Inc.*, 105 F.3d 192, 198 (4th Cir. 1997), stating:

> In determining on remand whether the jury's verdict was rendered in accordance with South Carolina law, the district court should look to South Carolina cases to determine the range of damages in cases analogous to the one at hand ... If the court believes a departure from the range is justified, it should provide the reasoning behind its view. If the court determines that there are no other comparable cases under South Carolina law, it should explain this determination as well. Such a decision in the district court will reduce the risk of caprice in large jury awards and will assure a

reviewing court that the trial court exercised its considered discretion under the applicable state law.

48. See, e.g., Stephen A. Salzburg, *Improving the Quality of Jury Decisionmaking*, in Verdict: Assessing the Civil Jury System 341, 349–371 (Robert E. Litan, Ed., 1994). See Giovanni Comandé, *Towards A Global Model For Adjudicating Personal Injury Damages: Bridging Europe And The United States*, 19 Temple International & Comparative Law Journal, no. 2, 2005, 241ff.

49. Giovanni Comandé, *Towards A Global Model For Adjudicating Personal Injury Damages: Bridging Europe And The United States*, 19 Temple International & Comparative Law Journal, no. 2, 2005, 241ff.

50. Sometimes courts already make express reference to a percentage of disability. See, e.g., Quantum Study, *Louisiana Personal Injury Awards*, 46 Loy. L. Rev. 651, (2000).

51. The suggestion of emphasizing the diversity among injuries and providing this information is not entirely new. *See, e.g.*, Roselle L. Wissler, Allen J. Hart, and Michael J. Saks, *Decisionmaking About General Damages: A Comparison of Jurors, Judges, and Lawyers*, 98 Mich. L. Rev., 751, 757 (1999), p. 817.

52. Also, the importance of age as a factor for differentiating awards for non-economic damages, is again stressed in § 905 of the Restatement. *See* Restatement (Second) of Torts § 905 cmt. i (1979) (discussing ramifications of the age of the injured may have on the measure of recovery). See also Giovanni Comandé, *Towards a Global Model for Adjudicating Personal Injury Damages: Bridging Europe and the United States*, 19 Temple International & Comparative Law Journal, no. 2, 2005, 241ff, on reasons suggesting the use of age as an objective factor to be taken into account.

53. See, e.g., Eleventh Circuit Pattern Jury Instructions, Civil Cases: Damages Instruction § 2.1 (West 2000); Fifth Circuit Pattern Jury Instructions, Civil Cases: Compensatory Damages §§ 15.2, 15.4 (West 1999); Louisiana Civil Law Treatise, Civil Jury Instructions § 18.01 (H. Alston Johnson 2000); New York Pattern Jury Instructions, Civil Cases § 2:280 (West 1998). Some other jurisdictions "disability" should be considered in determining damages. See, e.g., Alabama Pattern Jury Instructions, Civil § 11.04 (Ala. Pattern Jury Instructions Comm. 2005); Eleventh Circuit Pattern Jury Instructions, Civil Cases: Damages Instruction § 2.1 (West 2000); Fifth Circuit Pattern Jury Instructions, Civil Cases: Compensatory Damages § 15.4 (West 1999); Hawai'i Jury Instructions, Civil §§ 8.3, 8.60 (Hawai'i State Judiciary 1999); Illinois Pattern Jury Instructions, Civil § 30.04 (Ill. Sup. Ct. Comm. on Jury Instructions in Civil Cases 1995); Louisiana Civil Law Treatise, Civil Jury Instructions § 18.01 (H. Alston Johnson 2000); Ninth Circuit Manual of Model Civil Jury Instructions § 7.2 (West 1997); Washington Pattern Jury Instructions, Civil § 30.05 (Wash. Sup. Ct. Comm. on Jury Instructions, 5th ed. 1992); Wisconsin Jury Instructions, Civil § 1766 (Wisc. Civil Jury Instructions Comm. 2004); Wyoming Civil Pattern Jury Instructions § 4.01 (Wyoming Bar 2003).

54. See, e.g., Randall Bovbjerg, Frank A. Sloan, Avi Dor, Chee Ruey Hsieh, *Juries and Justice: Are Malpractice and Other Injuries Created Equal?*, 54 Law & Contemp. Probs. 5 (1991) (discussing a study using a six point scale); Patricia M. Danzon, *Medical Malpractice: Theory, Evidence, and Public Policy* 74–75 (1985). See

Nat'l Ass'n of Ins. Comm'rs (1980) Severity of Injury Scale (ranging from 1 for emotional injury only to 9 for death). See generally Nat'l Ass'n of Ins. Comm'rs, www.naic.org (last visited November 23, 2005). For a criticism of the use of this last scale see Gary T. Schwartz, *Proposals for Reforming Pain and Suffering Awards*, in Reforming the Civil Justice System, 416, 419 (Larry Kramer, Ed., 1996).

55. In this direction *See, e.g.*, Colorado Jury Instructions, Civil § 6:1A (Colo. Sup. Ct. Comm. on Civil Jury Instructions, 4th ed. 2002); Texas Pattern Jury Charges: General Negligence & Intentional Personal Torts § 7.2 (State Bar of Tx. Pattern Jury Charges Comm. 1998).

56. Use of the aggregate wisdom of past practice is quite reasonable – certainly more so than reinventing dollar values in each case ... linkage to past awards, in short, provides a helpful empirical foundation upon which to base – and justify – policy judgment." *See* Randall R. Bovbjerg, Frank A. Sloan, and James F. Blumstein, *Valuing Life and Limb in Tort: Scheduling "Pain and Suffering*, 83 Nw. U. L. Rev. 908 (1989) (discussing various advantages and concerns of scheduling damages), p. 961.

57. After all, several studies conclude juries' vertical variability is no greater than judicial one. *See generally* Steven. P. Croley and Jon D. Hanson, *The Non-Pecuniary Costs of Accidents: Pain-and-Suffering Damages in Tort Law*, 108 Harv. L. Rev. 1785 (1995), pp. 1906–1914.

58. See Giovanni Comandé, *Towards a Global Model for Adjudicating Personal Injury Damages: Bridging Europe and the United States*, 19 Temple International & Comparative Law Journal, no. 2, 2005, 241ff, for examples. *See* also 75A Am. Jur. 2d Trial § 554 (1991) (stating that counsel is permitted to suggest to the jurors all reasonable inferences that they may draw from the evidence so long as they understand that the argument of counsel is not evidence).

59. See, e.g., Prentice H. Marshall, A *View from the Bench: Practical Perspectives on Juries*, 1990 U. Chi. Legal F. 147, 158 (It is appropriate for the jury to assess the harm allegedly inflicted on the plaintiff in light of the values of the community in which it occurred. Jurors do just that.).

60. It reduces inefficiency (by reducing over-investment in liability avoidance that results in higher insurance costs). Consistency reduces lottery-like results that are often criticized in non-economic assessment and may also increase the incentives to settle. *See* Peter H. Schuck, *Mapping the Debate on Jury Reform*, in Verdict: Assessing the Civil Jury System (Robert E. Litan, Ed., 1994), p. 316 (suggesting that in certain circumstances uncertainty may increase the likelihood of settlement).

61. As a great Irish student taught me.

SCHEDULED DAMAGES AND THE AMERICAN TORT ENVIRONMENT

Steven J. Shapiro and A. E. Rodriguez

1. INTRODUCTION

In Chapter 10 in this volume, Comandé (2009) has proposed that American courts adapt "scheduling" for use by juries in awarding nonpecuniary damages in personal injury and wrongful death cases. Comandé suggests that American courts can develop schedules for awarding damages for non-pecuniary losses on the basis of the severity of the injury and the age of the injured party, based on data on prior awards by particular courts in specific jurisdictions. Comandé's proposal is shaped by the experiences of European jurisdictions that have developed scheduling for awarding nonpecuniary damages.

Comandé's justification for scheduling is based on the notion that individuals with injuries of a given level of severity should receive similar damages awards for nonpecuniary losses, which is horizontal equity. Explicit in Comandé's argument is a notion of vertical equity as well, i.e., individuals with more (less) severe injuries receive higher (lower) awards for nonpecuniary damages. However, Comandé's paper does not suggest how scheduling of awards for nonpecuniary damages fits into other economic goals of tort law, such as optimal deterrence.

The remainder of this chapter discusses scheduling of damages for nonpecuniary losses within the context of the current tort law system in the

Personal Injury and Wrongful Death Damages Calculations: Transatlantic Dialogue
Contemporary Studies in Economic and Financial Analysis, Volume 91, 277–289

ISSN: 1569-3759/doi:10.1108/S1569-3759(2009)0000091014

United States. This chapter compares scheduling with efforts by American jurisdictions to place caps on damages for nonpecuniary losses under the guise of tort reform.

We suggest that existing tort reform efforts in the United States have focused on simple caps on damages for nonpecuniary losses as a response to the concerns of the liability insurance industry that funds compensation in tort cases, particularly in medical malpractice and product liability cases, where damages awards are substantially higher. We ultimately view scheduled damages as a solution that also has problems compared to the status quo.

The remainder of this chapter consists of a discussion of the existing status of United States tort law regarding damages, including damages trends. Separate discussions follow of caps on damages and scheduled damages. The chapter then concludes with a case for scheduled damages as possibly a second-best solution.

This chapter analyzes alternative approaches to awarding nonpecuniary losses under the assumption that the American system of awarding damages for both pecuniary and nonpecuniary losses remains. In other words, if juries are still going to award damages for pecuniary and nonpecuniary losses, how can the current process be improved? We do not consider proposals for elimination of awards for certain or all types of nonpecuniary losses (e.g., Ausness, 1997). Punitive damages are not discussed in this chapter since such damages are distinct from compensatory damages for pecuniary and nonpecuniary losses.

2. DAMAGES LAW IN THE UNITED STATES

As noted by Huber (1988), tort law in the United States can be viewed as the law of accidents. The law and economics literature suggests that the purpose of awarding damages in tort actions is to

- compensate injured parties or survivors fully and fairly;
- deter harmful behavior; and
- punish for wrongdoing that may have caused an action (King & Smith, 1988).

In American tort law, a unique standard has appeared as a result of the decision by Judge Learned Hand in *United States v. Carroll Towing Company* (1947), which has become known as the Hand Rule. As formulated by Cooter (2003), the Hand Rule states that optimal precaution occurs when

$$B = PL \tag{1}$$

where B is the burden of precaution, P the probability of harm, and L the cost of accidental harm.

Cooter transforms Eq. (1) into

$$L = \frac{B}{P} \tag{2}$$

Eq. (2) then becomes the Hand Damages Rule.

Compensatory damages are intended to compensate injured parties or survivors fully. Under the Hand Rule, damages can conceptually be viewed as optimal (from the perspective of microeconomics!) when the injured party is indifferent between having the accident with compensation and not having the accident. It can be argued that this formulation of optimal damages is relevant in the "real world" when there are substitutes for the loss or losses caused by the injury in actual markets. When substitutes are readily available, the market price of the substitute measures the value of the loss. As an example, if an individual has her earnings reduced as a result of an injury, the labor market can provide readily available benchmarks for assessing loss. However, there are some losses caused by an injury for which there is no market. For example, if someone loses a leg or an arm in automobile accident, there is no relevant price in the market that allows one to estimate the appropriate compensation, especially if that individual continues to work after the accident. Such quandaries are reflected in the types of damages that can be awarded in personal injury and wrongful death cases.

In tort claims heard in federal and state courts in the United States, injured parties (in death cases, survivors or the decedent's estate) are entitled to compensatory damages that are both economic (pecuniary) and noneconomic (nonpecuniary) in nature. Economic damages tend to be for measurable losses such as diminished earnings or earnings capacity, lost services to the household by a severely injured individual or decedent and medical costs incurred or future costs of care. Noneconomic damages tend to be for such things as loss of consortium, pain and suffering, and loss of enjoyment of life.

For example, Connecticut statutes distinguish between "economic damages" and "noneconomic damages" in personal injury and wrongful death actions (Shapiro, 2006). In Connecticut, economic damages include medical care costs, rehabilitative services, custodial care, and loss of earnings or earnings capacity. By contrast, Connecticut states that noneconomic damages include all "nonpecuniary losses, but not limited to physical pain and suffering and mental and emotional suffering" (Shapiro, 2006). Connecticut statutes are a perfect example of the difficulties faced in defining nonpecuniary losses in a manner that is useful for American juries. There is no relevant market that one can refer to in trying to find benchmark metrics for determining losses due to physical or emotional pain and suffering. Connecticut also has an extensive case law that has long recognized an additional nonpecuniary loss in the form of lost enjoyment of life's activities for a decedent in wrongful death actions and more recently the same element of loss for injured parties in personal injury actions.

The problems faced in providing guidance to juries in awarding nonpecuniary damages are reflected in Massachusetts jury instructions in civil cases that state:

> Recovery for wrongful death represents damages to the survivors for the loss of value of decedent's life ... There is no special formula under the law to assess the plaintiff's damages ... It is your obligation to assess what is fair, adequate, and just. You must use your wisdom and judgment and your sense of basic justice to translate into dollars and cents the amount which will fully, fairly, and reasonably compensate the next of kin for the death of the decedent. You must be guided by your common sense and your conscience on the evidence of the case ... . (See Cooter & Ulen, 2004, p. 369)

Massachusetts's jury instructions are typical of the lack of coherent instructions provided to juries in order to compute damages in jurisdictions around the United States. By contrast, in the case of economic damages it is possible for plaintiffs and defendants to present arguments about how to project losses (e.g., earnings or medical care costs) by reference to market benchmarks, as well as how to discount those losses to present value.

It has been argued that the lack of guidance provided to juries in determining noneconomic damages is behind high and unpredictable awards for damages (Bovbjerg, 1991). As noted by Bovbjerg, Sloan, and Blumstein (1989), attorneys routinely present entirely subjective methods to juries, such as suggesting that the plaintiff be awarded a small amount per day. When the per diem is annualized and multiplied by remaining years of life expectancy, the result is an award. Small variations in per diems can result in large dollar differences in awards. Critics of the American tort law system have suggested that such arbitrary and unpredictable awards have led to increased insurance costs and reduced innovation (Huber & Litan, 1991). This unpredictability creates vertical and horizontal inequities for claimants as well.

As shown in Table 1, based on trends in jury awards in tort claims in the 75 most populous counties in the United States, the median jury award has declined by more than 50 percent from 1992 to 2005 (Langton & Cohen,

Table 1. Median Jury Trial Awards in Tort Claims in the 75 Most Populous Counties of the United States.

	1992	1996	2001	2005
All Tort Claims	$ 71,000	$ 37,000	$ 31,000	$ 33,000
Automobile	41,000	22,000	18,000	17,000
Premises Liability	81,000	70,000	67,000	94,000
Product Liability	154,000	409,000	597,000	749,000
Medical Malpractice	280,000	315,000	474,000	682,000

Source: Langton & Cohen, 2008.

2008). However, the overall trend in tort actions does not reflect the trend in product liability and medical malpractice litigation in which average awards are substantially higher than in other types of tort actions (in particular, automobile-related actions) and which have risen substantially between 1992 and 2005. As shown in Table 1, the median jury award in product liability litigation in the 75 most populous counties rose 386 percent, from $154,000 in 1992 to $749,000 in 2005, while the median jury award in medical malpractice litigation rose 144 percent from $280,000 in 1992 to $682,000 in 2005 (Langton & Cohen, 2008). By contrast, consumer prices, as measured by the United States Consumer Price Index for All Urban Consumers, rose 39 percent over the period from 1992 to 2005.

At the same time, there has been a concern in the political arena that the increase in jury awards in product liability and medical malpractice cases has focused on the difficulties faced by juries in measuring noneconomic damages. As a result, noneconomic damages in product liability and medical malpractice actions has been one of the areas that advocates of tort reform in the United States have focused on (American Tort Reform Association, 2008). Advocates of tort reform have promoted placing caps, i.e., dollar ceilings, on awards for nonpecuniary loss. As shown in Table 2, as of December 2008, 23 states have enacted caps on noneconomic damages either in all tort claims, in medical malpractice litigation, or for certain categories of nonpecuniary loss, such as pain and suffering (American Tort Reform Association, 2008).

As is discussed in the next section, damages caps are problematic from a horizontal and vertical equity perspective. This is not surprising since caps on noneconomic damages resulted from political action by the insurance industry, physician groups, and hospitals. In addition, empirical research suggests that caps may not have all of the desired effects of reducing damages in an efficient manner.

Table 2. States that Have Caps on Noneconomic Damages in All or Some Types of Tort Litigation as of December 2008.

State	Caps on Noneconomic Damages	State	Caps on Noneconomic Damages
Alabama	No[a]	Montana	Yes
Alaska	Yes	Nebraska	No
Arizona	No	Nevada	Yes
Arkansas	No	New Hampshire	No[a]
California	No	New Jersey	No
Colorado	Yes	New Mexico	No
Connecticut	No	New York	No
Delaware	No	North Carolina	No
District of Columbia	No	North Dakota	Yes
Florida	Yes	Ohio	Yes
Georgia	Yes	Oklahoma	Yes
Hawaii	Yes	Oregon	No[a]
Idaho	Yes	Pennsylvania	No
Illinois	Yes	Rhode Island	No
Indiana	No	South Carolina	Yes
Iowa	No	South Dakota	No
Kansas	Yes	Tennessee	No
Kentucky	No	Texas	Yes
Louisiana	No	Utah	Yes
Maine	No	Vermont	No
Maryland	Yes	Virginia	No
Massachusetts	No	Washington	No[a]
Michigan	Yes	West Virginia	Yes
Minnesota	Yes	Wisconsin	Yes
Mississippi	Yes	Wyoming	No
Missouri	Yes		

Source: American Tort Reform Association (2008).
[a]Previously enacted cap on noneconomic damages was struck down by state courts as unconstitutional.

3. CAPS ON DAMAGES FOR NONPECUNIARY LOSSES

In jurisdictions that have established dollar caps on damages for nonpecuniary losses, a dollar ceiling is placed on the total award for either all or some categories of noneconomic damages. For example, in 2003 Texas enacted legislation that limits the award of noneconomic damages against doctors and other healthcare practitioners in medical malpractice cases to $250,000 (American Tort Reform Association, 2008). In addition, the 2003 Texas legislation places a per-facility limit of $250,000 in noneconomic damages that can be accessed per individual healthcare facility, such as hospitals and nursing homes, with an overall cap of $500,000 applied to the parent entity of the facility (American Tort Reform Association, 2008).

The rationale for caps is that placing limits on losses leads to greater availability of liability insurance (Schuck, 1991), which presumably would be scarce without such caps. Even if scarcity of insurance is not a problem, advocates of caps on noneconomic damages suggest that the presumed increased predictability in awards leads to the removal of "ambiguity premiums" above the normal actuarially determined expected losses (Avraham, 2006). In addition, by truncating the distribution of possible awards, caps do increase the predictability of awards because lawyers and insurers have better knowledge of the range of possible awards due to the truncation of the range.

Caps on noneconomic damages have several problems. First, it is not clear to what extent caps actually impact most claims. As shown in Table 1, median awards have tended to be well below $100,000 in dollar terms in the 75 most populous counties, while caps tend to be set at $250,000 (American Tort Reform Association, 2008). Instead, caps seem to be more relevant for product liability and medical malpractice claims. If we assume that it is desirable to cover more claims through caps, then the answer is to arbitrarily lower the ceiling on noneconomic damages, although this could exacerbate vertical inequities.

Caps create vertical inequities as potential individuals with minor injuries will be unaffected while those with severe injuries (e.g., brain damage, paraplegia, and quadriplegia) will be limited in recovery (Viscusi, 1991). Since state statutes generally set damages caps in nominal terms, these effects are exacerbated over time when factoring in inflation.

For losses that fall below the damages ceiling, juries still have no guidance concerning how to determine the awards. Hence, horizontal inequities are not eliminated by caps, as they might be with scheduling that is related to severity of injury or age.

From the standpoint of economic efficiency, caps on noneconomic damages are not a panacea. As noted by Avraham (2006), caps on noneconomic damages distort the marginal deterrence associated with activities that would be associated with higher degrees of bodily harm. Individuals have less incentive to invest more in avoiding injuries as the resulting injuries do not necessarily increase the payouts of tortfeasors. In addition, as Avraham notes, risk-averse potential victims are less interested in insuring against minor losses, as opposed to major losses. With caps, the incentives to underinsure are increased.

Empirical evidence suggests that caps cause unintended consequences. In particular, where there are caps on noneconomic damages, plaintiff attorneys may have an incentive to pursue larger awards for economic damages in order to replace now restricted compensation for noneconomic damages. In an empirical study of jury trial verdicts from a nationwide database in medical malpractice cases, Sharkey (2005) found no statistically significant impact of caps on either the jury's total compensatory damages or the amount of compensatory damages entered into by the trial court following the jury verdict. Sharkey controlled for the independent effects of severity of injury, various litigant characteristics, state law and county demographic variables. Sharkey's results are consistent with higher economic damages awards serving as a substitute for lower awards for noneconomic damages.

Given the problems with damages caps, there is not sufficient evidence to support the notion that caps on noneconomic damages are associated with lower insurance premiums, a claim of advocates of caps. Zeiler (2005) notes in her review of the empirical literature on whether caps influence medical malpractice insurance premiums and losses that these studies do not answer this question. Existing literature provides contradictory conclusions concerning the direction of the effect of caps on premiums and losses. Zeiler's literature review suggests that it is difficult to isolate the effects of caps, when other types of tort reform have also been enacted. In addition, she notes that insurance company managers have incentives to lower insurance reserves when caps are imposed that are independent of actual expectations of future losses. Furthermore, Zeiler notes that it is difficult to assess the impact of caps on insurance premiums in medical malpractice cases unless the impacts of caps on claims filed and the number of patient injuries are analyzed simultaneously. Since Zeiler's review of the literature, Waters, Budetti, Claxton, and Lundy (2007) have reported a statistically significant reduction in the number of medical malpractice claims and the average payout per physician on malpractice claims caused by caps on noneconomic damages after controlling for other types of tort reform. However, the Waters et al. study only partially addresses the issues raised by Zeiler as there is no accounting for how the number of patient injuries is affected by caps on noneconomic damages or other elements of tort reform.

Caps on noneconomic damages are therefore not necessarily an improvement to a system of unconstrained noneconomic damages subject only to the opinion of a jury without guidance. Caps introduce their own inefficiencies. They do not address equity concerns. The unpredictability of awards is lessened only because of the truncation of awards for severe injuries. And empirical evidence is simply not conclusive in terms of caps causing reductions in insurance premiums, claims paid by insurance companies, and court awards.

4. SCHEDULED DAMAGES

As discussed by Comandé (2009), various forms of scheduling of nonpecuniary damages are being used in the United Kingdom, German, Italy, and France. All of the European systems rely on a medical evaluation that is matched to a monetary standard that is based on age and either by degree of impairment (in France and Italy) or by descriptive tables (United Kingdom and Germany). He suggests that all of the European countries that he examined based their findings on prior cases. He also suggests that a simple improvement would be for American juries to have the benefit of knowledge of prior jury awards

As has already been discussed, American tort reform has thus far only considered damages caps. However, there is a body of literature from American scholars that has proposed similar reforms in the United States. In particular, such proposals have emanated from Bovbjerg et al. (1989) and Blumstein, Bovbjerg, and Sloan (1991).

Bovbjerg et al. (1989) propose using information on past awards to develop a matrix of relative value scales plus a dollar numeraire based on an analysis of past awards. The matrix would be generally applied by juries based on evidence heard at trial concerning the nature of the plaintiff's injuries. The relative value scales would vary by severity of injury and age of the injured person. The relative values in the matrix would be multiplied by the dollar numeraire. Bovbjerg et al. demonstrate that the dollar numeraire and the relative value scale can be obtained from central tendencies derived from a multivariate regression analysis. As an alternative to strict reliance on information on past awards, Bovbjerg et al. suggest that the numeraire and the relative scale can be further adjusted according to what legislators view as politically acceptable or community standards of fairness. The appeal of the Bovbjerg et al. scheduling matrix is that horizontal equity is restored under this system since similar injuries receive similar damages awards. Vertical equity is preserved as more severe injuries receive higher awards.

The use of past information on jury awards is problematic, however. Schuck (1991) correctly points out that the main problem with using prior information on damages awards to construct damages schedules is that distortions built into the past are preserved in the schedules. To the extent that distortions are nonsystematic, the problems resulting from their use can be eliminated through large sample size, but this may not be possible in some jurisdictions. One way of increasing sample size is to include settlements, as well as jury verdicts, in order to develop the range of values. However, as Blumstein et al. (1991) note, data on settlements would not have the same value as data on jury verdicts that are subject to public scrutiny. In addition, as they note further, parties to a settlement are under no requirement to characterize the types of damages included in a settlement. Since most cases settle out of court, it is appealing to have information on settlements available to shape the schedules. However, according to Schuck (1991), this would require settlements to be regulated so that data can be collected that is comparable to verdicts.

Another problem with an award matrix is that it may increase incentives for individuals to pursue litigation, which could increase the case load handled by the courts. The potential for increased incentives is related to the increased certainty of the size of the award, once there is a determination of the severity of injury. But this could well be offset by an increased likelihood of settlement as some uncertainty is eliminated by reduction in the variability of awards.

As Avraham (2006) notes, the benefits of an explicit scheduling system are offset by administrative costs and the complexity associated with implementing such a system. In addition, once policymakers begin to make subjective judgments as to what the relative scales should be or what numeraire should be included, it will not be apparent to any observer where the schedules come from.

Bovbjerg et al. also propose that as an alternative method of scheduling, juries be presented with nonbinding injury scenarios that involve typical injuries and approved values (i.e., awards for noneconomic damages) that would be derived from past awards or via input from legislation or the judiciary. Bovbjerg et al. suggest a procedure in which juries would have access to a small number of scenarios representing a range of severity. As with the scheduling matrix, the use of such scenarios would allow for enhanced horizontal and vertical equity. The administrative costs and complexity of developing this type of system are similar to those associated with the scheduling matrix.

As an alternative scheduling mechanism, Bovbjerg et al. suggest that floors and caps be established for noneconomic damages based on severity of injury. This has been formalized by Blumstein et al. (1991) who suggest that individual states compile data on jury verdicts within their jurisdictions. The jury verdicts would include information on past and future economic damages, noneconomic losses, the nature of the injuries and adjustments in awards for comparative negligence, prior settlements by other defendants, joint and several liability, etc. The database would also include information on awards that are adjusted or upheld upon judicial review. Of particular interest to Blumstein et al. is for jurisdictions to be able to compile information on what are extreme values (25th percentile and 75th percentile) for "presumptively valid" noneconomic damages by type of injury. These would be based on a point scale ranging from 1 (for only emotional injuries) to 9 (death) and in which values 2 to 8 distinguish among degrees of temporary and permanent injuries. If there is a finding of liability, juries would be asked to consider the case's specific circumstances and would be supplied with boundary amounts by the judge in the matter. Awards outside the range provided by the schedule would have to be justified by the jury.

As Schuck (1991) suggests, further data are needed beyond what is specified by Blumstein et al. in order to develop similar situations concerning severity of injury. In addition to the nine-point injury scale, other factors such as the victim's age and duration of injury are legitimate reasons for variations in awards. The distortions caused by use of past awards are present in the Blumstein et al. suggested approach to scheduled damages.

A variation on the Bovbjerg et al. and Blumstein et al. scheduling of damages is the proposal by Avraham (2006) for schedules that are based on multiples of past and anticipated future medical costs associated with the case. Avraham's proposal is based on the hypothesis that noneconomic damages, such as pain and suffering and emotional distress, should be positively related to age-adjusted medical costs that are expected to be incurred by the claimant. The advantage of Avraham's proposal is that an objective measure, medical costs, replaces subjective measures like severity of injury. Unfortunately, Avraham's proposal requires the specification of arbitrary multiples of medical costs in order to derive a noneconomic damages figure that can be used by a jury during deliberations. It is possible to derive multiples based on central tendencies concerning the statistical relationship between medical costs awarded and noneconomic damages awarded suggested by past awards as a way around the arbitrary determination of multiples. However, as noted in other scheduling models, the alleged precision of statistics is an illusion given the problems with how past awards were determined. Avraham correctly notes that in some wrongful death cases medical costs are zero, even though an argument can be made that there was pain and suffering and loss of consortium.

Scheduled damages are an improvement over caps on damages and the status quo in improving horizontal and vertical equity for claimants. However, the legal literature has not formulated an approach to scheduling that does not force policymakers to use misinformation in past awards or arbitrary schedules set through the political process by legislators or the judiciary. Other than the approach by Avraham, there is a great deal of subjectivity in the use of severity-of-injury measures used to bracket suggested noneconomic loss figures.

5. CONCLUDING REMARKS

As Comandé (2009) eloquently argues in Chapter 10 in this volume, scheduled damages would be an improvement over the status quo from the standpoint of horizontal and vertical equity. But caps on damages do not cure the problems of distortions that result in horizontal and vertical inequity, and the implementation of caps does not lead to optimal deterrence and use of insurance.

At this juncture, the Avraham (2006) approach that treats noneconomic loss as a function of medical costs is probably the best of a series of second-best solutions. Further research needs to be conducted on the statistical relationship between noneconomic loss and the value of medical costs in awards in order to determine the benefits and costs of using Avraham's approach.

REFERENCES

American Tort Reform Association. (2008). Tort Reform Record. December 12, Washington, DC.

Ausness, R. C. (1997). An insurance-based compensation system for product-related injuries. *University of Pittsburgh Law Review*, *58*(3), 669–717.

Avraham, R. (2006). Putting a price on pain-and-suffering damages: A critique of the current approaches and a preliminary proposal for change. *Northwestern University Law Review*, *100*(1), 87–120.

Blumstein, J. F., Bovbjerg, R. R., & Sloan, F. A. (1991). Beyond tort reform: Developing better tools for assessing damages for personal injury. *Yale Journal on Regulation*, *8*(1), 171–212.

Bovbjerg, R. R. (1991). Problems and solutions in medical malpractice: Comments on chapters six and seven. In: P. W. Huber & R. E. Litan (Eds), *The Liability Maze: The Impact of Liability Law on Safety and Innovation*. Washington, DC: Brookings.

Bovbjerg, R. R., Sloan, F. A., & Blumstein, J. F. (1989). Valuing life and limb in tort: Scheduling pain and suffering. *Northwestern University Law Review*, *83*(1), 908–976.

Comandé, G. (2009). Doing away with inequality in lost enjoyment of life. In: J. O. Ward & R. J. Thornton (Eds), *Contemporary studies in economic and financial analysis, Volume 91, Personal injury and wrongful death damages calculations: Transatlantic dialogue*. Bingley: Emerald Press.

Cooter, R. (2003). Hand rule damages for incompensable losses. *San Diego Law Review, 40*, 1097–1121.

Cooter, R., & Ulen, T. (2004). *Law & economics*. Boston: Pearson Addison Wesley.

Huber, P. W. (1988). *Liability: The legal revolution and its consequences*. New York: Basic Books.

Huber, P. W., & Litan, R. E. (1991). Overview. In: P. W. Huber & R. E. Litan (Eds), *The liability maze: The impact of liability law on safety and innovation*. Washington, DC: Brookings.

King, E. M., & Smith, J. P. (1988). *Computing economic loss in cases of wrongful death*. Washington, DC: Rand Corporation.

Langton, L., & Cohen, T. H. (2008). *Civil justice survey of state courts, 2005: Civil bench and jury trials in state courts, 2005*. Bureau of Justice Statistics Special Report. United States Department of Justice, Washington, DC.

Schuck, P. H. (1991). Scheduled damages and insurance contracts for future services: A comment on Blumstein, Bovbjerg, and Sloan. *Yale Journal on Regulation, 8*(1), 213–221.

Shapiro, S. (2006). Assessing economic damages in personal injury and wrongful death litigation, the state of Connecticut. *Journal of Forensic Economics, 19*(1), 103–113.

Sharkey, C. M. (2005). Unintended consequences of medical malpractice damages caps. *New York University Law Review, 80*(2), 391–508.

United States v. Carroll Towing Company (1947). 159 F.2d 169; 1947 U.S. App. LEXIS 3226.

Viscusi, W. K. (1991). *Reforming products liability*. Cambridge: Harvard University Press.

Waters, T. M., Budetti, P. P., Claxton, G., & Lundy, J. P. (2007). Market watch: Impact of state tort reforms on physician malpractice payments. *Health Affairs, 26*(2), 500–509.

Zeiler, K. (2005). Turning from damages caps to information disclosure: An alternative to tort reform. *Yale Journal of Health Policy, Law and Ethics, 5*(1), 385–398.

EXAMPLES OF "SCHEDULES OF DAMAGES" USED IN EUROPE AND THE UNITED STATES

Robert Minnehan

1. INTRODUCTION

The use of "schedules of damages" to establish compensation amounts for injured parties appears to be more common in European personal injury or death compensation situations than in the similar legal situations in the United States. The major exception to this statement is the state-based system of workers' compensation covering employer liability in personal injury and death claims in the United States. Other chapters in this book largely concentrate on comparisons between the uses of Ogden Table multipliers in awarding pecuniary damages in the United Kingdom compared to actuarial methods for calculating such damages in the United States. The two chapters dealing with non-pecuniary damages and scheduled awards deal with methods used to award such damages in the United States and in Europe in individual civil torts. This chapter provides an overview of a number of scheduled damages schemes in both the United States and Europe for the purpose of comparison. The schemes selected address both general and special damages.

The two "compensatory" elements of damages are: (1) "general damages" to compensate for pain, suffering, and loss of pleasure or the amenities of

Personal Injury and Wrongful Death Damages Calculations: Transatlantic Dialogue
Contemporary Studies in Economic and Financial Analysis, Volume 91, 291–307

ISSN: 1569-3759/doi:10.1108/S1569-3759(2009)0000091015

life; these are also labeled as "non-pecuniary" damages since there usually is no monetary loss to survivors and (2) "special damages" which compensate for losses such as work earnings, property damage, medical costs, and in some cases the costs of hiring someone to provide replacement services for the injured or deceased party. These damages are labeled as pecuniary or economic damages.

In practice, there can be schedules for establishing or calculating both types of damages. For example, in the United Kingdom, there is a set of periodically updated guidelines for judges on "general damages" as well as a specific calculation procedure, also periodically updated, for the "special damages" category of earnings loss calculations labeled as the "Ogden tables." In contrast, tort damages in the United States are usually defined by state statutes or case law, and there is considerable variability in the measurement and award of such damages among the states. The resulting variance in the size of jury awards between different states in the United States can lead to "jurisdiction shopping" where attorneys attempt to move the filing of cases to a state or locality where there are few limits on award amounts. This lack of uniformity of awards between states is a concern to many in the United States. European scheduled damages systems attempt to create uniformity in awards between jurisdictions. The objective of this paper is to examine the unique features of a sample of schedules of damages systems drawn from Europe and the United States.

2. THE SCOPE OF SCHEDULES OF DAMAGES: GENERAL, SPECIAL, OR BOTH?

Some of the schedules of damages reviewed in this chapter provide both general and special damages compensation as a bundle with a single compensation amount. The Vioxx settlement in the United States fits in this category. Some compensation schedules provide both general and special damages calculations separately. The September 11 Victim Compensation Fund (VCF) of 2001 in the United States was a scheme with a large special damages component and a simple general damages component. The VCF was also a temporary and specific scheduled damages scheme, unlike the Northern Ireland Criminal Injuries Compensation Scheme of 2001 which provides a more complex general damages calculation for ongoing compensation claims.

3. EXAMPLES OF COMPLEX SCHEDULES OF DAMAGES FOR GENERAL DAMAGES

3.1. The British Court's "Guidelines for the Assessment of General Damages in Personal Injury Cases"

"Guidelines for the Assessment of General Damages in Personal Injury Cases" from the Judicial Studies Board (2006/2008) provide suggested compensation for personal injury cases for judges in the United Kingdom. The numbers are presented as a range of values rather than a fixed sum, as seen for the two VCF examples from Ireland and Great Britain. The text of the guidelines discusses how different case-specific conditions would indicate an award at the upper or lower end of the value range. This reference is based on actual case awards and is updated every second year. There are 255 categories of injury with value ranges included in this text. There are discussions of problems like "chronic pain" and "post-traumatic stress disorder" with some valuation guides. For example, the guidelines include a set of descriptions for asbestos-related disease providing general damages values ranging from £4,000 to £74,300 based on severity.

3.2. The Northern Ireland Criminal Injuries Compensation Scheme 2002

The VCF from the Compensation Agency for Northern Ireland (2002) provides a mechanism for the determination of the criminal damages award based on the injuries described in the formal tables for Tariff of Injuries. Awards are granted by level of injury and severity of injury, with awards ranging from £1,000 for a concussion to £280,000 for extremely serious brain damage. In the case of a death, there is a calculation for the loss of financial support for dependents based on a formula incorporating the ages of the decedent and survivors, earnings of the decedent and spouse, the degree of dependency of survivors on the decedent, and other characteristics of the decedent and survivors. The example in Table 1 shows this calculation for a family.

The financial loss, called the "dependency," is based on the deceased person's earnings, the surviving spouse's earnings, a deduction for personal consumption, and an adjusted Ogden Table multiplier to calculate the total amount of "dependency" loss. This dependency loss calculation in Table 1 illustrates the "special damages" value calculation for this sample case.

Table 1. Fatal Injury Calculation – Northern Ireland.

Background: husband age 32 died from a criminal injury (earnings of £265 net per week)		
Spouse age 30 working (earnings of £96 net per week)		
Two children, aged 5 and 3		
Dependency calculation		
Weekly joint income of £361; dependency is 80% of this (£289)		
Deduct wife's income of £96 to get loss of £193 per week (£10,036 per year)		
Period of future loss to age 65 is 33 years		
Indicative multiplier (Ogden tables) of 17, but reduced to 15 for contingencies		
Dependency loss is 15 times £10,036 for future	£150,540	a.
Deductions for collateral source items		
Widow's benefit of	£1,000	
Widowed mother's allowance: £3,060 per year to age 18 of youngest child		
Multiplier of 10	£30,600	
Widow's children's allowance		
Age 3, £575 per year, multiplier 10 to age 18	£5,750	
Age 5, £512 per year, multiplier 9 to age 18	£4,610	
Widow's pension from age 45, £920 per year		
Multiplier of (15–10)	£4,600	
Employer's pensions, taxable, only 50% subtracted		
Widow, £750 per year, multiplier 15	£11,250	
Younger child, £200 per year, multiplier 10	£2,000	
Older child, £200 per year, multiplier 9	£1,800	
Taxable gratuity to widow, £2,000 at 50%	£1,000	
Total deductions	£62,610	b.
Net dependency total	£87,930	a.–b.
Additions		
Bereavement support payments: 3 at £12,000	£36,000	
Younger child, loss of parental support, £2,500 × 10	£25,000	
Older child, loss of parental support, £2,500 × 9	£22,500	
Funeral expenses	£950	
Total additions	£84,450	c.
Total award to the family …	£172,380	a–b+c
Total compensation to the family Including the deducted collateral source items	£234,990	

Then there are deductions for collateral source items such as social security and pension to arrive at a "net dependency total." For the injured but surviving victim the "Tariff of Injuries" award includes the earnings loss for the first 28 weeks, plus noneconomic damages such as pain and suffering.

If the work loss exceeds 28 weeks, then a claim can be made for the loss of future earnings.

The general damages compensation, in the example in Table 1, includes "bereavement support" payments for the widow and two children of 12,000 pounds each as well as "loss of parental support" awards for the two children based on 2,500 pounds per year times an actuarial factor. These calculations are shown in the "Additions" section of Table 1.

The formulas for determining damages are found in the 2002 guides provided by the Compensation Agency for Northern Ireland. There is a proposed 2009 revision of the guide now under consideration.

3.3. From England, Scotland, and Wales – Another Victim Compensation Fund

This scheme from the Criminal Injuries Compensation Authority (CICA) (2008) of the United Kingdom has a more extensive list of compensated injuries in the "Tariff of Injuries" than that of Northern Ireland and slightly lower compensation levels for many of the same injuries. Awards under the CICA vary by level and severity of injury. For example, the award for a temporary injury could be as low as £1,000, with total deafness valued at £44,000. In the case of England, the maximum award is £250,000 for extremely serious brain damage.

For death or longer-term disability, additional claims can be made. The calculations are essentially identical to the Northern Ireland scheme. The issue of under-compensation with this British system based on the Ogden tables and other prescribed calculations has been discussed by Lewis, McNabb, Robinson, & Wass (2003). The compensation scheme began in 1964, and since then the Authority has paid out nearly £4 billion to more than one million claimants.

4. ANOTHER VARIATION ON A SCHEDULE FOR GENERAL DAMAGES FROM THE UNITED STATES: WORKER'S COMPENSATION LAWS

The U.S. workers' compensation laws and regulations provide many examples of schedules of damages. The general layout in a state's schedule of damages consists of two sets of specification: (1) to specify a set of rules for determining the weekly compensation amount for the injured person, where the rules generally show how to calculate a wage replacement number for the specific case based on recent past earnings and a minimum and maximum weekly payment and (2) to specify a schedule of damages expressed as weeks of compensation based on the type and severity of injury. These damages can be paid as a lump sum or received as a weekly amount.

Two examples of schedules of damages are shown in Table 2. The federal government's workers compensation schedule of weeks of award is similar to, but higher than, the Iowa schedule.[1]

The maximum weekly compensation rates vary surprisingly in the United States; an almost sixfold range existed in weekly state awards in 2007–2008.

Table 2. Two Examples of U.S. Workers Compensation Schedules.

Injury		Federal Workers Comp. Award in Weeks	Iowa Workers Comp. Award in Weeks
Both arms, or both hands, or both legs, or both eyes, or combs			500
Arm lost		312	250
Leg lost		288	220
Hand lost		244	190
Thumb lost		75	60
First finger lost		46	35
Second finger lost		30	30
Third finger lost		25	25
Fourth finger lost		15	20
Foot lost		205	150
Great toe lost		38	40
Toe other than great toe		16	15
Loss of hearing	Both ears	200	175
	One ear	52	50
Eye lost		160	140
Permanent disfigurement of face or head impairing future earnings			150
Value per week of work?		Based on individual's monthly pay times 66 2/3% rate adjusted to weekly basis	Based on 80% of employee's average spendable weekly earnings, subject to a cap of 184% of statewide average weekly wage.

5. USING A POINT SYSTEM TO CALCULATE DAMAGES: BELGIUM

Belgium has established a set of tables and procedures that create a reasonable degree of consistency in judicial decisions about compensation with a particular focus on standardizing general damages. These tables are comparable to schedules from other countries in their intended use. They are also prepared under the supervision of associations of judges and are applied to all types of accidents. The title of the tables is the "National Indicative Table." A chapter by de Kezel (2003) and the actual wording of the Belgium law, Le Droit Belge en Matiere d'Indemnisation des Accidents de la Circulation, provide the following example of compensation calculations and compensation schedules.

The example assumes that a 45-year-old male is injured. The medical report presents the opinion of a permanent disability rating of 60%. The earnings level is 24,700 euros per year. The expected working life is to age 65, meaning an earnings loss for the next 20 years.

The loss of earnings, the pecuniary loss or special damages loss, is projected in this formulation:

$$€24,700 \times 0.6 \times 14.34200 = 212,548.44 \text{ euros}$$

The value of 14.34200 is the annuity factor or coefficient for the 45-year-old male evaluated with a 3% interest or capitalization rate. This factor comes from a specified table from Belgium that is revised periodically.[2]

The non-pecuniary loss is based on a schedule of compensation per degree of disability or "permanent invalidity" which is shown in Table 3. The degree of disability is 60% and the age is 45; the projection formulation is

$$60 \times €750 = 45,000 \text{ euros}$$

The Belgian tables provide similar sets of formulas and guidelines for awards of lost support and bereavement to survivors in a death action. Belgium also has a schedule for damages for disfigurement, labeled as "aesthetic damage." This is a seven-point scale ranging from "minimal" to "catastrophic." In Belgium, the concept of subrogation rights against a tortfeasor is applicable, and there can be deductions from the claimant's compensation for items like social security benefits and private insurance benefits. But life insurance benefits purchased personally would not be deducted. There can be taxation for the receipt of replacement income, but not taxation on non-pecuniary damages.

Table 3. Compensation for Disability or Invalidity (in Euros (€) per 1% Degree of "Permanent Invalidity").

Age and Age Range	2001 Rules Compensation
15 and under	1,000 euros per 1%
25 years	937.5
30–35 years	875.0
40 years	812.5
45 years	750.0
50 years	687.5
55 years	625.0
60 years	562.5
65 years	437.5
70 years	375.0
75 years	312.5
80 years	250.0
85 years	187.5
Over 85 years	125.0

6. A SECOND EXAMPLE OF USING A POINT SYSTEM: FROM THE UNITED STATES – THE VIOXX VCF

Vioxx is a pain medication that was approved for relief of symptoms of osteoarthritis and management of acute pain in May 1999. It could be used to replace aspirin, ibuprofen, or naproxen as the medication of choice in some cases. However, Vioxx appeared to substantially increase the probability of cardiovascular events, such as heart attack and stroke, after 18 months of use compared to those (persons) taking a placebo or some other pain-reducing medication such as naproxen. Vioxx was withdrawn from markets worldwide in September 2004.

Lawsuits against Merck, the manufacturer of Vioxx, were filed because of heart attacks and sudden deaths, and the first jury verdict was for $253.4 million for the plaintiff. A national Vioxx litigation plaintiffs' steering committee was formed, and negotiations with Merck resulted in a November 2007 settlement agreement to create a (United States) nationwide settlement program to resolve the claims.[3] As of August 2008, almost 50,000 claims have been registered in the United States. The compensation scheme has each claimant provide health information that is then converted into a single numerical score. The scores of all registered and eligible claimants are then calculated, and the fund's amount of $4.85 billion is allocated based on the individual numerical scores.

This is a one-time distribution scheme which compensates for both general and special damages claims for those claimants who have agreed to join the settlement arrangement.[4] Every claimant had the option of joining the Vioxx settlement or proceeding to pursue a lawsuit independent of this settlement process – similar to the 9/11 VCF option. The $4.85 billion is divided into two pools of funds: $4.0 billion for the heart attack claimants and $850 million for ischemic stroke claimants. Each pool has a different scoring scheme for determining the final point score.

The U.S. federal government has a claim, or "lien," on compensation if the claimant also received financial help from the U.S. federal and state programs of Medicare and Medicaid for health services caused by Vioxx.[5] These liens will reduce compensation for the individual claimant.

The Vioxx Point System for awarding damages for heart attack victims is summarized in Table 4. There is a slightly different set of factors and percentage values for stroke victims.

This schedule of damages scheme, based on a detailed point system, at first appears to cover both general and special damages. There is a specific "waiver of claim for lost wages" form which is part of the application package. But a careful reading of the documentation reveals that there is a way to claim for special damages through the "extraordinary injury payments" clause.

7. A SIMPLER GENERAL DAMAGES SCHEDULE: FROM SPAIN – AN OVERALL COMPENSATION SYSTEM

Spain has several examples of schedules of general damages. These schedules identify a "basic compensation" amount for a degree of disability caused by an accident or an incident. In addition to this basic compensation, the victim can also make a claim for specific items like pecuniary loss related to a temporary or permanent loss of earnings, or for something labeled as a "cosmetic injury," in addition to the general damages amounts related to the severity of the disability.

One set of damages compensation numbers is based on a law relating to "Circulación de Vehículos de Motor." This is part of a compensation system labeled as the "ordinary system." A second system has been labeled the

Table 4. The Vioxx Point System.

Three factors affecting the "basis points" amount

1. Age at time of serious medical problem (30 or less to greater than 79 in 5 year intervals)
2. Duration/quantity of the use of Vioxx (42 pills or less to at least 639 pills in 6 levels of use)
3. Injury level (catheterization minimum; days of hospitalization, death maximum; 6 levels of injury)

Examples of "basis points" for heart attack (myocardial infarction, sudden cardiac death)

A. Age less than 30, Vioxx use for more than 30 months, death gets 1,000.0 points *Highest*
B. Age greater than 79, Vioxx use for more than 30 months, death gets 250.0 points
C. Age 35–39, Vioxx use for 6–18 months, hospitalized 10–14 days gets 357.29 points
D. Age 55–59, Vioxx use for 6–18 months, hospitalized 4–9 days gets 193.96 points
E. Age greater than 79, Vioxx use for less than 60 days, with ejection fraction greater than 50% and catheterization gets 39.20 points *Lowest*

Adjustment factors – variables that create an adjustment in point total[a]

a. Label adjustment: −20% to +15% depending upon dates Vioxx used or health event occurred
b. Consistency adjustment: based on regularity/frequency of Vioxx use in 12 months preceding health event (heart attack). Can vary from +20% for consistent use to −30% for lower use

Risk factor adjustments applied to "subtotal points" value – some examples

Smoking: regular smoker −30%; extreme smoking −50%
Cholesterol: controlled −20%; uncontrolled −30%
Hypertension: controlled −20%; uncontrolled −30%
Diabetes: controlled −20%; uncontrolled −30%
Obesity: body mass index (BMI) $\geqslant$30 kg/m = −17.5%; BMI$\geqslant$50 kg/m = −60%
Alcohol abuse: −45%
Prior MI or coronary artery bypass graft: −55%

[a]The label adjustment and consistency of use adjustment percentages are added together and the basis points are multiplied by [100% – sum of label and consistency adjustments] to get the "subtotal points."

"special system" and is applied when there are terrorist offenses. The compensation levels in both systems are shown in Table 5, which is derived from the Spanish Ministry of Justice, 2005, Council Directive document responding to the European Commission in the same year. The compensation for a victim of the March 11, 2004, train bombings in Madrid was higher than shown in Table 5. One published article stated that the "standard award" to parents for the loss of a child was about €400,000. Another article listed the award for the death of a breadwinner as £95,400, which does match the special system value of €138,233. But the article also identified the "maximum possible award" as £310,600, or about €446,906.

Table 5. Two Compensation Systems with Two Schedules of Damages.

Classification of Injury in Two Languages ...	Value for Aid by Classification		Special System – 2005 Values (€)	Ratio: Special to Ordinary (%)
	Ordinary System – 2005 values (€)			
"Spanish words" *English translation*		*Months equivalent*		
"Fallecimiento" *Death*	61,074	*130*	138,233	*226.3*
"Gran Invalidez" *Outstanding disability or great invalidity (two translations)*	65,772	*140*	390,658	*594.0*
"Incapacidad permanente absoluta" *Absolute permanent disability*	46,980	*100*	96,162	*204.7*
"Incapacidad permanente total" *Total permanent disability*	32,886	*70*	48,081	*146.2*
"Incapacidad permanente parcial" *Partial permanent disability*	23,490	*50*	36,061	*153.5*
"Lesiones permanentes no invalidantes" *Permanent non-disabling injuries*	See social security table		Same as ordinary system Limit is partial disability amount	
Other compensation items and comments	*Extra item to victim's children 20 monthly payments of €469.80 × no. of children*		*Extra for kidnapping victims: €12,020.24 for the act of kidnapping plus €180.30 per day, limit of €36,060.72*	
	Extra item: Compensation may be increased up to 30% in some cases		*Specific aid for medical treatment, prostheses or surgical operations if coverage not available from other sources*	
	Extra item: Psychological assistance with medical prescription up to €3,005.06 per person			
	With death: Compensation limited to the economically dependent such as children and co-habiting spouse/partner			

Note: The monthly payments amount is based on a "public income indicator with multiple effects" measure.

The average award in case of death was £154,000, which was about €221,582 when the article was published.[6]

8. GENERAL DAMAGES AND SPECIAL DAMAGES FOR A ONE-TIME PROGRAM: FROM THE UNITED STATES – THE 9/11 VCF

This scheme can be labeled as simple only in the case of a deceased victim who had no potential future earnings prospects. For such deceased persons, there was an award of $250,000, plus $100,000 for the spouse and for each dependent for general damages. However, for physical injury victims, the general damages awards ranged from just $500 to $6 million based on "the nature, severity, and duration of the injury and the individual circumstances of the claimant."[7]

For a working victim with earnings, there is a set of calculations for estimating loss of future earnings. The appealing aspect of this scheme is that it sets specifications for:

- assumptions about worklife,
- annual increases in earnings at each age,
- personal consumption for a deceased person,
- income tax rates for an adjustment of the award to a net-of-taxes amount,
- discount rates decreasing by age,
- a default pension rate as a percentage of earnings (if the pension was not known),
- a default medical insurance value assumed to be paid by the employer as a benefit, and
- a maximum earnings amount to include in the projection.[8]

The assumptions were gender neutral (except the worklife table was for males but was also used for females). Finally, the calculations could be done by an independent expert, or a victim could request that the VCF staff do the calculations.

The awards from the 9/11 VCF were relatively large compared to other award amounts discussed in this chapter. Table 6 shows award data for deceased and injured males and is from Feinberg (2005). Note that the highest awards were for the age 31–40 group.

As would be expected with these VCF calculations, the greater the victim's earned income the greater the average award. For deceased males

Table 6. Awards for Deceased and Injured Males.

Age Range	Claims for Deceased Males by Age		Claims for Physical Injury-Males	
	Number of claims	Average award ($)	Number of claims	Average award ($)
25 and under	96	1,743,255	26	141,640
26–30	253	2,261,190	117	496,378
31–40	842	2,787,425	776	499,101
41–50	630	2,252,152	988	378,949
51–60	299	1,428,736	307	286,486
61–70	57	1,020,348	43	153,017
Over 70	11	595,951	5	33,531
Total claims	2,188	2,283,916	2,262	405,907

earning less than $25,000, the average award was $788,022, while for the deceased males earning between $500,000 and $999,000 the average award was $4,749,654.

9. A SPECIAL TYPE OF GENERAL DAMAGES AWARD: FROM ITALY – A SCHEDULE OF DAMAGES FOR FAMILY MEMBERS OF A DECEASED VICTIM

One last example of a schedule of damages will be briefly discussed. Italy allows compensation for "danno morale da lutto," meaning "moral and physical suffering, pain, grief and sorrow, and mental and emotional distress caused by the death of the primary victim."[9] The family members eligible for compensation include parents, children, brothers and sisters, and other relatives living with the deceased. There is a difference in the schedule of compensation if the person was living with the victim. The range of compensation for a surviving spouse in Florence, for example, ranges from €77,500 to €196,300. Interestingly, instant death means that non-pecuniary losses cannot (generally) be claimed by heirs.

10. DISCUSSION AND SUMMARY

The schedules of damages discussed above provide examples of both general and special damages. The general damages examples show a considerable range in complexity. The three examples from the British and Irish courts and victim compensation agencies use multiple categories for injuries, have subcategories within these categories, and have scaling of damages based on severity factors. The British court system schedule provides a suggested range for damages payments; the two victim compensation schedules have 25 and 29 levels of fixed compensation, respectively.

The worker's compensation examples from the United States show a multiple-category description of injuries where compensation is specified in terms of weeks of payments and where the weekly payment amount is based on the injured person's earnings level. The U.S. worker's compensation system has this general damages component defined for the particular state or employer, but there is also a special damages component which pays for ongoing earnings loss and ongoing medical expenses related to the injury.

There are two examples of a "point" system being used to establish general damages. Belgium uses a determination of the percentage of "permanent invalidity" and multiplies this percentage by a compensation amount which is age dependent. In Belgium, the injured party can also receive compensation for special damages. The Vioxx settlement example in the United States determines a point total for each applicant and then multiplies this total by a monetary value based on the sum of all the applicant points. In this Vioxx example, the compensation amount also covers the special damages; there is no separate compensation for most cases that can be claimed from Merck.

The two examples from Spain have a six-level schedule for general damages. They are based on the injury range from "permanent nondisabling injuries" to "permanent disability."

Two particular types of general damages issues arise in U.S. court cases where it may be useful to consider the European examples of general damages. In the examples described above, there are several schedules of general damages applicable to the extended family of relatives of deceased injured persons where the relationship of the relative to the deceased determines the damages value. The examples are from Belgium and Italy. In contrast, in the United States 9/11 VCF situation, the family of a deceased person with no earnings loss claim was compensated with $250,000 plus $100,000 for the spouse and each dependent. It should also be noted that there are multilevel schedules of general damages compensation for facial scarring or other disfigurement in countries like the United Kingdom and Belgium.

While most of the schedules of damages discussed in this chapter focus on general damages, several also address special damages. The Northern Ireland compensation calculation for lost earnings and the Ogden tables both address special damages by specifying methodologies. The earnings loss compensation calculations, as done in Belgium, use periodically updated actuarial and discounting factors relating to annuities. Other European countries use the annuity analogy for discounting earnings loss.

The U.S. procedures for calculating special damages vary by state and jurisdiction. The 9/11 VCF scheme set up a unique mechanism as to how the earnings loss was to be projected; this scheme was similar to the procedures and assumptions used in many states but had its own unique assumptions.

It should be noted that in European countries, there are often national systems of health services and income support which an accident victim can draw upon. This combination of health and income services reduces the potential financial burden imposed on an accident victim by injury. But the government provider or other providers often have the right to claim part of the eventual compensation for injury to offset their financial aid. Northern Ireland does subrogate loss awards for such support. The U.S. Vioxx example and the 9/11 VCF scheme also allow some reductions in the award amount if the victim or family had received collateral source payments and other types of financial support.

While this review of schedules of damages only covers selected examples from the United States and Europe, the review does suggest that such schedules provide broad ranges of compensation for plaintiffs in personal injury and death claims. As an alternative to individual claims, these broad-based attempts to compensate plaintiffs have the advantages of uniformity and simplicity and may speed up the resolution of the victim's claims as well as reduce legal costs. However, the question remains as to their adequacy in compensating the plaintiffs. The considerable variability of awards from plan to plan suggests that, although each plan may attempt to achieve internal consistency in awards based on the level and severity of injury, there is little consistency across plans.

NOTES

1. The federal worker's compensation schedule is specified in the Title 5 of the U.S. Government Code, section 8107(c). There are multiple references on the Internet. A specific U.S. reference with the detailed code is found at www.findus law.com while more details can be found on the U.S. Department of Labor website www.dol.gov/esa. This Department of Labor website also has information and statistics about all the states including tables showing the award amounts for injuries by state.

The Iowa state regulations are available on the Internet; and a useful summary is found at the Iowa Workforce Development Division of Workers' (2008)

Compensation website www.iowaworkforce.org/wc which has annual updates of the rules.

2. The actuarial factor comes from Levie (2003).

3. The law firm of Brown Greer is the administrator for this settlement. It has a website at www.browngreer.com/vioxxsettlement which has more information and the forms for application. This may not be a permanent website, however. It could disappear after the funds are disbursed, as did much of the 9/11 VCF materials.

4. There is a provision in the settlement agreement for "extraordinary injury payments" which allows extra compensation for "an injury that is not adequately reflected within the point grid" or where the claimant "has specified ... economic damages of at least $250,000" which can include "past or future out-of-pocket medical expenses" and "past lost wages" caused by a heart attack or stroke which have not been reimbursed and are not eligible for reimbursement. There is a total limit of $300 million for these extraordinary payments.

5. Medicare is a U.S. federal government health insurance program for the elderly or qualifying disabled persons. Medicaid is another U.S. government health insurance program with both federal and state funding and is administered by the individual states. The Medicaid coverage is focused on low-income families and also disabled persons with higher medical costs.

6. The first article was in the *Sunday Telegraph* of February 19, 2007, authored by Graham Keeley and titled "Terror Suspect Claimed Compensation Payout for Daughter's Bomb Death." The second article did a basic comparison of VCF systems and is titled "Add Insult to Injury," by Rob Blackhurst, *Financial Times*, July 1–2, 2006.

7. This excerpted text and information about physical injury victims was found on page 43 of Feinberg (2004, Vol. I). This volume is available on the Internet at www.usdoj.gov/final_report.pdf

8. The specific instructions for projecting an earnings loss are found in Exhibit E of Feinberg (2004, Vol. II). It was found at www.usdoj.gov/final_report_vols.pdf

9. See Bona (2005).

REFERENCES

Bona, M. (2005). Fatal accidents and secondary victims – compensation in Italy. In: M. Bona, P. Mead & S. Lindenbergh (Eds), *Fatal accidents & secondary victims* (pp. 219–263). St. Albans: XPL Press.

Compensation Agency for Northern Ireland. (2002). *The Northern Ireland criminal injuries compensation scheme 2002*. This publication can be found on the Internet. There are a series of additional publications on the Internet from this agency including: "*A guide to the Northern Ireland criminal injuries compensation scheme 2002*"; "*A guide to applicants for compensation in fatal cases*"; and "*A guide to applicants for loss of earnings and special expenses*".

Criminal Injuries Compensation Authority. (2008). *The criminal injuries compensation scheme 2008 and a guide to the criminal injuries compensation scheme 2008*. These two publications recently appeared on the Internet.

de Kezel, E. (2003). Personal injury compensation in Belgium. In: M. Bona & P. Mead (Eds), *Personal injury compensation in Europe* (pp. 39–72). Deventer: Kluwer.

Feinberg, K. (2004). *Final report of the special master for the September 11th victim compensation fund of 2001* (Vols. I and II).

Feinberg, K. R. (2005). *What is life worth?* New York: Public affairs.

Iowa Workforce Development Division of Workers' Compensation website, Questions and Answers about Workers' Compensation Law for Injured Workers, 2008. Avialable at: www.iowaworkforce.org/wc (Also see Iowa Workers' Compensation Manual available at the same website).

Le Droit Belge en Matiere d'lndemnisation des Accidents de la Circulation. Available at: www.fcga-gmwf.be/documents (An English language translation is available using Google).

Levie, G. (2003). *Life tables: Sterftetafels – 1998–2000*. Louvain-La-Neuve, Belgium: Emile Bruylant.

Lewis, R., McNabb, R., Robinson, H., & Wass, V. (2003). Loss of earnings following personal injury: Do the courts adequately compensate injured parties?. *The Economic Journal, 113*(November), F568–F584.

Spanish Ministry of Justice. (2005). *Council directive 2004/80/EC of April 29, 2004 relating to compensation of crime victims*. Madrid. Found on the Internet using Google search term "Council directive 2004/80/ec spain".

The Judicial Studies Board. (2006). *Guidelines for the assessment of general damages in personal injury cases* (8th ed.). Oxford University Press.

INTERNATIONAL DATA AND THE FORENSIC ECONOMIST: A GUIDE TO SOURCES AND USES

Michael J. Piette and David R. Williams

1. INTRODUCTION

Forensic economists are often asked to calculate economic damages in cases that are tried in the United States but involve the death or injury of a citizen or resident of a foreign country. Commonly called *international cases*, they can range from a single tourist who is killed or injured while visiting the United States to mass torts such as plane crashes or product liability claims. The single plaintiff cases are typically relegated to state courts, whereas the Federal District Courts are often deemed to have jurisdiction over the determination of liability and subsequent economic damages in mass torts. In these and other types of international cases, macroeconomic data compiled by various governmental or private sources within the United States are of very limited use to the forensic economist preparing economic loss estimates. The decedent or injured party's economic, demographic, and social environment will in all likelihood differ significantly from individuals living in the United States. Rather, they are impacted by the macroeconomic conditions of their country of domicile or residence.

As in the United States, economic loss estimates in international cases can only be accomplished when relevant data are available. It is locating and

Personal Injury and Wrongful Death Damages Calculations: Transatlantic Dialogue
Contemporary Studies in Economic and Financial Analysis, Volume 91, 309–320

ISSN: 1569-3759/doi:10.1108/S1569-3759(2009)0000091016

appropriately applying the underlying data to the case at hand that presents the greatest challenge to the forensic economist when working in the context of an international case. The purpose of this chapter is to provide an overview of the data sources that are available to assist the forensic economist in preparing reasonable economic loss estimates in international cases.

The chapter is organized as follows. Section 2 provides details regarding the sources of various types of data that are useful to the forensic economist in determining economic losses, along with an indication of some of the limitations of the data. Section 3 presents special issues relevant to international cases. Summary and concluding comments are offered in the last section of the chapter.

2. DATA SOURCES IN INTERNATIONAL CASES

This section presents some of the most useful data sources available to the forensic economist. They have been divided into three categories: (1) "official" or primary data, (2) nonprimary or secondary/tertiary data, and (3) private/proprietary data sources. The forensic economist working on an international case may need to draw upon a wide array of these categories of data sources simultaneously. These sources will often include primary data compiled and maintained by national governments (most often a central bank and/or an economic/statistical agency) and from nonprimary data reported by quasigovernmental agencies of various types such as the International Monetary Fund (IMF), the United Nations (UN), and the World Bank. Additionally, data are sometimes obtainable from private/ proprietary sources, including large accounting firms or from a variety of specialized private consulting companies. In each case, however, data quality and compatibility can be a concern, particularly in the context of Federal District Court and possible *Daubert* challenges.

2.1. Official or Primary Data Sources

Official or primary data are typically available from government agencies. As such, these data are part of large, scientifically structured surveys and databases prepared and administrated by the governmental agency and are based on internationally accepted methodologies. The advantage of primary data sources is that they address in detail a specific research question, are relatively current, and are from a known entity. These are important considerations if the economist's analyses are challenged.

2.1.1. Central Banks[1]

A primary source of macroeconomic data on a foreign country is that country's central bank. In many instances, only a limited amount of data on a foreign country will be available from such traditional data sources such as the IMF, the UN, and/or the World Bank. In these instances, that country's central bank may be the only source. Even the most underdeveloped or emerging market country will have a central bank where macroeconomic statistics are kept. In fact, the country's central bank is usually the source for some of the macroeconomic data that are provided to the IMF, the UN, or the World Bank, which in turn reports it as a secondary data source.

2.1.2. Governmental Statistical Agencies and Institutions[2]

Many countries have government statistical agencies and institutions that publish a substantial quantity of detailed historical macroeconomic data. These entities are typically the primary data sources relied upon by the IMF, the UN, and/or the World Bank. Making contact with economists in these types of agencies and institutions will often yield much of the basic information needed by a forensic economist with an international case.

2.2. Nonprimary Data Sources: Secondary and Tertiary Data

Nonprimary data include both secondary and tertiary data sources. These are data that are already in existence from the primary sources. They are simply reprinted or reported in a different format and, most often, in conjunction with other types of data.

2.2.1. International Monetary Fund (IMF)[3]

Although it is not a primary data source, the IMF publication *International Financial Statistics* (IFS) is an excellent starting point for an economist seeking a large amount of macroeconomic time series data on a foreign country reported in one place. The macroeconomic data contained in the IFS (from Albania to Zimbabwe) include the following: exchange rates (end of period and period averages), interest rates (including treasury bill and government bond yields, short and long term), consumer prices, wages (average monthly earnings), unemployment rates, labor force, employment, unemployment, total population, GDP and GDP deflator. It should be noted that, although data are generally available for most developed countries, there are likely to be some gaps in the data available for developing countries. When the data are available, however, one of the decisive advantages to the IMF data is that they are collected, tabulated, and presented in a standardized manner, thus allowing for year-to-year and country-to-country comparisons. Equally important, the data collected and reported by the IMF are all from primary data sources.

The two main IFS publications are (1) the *Annual Yearbook*, which contains calendar year time series data going back approximately ten to twelve years, and (2) the *Monthly Update*, which has monthly data going back approximately nine months, quarterly data for the past two years, and annual data going back approximately seven years. A third IFS publication, *Country Notes*, should also be consulted. This publication discusses each of the footnotes to the economic variables listed in the IFS on a country-by-country basis. It is also possible to speak to specific country economists at the IMF by calling the IMF at (202) 623-7000 and asking to be transferred to an economist dealing with a specific country.

2.2.2. World Bank[4]

The World Bank publishes a useful set of data called the *World Tables*. These data are published annually in a time series format starting approximately 20 years in the past. Included in the macroeconomic data that would be of interest to the forensic economist working on an international case are GNP per capita, GDP deflator, CPI, real earnings per employee, and life expectancy from birth. Like the IMF data, the information collected and reported by the World Bank are also from primary data sources. For some data, such as GDP figures expressed in U.S. dollars, the Bank has developed a methodology to convert the local currency figures into U.S. dollars based on purchasing-power-parity-adjusted exchange rates, which corrects for currency misalignments.

2.2.3. United Nations Data Sources

The question of life expectancy often arises in an international case in situations involving a personal injury and the need for a life care plan and/or valuing a stream of lost household services. In this context, the life expectancy of the plaintiff is a key consideration. In any of these situations, a source of mortality data, by age and gender is required. Perhaps the best source of this type of data is the United Nation's (UN) World Health Organization (WHO) and the WHO Statistical Information System (WHOSIS).[5] At the present time, the WHO maintains life expectancy data for 192 counties (from Afghanistan to Zimbabwe). The life expectancy data can be obtained for five-year intervals for historical years (1950–1995), recent years (2000–2005), as well as projections (2005–2010 and beyond). The WHO data are presented from birth and in five-year age bands (e.g., age 10–15, age 15–20). While not perfect, the data will allow the economist to estimate life expectancy from a given age or to calculate the probability of living from one year to the next.[6]

The UN also publishes an annual data set entitled the *Statistical Yearbook*. These data are provided in a time series format over the past 10 years and include exchange rates, GDP per capita, short-term treasury bills, unemployment rates, manufacturing wage rates, and the CPI. It should be noted, however, that many data series are sourced as the IMF or the International Labour Organization (discussed below), making the UN *Statistical Yearbook* a tertiary data source. Also, due to data revisions by the primary sources, nonprimary publications may show different figures for some of the data.

There are five regional economic commissions operating under the umbrella of the UN. Perhaps the best known of these commissions is the Economic Commission for Latin America and the Caribbean (ECLAC). ECLAC publishes annually three main sources of macroeconomic data for this region, namely: (1) *Statistical Yearbook for Latin America and the Caribbean,* (2) *Preliminary Overview of the Economies of Latin America and the Caribbean,* and (3) *Economic Survey of Latin America and the Caribbean.* The first publication, *Statistical Yearbook for Latin America and the Caribbean,* has for each country life expectancy from birth (male and female) historically and forecasts for the 2005–2010 and 2010–2015 time periods, as well as labor force participation rates (male and female) historically and projections for 2010 and 2015. It also reports age brackets relative to labor market participation, unemployment rates by gender and by years of schooling, as well as time series data on real per capita GDP, real GDP growth rates, and consumer price inflation rates. The second publication, *Preliminary Overview of the Economies of Latin America and the Caribbean,* gives a country-by-country detailed economic and political snapshot and economic outlook. The third publication, *Economic Survey of Latin America and the Caribbean,* is similar to the second in that it also has country-by-country economic analysis and macroeconomic statistics. An added feature of this publication is that there is a CD-ROM with very detailed macroeconomic data available.[7]

The UN also supports the Economic Commission for Africa (ECA). This commission prepares an annual publication entitled *Economic Report on*

Africa that contains economic data for each country and includes monthly wages by sector and unemployment rates by gender and race. Individual country reports are also available at the ECA website.[8]

UN data on Europe are available from the Economic Commission for Europe (ECE). Macroeconomic, gender, and social data are available on ECE's website through an online statistical database.[9]

A good source of UN data on the Pacific Rim is the Economic and Social Commission for Asia and the Pacific (ESCAP). There are various publications and online data available from ESCAP for member countries in this region.[10]

Lastly, the UN provides data for Western Asia via the Economic and Social Commission for Western Asia (ESCWA). This commission provides an annual publication entitled *Statistical Abstract of the ESCWA Region*. It is available for purchase and contains a variety of macroeconomic data for countries in this region. Other ESCWA publications include *Vital Statistics in the UNESCWA Region*, *Compendium of Social Statistics and Indicators*, and *Summary: Survey of Economic and Social Developments in the ESCWA Region*. These sources provide inflation and real GDP growth data, history and forecast, by country in the region.[11]

2.2.4. International Labour Organization (ILO)[12]

The ILO compiles an annual publication called the *Yearbook of Labour Statistics*. The *Yearbook* contains detailed time series data on wages by occupation and/or industry, including manufacturing, by ISIC (International Standard Industrial Classification) code and CPI data (overall and for food, utilities, clothing, and rent) for approximately 10 years. The ILO also publishes the *Bulletin of Labour Statistics*, which contains similar data and articles in the international labor arena.

2.2.5. Central Intelligence Agency (CIA)[13]

The CIA publishes online *The World Factbook* that has a very general overview of a country's economic, social, and political history. Although this source is lacking in detailed time series data, it is nevertheless useful for a general overview and an economic snapshot of a country, particularly political information. *The Factbook* contains data on life expectancy from birth (male and female), inflation, GDP, real GDP growth rate, GDP per capita, unemployment rate, and exchange rate information on the country in question.

2.2.6. European Commission (EC)[14]

The EC publishes annually the *Eurostat Yearbook* and *The Statistical Guide to Europe*. The EC website also has an abundance of macroeconomic data available for downloading at no charge after a short registration process is completed.

2.2.7. The Statistical Abstract of the World

This publication is only available in hardcopy and is useful for gathering general background data on a specific country, without providing detailed time series data. It is similar in use to the forensic economist as the CIA website.

2.3. Private/Proprietary Data Sources

Several of the largest accounting and law firms have offices in many countries throughout the world and may publish useful information on specific countries. For example, BDO Seidman, LLP publishes a series of booklets entitled *Doing Business in…* . Although these publications may be somewhat lacking in time series macroeconomic data, they are nevertheless one of the most useful sources for understanding the basic accounting practices, individual and corporate tax structures, and national/private retirement information and pension structures in a particular country. These types of booklets are sometimes out of date. In that case, by contacting a United States office of one of the firms, the forensic economist may be able to reach a member of the accounting firm specializing in the relevant country.

In addition to accounting firms, private consulting firms or other private consulting sources in foreign countries sometimes perform services that meet the needs of a forensic economist in an international case. First, the consulting firm may engage in "data gathering" activities upon request and for a fee, fulfilling much of the data needs discussed in this chapter. Second, the consulting firm may already be in the "data collection" business, generating surveys or producing studies of various types for either the private or the public sector in that country. Relying on private consulting sources for international data can be a risky proposition, however, sometimes leading to a challenge under *Daubert* in federal cases. In our experience, the use of private consulting firms or private consulting sources in international cases should be approached very cautiously on a case-by-case basis.

Business publications can also be a source of data in international cases. For example, *The Economist*, a well known weekly world economic and political magazine, has a substantial statistical section in the back of each issue. Included in the statistical data are current and past year exchange rates, current interest rates on government 3-month and 10-year bonds, current GDP and a one-year projection, and CPI current and one year ago.[15]

3. SPECIAL ISSUES AND RELATED DATA NEEDS

A potentially difficult aspect of international cases occurs when the allegations involve a wrongful death. In most jurisdictions, there is a statutory requirement that the expected income of the decedent must be reduced by the decedent's "personal consumption." In this situation, one of the most significant data challenges facing a forensic economist is determining personal consumption, either as an absolute dollar amount or as a percentage of anticipated income. In the United States, a large number of economists rely on the Ruble, Patton, and Nelson studies (based on the Consumer Expenditure Survey (CES)) that have been published and updated frequently in the *Journal of Forensic Economics*. Other economists utilize the CES directly as the source of data relevant to the determination of personal consumption. Rarely have comparable studies been completed for foreign countries. In an ideal world, the best possible scenario would be to have CES-type micro data available for the foreign country, perform the regression analysis, and replicate the Ruble, Patton, and Nelson tables. In the authors' experiences, these types of data are rarely available. In the very few cases where the data are available, it is a cumbersome and time-consuming project to complete accurately.

A first step to obtaining the data necessary to undertake a personal consumption adjustment in a wrongful death is to determine which governmental entity produces the relevant data. It is not uncommon to find that this same government entity may prepare something similar to the CES as found in the United States. An issue, however, is whether the governmental entity is willing to release the underlying information. If available, these data may allow the economist to construct estimates of the personal consumption adjustment. This approach is discussed in detail below using Venezuela as an example.

Often a forensic economist faced with the personal consumption deduction in a foreign case will have to make do with a "second best solution," but still a solution that will yield reasonable estimates of personal consumption of a decedent. For example, Table A1 illustrates some of the data on consumption in Venezuela available from the country's Central Bank. The table is useful because it indicates consumption across four quartiles of family income. Although the data are not prepared at the same level of detailed expenditure categories as the United States CES in terms of income and/or family size, the Venezuelan data nevertheless provides sufficient detail to prepare reasonable personal consumption estimates. Using Table A1, personal consumption deductions in Venezuela can be computed.[16]

Another issue, but nowhere near as problematic as the personal consumption issue, pertains to countries where life expectancy from a given age is not available; instead, only life expectancy from birth is obtainable. This latter situation is common in lesser developed countries, where macroeconomic data are scarce in general. In this situation it is possible to arrive at a reasonable approximation of a life expectancy from a given age in that country by comparing the life expectancy at birth between that country and the United States. The forensic economist can use the percentage difference at birth between that country and the United States and then use the United States life expectancy tables for that given age and apply the percentage difference at birth to that given age, as appropriate.

4. SUMMARY AND CONCLUSIONS

This paper provides a summary of the data sources that are available to forensic economists when the task requires estimation of economic losses in an *international case* involving the injury or death of a foreign national. Data collection and availability, as well as language barriers and institutional and cultural differences, can make the calculation of economic losses in international cases a difficult task. It would be foolhardy, however, for the economist to simply rely on United States data when analyzing an international case based solely on the perceived difficulty of obtaining the requisite macroeconomic data from the plaintiffs' country of domicile. Rather, it is the obligation of the forensic economist to be as familiar as possible with the available data sources and to utilize them with appropriate care. It is our hope that the information contained in this chapter will assist the economist who is willing to undertake international case analyses.

NOTES

1. Examples of central bank websites include:

Brazil www.bcb.gov.br

Guyana www.bankofguyana.org.gy

United Arab Emirates www.uaecb.gov.ae

A listing of central bank websites from around the world (from Albania to Zimbabwe) can be found at www.bis.org/cbanks.htm

2. Examples of government statistical agency websites include:

United Kingdom www.statistics.gov.uk

Guyana www.statisticsguyana.gov.gy

St. Lucia www.stats.gov.lc

A listing of government statistical agency websites from around the world (from Afghanistan to Zambia) can be found at www.bls.gov/bls/other.htm

3. The IMF website is www.imf.org. The three IMF publications can be obtained through the website, by contacting publications@imf.org, or by calling the IMF Publication Service at (202) 623–7430. Available by subscription are either a hardcopy, a CD-ROM, or, alternatively, online access to the IFS database. All of these sources contain time series data going back to 1948. Discounts for university faculty and students are available for subscribers by any of the three methods. Single copies of the relevant publications are also available without subscribing.

4. The World Bank website is at www.worldbank.org

5. The United Nations and the World Health Organization websites are at www3.who.int and www.un.org, respectively.

6. Another possible source of life expectancy is from various groups of actuaries. A good starting point for basic information and links is the Society of Actuaries (www.soa.org) in the United States. More importantly, most developed countries have at least one group of actuaries who are actively involved in preparing life expectancy estimates. For example, in the United Kingdom the Institute of Actuaries can be located online at www.actuaries.org.uk. Other organizations of actuaries in other countries can be located at similar websites.

7. On the ECLAC website www.eclac.cl, click on the English version and then go to "statistical information." All the publications are downloadable at no charge. However, the CD-ROM with the third publication is not downloadable and is only available with the hardcopy purchase of the publication.

8. The main ECA website is www.uneca.org. The *Economic Report on Africa 2005* (http://www.uneca.org/era2005/full.pdf) is downloadable at no charge.

9. The ECE website is www.unece.org. The ECE has its online statistical data (called stat@unece) available at www.unece.org/stats/data.htm, which is free to users after a simple registration is completed. The ECE also has a website with excellent links (www.unece.org/stats/links.htm#national), which contains economic data on countries throughout the world. The data at this link are arguably even better than the two websites that list central banks and economic statistical agencies throughout the world, because this website also has available regional data within the country.

10. The main ESCAP website is www.unescap.org. The online data are available by country at www.unescap.org/stat/data/statind/areaSectorIndicators.aspx. The

publication *Statistical Indicators for Asia and the Pacific* is available to download at no charge from the website. The online data and data in the publication provide monthly economic, financial, and demographic data for member countries in the region.

11. The main ESCWA website is located at www.escwa.org.lb. Data at this site are downloadable at no charge. (See, for example, http://www.escwa.org.lb/information/publications/edit/upload/ead-2006-1.pdf)

12. The International Labor Organization (ILO) website is www.ilo.org and has information on obtaining either the *Yearbook of Labour Statistics* and/or the *Bulletin of Labour Statistics*.

13. The Central Intelligence Agency website is at www.cia.gov.

14. The European Commission (EC) website is at http://ec.europa.eu/index_-en.htm. A CD-ROM containing macroeconomic data on the member countries is also available.

15. *The Economist* website is www.economist.com. Available under a section entitled *Indicators* are subscriptions to an economic database called *Country Data*. These data are compiled for 150 countries throughout the world for up to 320 economic indicators, including historical data back to 1980 and forecasts up to 2030 for 60 of the most important developed countries from the Economist Intelligence Unit (EIU). The website also has data on global house price indices and the now famous *Big Mac Index*. The latter is a "burgernomics index" that compares the cost of a standard Big Mac throughout the world and concludes whether a country's currency is under- or overvalued relative to the U.S. dollar using the purchasing power parity (PPP) principle.

16. For example, consider an income level in the fourth quartile and a decedent in a family size of five. The first step is to deduct as joint consumption from 100% the sum of the housing components of housing (17.30%), housing services (3.26%), and furniture, home equipment, and maintenance (6.15%). In other words, 100%–(17.30%+3.26%+6.15%) = 73.29%. Assuming a family size of five, an approximation of the personal consumption of a decedent would be 14.66% (73.29% ÷ 5). If the family size had been four, an approximation of the personal consumption of a decedent would be 18.32% (or 72.29% ÷ 4).

ACKNOWLEDGMENTS

The authors thank Manuel Lasaga of Strategic Information Analysis, Miami, FL, for his insightful comments.

APPENDIX

Table A1. Consumption Data (Venezuela).

Categories	First Income Quartile	Second Income Quartile	Third Income Quartile	Fourth Income Quartile	Average
Food and Nonalcoholic beverages	44.18%	36.88%	27.40%	16.60%	23.90%
Alcoholic beverages	0.97%	1.05%	0.88%	0.86%	0.90%
Tobacco	0.82%	0.79%	0.70%	0.41%	0.56%
Housing	9.35%	11.56%	12.77%	17.30%	14.89%
Housing services	3.44%	3.68%	3.86%	3.26%	3.46%
Furniture, home equipment, and maintenance	3.91%	4.69%	4.83%	6.15%	5.48%
Transportation	5.52%	6.72%	8.74%	17.41%	13.12%
Communications	2.49%	3.38%	4.34%	6.18%	5.11%
Educational services	2.83%	3.95%	4.74%	5.23%	4.76%
Clothing	4.78%	5.88%	5.52%	3.60%	4.39%
Shoes	2.67%	2.64%	2.83%	1.53%	2.06%
Personal care	4.82%	4.62%	3.30%	2.31%	3.03%
Culture and entertainment	4.30%	3.46%	4.46%	5.79%	5.07%
Restaurants and hotels	6.18%	6.29%	5.58%	6.14%	6.04%
Medicine	2.28%	1.42%	2.30%	1.18%	1.55%
Medical services	0.54%	1.01%	1.18%	1.41%	1.24%
Hospital services	0.07%	0.43%	3.45%	0.72%	1.24%
Therapeutic equipment and machines	0.21%	0.20%	0.10%	0.17%	0.16%
Insurance	0.25%	0.93%	1.97%	2.90%	2.22%
Other goods and services	0.37%	0.64%	1.06%	0.85%	0.83%
Total	100.00%	100.00%	100.00%	100.00%	100.00%

Source: Based on Banco Central de Venezuela, II Encuesta Nacional de Presupuestos Familiares 1997/98 (Consumer Expenditure Survey).

ABOUT THE AUTHORS

Gary R. Albrecht, Ph.D., North Carolina is an economist at Albrecht Economics located in Winston-Salem. He specializes in economic forecasting and forensic economics. He has been an Assistant and Adjunct Associate Professor at Wake Forest University, and he was the Director of Econometric Modeling at the University of Kansas. He is a past vice president of the National Association of Forensic Economics. His research has been published in the *Journal of Forensic Economics*, *Journal of Legal Economics*, *Trial Briefs*, and *The Earnings Analyst*, in addition to his authoring various economic research reports and book chapters. He holds a Ph.D. degree in Economics from Indiana University.

Zoltan Butt is a research assistant in actuarial science at Cass Business School, City University London. He graduated from Middlesex University with a B.Sc. (Hons.) degree in Mathematics in Society with distinction, while also winning the Institute of Mathematics and IT Applications prize in 1998. While at City University, he has coauthored many articles in various fields of insurance modeling, such as mortality dynamics and forecasting, income protection, long-term care, as well as in the field of labor economics. He has also been studying for his Ph.D. degree in the area of mortality models for heterogeneous populations. During 2006, he was closely involved in the reassessment of the approaches used for estimating damages for the loss of future earnings following personal injury or fatal accidents in the United Kingdom. He has successfully contributed to the introduction of new methodologies in the estimation of future labor-market-related risks for able-bodied and disabled workers. In addition to theoretical research, he is also interested in working with large data sets and the programming of statistical applications.

James E. Ciecka received his Ph.D. in economics from Purdue University. He is professor of economics at DePaul University in Chicago, IL, where he teaches microeconomics, mathematical economics, and econometrics. Professor Ciecka has published refereed papers on a variety of topics, but his research interest for the past several years has been in Markov process models of labor force activity. He has coauthored several worklife expectancy tables based on the increment–decrement model. His most important research has been, and continues to be, with Gary R. Skoog on the probability distributions of labor force variables such as years of activity and years to final labor force separation. Together they have published theoretical papers and a comprehensive set of tables for years of labor force activity, including characteristics such as mean years of activity (worklife), median and modal years of activity, standard deviation, skewness, kurtosis, and various probability intervals for years of labor market activity. A related set of tables deals with years to final labor force separation. Current work with Gary Skoog includes analysis of retirement-related variables such as years spent in retirement and years to retirement. He is an executive editor of the *Journal of Forensic Economics*.

Giovanni Comandé, Esq., is full professor of Private Comparative Law at Scuola Superiore S. Anna Pisa, Italy. He is also director of the Lider-Lab. He received his LL.L. from the University of Pisa, an M.A. and LL.M. from Harvard Law School, and a Ph.D. from the Scuola Superiore Sant'Anna. Professor Comandé has served as visiting professor at the Université Paris II, Wake Forest University School of Law, and the University of South Carolina School of Law. He is a member of the Italian State Bar in Pisa and a member of the New York State Bar. He is a member of the European Group on Tort Law for the drafting of Principles of European Tort Law and is a member of the European Center for Law and Insurance. Professor Comandé has served as scientific director of research projects funded by the Italian Ministry of Science and Education, the Italian National Council of Research, the European Science Foundation, and the European Union. His main fields of interest are comparative law, tort law, European private law, insurance law, information society law, health law, free circulation, and immigration. Giovanni is editor or coeditor of eight collective works, author of articles and notes published in major Italian law reviews, and contributor to collective publications in Italian, English, and Spanish on medical malpractice and insurance, privacy and e-commerce, tort law, and information technology.

Richard Cropper is an independent financial adviser who specializes in providing advice to recipients of personal injury damages. He has provided expert advice to the courts in the United Kingdom since 1993, initially with regard to the viability of structured settlements and later with regard to periodical payments since their inception in 2005. With Dr. Victoria Wass he was the financial expert for the claimants in the test cases in respect of the indexation of earnings-based annual payments for care. Committed to the development of the financial aspects of the law, he continues to seek equitable solutions to other areas, such as the *Roberts v. Johnstone* approach to the need for accommodation. He regularly lectures on the issues of periodical payments, conventional lump sums, and statutory funding of care to solicitors and legal bodies.

Steven Haberman is professor of actuarial science, director and deputy dean of Cass Business School, City University. He graduated in mathematics from the University of Cambridge, qualifying as a fellow of the Institute of Actuaries in 1975, and subsequently obtained his Ph.D. and D.Sc. in actuarial science from City University. He has worked at Prudential Assurance and for the Government Actuary's Department, and has been a member of the Council of the Institute of Actuaries. He is a member of the Financial Reporting Council's Board of Actuarial Standards and the ABI's Research Advisory Panel. He was a member of the External Advisory Panel to the Morris Review of the Actuarial Profession. He has written over 150 papers on a wide range of topics, including mortality and morbidity models, annuities, insurance pricing and pensions. His papers have won research prizes from the Institute of Actuaries and the Society of Actuaries (United States). He is coauthor of five books, including *Modelling Longevity Dynamics for Pensions and Annuity Business* (2009), *Modern Actuarial Theory and Practice* (2005 – 2nd edition), and *Actuarial Models for Disability Insurance* (1999). He is one of the founding editors of the *Journal of Pension Economics and Finance*.

Matthias Kelly, QC, is a practicing barrister, former chairman of the Bar of England and Wales (2003), and former chairman of the Personal Injuries Bar Association of England and Wales. Mr Kelly has played a central role in the adoption of actuarial methods in the calculation of personal injury damages through his practice in the courts and in his contributions to the Ogden Working Groups and the Law Commission of the United Kingdom.

Kurt V. Krueger, Ph.D., is an economist at John Ward Economics located in Prairie Village, Kansas. He specializes in forensic economics and economic demography. He is the managing editor of the *Journal of Forensic Economics*, and he is a past vice president of the National Association of Forensic Economics. He has published in *Medical Care*, *Journal of Forensic Economics*, *Journal of Legal Economics*, *Litigation Economics Digest*, *Litigation Economics Review*, and *The Earnings Analyst*, in addition to authoring economic research reports, book chapters, and one book on catastrophic injury damages. He holds a Ph.D. degree in economics from the University of Missouri-Kansas City.

Robert McNabb, B.Sc., M.A., Ph.D., is professor of economics and dean at Cardiff Business School, Cardiff University. Professor McNabb has held visiting and advisory posts with a number of international organizations including the OECD, the UN, and the Office for National Statistics (United Kingdom). He has published extensively in the areas of gender and earnings determination, personnel economics, forensic economics, and macroeconomics in such journals as the *Economic Journal, Economica, Oxford Economic Papers, Organization Studies*, the *International Journal of Human Resources*, and the *Journal of Management Studies*. He has published several books including *Personnel Economics* (with Ed Lazear) and *Macroeconomics: European Edition* (with Andy Abel and Ben Bernanke).

Robert Minnehan has a Ph.D. degree from the University of California at Berkeley and a B.S. degree in civil engineering from the University of Washington. His publications include papers and reports on environmental engineering and management of government programs. Dr. Minnehan provides forensic economic consulting services primarily to attorneys in the State of Delaware, but also does some cases for attorneys in Maryland and Pennsylvania. He began consulting in 1972 while a faculty member at the University of Delaware, and his business grew to become a full-time occupation in 1990. He does work for both plaintiffs and defense, although his work in the continuing asbestos casework has been mostly for the defense since 1984. He has a particular interest in cases involving pension loss.

Michael J. Piette is president of *Analytical Economics, Inc*. in Tallahassee, FL. Dr. Piette specializes in the estimation of economic damages resulting from personal injury and wrongful death claims, including mass torts such as airline disasters. He has prepared analyses in medical malpractice cases as well as in cases involving allegations of employment discrimination. Dr. Piette has testified throughout the country for both plaintiffs and defendants for over 20 years. He is a past president of the National Association of Forensic Economics and an editor emeritus of the *Journal of Forensic Economics*. He has also taught in the graduate program at Florida State University. Dr. Piette has authored over 50 peer-reviewed articles during his career, including research published in the *Journal of Forensic Economics* and the *Journal of Legal Economics*. He earned an MBA in finance and a Ph.D. in economics, both from Florida State University.

A. E. Rodriguez is an associate professor in the Department of Economics and Finance of the University of New Haven. He works in antitrust, discrimination, and other forensic economics areas. He earned a Bachelor of Science in Chemical Engineering and a Ph.D. in Economics from the University of Texas at Austin.

Steven J. Shapiro, Ph.D., is professor of finance and director of the Risk Management Center at New York Institute of Technology. Dr. Shapiro is a former at-large vice president of the National Association of Forensic Economics (NAFE). He is an executive editor of the *Journal of Forensic Economics* and former editor of the *Litigation Economics Review*. He has published articles in refereed journals on damages estimation, use of statistical methods to assess the suitability of investments, valuation of employee stock options, and the appraisal of closely held businesses. He is also coauthor of a textbook on sport finance. Dr. Shapiro has been providing expert testimony on economic damages for plaintiff and defendants since 1988.

Gary R. Skoog earned a Ph.D. in economics from the University of Minnesota in 1976 and a BA from the University of Michigan in economics and actuarial science in 1968. He has taught at the University of Minnesota, the University of Wisconsin, the University of Chicago, and currently De Paul University. He heads Legal Econometrics, Inc. located in Glenview, IL, a northern suburb of Chicago and is the immediate past president of the National Association of Forensic Economics. He has taught graduate courses in microeconomics, macroeconomics, statistical analysis, business and economic forecasting, applied time series, econometric theory, and undergraduate principles.

His forensic economics research has centered on issues related to worklife expectancy – its general theory and its application and misapplication, especially regarding disability. He has published, alone or with coauthors, in *Econometrica*, *Economics Letters*, the *Journal of Forensic Economics*, the *Journal of Legal Economics*, the *Litigation Economics Review*, the *Earnings Analyst*, and the Minneapolis Federal Reserve *Staff Papers*. His consulting is broadly based in economics and statistics and has included, in addition to personal injury/wrongful death cases, antitrust, major league baseball salary arbitration, copyright damages, liability and damages in employment discrimination, lost business profits, patent damages, and statistical hypothesis and significance testing.

Robert J. Thornton is MacFarlane Professor of Economics at Lehigh University. His areas of research include labor market discrimination, unions and collective bargaining, occupational licensing, and forensic economics. He has written or edited a number of books and collective volumes, most recently *Fundamentals of Labor Economics* (with Thomas Hyclak and Geraint Johnes) and *Developments in Litigation Economics* (with Patrick Gaughan). He has also published many articles, which have appeared in such journals as the *Journal of Forensic Economics*, *Industrial and Labor Relations Review*, *Journal of Human Resources*, *Industrial Relations, Journal of Economic Perspectives*, and the *Oxford Bulletin of Economics and Statistics*. He has been a practicing forensic economist since 1974 and served as national president of the National Association of Forensic Economics in 1989–1990.

Richard Verrall is professor of actuarial statistics and Associate Dean for Research, Knowledge Transfer and International Affairs at Cass Business School, City University London. He read Mathematics at St John's College Cambridge, and was awarded an M.Sc. in Statistics, with Distinction, by University College London. His Ph.D. dissertation from City University was on claims reserving in general insurance, and he has since published many papers in this area. His focus has been on the application of statistical methods to insurance problems, and the research carried out in relation to the 6th edition of the Ogden Tables is an example of this. In 1999, he was made an honorary fellow of the Institute of Actuaries.

John O. Ward, Ph.D, is professor emeritus of Economics at the University of Missouri-Kansas City. He was the first president of the National Association of Forensic Economics, editor and coeditor of the *Journal of Forensic Economics* from 1987 to 2004, and editor of the *Journal of Legal Economics* from 2007 to 2009. At the University of Missouri-Kansas City, Dr. Ward served as chair of the Department of Economics as well as associate dean of the College of Arts and Sciences. Dr. Ward organized the first NAFE International Meetings and has published over 50 papers in refereed journals in the field of forensic economics, 12 book chapters, as well as 6 edited or authored books in the field of forensic economics. He has been a practicing forensic economist through his firm, John Ward Economics, since 1978.

Victoria Wass is a labor economist at Cardiff Business School with research interests in earnings and employment determination. She has worked as a forensic economist in the United Kingdom since 1994, initially advising in a series of test cases to determine loss of future earnings for coal miners affected by respiratory disease who had been made redundant from the declining sector in the mid-1980s. In 2006 and 2007, she was the lead expert for the claimants in a second series of test cases on the issue of the indexation of earnings-based annual payments for care. The sixth edition of the Ogden Tables published in May 2007 includes worklife expectancies adjusted for the effects of disability based on joint research with Richard Verrall, Steven Haberman, and Zoltan Butt. She is a regular contributor to training programs and workshops on damages and to the *Journal of Personal Injury Law*. She has been invited to join the Ogden Working Party in preparation for publication of the seventh edition.

Shane Whelan is an actuary with extensive experience of both civil litigation and of the investment industry in Ireland, where he has worked as an investment analyst, fund manager, and strategist for over a decade. He became a lecturer in actuarial science and statistics at University College Dublin in September 2001, and subsequently the Head of Department. Shane has presented and published many papers on actuarial and investment topics to professional and academic audiences, and his research has been noted by prizes from the Institute of Actuaries (United Kingdom) and the Worshipful Company of Actuaries (a guild in the City of London). Shane has a mathematical science degree from University College Dublin, a doctorate from Heriot-Watt University in Edinburgh, and he has played an active role in the actuarial profession both in Ireland and the United Kingdom.

David R. Williams is the president of *Florida Economics Consulting Group, Inc.* in Miami, FL. Dr. Williams specializes in the calculation of economic losses in wrongful death, personal injury, discrimination, and business loss situations. He has been the acting chief economist in the Governor's Office, State of Florida; a senior research fellow at Florida International University, on the Board of Economists for *FLORIDA TREND* magazine; and has taught at the University of Miami. Dr. Williams has published articles in the *Litigation Economics Digest* and the *Journal of Forensic Economics*.